WAR
in the
PACIFIC
Pearl Harbor to Tokyo Bay

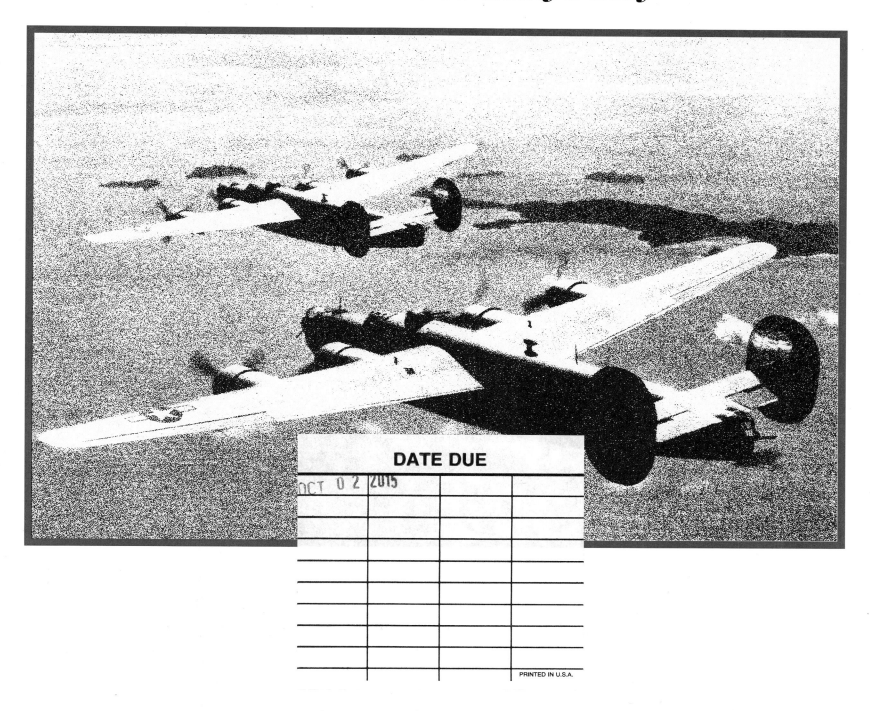

DATE DUE			
OCT 0 2 2015			
		PRINTED IN U.S.A.	

940.54
NAL

WAR in the PACIFIC

Pearl Harbor to Tokyo Bay

The story of the bitter struggle in the Pacific
theater of World War II. Featuring commissioned
photographs of artifacts from all
the major combatants

**Consultant Editor
BERNARD C. NALTY**

**Technical Advisor
RUSS A. PRITCHARD**

University of Oklahoma Press

Norman

WAR IN THE PACIFIC
Pearl Harbor to Tokyo Bay

ISBN 0-8061-3199-3

Oklahoma Paperbacks editions published
1999 by the University of Oklahoma Press,
Norman, Publishing Division of the
University, by special arrangement with
Salamander Books Ltd, 8 Blenheim Court,
Brewery Road, London N7 9NT,
United Kingdom.

1 2 3 4 5 6 7 8 9 10

© Salamander Books Ltd 1991

All rights reserved. No part of this book may
be reproduced, stored in a retrieval system or
transmited in any form or by any means,
electronic, mechanical, photocopying,
recording or otherwise, without prior
permission of Salamander Books Ltd.

All correspondence concerning the content of
this volume should be addressed to
Salamander Books Ltd.

Credits

Editor: Tony Hall

Designer: Paul Johnson

Indexer: David Linton

Japanese translations: First Edition, Cambridge

Picture research: Tony Moore (London),
Helen Purves (Tokyo)

Color artwork: Jeff Burn (figures);
Tony Gibbons (submarine);
Stephen Seymour (aircraft)
© Salamander Books Ltd

Map artworks and Pearl Harbor diorama:
Geoff Denney Associates
© Salamander Books Ltd

Diagram artwork: Kevin Jones Associates
© Salamander Books Ltd

Commissioned color photography:
Don Eiler, Richmond, Virginia
© Salamander Books Ltd;
except pp. 42-43 (main picture) by
Chapman Collings & Partners, London
© Salamander Books Ltd

Retouched photographs:
pp. 294-295, by Alan Hollingbery
© Salamander Books Ltd

Filmsetting: The Old Mill, London

Color reproduction: Scantrans Pte Ltd,
Singapore

Printed in Spain

Publisher's Acknowledgments

In the preparation of this volume we have
been extremely fortunate to receive the
advice and support from militaria collectors
and museum directors and their staffs in the
United States. We would also like to thank in
particular: Sr. Stanley L. Falk; the staff of the
Photographic Stills Department, National
Archives, Washington DC; and Toshiyuki
Maesaka of the Mainichi Newspaper, Tokyo.
We sould also like to extend a very special
thanks to the consultant, Bernard C. Nalty;
technical and arms advisor Russ Pritchard;
and photographer Don Eiler, for their
invaluable contributions to the
success of this book.

A Salamander Book

Contents

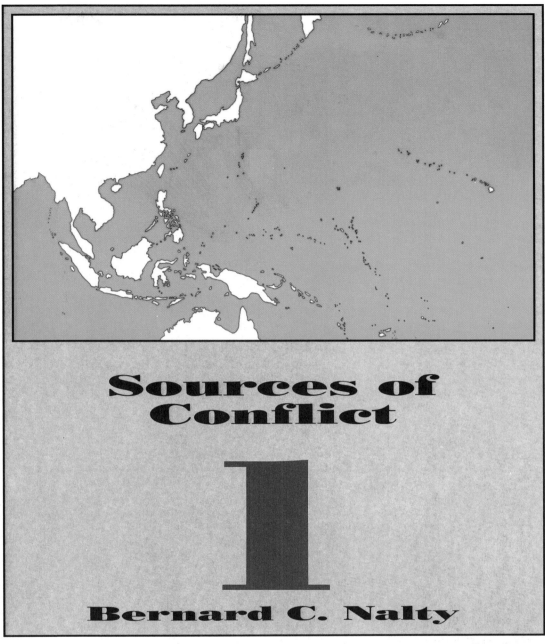

Sources of Conflict

1

Bernard C. Nalty

Although the vast Pacific Ocean separated Japan from the United States, the interests of the two nations remained tightly intertwined for the better part of a century. In 1853, the visit of an American naval squadron provided the catalyst for the modernization of Japan. In 1945, after a bloody war, an instrument of surrender, signed on the deck of an American battleship, propelled Japan into a democratic era.

Commodore Matthew C. Perry dropped anchor in Tokyo Bay, then called Yedo Bay, in 1853 to deliver a demand from President Franklin Pierce for a treaty to ensure trade and to extend protection to shipwrecked seamen, whom the Japanese had killed or mistreated in order to preserve Japan from foreign corruption. The nation's feudal rulers, impressed by the American flotilla, signed the agreement, but opposition to the pact rapidly coalesced. The opponents pinned their hopes on the emperor, who, they believed, would revert to a policy of isolation. Ironically, the proponents of change succeeded in using the office of emperor to legitimize the modernization of Japan. An oligarchy created a centralized government, nominally headed by an all-powerful emperor but actually dominated by this small group of advisers. Under the Emperor Meiji, the first ruler of modern Japan, who acceded to the throne in 1868, the nation took on the trappings of a constitutional monarchy, on the European model, but the oligarchs who wrote the constitution made sure that the Diet, or national legislature, had no real control over policy. Until the summer of 1945, when Emperor Hirohito shattered precedent to save his nation from destruction, Japan followed a course shaped by the cadre of military and civilian advisers who happened to be closest to the throne.

The new Japan promptly began expanding beyond the confines of the Home Islands of Honshu, Kyushu, Shikoku, and Hokkaido. The Japanese first claimed the Bonin Islands and Okinawa in the south and then cast covetous eyes upon the Kurile Islands and Sakhalin to the north, where Russia had a conflicting interest. The two nations compromised, with Japan taking over the Kuriles and Russian Sakhalin. Another object of

Japanese ambitions, Korea, lay within China's sphere of influence; but in 1894, Japan overthrew the Korean government, appointed a puppet regime, and defeated the Chinese forces trying to restore the old order.

Whereas Japan expanded step by step, the United States burst on the Far Eastern scene with dazzling suddenness. Victory over Spain in 1898 propelled the United States into world prominence as the master of an empire stretching from Puerto Rico to the Philippines. The island of Cuba where the United States had intervened to bring independence from Spain, became, in effect, an American protectorate. The peace treaty signed at Paris in 1898 contained a combination of Spanish indemnities and American payments that left the United States in control of Puerto Rico, conquered by American troops; Guam, where an expedition bound for the Philippines had put in and raised the flag; and the Philippine Islands, where some seven years of campaigning proved necessary to suppress an independence movement and impose control.

The destruction of Spain's Pacific Empire — Germany purchased what did not go to the United States — coincided with the collapse of Chinese authority on the Asian mainland, a decline foreshadowed when Japan wrested Korea from the hands of the Chinese. Events in China spawned conditions that resulted in military cooperation between the two emerging Far Eastern powers, the United States and Japan. In 1900, as imperial power crumbled under foreign pressure, a group of militant Chinese, the Righteous Fist of Harmony, nicknamed the Boxers, attempted to expel the foreigners. The Boxers laid siege to the foreign legations at Peking (Beijing), and when the Chinese government, which secretly supported the uprising, made no move to protect the foreigners, a hastily organized international expedition, including Americans and Japanese, set out to the rescue. The relief column, however, soon found itself cut off from the other foreign troops at Tientsin (Tianjin) and a force of 18,000 men from a half-dozen nations had to be dispatched to break the sieges of Tientsin and then Peking. At Tientsin, Japanese troops broke through and led the other contingents into the city, but at Peking the Russians spearheaded the attack.

Japan soon was at odds with two of the nations that had helped it suppress the Boxers — Russia and the United States. Even as Japanese and American troops soldiered together in the international expedition, question of race and competition for jobs were souring relations between the two powers. A treaty signed in 1894 resulted in a reciprocal grant of most favored nation status. As a result, Japanese enjoyed the right to enter the United States, though not the privilege of becoming naturalized citizens. Moreover, a clause in the agreement enabled the United States to exclude laborers who might compete with Americans for jobs. Repeated American protests that most Japanese immigrants belonged in this prohibited category persuaded Japan to impose voluntary restrictions in 1900, but laborers continued to enter the continental United States by way of Canada, Mexico, and even Hawaii. Consequently, a Japanese and Korean Exclusion League came into being on the Pacific Coast, where prejudice against Asians was strong and competition for jobs fierce. In the fall of 1906, when the schools of San Francisco reopened after the disastrous April

Below: American troops enter Havana on January 1, 1899, and end Spanish rule in Cuba. The Spanish-American War also gave ownership of the Philippine and other Pacific islands to the Americans, thereby making the United States a Pacific power.

earthquake, all Asian pupils were segregated in a special Oriental school. The Japanese government protested that this action violated the treaty of 1894, and President Theodore Roosevelt fashioned a compromise whereby the San Francisco school board rescinded its order, the United States Congress enacted an immigration law empowering the federal government to bar any immigrants — clearly the Japanese — who might adversely affect "labor conditions," and Japan entered into a "Gentlemen's Agreement" to cooperate in preventing Japanese workers from

Below: Japan appreciated the importance of naval power early in its rise to Pacific importance, and quickly built a capable navy; initially using British-built ships such as this pre-dreadnought battleship, the 12,533-ton *Fuji*, with her four 12-inch guns.

Above: The Russo-Japanese War of 1904-5 marked Japan's emergence as a world power. Though Russian positions such as this outside Port Arthur checked the Japanese for a time, Japan finally secured a decisive victory over the Tsarist empire.

emigrating to the United States.

Throughout much of the bitter agitation over racial discrimination against Japanese on the West Coast of the United States, Japan faced a more dangerous threat closer to home, as the military rivalry with Russia reached flashpoint. Although briefly allied against the Boxers, the two nations competed to fill the void caused by the decline of China. In 1895, five years before the relief of the besieged embassies at Peking, China had yielded to pressure and granted Russia the rights to Port Arthur (Lushun), near Darien (Luda)

Above: Theodore Roosevelt used the fame he gained with the "Rough Riders" in Cuba as one of the platforms for his successful presidential campaign. Among Roosevelt's greatest achievements was the Panama Canal linking the Caribbean with the Pacific.

on the Liaotung (Liaodung) Peninsula. In 1902 Japan sought to neutralize the Russian move by entering into an alliance with Great Britain, which for some 20 years remained the keystone of Japanese foreign policy.

Japan soon concluded, however, that diplomacy alone could not provide security against Russia, and in 1904, without a formal declaration of war, the Japanese navy attacked the Russian squadron at Port Arthur, winning the first in a series of victories. The most spectacular success occurred in the Strait of Tsushima, where in May 1905 a Japanese fleet annihilated the outnumbered Russian Baltic Squadron, its equipment in disrepair after an exhausting voyage halfway around the world. Among those who fought that day under the victorious Adm. Heihachiro

Togo was a young midshipman, Isoroku Takono, later adopted by the Yamamoto family, who lost two fingers of his left hand when an overheated gun exploded. Yamamoto would be a key figure in shaping and executing Japanese strategy in World War II.

Neither the overwhelming triumph of Togo, nor the victories at Port Arthur and Mukden, forced Russia to surrender. Lengthening casualty lists and mounting costs placed Japan in increasing peril as an inefficient but powerful enemy began bringing its resources to bear. When President Theodore Roosevelt offered to mediate, the war-weary combatants accepted his offer, Japan because the nation was being bled white, and Russia because of the danger of revolution at home. The American Chief Executive admired Japan's success against a potentially more powerful enemy — he had an instinctive sympathy for the underdog — and he may also have been embarrassed by California's persistent discrimina-

tion against Japanese. Whatever his motivation, however, he believed that Japan received fair treatment in the peace settlement he helped fashion at Portsmouth, New Hampshire, in 1905. The Treaty of Portsmouth, which earned Roosevelt the Nobel Prize for peace, undoubtedly saved Japan from economic ruin and may also have staved off social disintegration in Russia, but it did not satisfy the government in Tokyo. Japan received hegemony over northeastern Asia and possession of Port Arthur and the northern half of Sakhalin Island, but did not get the large cash indemnity that it desperately wanted, and for this it blamed Roosevelt.

The president now realized that Japan had become the dominant power in the Far East and a threat to the newly acquired Philippines. Moreover, Japanese immigration to the United States remained a source of friction. As a result, Roosevelt sent the American battle fleet on a cruise around the world, from

December 1907 to February 1909, as a show of strength, and followed up the "Gentlemen's Agreement" to restrict immigration from Japan with a pact that in effect confirmed the dominant Japanese interests in northeast Asia, in return for recognition of American control over the Philippines.

Both the United States and Japan sided with the Allies in World War I. For Japan, the conflict presented an opportunity to absorb the German holdings in China and the islands in the central Pacific that Germany had bought from Spain. Whereas Japan acquired territory, the United States sought to restore the balance of power in Europe, described grandiloquently as making the world safe for democracy, and had no specific territorial ambitions. The Treaty of Versailles that officially ended the war in 1919 awarded Japan trusteeship over Tinian and Saipan in the Marianas, as well as the Palaus, the Carolines, and the Marshalls; an arrangement confirmed by

Above: Japanese infantry played a major part in the China Relief Expedition of 1900, to rescue the legations that were taken under siege in Peking during the "Boxer Rebellion." They acquired a good record as reliable and disciplined troops.

Top right: The Treaty of Versailles brought a political end to World War I, but also set up a situation fraught with problems for the future. This is Count Brockdorff-Rautzau leaving the Trianon Palace after receiving the Allied demands on Germany in May 1919.

Above: Known as "The Great White Fleet" for the color of its ships, the US Navy's battle fleet circumnavigated the world between 1907 and 1909 in a striking display of emerging American naval power and its capacity for global power projection.

Visions of War

The Japanese victory over Russia in 1905 awakened concern in the United States that this emerging Asian power was casting covetous eyes upon the Philippine Islands, an American possession since the war with Spain in 1898. Even as representatives of Japan and Imperial Russia were negotiating a treaty of peace at Portsmouth, New Hampshire, through the mediation of an American president, Theodore Roosevelt, another American was putting the finishing touches on a futuristic novel, *The Valor of Ignorance*, in which a vigorous and ambitious Japan attacked a complacent, even decadent, United States. The writer was Homer Lea, an admirer of Napoleon, who, despite physical frailty, commanded a Chinese army and served as an adviser to Sun Yat-sen (Sun Zhong Shan), hailed as the founder of modern China. Concerned by what he perceived as a decline in the classic American virtues of discipline, self-sacrifice, and patriotism, Lea predicted that Japan, in a lightning-like campaign of three or four months, could overrun the American possessions of the Philippines, Guam, and Hawaii before invading the mainland and conquering the states of Oregon and Washington. The United States would mass its army near San Francisco for a decisive battle, which might well be lost unless Americans recaptured the spirit of past generations.

Whereas Lea brooded about the moral fiber of the nation, Hector Bywater, a British journalist specializing in naval and military matters, concentrated upon Japanese strategy in a war against the United States. In his 1925 novel, *The Great Pacific War*, Bywater predicted that Japan would strike first, as it had done in surprising the Russian forces at Port Arthur, detonating an explosives-laden freighter in the Panama Canal and severing the link between Atlantic and Pacific. Japanese forces could thus dominate the Pacific west of Hawaii, attack Dutch

Harbor in Alaska, bomb the cities of California from aircraft carriers, and repulse an American counterattack into the Bonin Islands. American strength would ultimately prevail, however, once the Atlantic squadron had fought its way through the Strait of Magellan and joined the naval units already in the Pacific. He described how the American fleet would seize Truk and shatter the Japanese navy in a major battle off the island of Yap. Once the United States had gained control of the Pacific, Japan could not sustain its conquests and had no choice except surrender.

Yet another vision of a war between the United States and Japan may be found in the writings of Brig. Gen. William L. "Billy" Mitchell, who vigorously — at times recklessly — advocated an independent American air arm, patterned after the British Royal Air Force, in a department of aeronautics headed by a cabinet officer. Mitchell's intemperate criticism of the handling of aviation by the Army and Navy resulted

Above: "Billy" Mitchell was convinced of the vulnerability of the US Navy's surface ships to air attack, and advocated such views so controversially that he was court-martialed and suspended from the army.

in his conviction by court-martial on the charge of conduct prejudicial to good order and discipline. Mitchell became convinced that Japan could overcome the American advantage in raw material and industrial capacity by making full use of the most modern and deadliest of weapons, the airplane. Under the umbrella of air power, Japan could, he believed, advance island by island across the Pacific to Hawaii and perhaps beyond. Indeed, by using aircraft carriers and submarines, the Japanese were capable of neutralizing the base at Pearl Harbor at the onset of war. Should Japan attack Pearl Harbor, whether at the outbreak of a conflict or after advancing across the Pacific, Mitchell predicted that the division of responsibility between the Army and Navy would prove a severe handicap in defending the base.

mandate of the postwar League of Nations. Having taken over the German holdings in China, the Japanese succeeded in asserting economic domination over Manchuria, all the while paying lip service to the Open Door — the policy of ensuring equal economic opportunity in China for all foreign nations, which had become a shibboleth of American foreign policy.

Japan thus emerged from World War I as an empire. The islands entrusted to it by the League of Nations lay athwart the lines of communication between Hawaii and the Philippines, which was a

Right: One of the early sessions of the Council of the League of Nations, which took place at San Sebastian, Spain, in August 1920. The council confirmed the Japanese mandate over several Pacific island groups conferred by the Treaty of Versailles.

cause of concern to the United States. Great Britain, exhausted by the recent war, worried that the emergence of Japan as a major naval power would jeopardize its colonies of Hong Kong, Malaya and Burma. China, threatened more directly by Japan, feared for its existence. Against this backdrop, President Warren G. Harding of the United States convened the Washington Naval Conference in 1921. His Secretary of State, Charles Evans Hughes, hoped through negotiations among the interested powers to prevent a naval armaments race, keep Great Britain from siding with Japan in the event of a war in the western Pacific, and reduce the possibility of such a conflict. During the conference, the United States achieved everything it sought, in part because a group of cryptanalysts headed by Herbert O. Yardley had broken the Japanese diplomatic code, so that the American negotiators knew the instructions of the government in Tokyo almost as soon as their Japanese counterparts did. The Washington Naval Conference produced a treaty that established a tonnage ratio for capital ships — battleships,

Below: In February 1932 the Japanese declared the independence of Manchuria under Pu Yi, the former Chinese emperor, as the Japanese-protected puppet state of Manchukuo. This is Pu Yi with Emperor Hirohito on a state visit to Japan in April 1935.

Above: A major feature of American policy for the Pacific in the 1920s was the need to deter any possible alliance of Great Britain with Japan, which would have opened the possibility of operations in the Pacific by British battle squadrons such as this.

aircraft carriers, and cruisers — of 5:5:3 among the United States, Great Britain, and Japan and 1.7 for France and Italy. (Germany was forbidden any capital ships under the terms of the Versailles Treaty.) This apportionment of tonnage was designed to prevent any one nation from becoming the dominant naval power in the western Pacific. Since both the United States and the United Kingdom had naval commitments elsewhere, the two nations would have to act in concert if their fleets were to overcome the smaller Imperial Japanese Navy. As a further means of maintaining stability in the region, the treaty prevented the United States, Great Britain, and Japan from fortifying their outlying possessions. Excluded from this category was Singapore.

Pressure from the United States and Canada persuaded Great Britain to allow the alliance with Japan to lapse. To replace this bilateral pact, in 1921 the United States, Great Britain, France, and Japan fashioned a brand new agreement that guaranteed their territories, called for the peaceful resolution of differences among the signatories, and proposed joint action to meet aggression by any other power. These four powers took a further step to preserve peace in the western Pacific when they joined Italy, Portugal, Belgium, France, and the Netherlands in signing the Nine Power Treaty of 1922 which endorsed, but did not guarantee, the independence of China. In effect, this pact recognized the principle of the Open Door, which the United States and Great Britain had supported since the 1890s and Japan had more recently endorsed.

Although Japan accepted naval limitation and international cooperation in the early 1920s, the nation's attitude hardened as the decade wore on. The ratio of 5:5:3 became a symbol of national humiliation, and was branded as "the navy's failure" by a group of aggressive army officers intent upon seizing an economic bridgehead on the Asian mainland. Increasingly the army championed expansion at the expense of China, and the idea grew in popularity as the Great Depression spread worldwide and fixed its grip upon Japan. As a source of raw materials and a market for manufactured goods, China seemed to hold the answer to Japan's economic woes.

Those who believed that conquest could restore the economy soon found themselves in a race against time. On the mainland, Chiang Kai-shek (Jiang Jieshi) seemed to be making progress toward unifying China; merging the feudal states, each with its own war lord, into a modern nation. This process, if brought to completion, boded ill for the Japanese and other foreigners who had staked out claims. In September 1931, Japan's militarists struck. A bomb, allegedly planted by Chinese terrorists, exploded on the right of way of the Japanese-owned Manchurian railway, giving the Japanese army an excuse to invade Chinese territory to protect the property of Japanese citizens. Unable to oppose the invasion, China appealed to the League of Nations, which investigated the Chinese complaint, concluded that Japan had no justification for its action, but did nothing to redress the wrong. Although the League contented itself with the mildest of reprimands, Japan angrily withdrew from the organization. The United States lodged a protest through diplomatic channels, but the administration of President Herbert Hoover placed an infinitely higher priority on economic recovery than on preserving the territorial integrity of China.

The conquest of Manchuria, which became the Japanese territory of Manchukuo, reflected the ascendancy of the most militant elements of the army in Japanese politics. The radical army officers intended to control the government and manipulate Emperor Hirohito, who had ascended the throne in 1926, as they led Japan into a golden age of military and economic dominance in Asia. Some of the military men, like Hideki Tojo, who would serve as prime minister during much of World War II, were prepared to work within the

CHINESE NATIONALIST OFFICER, 1930s

The vastness of China and the military organization of Nationalist forces meant that uniforms and equipment varied greatly from one military area to another. The German influence at this time was a strong one, as can be seen by the Mauser *Schnellfeuer* pistol, being carried here as in a machine-pistol configuration with its stock/holster attached. Other equipment includes a captured Japanese water bottle.

September 1 1939

UNION OF SOVIET SOCIALIST REPUBLICS

ALASKA

Sakhalin

Kurile Islands

Aleutian Islands (US)

OUTER MONGOLIA

MANCHURIA
(MANCHUKUO)

INNER MONGOLIA

TIBET

CHINA

JAPAN

INDIA
(B)

Ryukyu
Islands

Okinawa

BURMA
(B)

Bonin
Islands

Volcano
Islands

Marcus
Island

Midway (US)

INDO
CHINA
(F)

Iwo Jima

FORMOSA

HAINAN

THAILAND

Marianas Islands

Wake (US)

Hawaiian
Islands (US)

PHILIPPINE
ISLANDS
(US)

JAPANESE MANDATES

Guam (US)

Andaman
Islands
(B)

Marshall Islands

Palmyra (US)

MALAYA (B)

Caroline Islands

Gilbert Islands (B)

Christmas
Island (B)

BORNEO
(D)

SUMATRA (D)

AUSTRALIAN MANDATE

Canton (US)

NEW
GUINEA
(D)

(B)

Solomon
Islands

JAVA (D)

Samoa
(US and NZ mandate)

New Hebrides
(F)

Fiji Islands (B)

AUSTRALIA

New Caledonia (F)

TASMANIA

NEW ZEALAND

POSSESSIONS AND THE BALANCE OF POWER IN ASIA AND THE PACIFIC, 1939

This is the territorial position in the Pacific and Far East just prior to the outbreak of war in Europe. European powers such as Britain, France and the Netherlands had long held colonies in the region, drawn by the enormous trade markets — particularly that of China — and the wealth of raw materials available. Japan and the United States began their own expansionism here during the latter part of the nineteenth century, mostly for the same reasons. America secured the Philippines from Spain in 1898, while Japan gained Formosa from China in 1894. In 1905 in a war with

Tsarist Russia the Japanese inflicted a crushing defeat which opened up the whole of southern Manchuria, a move which threatened America's trade with China.

The outbreak of World War I did nothing to alleviate strained relations. Within days of its outbreak, Japan — then a British ally — had declared war on Imperial Germany and seized it's possessions in China. If this were not bad enough, the islands of the Marshalls, Carolines and Marianas formally in German hands were also siezed, thus effectively blocking direct passage from America's West Coast to the Philippines.

The post-war settlements did nothing ease this state of affairs and the deterioration in

international politics and the Great Depression of the 1930s simply made a bad situation worse. In a move on its own authority, the Japanese Army took over Manchuria in 1931, and in 1937 invaded China. At this time, events in Europe once more took a hand. Hitler's invasion of Poland plunged the continent into war and opened up the European possessions in the Pacific to Japanese pressure. On September 27, 1940 Japan joined the Axis with Germany and Italy, but would do little else while the Soviets threatened her in Manchuria. The German invasion of Russia changed all that, however, and by September 1941 Japan was laying her plans for all-out war in the Pacific.

Above: Soldiers of a Japanese motorized formation prepare their weapons before departure to Manchuria. The Japanese took Manchuria, an area important for raw materials, from the Chinese between September 1931 and February 1932.

Below: The Japanese foreign ministry is surrounded by soldiers during the military revolt of February 26, 1936, launched by young army officers unhappy with the civilian government's lack of determination for a speedy conquest of China.

existing political and economic structure, but others had less patience. The true firebrands proposed nothing less than the overthrow of the industrialists and politicians who, they believed, served the emperor badly and prevented Japan from achieving true greatness.

In 1936, five years after the conquest of Manchuria, a group of Japanese army officers mutinied, killed two of Hirohito's principal advisers, and wounded a third, Adm. Kantaro Suzuki, who lived to serve as prime minister in August 1945 as World War II drew to an end. The high command did not rally behind the plotters, who had gone too far for most of the senior officers. The task of settling the issue without compromising the honor of the officer corps fell to Maj. Gen. Tomoyuki Yamashita, who would achieve prominence in World War II as the conqueror of Malaya. Yamashita tended to be more radical than Tojo, and for that reason he proved an effective intermediary in persuading the leaders of the mutiny to commit ritual suicide, thus avoiding a trial that might have demoralized the army.

The Imperial Japanese Navy showed less enthusiasm than the army for waging a war of aggression, possibly because the soldiers thought mainly in terms of a war on the mainland of Asia against Chinese forces that were almost all

American Navy backed by the industrial might of the United States. Indeed, a strong faction within the naval ill-trained and poorly armed, while the navy planned for a war against the establishment continued to believe in naval limitation, although with a tonnage ratio more favorable to Japan. The so-called "Treaty Faction" included Yamamoto, who by 1930 was clearly on the fast track to flag rank.

During the 1920s, Yamamoto had served two tours in the United States, one as an assistant naval attaché at Washington and the other as a language student at Harvard University. At the capital, he became interested in air power. During his assignment to the attaché's office, the United States Navy experimented with its first aircraft carrier, a converted collier rechristened USS *Langley*, and Brig. Gen. William L. "Billy" Mitchell of the Army air service sank a number of ships, including obsolete battleships, anchored as targets for land-based bombers. Inspired by these developments, Yamamoto came to believe that airplanes and aircraft carriers were the weapons of the future.

While studying at Harvard, Yamamoto attended few formal classes but roamed North America from the automobile factories of Detroit to the oil fields of Texas and Mexico, an experience that impressed him with the industrial resources and mineral wealth at the disposal of the United States. He became convinced that a war with the United States would prove disastrous for Japan. Japanese diplomacy, he maintained, should seek a balance of power in the Pacific that would deter either nation from attacking the other. For Yamamoto, agreed tonnage ratios afforded the likeliest means of maintaining that equilibrium.

The views of the Treaty Faction did not prevail. The government of Japan dared not extend the agreement on the 5:5:3 ratio, which the populace had come to see as a proof of submission to the United States and Great Britain. A change in the ratio to increase Japanese tonnage might have saved the principle of naval limitation, but the British and American governments would make only minor concessions. In 1930, Yamamoto served as technical adviser to a Japanese negotiating team that obtained agreement to a five-year extension that permitted Japan to build as many submarines as the Americans or British and established a 10:10:7 ratio for cruisers. The hated proportion of 5:5:3 continued, however, to prevail for battleships and aircraft carriers. As the pact signed in 1930 drew to an end, Yamamoto took part in another attempt to modify the old ratio; the Treaty Faction empowered him to propose the

Right: The Japanese forces developed considerable tactical skills during their war with China. Seen here is Gen. Tsuitsui, commanding in northern China in July 1937. His forces captured Peking and Tientsin on July 28 and 29 of that year.

Above: The *Langley*, seen here with Vought VE-7 fighters on her deck, was converted in 1922 from the collier *Jupiter*. The *Langley* was a harbinger of naval air power to come, and her successors made obsolete battleships such as those in the background.

Right: During the war with China, the air arms of the Imperial Japanese Navy and Army made extensive use of aircraft for a variety of tactical and strategic tasks, and decided that range and agility were more important than firepower and protection.

abolition of the aircraft carrier in the hope of jump-starting the talks, but to no avail. Unable to obtain a satisfactory ratio, Japan broke off the talks and in 1937 approved the construction of the world's largest battleships, the 72,000-ton *Yamato* and *Musashi*.

Having cast aside naval limitation and launched a program of warship construction, Japan began searching for allies. Since the Soviet Union posed a threat to Manchukuo, in 1936 Japan aligned itself with Nazi Germany and Fascist Italy in the Anti-Comintern Pact, an agreement that imposed no military obligations but merely called for cooperation in preventing the export of Soviet Communism. While Japan's diplomats sought to protect Manchukuo by adhering to the Anti-Comintern pact, the army used the territory as a springboard for an assault on China. Japanese haughtiness and Chinese pride rendered such a conflict all but inevitable; firing erupted at the

Left: Japanese soldiers move up toward the front line past an honor guard of garrison troops in an occupied village. The ruthless treatment of Chinese civilians by such troops sowed an intense hatred of the Japanese among the Chinese.

Above: The Japanese forces enjoyed virtually complete *materiel* superiority over the Chinese. This piece of artillery, firing on Chinese in a mountain position, is a lightweight weapon produced specifically for this role.

Marco Polo bridge near Peking in July 1937, and the war began.

The administration of President Franklin D. Roosevelt tried to maintain correct, though not cordial, relations with Japan, in the hope that the mounting costs of a war in the vastness of China would discredit the militarists and bring to power a government willing to write off the venture as a bad gamble. Unfortunately, the United States had little influence on Japanese behavior, as demonstrated in December 1937, when naval aviators sank the clearly marked American gunboat, USS *Panay*, as it escorted a convoy of Standard Oil tankers, and then machine-gunned the crew members who sought concealment among the reeds on the banks of the Yangtze (Chang Jiang) River. Two sailors and a civilian passenger died as a result

Right: Japanese advances on major cities often resulted in a mass exodus of the population. Here civilians return to Canton after its capture by the Japanese subsequent to an amphibious landing near Hong Kong during October 1938.

of the attack, and 11 members of the crew were wounded. Japanese authorities sent ships to pick up the survivors and promptly apologized for what they described as a tragic accident. Yamamoto himself, who was now a vice minister in the navy ministry, promised to take "redoubled precautions" to prevent a similar incident in the future. The Japanese response served to defuse a potentially explosive situation, but less dramatic confrontations continued to occur as Americans tried to conduct business as usual in the midst of an increasingly violent war.

The mounting tensions in the Far East coincided with a growing danger in Europe, where Adolf Hitler consolidated his power over Germany in 1933 and 1934, began a systematic persecution of the nation's Jews, and rearmed in defiance of the Treaty of Versailles. He intervened in the Spanish Civil War and by the summer of 1939 absorbed Austria and Czechoslovakia. A non-aggression treaty with the Soviet Union gave Hitler the opportunity to attack Poland, but to his surprise France and Great Britain came to the aid of the Poles, and World War II began in September 1939. By the end of June of the following year, German forces had overrun western Europe from Norway to the Pyrenees, driving

Right: Between July 11 and August 10, 1938, the Japanese tried to take the Lake Khasan area in the ill-defined border region between Manchukuo, Korea, and Siberia, but were halted by Soviets using tanks such as the highly effective BT-7 seen here.

the British from the continent. During 1941, Hitler overwhelmed Yugoslavia and crushed the resistance of the Greeks, who had checked an invasion by his Italian ally. He also launched an attack across the North African desert toward the Suez Canal and in June attacked the Soviet Union. The American government concluded that Hitler's Germany was the most dangerous potential enemy, and President Franklin Roosevelt sought to marshal the nation's industries to aid the foes of Nazism.

Although Hitler seemed the greater threat to world order, Japan could not be ignored. The Roosevelt administration continued to use diplomatic and economic pressure in an attempt to restrain the Japanese. The United States government allowed the commercial treaty with Japan to expire, extended credit to China to help finance resistance to the Japanese invasion, and imposed an embargo on a lengthening list of war materials destined for Japan, including aluminium for aircraft production and aviation gasoline. Protests and material shortages could not, however, have a decisive effect on Japan's deter-

mined militarists who had already demonstrated their willingness to kill their opponents.

In April 1940, before Hitler's army had advanced to the Channel coast, Roosevelt decided to reinforce the diplomatic and economic measures with a modest show of force. He directed that the United States Fleet, after completing its annual exercises, remain in Hawaiian waters, shifting its home port from San Pedro, California, to Pearl Harbor. "Why are we here?" asked Adm. James O. Richardson, the fleet's commander, who objected to massing his ships at the end of a vulnerable supply line stretching halfway across the Pacific. "You are there," replied Adm. Harold R. Stark, the Chief of Naval Operations, "because of the deterrent effect it is thought your presence may have on the Japs going into the East Indies."

As Stark's reply indicated, the German conquest of France and the Netherlands, along with the British withdrawal from the continent, afforded Japan an opportunity to seize the colonies of the Netherlands East Indies, French Indochina, and British Malaya and Burma. Indeed, following the collapse of France in June 1940, Japan extorted the first in a series of concessions in Indochina that soon included the right to build airfields, access to the rice harvest, and use of the airport at Saigon (Ho Chi Minh City).

The American economic restrictions were having an effect, though not the desired one of inspiring a sober reconsideration of Japan's expansionist policy. Indeed, Japanese tended to see American concern for the Open Door and support of China, which the trade measures dramatized, as especially offensive examples of meddling in Japan's natural sphere of interest. In the summer of 1940, when Hitler's triumph in western Europe persuaded the United States to embark on a massive program of naval construction, the Japanese assumed that the resulting "Two-Ocean Navy" would be used against them. A naval arms race with the United States loomed on the horizon.

As Japanese-American relations thus deteriorated, the Anti-Comintern Pact no longer afforded protection against Soviet designs on Manchukuo, for in August 1939, Germany and the Soviet Union had signed their non-aggression pact. In these circumstances, Japan sought to neutralize the threat to Manchukuo, for Japanese and Soviet troops had clashed in 1938 and 1939 on the border between Manchukuo and the Soviet Republic of Mongolia. The answer seemed to lie in a military alliance with Hitler, while reaching an accommodation with Joseph Stalin. In September 1940, Japan, Germany, and Italy acceded to the Tripartite Pact, by which they agreed to go to the aid of any partner attacked by a power not already involved in the European conflict or the war in China. Japan obtained further assurance of a free hand in Asia by negotiating a non-aggression treaty with Soviet Union, signed in April 1941.

Although the Japanese army tended to applaud the alliance with Hitler and Benito Mussolini, the Italian leader, elements within the navy opposed the idea. The Navy Minister, Adm. Mitsumasa Yonai, warned that his service, still too weak to defeat the fleets of Great Britain and the United States, could expect no help from Germany or Italy, whose navies were fully committed in the Mediterranean and Atlantic. The alliance with Germany and Italy, he pointed out, would antagonize the United States and Great Britain without reinforcing Japanese naval strength in the Pacific.

The attitude of the naval leadership began to change, however, as symbolized by the conversion of Adm. Yamamoto from an opponent of a war with the United States to an architect of Japanese strategy. As Japan drew closer to Germany, Yamamoto warned that : "A war between Japan and the United States would be a major calamity for the world, and for Japan it would mean, after several years of war already [in China], acquiring yet another powerful enemy — an extremely perilous matter for the nation . . . . It is necessary, therefore, that both Japan and America should seek every means to avoid a direct clash, and Japan should under no circumstances make an alliance with Germany." But alliance was made, and Japan drifted closer to war with the United States. In these circumstances, Yamamoto became convinced that every Japanese, himself included, had to fall in line behind the emperor, whatever the risk to the nation. In April 1941, he wrote to a friend, "if by any chance there should be a war between Japan and America within the year, I am ready to carry out my duties in a way that'll have you all saying 'Good old Iso[roku]'."

Before he wrote this letter, perhaps as early as January, Yamamoto concluded that he could best carry out his duties to emperor and country by attacking the American Pacific Fleet at Pearl Harbor, gaining time for Japan to seize the Philippines, Malaya, Burma, and the Netherlands East Indies and thus acquire an empire rich in oil, ore, rice, and other resources. Other officers, especially in the army, believed that Japan's warrior tradition would prevail in such a conflict; the Americans, they said, lacked the discipline and courage to recover from the initial Japanese victories. The United States would not pay the price in blood and treasure to roll back the tide; the war would end in a negotiated settlement that accepted Japanese domination of the western Pacific.

Below: At the time of France's defeat in June 1940, Japan demanded and received the right to land troops in French Indochina. These troops are marching into Saigon during July 29, and such moves soon closed one of two Chinese lifelines to the outside world.

Above: The relationship between Japan and Germany was signalled by events such as a Japanese art exhibition held in Berlin in February 1939, when Hitler was greeted by Ambassador Oshima. In September 1940, Japan, Germany and Italy signed the Axis agreement.

Such were the predictions of the optimists, but Yamamoto entertained no such illusions. He had lived in the United States and knew firsthand of its overwhelming industrial power and vast natural resources. If war should come, he wrote, "I shall run wild for the first six months or a year, but I have no confidence for the second and third years."

Instead of going to war in the expectation that the United States would lose heart, Yamamoto urged that Japan prepare for a long and bloody war and resolve to do whatever was necessary to win. Taking "Guam and the Philippines, nor even Hawaii and San Francisco," would not be enough; Japan he said, "would have to march into Washington and sign the treaty in the White House."

The road to war began running sharply downhill in July 1941, when Japan, after nibbling away at French Indochina, decided to bolt down what remained. President Roosevelt reacted by imposing an embargo on the shipment of American oil to Japan and then by freezing Japanese assets in the United States. The United Kingdom and the Netherlands government in exile also impounded Japanese funds, so that Japan could no longer buy oil from the usual Dutch or American suppliers. Imports of crude oil and petroleum products, which totaled almost 40 million barrels during the year ending in March 1941, slowed overnight to a comparative trickle from Latin America and the Near East. In the fall of 1941, Japan's oil reserves amounted to some 50 million barrels, but the fleet burned 2,900 barrels during each hour's steaming. The temptation to invest the reserve in a war of conquest that would gain the oil of the Netherlands East Indies proved irresistible. Economic pressure designed to discourage aggression actually accelerated the movement toward war.

Above: Japan's path to war became firmer with the advent of a militaristic government on October 17, 1941 under Gen. Hideki Tojo (front center). His two main props were the army and navy chiefs of staff, Marshal Hajime Sugiyama and Adm. Osami Nagano.

Despite heightening tensions, the Japanese prime minister, Prince Fumimaro Konoye, still hoped to avoid hostilities and tried through diplomacy to persuade the United States to accept Japanese hegemony in the Far East. The army grew impatient, however, and decided that Konoye lacked the resolve needed to prosecute a war with the United States. After consultations with his principal advisers, including Minister of War Hideki Tojo, Konoye stepped aside, and on October 17, Tojo replaced him. At Washington, the Japanese ambassador, Adm. Kichisaburo Nomura, joined in November 1941 by a special emissary, Saburo Kurusu, persisted in trying to talk the United States into giving Japan a free hand, even though the two diplomats could offer no concessions. An agreement, moreover, had to be reached by a specific date, initially November 25 but postponed to the 29th, though the Japanese negotiators did not realize that the alternative would be war.

While Yamamoto, his navy colleagues, and the army leadership made their plans, and the diplomats pursued their talks, American intelligence was intercepting, decoding, and translating Japanese diplomatic traffic. During the summer of 1940, the Army's Signal Intelligence Service, under Lt. Col. William F. Friedman, had succeeded in breaking the Japanese Purple code, a demanding task that resulted in Friedman's nervous collapse and temporary hospitalization. As Purple decoding machines became available, one went to the Philippines, one to Hawaii, and two to London, while four remained at Washington. Friedman's machines enabled the United States to eavesdrop on the Japanese Foreign Office, so that American officials sometimes read Nomura's instructions from Tokyo before he did. No wonder the product of the cryptanalysts was called Magic. Other diplomatic codes less difficult than Purple also proved vulnerable to this kind of cryptanalytical assault.

Unfortunately, Japanese naval codes remained unbroken for the present. Unable to decipher Yamamoto's messages to his fleet, the Americans had to try to draw conclusions from the volume and source of the traffic and the call signs and transmitting characteristics of the radio operators. This technique was vulnerable to rudimentary countermeasures, such as changing call signs or imposing radio silence, which masked the sailing of the Pearl Harbor task force and its approach to the objective.

As the Japanese steamed toward Hawaii, peacetime routine prevailed on the ships of the Pacific Fleet. The usual Saturday morning inspection took place on December 6. Rear Adm. H. Fairfax Leary checked the shaves, haircuts, and uniforms of the sailors of the light cruiser *Phoenix* and then made a white-glove inspection of the ship. On board the battleship *California*, the crew prepared for a more extensive inspection scheduled for the coming week by removing the covers to a half-a-dozen hatches leading to the double bottom. When the Japanese attacked on December 7, *Phoenix* came through undamaged except for a single bullet hole in the superstructure; *California*, however, flooded when hit by deep-running torpedoes, in part because of the open hatches, and settled into the mud of Pearl Harbor.

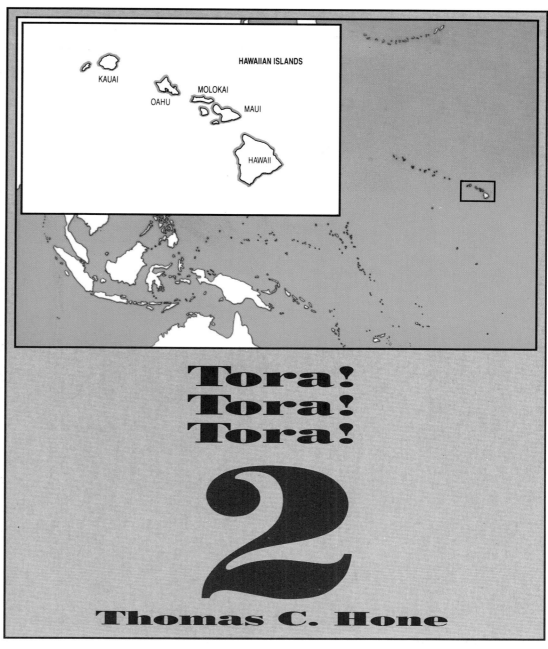

Tora! Tora! Tora!

2

Thomas C. Hone

Japan's attack on Pearl Harbor should not have surprised senior officers of the United States Navy. Not since England and France had fought for control of the seas in their colonial wars of the eighteenth century had two nations planned so assiduously for a clash at sea as Japan and the United States in the years before World War II. Once the United States became a colonial power in Asia, after the Spanish-American War, the US Navy had to plan to hold the Philippines in the face of threats from foreign powers. After World War I, the only nation with a navy able to challenge the US Navy in the Pacific and with any reason to do so was Japan. Japan controlled resources in Korea and wanted control over Manchuria and, eventually, China. The United States consistently opposed Japanese policy. The real question was not whether the navies of the two nations would fight, but when.

Between the end of the World War I and the termination, by the government of the United States in July 1939, of the commercial treaty linking the two nations, both navies planned carefully for a trans-Pacific war. Their strategic situations were quite different. Japan was Asia's Britain — an island kingdom vulnerable to blockade and starvation. To make matters potentially even worse, Japan's merchant fleet was not as large as Britain's, and her industrial output was not quite the equal of Italy, let alone the United Kingdom. On the positive side, Japan's likely enemy, the United States, was very far away. It is just over 4,500 nautical miles (8,100km) from San Francisco to Yokohama. The distance from San Diego, a major American naval base on the Pacific coast, to Manila is 6,500 nautical miles (11,700km). From Yokohama to Manila, on the other hand, is just about 1,750 nautical miles (3,150km). Pearl Harbor is nearly 4,700 nautical miles (8,460km) from the Panama Canal, 2,200 (3,960km) from San Diego, 3,300 (5,940km) from Guam, in the Marianas, and 1,970 (3,546km) from Wotje, the Japanese anchorage in the Marshall Islands. These great Pacific distances dominated both Japanese and American naval planning between the first and second World Wars.

Given the industrial power of the United States, Japan's only hope was to wage a war of attrition, wearing down American strength until the government of the United States accepted a compromise peace. A more aggressive strategy was blocked by Japan's signing of the five-power naval limitation agreement when the Washington Conference ended in 1922. That agreement set ratios and limits to the warship tonnages allowed the signatories (Great Britain, the United States, Japan, France, and Italy). The ratio of battleship tonnage for Great Britain, the United States, and Japan was 5:5:3, which meant, in practice, that the United States Fleet would have 15 battleships to the Imperial Japanese Navy's ten. Japan did somewhat better on cruiser tonnage, when the ratio among the three major navies was adjusted to 10:10:7. For aircraft carriers, then largely experimental, the ratio was the same as for battleships, with a cap of 135,000 tons for the United States and Great Britain and 81,000 tons for Japan. These limits forced the Imperial Navy to develop a defensive strategy for war with the United States.

The Versailles conference, which ended World War I, gave Japan jurisdiction over several former German possessions in the Pacific, including the Marianas (except Guam, which belonged to the United States), the Carolines, and the Marshalls. Soon afterward, the newly formed League of Nations affirmed the Japanese mandate over these islands, which stood athwart the direct route to the Philippines from Hawaii. Though Japan controlled them, successive Japanese governments pledged not to fortify them in exchange for a commitment by the United States not to modernize its defenses in the Philippines. Possession of these islands was a two-edged sword. On the one hand, Japanese forces could use them to block any thrust by the United States Navy to the Philippines. On the other, the United States could seize bases there in the event of war and then use those bases as way-stations on the road back to the Philippines.

Both Japanese and American naval planners believed that the Philippines could not be held in the face of a concerted Japanese attack. The best the limited number of United States troops might do was to hold the island forts in Manila Bay, denying that anchorage to the Imperial Fleet. It was not clear, however, how long they might hold out, and around that question spun the major issues of United States Navy war planning. Should the United States try to reinforce the Philippines quickly, aiming for a quick, decisive confrontation with the Japanese fleet? Or, should the US Navy move cautiously, conquering anchorages and bases in the Marshalls and Carolines, gradually building up its strength until it could fight the Imperial Fleet in a showdown in Philippine waters? For the Japanese Navy, the new island possessions were welcome as bases (Truk, in the Carolines, for

Above: Kobe was a major Japanese trading port and also the home of the Kawasaki shipyards where many of Japan's major warships were built. Of the six carriers involved in the Pearl Harbor attack, the *Zuikaku* was built here.

example, is a magnificent anchorage) but also a problem: they had to be supplied. In wartime, they might be isolated and cut off, leaving smaller contingents of the Imperial Fleet to face larger contingents of an attacking American force.

Distances were, as usual, everything. From Yokohama to Truk is over 1,800 nautical miles (3,240km); Yokohama to Saipan, in the Marianas, is almost 1,300 nautical miles (2,340km). Yokohama to Wotje, in the Marshalls, is more than 2,300 nautical miles (4,140km), which meant that an American task force could reach the Marshalls from Hawaii faster than reinforcements from Japan. Japanese Navy planners faced a dilemma. If they dispersed their smaller fleet, it might be defeated piecemeal by a concentrated and larger American force. If they held their forces back, however, waiting to strike the decisive blow, they might not be able to reach the scene of action in time to prevent the United States Navy (and its Marine Corps) from conquering a base that, properly reinforced, could serve as the next stepping stone on the way to the Philippines and the Japanese Home Islands. United States Navy planners had their own problems. The naval agreements which kept the Imperial Fleet smaller than the United States Navy also limited the immediate wartime potential of the latter. American interwar fleet exercises always showed that the United States Navy needed more ships and aircraft if it were to overcome Japanese forces at great distances from secure American bases. In the 1920s and 30s, Pearl Harbor

lacked machine shops, a trained labor force, and adequate supplies of fuel to support a fleet thrust westward. Ships damaged by torpedoes and bombs would have to return to San Diego for repair, and replacement aircraft would have to be shuttled out in cargo ships to the advancing force across thousands of miles of open water, under constant threat of Japanese submarine or surface raider attack.

Planners in the two navies wrestled with these problems for years. Their conclusions shaped the characteristics of the ships built in peacetime for the coming trans-Pacific war. The United States Navy's "treaty" cruisers, for example, built to the limits (10,000 tons and 8-inch guns) set by the naval arms control agreement signed in 1922, had great endurance and guns of great range, but they were lightly armored until the *New Orleans* class of 1930. Their Japanese counterparts, such as the *Furutakas* and *Aobas*, were built for speed, so they could decline battle if outnumbered. However, the latter were eventually equipped with very large (24-inch diameter), very long range (20 nautical miles — 36km), Type 93 torpedoes, each of which was — for a destroyer or light cruiser — a shipkiller. The reason was simple: the United States Navy had the advantage in the daytime, and the Japanese at night. On clear, central Pacific days, the US Navy's advantage in battleship and cruiser broadside weight would eventually tell. To counter it, Japanese planners designed fast surface ships and an anti-ship torpedo which could wreak havoc by night upon American forces steaming in defensive formations.

Both navies were spurred by the need to overcome great distances and the limits on numbers and sizes of ships,

Above: The *Omaha* was a light cruiser designed to treaty limitations, and was lead ship of a ten-ship class. All survived the war with armament that differed considerably from the original fit of twelve 6-in guns in two twin and eight single mountings.

Right: Seen in 1925, the *Akagi* was converted to a fleet carrier under the terms of the Washington naval agreement. Her sister *Amagi* was lost in a 1923 earthquake before completion, and the incomplete battleship *Kaga* was then converted in her stead.

which put a premium on packing as much fighting power into a ship as possible. These pressures also affected aircraft carrier design. At the Washington conference of 1921-2, for example, the US Navy and the Imperial Navy were allowed to convert two battlecruisers or battleships then building to large aircraft carriers. These ships eventually emerged as carriers *Lexington, Saratoga, Kaga,* and *Akagi.* The former US Navy battlecruisers were especially useful because of their great steaming ranges 10,500 nautical miles (18,900km) at 15 knots, and the ability to survive damage (*Lexington* was torpedoed twice at Coral Sea in May 1942 and still steamed at 25 knots). Their Japanese counterparts had less range 8,000 (14,400km) nautical miles at 14 knots but were otherwise similar. All four ships, though not designed as carriers from the keel up and therefore less than ideal, had the size to accept the increasingly large and heavy planes which their respective industries supplied as the interwar years passed.

Carriers commissioned after the conversions tended to be much smaller. The American *Ranger,* laid down in 1931, was only 14,500 tons standard displacement (the treaty measure). *Ryujo, Ranger's* Japanese contemporary, was even lighter: 8,000 tons standard displacement. Both navies wanted to maximize

the number of carriers that could be built under treaty limits. Exercises had shown air-minded officers in both fleets that, in battle, the side with the most (and most effective) planes in the air usually won. Accordingly, aviators pressed for more carriers; since more decks meant more planes in the air more quickly. However, the size of carriers depended upon the size and weight of the aircraft they carried, and planes kept getting larger and heavier in the years just before 1941. The Boeing F3B-1 biplane fighter of 1928, for example, weighed 2,950 pounds (1,180kg). The Grumman F4F-4 Wildcat of 1941 tipped the scales at 7,975 pounds (3,190kg). The Nakajima A2N1 of 1931 weighed 3,416 pounds (1,366kg). The Mitsubishi A6M2 Zero of 1939 was up to 5,139 pounds (2,055kg). Like the fighters, dive bombers and

Right: Designed to meet treaty limitations, the *Ranger* was smaller than the earlier battlecruiser conversions, but was designed from the keel up as a carrier. The three folding funnels on each side proved an inadequate arrangement.

torpedo planes grew larger and heavier. Carriers had to increase in tonnage to operate larger, faster, more potent planes. *Ranger* was followed by *Enterprise* (laid down in 1934), of 19,800 tons; *Ryujo* was succeeded by *Soryu* (also laid down in 1934), of 15,900 tons.

As carriers and their planes grew larger and more powerful, carrier tactics also improved. In Fleet Problem IX, staged in 1929 near the Panama Canal, *Saratoga* proved that a large carrier could strike effectively and independently deep into enemy areas. From that time until 1941 — and even through 1942 — both navies worked to invent the best ways of deploying, maneuvering, and defending their aircraft carriers. In the 1930s, carriers had to rely almost exclusively on their own antiaircraft guns and those of their escorts to shield them from an enemy's air attack. This was not a really effective defense. As a result, in exercises, the carrier which found its opponent first usually delivered the knockout blow. Carriers were fragile. Their power was in their air groups, usually two or three squadrons of attack aircraft (dive bombers and torpedo planes) and one squadron of fighters. The ships themselves were floating magazines, filled with munitions and highly volatile aviation gas for their planes.

By 1939, carrier aircraft could conduct highly coordinated strikes on enemy carriers and other ships. Attacks could be mounted quickly, and planes often practiced pre-dawn take-offs, using short-range radio once airborne to tighten their formations. After 1937, Japanese carrier aircraft battled Chinese air units, gaining wartime experience in aircraft tactics and in the launching and recovery of fully armed and (sometimes) damaged planes. By the end of the 1930s, the striking power of carriers was acknowledged in both navies. Adm. Isoroku Yamamoto, later commander-in-chief of Japan's Combined Fleet, made his reputation as an innovative leader in naval aviation. He firmly believed that long range and offensive power were the keys to victory

MITSUBISHI A6M ZERO-SEN ("ZEKE")

From the overwhelming onslaught against China to the desperate, last-ditch attacks on wave upon wave of the USAAF's bombers, the Mitsubishi A6M Zero-Sen ("Zeke") came to symbolize the undoubted tenacity of Japanese air power during the war in the Pacific. Well over 10,000 examples of this highly-maneuverable warrior were built, with their "blooding" in combat coming on September 13, 1940, over China. But it was against Allied forces, especially the US Navy during the first six months of the Pacific War, that the Zero reigned supreme, outflying and outfighting its victims. In time, however, its prowess was surpassed as the sun set on the Japanese empire.

in carrier-on-carrier battles, and he forced Japan's aircraft manufacturers to build planes that flew farther and carried at least equivalent ordnance loads when compared with their US Navy counterparts. He helped mold a force well suited to taking the initiative at the beginning of a conflict.

Supporting the carriers were other forms of naval aviation. The US Navy had agreed with the US Army in 1931 not to develop land-based bombers, but the Navy had built up a force of long-range seaplanes, including, by 1941, impressive numbers of the PBY Catalina, which could (and early in World War II actually did) stage high-altitude formation bombing raids like those conducted by B-17s. The Imperial Japanese Navy had its own similar seaplanes, as well as an impressive land-based bomber force. As with its cruiser and destroyer designs, its land-based bombers reflected Japanese battle tactics. Assuming that the US Navy would launch an offensive to rescue the defenders of the Philippines, the Japanese navy planned to whittle American numbers down through submarine attacks, night raids conducted by land-based bombers, and torpedo assaults launched during the dark by groups of cruisers and destroyers. After wearing the United States Fleet down — equalizing the strength in battleships and carriers — the imperial fleet would wade in for the final, conclusive battle. A decisive Japanese victory there would leave the United States with little choice (so the argument ran) but to accept a compromise peace.

Unfolding events disrupted this planning. First, the Pacific Ocean no longer monopolized the interests of American strategists, who turned during the 1930 to the Atlantic as well. A rearmed Germany, allied with Italy, confronted France and Britain in Europe. The threat of war there forced the US Navy in 1939 to abandon its traditional war plan (called Orange) against Japan in favor of a series of plans (dubbed Rainbow) covering a number of possibilities and belligerents. In the crucial year of 1940, moreover, Japan fortified the Marshall Islands. The American President, Franklin D. Roosevelt, reacted by ordering the United States Fleet to remain in Hawaii after completing its annual war problem. In May and June of that year, German armies rolled over British and French forces, compelling both Washington and Tokyo to reassess their long-range plans. In response, the United States Congress authorized construction of what was called a "two-ocean" navy: 9 new battleships, 6 battle cruisers, 8 heavy cruisers, 34 light cruisers, 11 large aircraft carriers, 5 small carriers, 179 destroyers, 67 submarines, and a large force of support and amphibious ships. Justified at home by the potential threat from Germany, the proposed fleet was seen as something very different in Japan. There, the military leadership

Above: Introduced in 1928 as the primary type of carrier-borne fighter until 1932, the Boeing F3B-1 came in the middle of a line of evolutionary Boeing fighters. This machine served with VB-1B (technically a bomber unit) on the *Lexington*.

Below: The Consolidated PBY was a truly exceptional patrol seaplane developed before the war, and reached a high point of development with this PBY-5A version, which added wheeled landing gear to give this versatile type an amphibious capability.

perceived the huge building program as part of a larger plan to give the US Navy clear superiority in the waters near Japan. In response, Japan joined the Axis (September 1940), taking advantage of Germany's defeat of France to gain bases in French Indochina.

By the end of 1940, Adm. Yamamoto, now head of Japan's Combined Fleet, thought seriously of abandoning the Japanese navy's accepted strategy of a fighting, drawn-out defense against an American offensive. His thinking reflected a change in Japan's strategic

goals. The United States was just one of several potential enemies. The German government had informed Japanese leaders that Britain's military officials believed that their forces were too slim to hold Malaya if Japan attacked. Assuming that were true, Malaya and the Netherlands East Indies provided opportunities for easy conquests that would give Japan a secure supply of oil and other needed resources, offsetting the constraining effect of the ever-tightening American economic boycott. With the Royal Navy hard-pressed in the

Below: Yamamoto's belief in air-dropped torpedoes for Pearl Harbor was confirmed by the success of such weapons in the British raid of November 1941 on Italian ships in Taranto harbor, where a reconnaissance photograph reveals two damaged cruisers.

Above: Though in no way a democratic nation, Japan appreciated the importance of giving its citizens a sense of involvement with the military with episodes such as this 1930 naval display. Here ordinary Japanese are seen on a Japanese warship.

Atlantic and the Mediterranean, Singapore posed a diminished threat. The danger that the Imperial Fleet would have to fight a multi-front campaign while still trying to consolidate its conquest of the Philippines seemed much reduced.

The position of the United States was also changing. In November 1940, President Roosevelt had accepted "Plan D", based on the fourth paragraph, lettered D, of a proposal by Chief of Naval Operations Adm. Harold R. Stark that America's primary goal, in the event of a world war, should be the defeat of Germany. The American decision to focus first on Europe gave Japan a great opportunity, and Adm. Yamamoto capitalized on it. In January 1941, the Combined Fleet formally requested the Imperial Navy Ministry to supply the Fleet's carrier torpedo planes with weapons that could be launched in the 40-to-45-foot (12-13m) depths of Pearl Harbor. This proved quite a challenge. Aircraft torpedoes usually sank below that depth before stabilizing on shallow runs to their targets. However, Royal Navy torpedo planes had used shallow-running torpedoes in their attack on the Italian battle fleet in Taranto in November 1940, with spectacular results, so Yamamoto thought the gamble well worth the risk.

Also that January, the admiral revealed to a colleague his plans to change

Japanese battle plans completely — to forego attrition in the mandated islands as the prelude to a decisive battle, and move offensively against the United States Fleet in Hawaii while attacking Singapore and the Philippines. By February, Yamamoto's staff had formulated a draft plan for the Pearl Harbor operation, and the admiral submitted it to Cdr. Minoru Genda, a young aviator with a brilliant grasp of carrier aircraft tactics. Genda became convinced the attack would work, provided sufficient aircraft were massed for the operation. He also persuaded Yamamoto that the primary target of the attack should be the US Navy's aircraft carriers, and he argued unsuccessfully for an amphibious assault on Oahu. Genda's goal was a "knock-out blow". His chief, however, remained content with a "knock-down blow".

That same month, the United States Navy formally acknowledged the shift in American strategy toward Europe by dividing the United States Fleet into Atlantic and Pacific commands. In

March, the military chiefs of the United States and Great Britain formally and secretly agreed to take a defensive but coordinated stand against further Japanese moves in the Pacific. They agreed on little else. There would be no unified Pacific command, and no joint strategy. However, the Congress, at Roosevelt's urging, approved the Lend-Lease Act in March, allowing Great Britain to tap US industry without paying for its purchases immediately in cash.

In April, Adm. Yamamoto formed the First Air Fleet, the striking force of Japan's six largest aircraft carriers that would attack Pearl Harbor that December. In support of its move south and east, Japan signed a neutrality pact with the Soviet Union in April, protecting Manchukuo and Korea from attack and further directing the coming theater of war to the South Pacific. At the end of the month, Yamamoto submitted his plan for multiple offensives (including the Pearl Harbor attack) to the Imperial Fleet's General Staff. His plans gained support from an American decision to

Right: Yamamoto, seated in the center of the front row in this photograph of a meeting of Japan's senior naval leaders in November 1940, did not have an altogether easy task in overcoming the objections of his less far-sighted superior, Adm. Nagano.

shift three battleships, an aircraft carrier, and supporting cruisers and destroyers to the newly formed Atlantic Fleet. Adm. Husband Kimmel was no longer in charge of the United States Fleet. The ships that remained under his command now constituted the Pacific Fleet, but Kimmel and his staff did not think the force in Hawaii could deter Japan from a move against the Philippines or Southeast Asia.

President Roosevelt froze Japan's assets in the United States in July, announced that the United States would send a military mission to China, and cut the flow of oil to Japan to a trickle. His goal was to influence Japan without provoking her. He failed. He had no influence whatsoever with the men who now mattered: the staff officers in Tokyo analyzing Yamamoto's plans. In September, a series of war games, in which the senior Japanese naval officers took part, tested Yamamoto's proposals. Based on the results of the games, the General Staff recommended against the Pearl Harbor attack. The Imperial Navy had only 11 carriers. In sending the six best against Pearl Harbor, Yamamoto was risking everything on one throw of the dice. Moreover, in striking at Pearl Harbor, Yamamoto was placing heavy burdens on the air and naval units left to cover the invasions of the Philippines, Malaya, and the Netherlands East Indies. Equal losses at Pearl Harbor — three Japanese carriers for three American — would threaten the whole enterprise. Yamamoto was no fool, however. He well understood the risk.

Above: A cheerier moment late in November 1941 for Japan's ambassador to Washington, the politically moderate Adm. Kichisaburo Nomura (right) and the more hard-line special envoy Saburu Kurusu, who arrived on November 15.

He also understood better than any other senior naval commander in the region what advances in aviation had done to the traditional plans of the American and Japanese navies. Yamamoto had no doubt that Japan's ultimate goal was still a negotiated settlement with the United States. However, he also knew that the increases in range and striking power of carrier and land-based planes gave him the chance to do with aviation what the naval limitation agreements prevented him from doing with a surface fleet — to be in all the places that mattered in sufficient strength to keep the military initiative. To conquer both the resources needed by Japan and a buffer zone between Japan and the United States, Yamamoto needed to be able to "run free" for about six months. Then, his initial objectives in hand, he could adopt the traditional waiting game. There was really no other alternative, and Yamamoto threatened to resign if the General Staff did not set aside its reservations.

A similar understanding of the impact of long-range aviation was shaping the policies of the War Department in the United States. While the Washington agreements were in effect, the US Army was not allowed to improve or enlarge its Philippine defenses. After Japan withdrew from the agreements in 1936, Congress declined to appropriate funds for Philippine fortifications because the United States was scheduled to grant independence to the islands in 1946 and because the Army and Navy did not think that scarce military appropriations should be diverted to what was regarded as a lost cause. However, in 1941 the Army's B-17 four-engined bomber looked like just the mobile weapon which might make defense of the Philippines feasible. The heavy bombers had demonstrated that they could find and

attack ships at sea, although under admittedly artificial conditions, and they had the range to reach Japanese airfields on Formosa. Secretary of War Henry L. Stimson and Gen. Douglas MacArthur (who had been recalled from retirement to lead US and Philippine troops) were convinced that land-based air power could take up the slack left by the transfer of American aircraft carriers to the Atlantic. In September, the first B-17s landed at Clark Field on the island of Luzon, near Manila. MacArthur hoped to have 300 of them by April 1942. When Pearl Harbor was attacked, he had 35.

It was too little, too late. On November 5, the Japanese set a date for the Pearl Harbor attack; on the 26th, the Pearl Harbor Striking Force left its anchorage in Etorofu, in the Kurile Islands. The Force, commanded by Vice Adm. Chuichi Nagumo, was built around the following carriers: *Akagi* (commissioned 1927 and later modernized), *Kaga* (1928, also modernized), *Hiryu* (1939), *Soryu* (1937), *Shokaku*, and *Zuikaku* (both commissioned 1941). These ships carried 423 aircraft, their maximum complement. Escorting them were the modernized battle cruisers *Hiei* and *Kirishima*, two heavy cruisers (*Tone* and *Chikuma*), and a squadron of nine *Kagero* class destroyers. Patrolling ahead of the Striking Force were three *I* class submarines; supporting it were eight tankers and supply ships. Steaming at latitude 43 degrees North, the Force turned southeast on December 3, and headed for a point 275 miles (440km) north of Oahu.

Above: The American diplomat with the difficult task of putting the American point of view to the Japanese was the ambassador in Tokyo, Joseph C. Grew, who later became Under-Secretary of State dealing with problems relating to Japan's surrender.

Above: The man charged with implementing the Japanese plan for the attack on Pearl Harbor was Vice Adm. Chuichi Nagumo, an officer perhaps too cautious to take the maximum advantage of the opportunities that his airmen created at Pearl Harbor.

Proceeding separately to Hawaiian waters (via the Marshalls) was the Advance Expeditionary Force: 27 large, long-range submarines — 11 with small aircraft and five carrying midget submarines for use inside Pearl Harbor. Each midget carried two torpedoes. The large submarines were to remain off Oahu after the initial attack; their job was to ambush any ships which the aircraft could not sink. The whole plan was bold. Adm. Nagumo did not assume that he could approach undetected; he had orders to attack even if detected in his final approach to Pearl Harbor. If US ships left the harbor during his approach, he was to find and sink them. He was not to assume complete surprise. The chance that the midget submarines and the aircraft of Nagumo's force might not strike simultaneously was accepted as worth the risk. Soon after 6:00 A.M. on December 7, the six carriers turned into the wind and launched the first wave of 183 planes. Another 170 aircraft were launched in a second wave an hour later. Of the 353 planes sent against Pearl Harbor, 50 carried 40-centimeter armorpiercing shells converted to bombs for use against battleships, 40 carried torpedoes with 450-pound warheads, 50 were level bombers with 250-kilogram high explosive bombs, 80 were Zero fighters, and the rest were dive bombers.

At anchor in Pearl Harbor were 70 warships, including 8 battleships, 2 heavy cruisers, 6 light cruisers, 29 destroyers, and 5 submarines. There were also 24 auxiliaries, among them 10 destroyer and submarine tenders, 2 oilers, 3 repair ships, and a hospital ship. Adm. Kimmel and the Army commander in Hawaii, Maj. Gen. Walter Short, had already been sent several "war warnings" by their superiors in Washington. As recently as November 27, Chief of Naval Operations Stark had cautioned Kimmel, largely on the basis of intercepted Japanese diplomatic traffic, that Japan was expected to make an

Above: Photographed in 1936, the *Kaga* is seen in her definitive form with funnels angled out and down from her midships section. With her half-sister *Akagi*, the *Kaga* formed the 1st Carrier Division of Nagumo's Pearl Harbor Strike Force.

Below: Seen in 1938, the *Hiryu* was slightly more conventional in appearance than the *Kaga*, but still had lateral funnels, in this instance two units forward of the island. With her sister *Soryu*, the *Hiryu* formed the 2nd Carrier Division.

Left: Aircrew move to their machines in preparation for the Pearl Harbor attack. At this time the flight skills of Japanese naval aircrew were equal to those anywhere in the world, and their tactical abilities were decidedly superior.

"aggressive move" in a matter of days. However, Stark had also said that the evidence "indicates an amphibious expedition against either the Philippines, Thai or Kra Peninsula or possibly Borneo". As Stark's warnings demonstrated, the cryptanalysts who had broken the Japanese diplomatic codes could chart the breakdown of relations between the United States and Japan, but they tended to produce vague and sometimes contradictory indications of a Japanese attack 'somewhere' in the Pacific. Since October, the Navy's signal intelligence station on the island of Corregidor in Manila Bay had been monitoring Japanese naval and merchant marine communications in ports such as Shanghai and in the South China Sea. The Japanese clearly were on the move, but the volume and sources of radio traffic pointed toward a southward advance, since Nagumo's force maintained strict radio silence as it steamed eastward.

Pearl Harbor was calm. Though painted a warlike dark grey, the battleships were not protected by antitorpedo nets and their ready-to-use

Left: With their engines warmed up and running in the most economical mode, Mitsubishi A6M2 Zero fighters await the order to take-off from the carrier *Hiryu* as escorts for the Aichi D3A dive-bombers and Nakajima B5N torpedo bombers.

antiaircraft ammunition was stored in locked boxes. There were no barrage balloons over the harbor, nor was there equipment to put up an effective smoke screen over the anchored ships. Many officers and enlisted personnel were ashore. The Navy had two seaplane bases on Oahu — one in Pearl Harbor and the other at Kaneohe Bay — plus an airfield on Ford Island, in the center of the harbor, for its carrier planes. There was also a Marine Corps airfield at Ewa. Not one of these fields could put up an effective defense.

The Army was responsible for antiaircraft protection, but many of its artillery units had been depleted in order to build up the defenses of the Philippines. There were two large Army airfields on Oahu: Hickam, next to Pearl Harbor, and Wheeler, in the center of the island. There were also two small auxiliary fields, Bellows and Haleiwa. Based mostly at Hickam and Wheeler were 64 modern, flyable P-40 fighters, six combat-ready B-17s, and 21 obsolete B-18 twin-engine bombers. All told, the Navy and Marine Corps had about 150 planes on Oahu, while the Army counted 143. However, most of the flyable Army planes stood precisely aligned on taxiways away from recently built revetments. They were so exposed because Gen. Short feared sabotage more than attack, despite the fact that both he and Adm. Kimmel had been warned by their senior aviation officers the previous March that Oahu was poorly prepared to ward off an attack.

If Oahu had been alert, the first efforts of the Japanese midget subs would have given the whole game away. Launched after midnight December 6-7, the five small subs gamely approached the antisubmarine net stretched across the narrow entrance to Pearl Harbor. At 3:42 A.M., a small minesweeper patrolling the entrance spotted the periscope of one of the midgets. The minesweeper summoned the World War I destroyer *Ward*, which searched the area for the next two hours. Soon after 6:00 A.M., a patrolling PBY flying boat sighted and marked the same or another midget (the

Above: A heavily laden Nakajima B5N bomber claws for altitude just after leaving the flight deck of its carrier for the attack on Pearl Harbor. The type was used for torpedo and level bombing, in the latter role using converted armor-piercing naval shells.

Above: The ship targeting detail on this captured Japanese chart of Pearl Harbor reveals the high quality of the naval intelligence received from Japanese agents on Oahu, who could watch the fleet anchorage from a number of positions.

Above: Adm. Husband E. Kimmel was the commander-in-chief of the US Navy's Pacific Fleet with his headquarters at Pearl Harbor. Though alerted to the possibility of war with Japan, Kimmel had not brought his command to a high state of preparation.

Above: Kimmel's army counterpart was Lt. Gen. Walter C. Short. Like Kimmel, Short had failed to ensure that his command was prepared for war, and was therefore relieved of his command less than a fortnight after the Pearl Harbor disaster.

midgets were hard for their crews to control) attempting to follow repair ship *Antares* into the harbor. *Ward* attacked the small sub at 6:45 A.M. Nine minutes later, William W. Outerbridge, *Ward*'s captain, who had been summoned to the bridge from his cabin, notified the Commandant of Hawaii's naval district (the officer responsible for the harbor's defenses) that it had fired upon, rammed, and sunk a submarine. The antisubmarine net, opened at 5:00 A.M. for routine morning traffic, was still open. Even worse, Adm. Kimmel's staff was not told of the attack until 7:25 A.M. Kimmel and Gen. Short should already have been alerted. An Army air search radar on Kahuku Point, above the northern shore of Oahu, had detected, at 6:45

A.M., the cruiser float planes sent as scouts ahead of the Striking Force's first wave of attacking aircraft. Half an hour later, the same radar picked up the main body of Japanese planes, 132 miles (211km) north of Oahu. Both radar sightings were reported to a central plotting station, but the young officer there (filling in temporarily for the regular duty officer) thought that the radar was just picking up a flight of B-17s due in that morning from California. At 7:53 A.M., the senior officer with the first wave radioed Nagumo "Tora, Tora, Tora" (Tiger, Tiger, Tiger) — telling the admiral that surprise had been achieved.

Two minutes later, the first wave started attacking Pearl Harbor and Oahu. Torpedo planes struck the

Map A
December 7 1941

KAUAI

NIIHAU

OAHU

Pearl Harbor

MOLOKAI

LANAI   MAUI

KAHOOLAWE

HAWAIIAN ISLANDS

HAWAII

First Wave 07:40   Attack ordered 07:53   B

Mokuleta Field   Haleiwa Field

Wheeler Field

Kaneohe NAS

Pearl Harbor

Hickam Field

Bellows Field

Ewa   Honolulu

Second Wave 08:50   Attack ordered 08:55   C

Haleiwa Field

Mokuleta Field

Wheeler Field

Kaneohe NAS

Pearl Harbor

Hickam Field

Bellows Field

Ewa   Honolulu

D

Pearl City

FORD ISLAND

US Naval Station and Fleet HQ

THE ATTACK ON PEARL HARBOR

Map A
At 6:00 A.M., local time, December 7, 1941, in rough seas, the first Japanese aircraft of the First Air Fleet took off from the carriers of the Pearl Harbor Striking Force, lying 274 miles (440km) north of Oahu. The fighters were launched first, then the level bombers, then the dive bombers followed by the torpedo bombers; a second force of fighters acting as aerial cover completed the first wave. The whole operation took a little over 15 minutes to complete. At about 6:20 the assembled aircraft headed for Pearl Harbor. Because of the sheer number of aircraft to be launched, a second wave began taking off at 7:15. In total 353 planes were flying into the attack.

Map B
The first wave reached the north coast of Oahu at 7:53 A.M. and the attack order was given by Cdr. Mitsuo Fuchida. Complete surprise was achieved — in those first minutes there wasn't even antiaircraft fire. As planned the attacking aircraft divided into two groups.

The fighters and dive bombers concentrated on Wheeler Field, Kaneohe Naval Air Station, and Bellows Field, while the torpedo bombers and level bombers attacked Ford Island, Ewa and Hickam Field.

Map C
The second wave reached the Oahu coast at about 8:50 A.M. some thirty minutes after the first had finished their attack and had headed back towards the carriers. This second attack went in at 8:55 against fierce antiaircraft fire. The initial shock of the defenders had worn off sufficiently during the brief lull in attacks and now every weapon that could be pointed skyward was aimed at the Japanese aircraft, the Americans even managed to get a number of P-40 fighters aloft from Haleiwa Field to the north. As in the first wave, the attackers divided their forces. Dive bombers and accompanying fighters attacked Ford Island and the ships still afloat in the harbor, while the high level bombers came up from the south and hit Hickam Field. The attack lasted until 9:55. The aircraft had returned to their carriers by 12:15 P.M. and the Striking Force was heading for home by 13:00 P.M.

Map D
The attack of the first wave on Ford Island. The torpedo bombers came up from the south towards Battleship Row, where seven battleships of the Pacific Fleet were moored, while fighters and dive bombers attacked ground installations and aircraft.

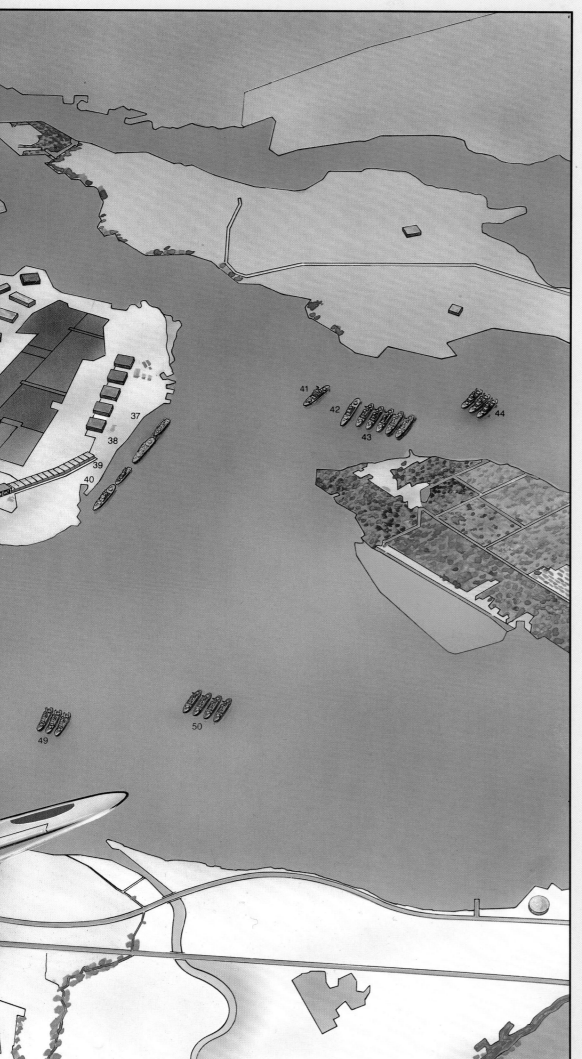

SHIPS' POSITIONS IN PEARL HARBOR ON DECEMBER 7, 1941

View from the air looking south

1 Auxiliary Vessel CASTOR
2 Auxiliary Vessel SUMNER
3 Submarine Tender PELIAS
4 Submarines NARWHAL, DOLPHIN & TAUTOG and Tenders THORNTON & HULBERT
5 Destroyer BAGLEY
6 Light Cruiser ST. LOUIS
7 Light Cruiser HONOLULU*
   Damaged; returned to service
8 Minesweeper GREBE and Destroyers SCHLEY, SICARD & PRUITT
9 Heavy Cruiser SAN FRANCISCO
10 Destroyers TRACY, PREBLE & CUMMINGS
11 Heavy Cruiser NEW ORLEANS
12 Oiler RAMAPO
13 Repair Vessel RIGEL
14 Seaplane Tender SWAN
15 Destroyer MUGFORD
16 Destroyer JARVIS
17 Gunboat SACRAMENTO
18 Auxiliary Vessel ARGONNE
19 Light Cruiser HELENA*
   Heavily damaged; returned to service
20 Minelayer OGLALA*
   Capsized; refitted as repair vessel
21 Submarine CACHALOT
22 Battleship PENNSYLVANIA*
   Damaged; returned to service December 1941
23 Destroyer CASSIN*
   Capsized; returned to service with new hull, November 1943
24 Destroyer DOWNES*
   Heavily damaged; returned to service with new hull, February 1944
25 Destroyer SHAW*
   Sunk; returned to service with new bow section, September 1942
26 Minesweepers BOBOLINK, VIREO, TURKEY, RAIL & TERN
27 Seaplane Tender AVOCET
28 Battleship CALIFORNIA*
   Sunk upright; returned to service September 1943
29 Oiler NEOSHO
30 Battleship OKLAHOMA*
   Capsized; sold for scrap December 1946; sunk in storm en route to West Coast, 1947
31 Battleship MARYLAND*
   Damaged; returned to service December 1941
32 Battleship WEST VIRGINIA*
   Sunk upright; returned to service July 1944
33 Battleship TENNESSEE*
   Damaged; returned to service December 1941
34 Repair Vessel VESTAL*
   Heavily damaged and beached; returned to service February 1942
35 Battleship ARIZONA*
   Sunk; rests as war grave
36 Battleship NEVADA*
   Heavily damaged and beached; returned to service December 1942
37 Seaplane Tender TANGIER
38 Target Battleship UTAH*
   Capsized; rests as war grave
39 Light Cruiser RALEIGH*
   Torpedoed; returned to service
40 Light Cruiser DETROIT
41 Seaplane Tender CURTISS*
   Damaged; returned to service
42 Repair Vessel MEDUSA
43 Destroyers TREVER, BREESE, ZANE, PERRY & WASMUTH
44 Destroyers RAMSAY, GAMBLE & MONTGOMERY
45 Destroyer CHEW
46 Destroyer ALLEN
47 Hospital Vessel SOLACE
48 Tender DOBBIN and Destroyers WORDEN, HULL, DEWEY, PHELPS & MACDONOUGH
49 Destroyers PATTERSON, RALPH TALBOT & HENLEY
50 Destroyers AYLWIN, FARRAGUT, DALE & MONAGHAN
51 Light Cruiser PHOENIX
52 Destroyer BLUE
53 Tender WHITNEY and Destroyers TUCKER, CONYNGHAM, REID, CASE & SELFRIDGE

anchored ships while dive bombers and fighters attacked the American aircraft lined up on the ground. As the first torpedo planes pulled away, other Type 97s, flying at 10,000 feet (3,000m), released their converted 40-centimeter shells. Within minutes, Japanese planes were swarming all over their primary targets, and inflicting terrible damage.

The primary targets of the first wave were the seven battleships berthed at mooring quays along the southeast side of Ford Island, opposite the Navy yard piers. *Nevada* (launched in 1914) was hit by a torpedo on her port side 14 feet (4m) above her keel, between her two forward 14-inch turrets. *Arizona* (launched in 1915) was apparently also torpedoed forward. A motion picture film taken at the time shows fuel oil from this hit burning on the water around her bow. *Oklahoma* (also launched in 1914) was struck on the port side four times in a matter of minutes. She listed so rapidly that the third and fourth torpedoes detonated above her side armor belt. *West Virginia* (launched in 1921) had her port side ripped open by six torpedo explosions. A seventh torpedo crashed into the battleship's rudder and tore it free. Two torpedoes hit *California* (launched in 1919). The first cut a gash below the waterline between number two turret and the bridge; the second blew out side plating beneath the after superimposed 14-inch turret. Other torpedo planes went after the ships in the anchorages on the opposite side of Ford Island, holing the disarmed battleship *Utah* (a target ship) twice and light cruiser *Raleigh* (launched in 1922) once.

By ten minutes after eight o'clock *Oklahoma* was capsizing to port, *West Virginia* appeared to be headed for the same fate, and *Utah* lay on her side. But worse was to come. When the high-altitude bombers carrying the converted armor-piercing shells dropped their loads, one of shells plummeted through *Arizona*'s two armored decks and ignited her forward main battery magazines, containing 1,232 silk-wrapped cartridges of smokeless powder. The force of the explosion was tremendous. From her second turret forward, *Arizona*'s sides were blown completely out, and the ship's armored decks and turrets dropped straight down onto the wreckage which had formed *Arizona*'s forecastle. An all-consuming fire followed the thunderous detonation. *Tennessee* (sister to *California*, and anchored inboard of *West Virginia*) and hapless *West Virginia* were also hit by converted shells. Two struck the latter. One was stopped — unexploded — by her armored deck; the second crashed through the roof of her superimposed 16-inch turret aft but broke up. Two also fell on *Tennessee*. One broke through a turret roof but caused only local damage; the other blew up after striking the middle barrel of one of the ship's three-gun, 14-inch turrets.

By 8.30 A.M., "Battleship Row" was

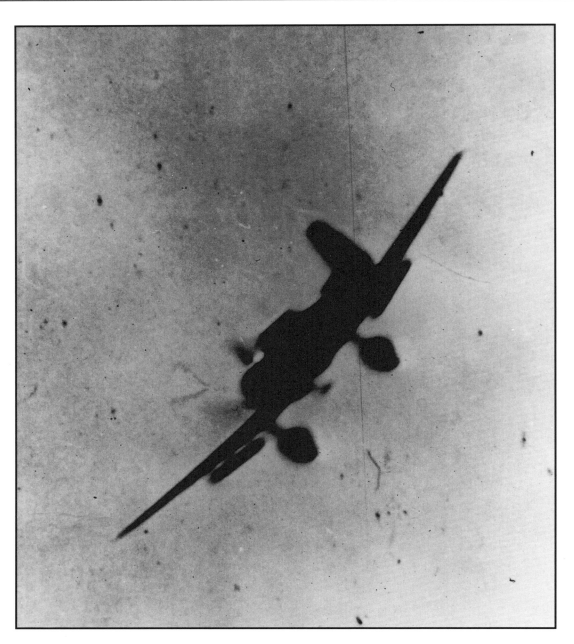

Above: Later known to the Allies as the "Val", the Aichi D3A1 was the Japanese Navy's primary carrier-borne dive-bomber in late 1941. Some 126 D3A1s were involved in the Pearl Harbor operation, each carrying one 500-pound bomb as offensive armament.

Below: Lying off Ford Island in Battleship Row, from left to right, were the six battleships *Nevada*, *Arizona* (inshore of the repair ship *Vestal*), *West Virginia* and *Tennessee*, and *Oklahoma* and *Maryland*. The *Arizona* was completely destroyed.

chaos. *Oklahoma* had rolled 150 degrees to port until her superstructure jammed in the harbor bottom. Only the turn of her bilge and part of her keel showed above water. *West Virginia* also rested on the bottom, but still upright. Prompt counterflooding, and the retarding pressure exerted by the bulk of *Tennessee* as the two ships wedged together, had kept the listing *West Virginia* from going all the way over. However, she was smothered by oil fires which were gutting her superstructure and threatening to trigger an explosion in her unflooded forward 16-inch powder magazines. *Nevada* was down by the head and on fire forward. *Arizona* was a hideous

wreck; over one thousand men were dead in her.

The Japanese did not overlook other targets. One Japanese torpedo plane crossed Ford Island from the northwest and launched a torpedo at light cruiser *Helena* (launched in 1938) anchored alongside a Navy Yard pier. The torpedo hit the cruiser amidships; the concussion from the explosion so damaged the neighboring old minelayer *Oglala*, however, that the latter rolled over. Ford Island's seaplane ramps and hangars were also given a good working over. For good measure, a midget sub that had penetrated the harbor tried to attack seaplane tender *Curtiss* at 8:39 A.M.

Fired upon by the anchored tender, the sub was rammed and depth charged by destroyer *Monaghan*, which had been on its way to reinforce *Ward*.

The second group of attacking planes struck their targets just before 9:00 A.M. Dive bombers attacked battleship *Pennsylvania* (sister ship of *Arizona* and flagship of the Pacific Fleet) and two destroyers high and dry in Pearl Harbor's concrete drydock. One 250-kilogram bomb landed on the battleship amidships, doing superficial damage. However, other bombs ruptured the fuel tanks of the destroyers, starting a severe fire in the bottom of the drydock. Flooding the drydock only made matters

Above: Taken only moments after her forward magazine exploded, this photograph of the *Arizona* indicates the devastation before the ship sank. More than 1,000 American sailors were killed in the destruction of this *Pennsylvania* class battleship of 1915.

Below: Seen from the shore, the Japanese attack on Pearl Harbor gave the impression that almost nothing and no one could survive. Yet the Japanese failure to destroy repair facilities meant that many American ships were soon back in fighting trim.

Above: A motor launch moves in to rescue survivors from the water alongside the *West Virginia*, which suffered considerable structural damage amidships from torpedo hits and then settled on the bottom. Inshore of her, the *Tennessee* suffered less damage.

US ARMY PERSONNEL, PEARL HARBOR

Taken by surprise as they were on that fateful Sunday morning, the troops who defended Pearl Harbor were not prepared for combat. Troops on garrison duty like these simply grabbed what weapons they had and began to fight back. These two are armed with the .30 caliber Model 1903 rifle and carry on their waist belts the Model 1910 bayonet and ammunition pouches. The sergeant also wears the pre-war British-style steel helmet.

Above: The Japanese also struck at Oahu's airfields. This post-attack scene at one of the two naval air stations (Ford Island and Kaneohe Bay) shows a Consolidated PBY and a Vought OS2U Kingfisher against a backdrop of burning aircraft and installations.

Below: This improvised antiaircraft position, in a bomb crater at NAS Kaneohe Bay has .30-cal machine guns on high-angle mountings. It would have been able to achieve little against anything but a very low-level attacker flying at low speed.

Above: Naval Air Station Kaneohe Bay lay on the eastern side of Oahu. It was attacked by some Japanese first-wave aircraft, but was right on the path of the second attack wave, and this aerial photograph shows the extent of the damage caused by Japanese bombing.

worse, for the burning oil rose with the water, turning the destroyers into blackened hulks. At about the same time, the damaged *Nevada* attempted to sortie from Pearl Harbor. The ship had raised steam before any of the other battleships because her engineers had kept more of her boilers active than was the usual habit while in port. Under the command of a reservist, Lt. Cdr. J. F. Thomas, with her helm under the hand of a veteran chief quartermaster, Robert Sedberry, *Nevada* swung clear of the burning *Arizona*, passed "Battleship Row", and headed as quickly as she could for the harbor entrance.

Dive bombers lining up to strike drydocked *Pennsylvania* turned their fury instead on *Nevada*, and the wounded battleship was quickly obscured by columns of water thrown up by the explosions of 250-kilogram bombs. *Nevada* sustained more hits. Her bow was now so badly damaged that water was flowing in above her belt of anti-torpedo armor and running along her armored deck to cascade down through ventilation trunks into boiler rooms. To keep *Nevada* from sinking in the harbor entrance, the senior admiral on the scene ordered the burning battleship beached, where she slowly filled with water. *Maryland*, sister to *West Virginia* and nestled inboard of *Oklahoma*, was hit by two of the modified 40-centimeter shells. Neither caused serious damage. *California*, hit by two bombs as well as by two torpedoes, would have stayed afloat had her crew and her defenses been properly prepared, but the crew was ordered to

Right: Taken during the Pearl Harbor raid, this Japanese photograph reveals some of the damage inflicted on Wheeler Field, the USAAF's most important fighter airfield on Oahu. Note the aircraft arranged in the neat rows that greatly eased the attackers' task.

Above: The Japanese committed five "Type A" midget submarines (each with two 18-in torpedoes) to the Pearl Harbor attack. All were lost or abandoned without gaining any successes. This boat was beached near Bellows Field on the eastern side of Oahu.

Below: Firefighters play the jets of high-pressure hoses onto the superstructure of the burning *Nevada*, which was deliberately beached at Hospital Point to avoid blocking the deep channel as she settled deeper into the water while trying to reach the sea.

abandon their ship just as they were raising the power necessary to drive her pumps. Burning oil from *Arizona* and *West Virginia* had drifted down on the battleship at just the wrong time. As a result, *California* also gradually filled with water.

By 10:00 A.M. the attack was over. Aviators returning to the Striking Force pressed Adm. Nagumo to order yet another strike. Only then, they argued, could Pearl Harbor's docks, machine shops (built only recently), and tank farm be smashed. Nagumo demurred. He still had no idea where carriers *Lexington* and *Enterprise* were. They could surprise him at any time. Although his air units had lost only 39 planes, many more had been damaged, if only lightly. Attacking Pearl Harbor again would put his offensive power over Oahu just when he might need it to hit the American carriers, his primary target. Beyond that risk was the certain cost in lost and damaged aircraft — planes which his force might need on the return voyage. Nagumo chose to retire. In its wake, his command left five battleships and three destroyers sunk or sinking, three battleships and two cruisers damaged, nearly 200 Army and Navy aircraft destroyed, and 3,478 killed or wounded military personnel. It was a stunning victory.

American commentators and historians have argued that Pearl Harbor was a tactical victory but a strategic error for Japan. The attack united public opinion in the United States in favor of war and also failed to catch the US Navy's carriers, though *Enterprise* was so close that some of her aircraft flew into Ford Island during the closing moments of the Japanese assault. However, Yamamoto's gamble did buy time. Carrier *Yorktown*, sister of *Enterprise*, left the Atlantic ten days after the attack on Pearl Harbor and took two weeks to reach San Diego via the Panama Canal. *Saratoga*, absent from Pearl Harbor on December 7, was torpedoed by a Japanese submarine on January 11, 1942, and was out of action, under repair, until May 22. Yamamoto's goal was to shove the US Navy aside while Japanese forces encircled the Philippines and conquered Malaya and the Netherlands East Indies. He achieved it. Had circumstance put one or more of the US carriers in Pearl Harbor on December 7, American commentators on the battle might have taken a different view of the larger outcome. Midway, the decisive carrier battle of the war, could not have been won by the US Navy if the losses sustained at Pearl Harbor had included a carrier.

Beyond that, American commentators fail to consider the dilemma facing Adm. Kimmel. He had been told he had to remain in Hawaiian waters. He had also

Left: The *California* began to settle after receiving two torpedo hits. Threatened by a blaze of floating oil, the ship was temporarily abandoned after 10.00 A.M. but then reboarded after the wind had changed direction and blown away the threat.

Above: Built as a destroyer in 1919, but converted into a high-speed minesweeper by the time of Pearl Harbor, the *Chandler* managed to put to sea in search of the enemy with an armament of just three 3-in guns. Fortunately for her she didn't find them.

Below: American personnel survey the wreckage of one of the 39 Japanese aircraft lost during the Pearl Harbor attack. In *materiel* terms this was indeed a very small price that the Japanese had to pay. Other aircraft were damaged but returned safely.

been denied the forces necessary to take the offensive, in part because of demands of the Atlantic. He was not even allowed to pull his veteran battleships back to San Pedro or San Diego, where they would not drain his oil stocks in Hawaii. Kimmel actually had two fleets: one built around three fast carriers, the other composed of the slow battleships and their escorts. With this heterogeneous force, he was expected to undertake some sort of action against the Imperial Japanese Navy if war should come. His staff put together a foray against the Marshalls, but it was fortunate that the Japanese attack kept him from implementing it. The Pacific Fleet, even at pre-attack strength, would have been outnumbered two-to-one in carriers, in waters teeming with Japanese submarines and scouted by land-based Japanese military aviation.

In his own defense, Adm. Kimmel later argued that he would have been prepared if he had been given access to the closely held Magic intercepts of Japan's diplomatic code. The admiral was understandably bitter, but the diplomatic messages from Tokyo to Washington did not reveal that the Striking Force was on its way to Pearl Harbor. The only hint that something might happen in Hawaii was Tokyo's request that its consulate on Oahu send it information about the ships anchored in Pearl Harbor. The fact that other Japanese diplomatic posts were asked to forward

Below: The American forces lost 188 aircraft on Oahu. Many of these, however, were obsolescent types such as these Curtiss P-36 fighters of the USAAF, whose loss was insignificant in the longer term. Another 159 American aircraft were badly damaged.

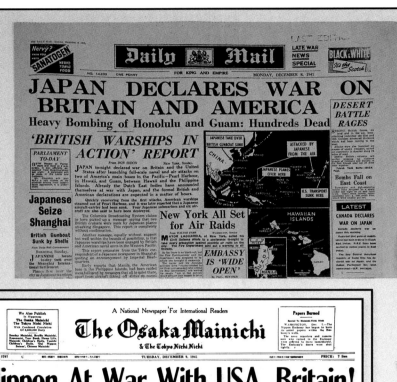

The Outbreak of the Pacific War. Newspapers of December 7-9, 1941

Close study will reveal some examples of journalistic license based on rumor and fear rather than hard fact — take for example the early reports of Japanese paratroopers on Oahu and Honolulu

1 *Daily Mail*, dated Monday December 8, 1941, published in London
2 *Daily Express*, dated December 8, 1941, published in London
3 *Daily Mirror* dated December 8, 1941, published in London
4 *San Francisco Chronicle*,

Extra edition, published December 8, 1941
5 *Honolulu Star-Bulletin*, Extra edition, published Sunday, December 7, 1941
6 *St. Louis Post-Dispatch*, evening paper, seventh Extra edition, published December 8, 1941
7 *New York Times*, published Tuesday, December 9, 1941
8 *The Osaka Mainichi*, a Japanese English-language newspaper, published in Tokyo, Tuesday December 9, 1941

John Frost Historical Newspaper Service, 1-7; The Mainichi Newspaper, Tokyo, 8

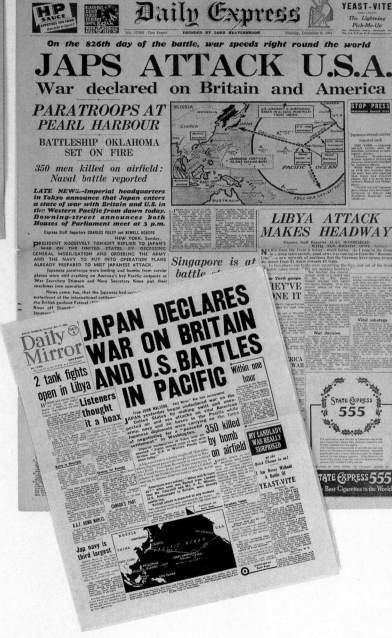

These newspapers report the moment that Japan went to war with the United States and the Allies, from three totally contrasting points of view. On December 11, the newspapers would follow this up with reports that both Italy and Nazi Germany had also declared war on the United States, in support of Japan's ambitions in the Pacific. Global war had broken out and war in the Pacific was to be only a part of it.

similar information did not make the messages from Oahu stand out. Finally, the Imperial Navy changed its operational codes suddenly at the beginning of December. This was taken as a clue that something was up, but radio traffic analysis continued to direct leaders in Washington towards the Philippines and Malaya.

The truth is that Kimmel was surprised because he did not see the strategic situation as Yamamoto did. Kimmel did not think his command was a serious threat to the Japanese, and he also failed to sense the possibility that Yamamoto had changed Japan's strategy

from defensive at the outset to a surprise attack followed by a prolonged defense. To protect his country's rapid thrust south and west, Yamamoto needed to eliminate any threat from the east — from Hawaii. The Imperial Fleet could not be everywhere at once in strength, so Yamamoto first sent it, in overwhelming force, against his primary enemy. The test of a senior commander is his ability to perceive the enemy's strategy and act against it, no matter what the odds. Kimmel's situation was impossible. He could neither run nor fight to win. But he did not have to suffer so crushing a defeat. No excuse offered on his behalf

can obscure the fact that he was undone by his military opponent.

Pearl Harbor produced far more than its fair share of myths. The worst was that President Roosevelt knew of the attack ahead of time; some of his bitterest critics alleged that he deliberately set it up in order to cover his undeclared "private war" against Hitler in the Atlantic. There is no evidence for this at all. Roosevelt was indeed preoccupied by events in the Atlantic. The destroyer *Greer* had been torpedoed in the North Atlantic in September by a German U-boat, and the US Navy to all intents and purposes, had been a belligerent since that time. The destroyer *Reuben James* had been lost to submarine attack near Iceland at the end of October. US Navy ships were attacking submarines on sight. But the president knew the United States was not prepared for a two-ocean war. He was trying to pressure Japan without provoking war. If he was guilty of anything, it was in believing that his administration's policies gave him some control over the actions of the Japanese government.

A related myth is that Navy code-breakers had learned of the approaching Japanese Striking Force, but failed to get the message to Hawaii intime, either because of the president's interference of because of bureaucratic incompetence. There is no evidence for this claim either. The Striking Force maintained radio silence throughout its approach to Hawaii. A third myth, widely held after the attack, was that Hawaiians of Japanese ancestry had supplied information and even directions to Nagumo's Striking Force. This was an outright falsehood, promulgated by white Hawaiian officials and suspicious Army intelligence officers to justify a decree of martial law on Oahu and the internment of Japanese-American citizens on the US mainland. The air attack on Hawaii was a tremendous shock. Eyewitnesses were staggered by the

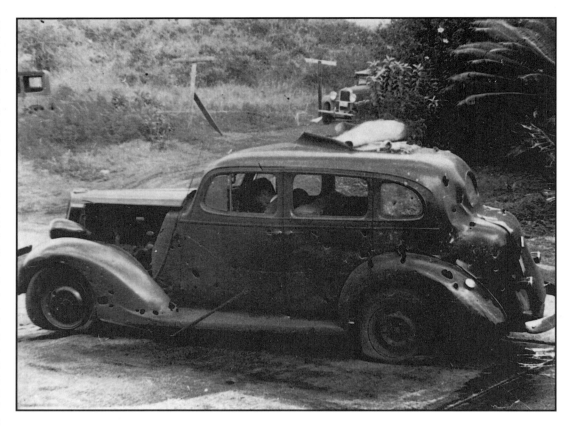

Above: For obvious military reasons, the Japanese tried to restrict their attacks to military targets. Civilian casualties numbered 68 killed and 35 wounded, some of them victims of antiaircraft shells that failed to explode and plunged to earth.

Below: The body of an American sailor washed up on the beach. This unfortunate was just one of 3,478 military personnel killed or wounded in the disaster at Pearl Harbor, the vast majority of them US Navy and US Marine Corps personnel.

blow, and many military and civilian leaders on Oahu feared that the air strike was only a prelude to invasion. Wild rumours swept Oahu, the panic they caused made worse by a radio blackout ordered by the military authorities.

Neither was it true that Japanese aircraft had bombed Honolulu. Of the 40 explosions in the city during the attack,

Below: Congressional leaders watch intently on December 8 as President Roosevelt signs the bill that declared the United States to be in a state of war with the Japanese empire. War with Germany and Italy followed just three days later.

39 were definitely caused by large antiaircraft shells which had failed to detonate in the air. Similarly, battleship *Arizona* was not blown apart by a bomb which went down her smokestack. All American battleships had thick armor gratings over the outlets for their boiler fire exhausts, and *Arizona*'s was never pierced. Yet such rumors persisted because they reassured people who were angry, confused and afraid. The terrible Japanese had bombed civilians in Honolulu as they had smashed Nanking, in China. *Arizona* had been shattered by a lucky shot, not in a well

Above: A somber President Roosevelt addresses an emergency session of Congress on December 8, asking for a declaration of war against Japan for its attack against Pearl Harbor — "a date which will live in infamy."

executed attack staged by highly skilled professional pilots. Such myths allowed people to avoid the hard questions of responsibility.

Did the Japanese pass up an opportunity by not returning to attack? Yes. Though US antiaircraft fire improved decidedly once the initial shock of the surprise wore off, Japanese aircraft would have been able to return and smash the tank farm and the Navy Yard shops. They might even have discovered *Enterprise*, only 200 miles (320km) west of Oahu as the second flight of Japanese planes worked over Pearl Harbor. Was the ultimate cost of the surprise attack balanced by its benefits? No. The effect of the attack on American public opinion was electric. The surprise nature of the attack reinforced an already widely accepted image of the Japanese as cunning and unscrupulous. Moreover, the damage inflicted on the Pacific Fleet was largely made good through repair and salvage. Only *Arizona* and *Oklahoma* of the major ships were total losses. *Arizona*, stripped of her superstructure, still reposes on the bottom of the harbor; *Utah* lies there, too. *Oklahoma* was rolled upright and floated in an impressive feat of salvage, but her hulk sank in deep water while being towed to the mainland for scrapping. During the course of the war Pearl Harbor was never blockaded or rendered ineffective as a fleet base.

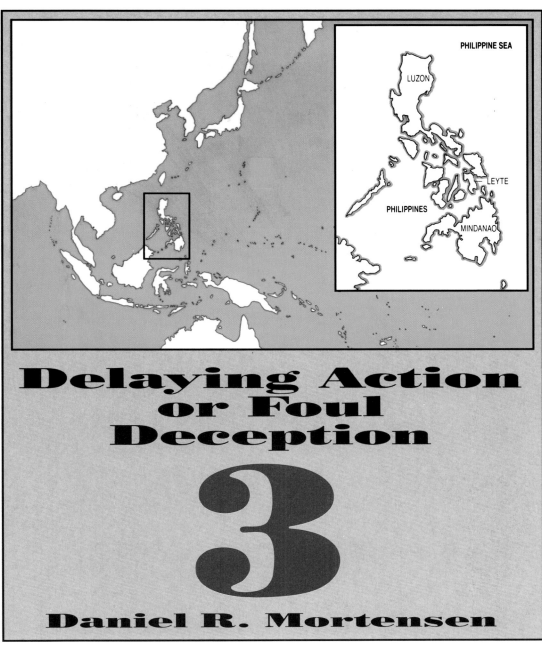

Delaying Action or Foul Deception

3

Daniel R. Mortensen

Shortly after 3:00 on the morning of December 8, 1941, the phone rang beside Lt. Gen. Douglas MacArthur's bed in his Manila penthouse. The caller reported a Japanese air attack at Pearl Harbor, where, because of the time zones and the international date line, it was 9:00 A.M. on December 7. Despite the puzzling juxtaposition of times and dates, MacArthur and other military leaders at Manila got the news as the last wave of Japanese bombers attacked Pearl Harbor. The dramatic events unfolding on December 7 in Hawaii routed the American military leaders in Manila from their beds long before the light of the rising sun touched MacArthur's headquarters.

The principals gathered in MacArthur's offices to address the problem of defending an archipelago of nine major and over seven thousand lesser islands, lying eastward across the South China Sea from French Indochina, south of Formosa, and north of the central Netherlands East Indies. Some of the officers clustered around MacArthur played a greater role than others in the emergency, but all of them participated in the

decisions that contributed to the impending disaster, a tragedy that had its inception long before the war began.

Rear Adm. Thomas C. Hart, MacArthur's naval counterpart, heard about the Japanese attack from Adm. Husband E. Kimmel's headquarters in Honolulu before the general got word, but typically of interservice relations, the navy did not inform the army. Hart's pathetically small Asiatic Fleet — three cruisers, 13 destroyers, 18 submarines (reinforced to 29), and a few patrol torpedo (PT) boats — could not stand up to the Imperial Japanese Navy. Joint Army-Navy war plans adopted in May 1941 directed Hart to support the Army in the defense of the Philippines by attacking the Japanese fleet, especially in the event of an amphibious landing, and to help keep open the sea lanes. The plan also permitted Hart, in the event the Japanese Navy appeared in overwhelming strength, to abandon the mission of supporting the Army and move his forces south to a safer anchorage in British Malaya or the Netherlands East Indies, where he could await reinforcements.

Japanese occupation of Indochina in

Japanese Personal Patriotic Flags and Designation Pennants

1 Personal patriotic flag of a soldier named Nakayama. The flag was given to him on his departure to war, and is covered with exhortations to victory and loyalty to his country, as well as wishes for his good fortune in the war. It is signed by representatives of both his village and graduating class. Oddly to the Western mind, none of these personal messages includes a wish for his safe return.
2 Battle flag with honors.

From the left: Mindanao, Mindoro, Leyte, Panay, Hollandia, Godenough Island
3 Personal patriotic flag. The slogans congratulate the soldier on his spring enlistment and exhort him to the suicide spirit
4 Navy identification pennant
5 Unit identification pennant. The slogan reads: Number one (the best) spear
6 Identification pennant; the drawing of the tiger does not appear to have any special significance

Eugene Gibson: 1-3, 5;
Andrew L. Chernak: 4, 6

When they left home for war, many Japanese soldiers were presented with small national flags adorned with various patriotic slogans, prayers, and wishes for success. These flags were carried by the individual soldier and became prized war souvenirs to Allied soldiers. Although much of the sentiment is difficult to translate into English, such personal keepsakes and messages were treasured by the Japanese soldier — bolstering his morale when fighting against incredible odds.

July 1941 all but encircled the Philippines, for Japan governed Formosa to the north, and to the east the islands mandated to Japan by the League of Nations — the Marianas except for Guam, the Carolines, the Palaus, and the Marshalls — stood athwart the most direct route from Hawaii and the United States. Even so, MacArthur claimed that the Philippines could be defended. The Army officer's infectious optimism influenced Hart who suggested to the Navy Department that the Asiatic Fleet concentrate in Manila Bay rather than move out of harm's way to the south. Hart accepted the idea that expansion of the Far East

Air Forces improved prospects for the successful defense of Manila Bay, agreed with MacArthur that the Americans were morally obligated to hold the islands, and suggested that the concentration of Allied warships to the south might prove fruitless, since no plans had been made for their further employment. The Navy Department did not respond until late November, when it unequivocally rejected Hart's suggestion, telling him to pull out of the Philippines. The admiral sent nine destroyers and one cruiser south to Tarakan and Balikpapan in Borneo, and two cruisers and other ships to the southern Philip-

pines, but the sudden outbreak of war on December 8 caught four destroyers, 9 submarines, and several auxiliary ships at Cavite Navy Yard, just south of Manila. Hart abandoned hope of doing battle with the Japanese; he had neither the ships nor the secure base he needed to take the offensive. Still, Hart went to work getting his naval facilities — especially the floating workshop USS *Canopus* — set up to help the Army and in reinforcing the antiaircraft defenses of Manila, Cavite, and other points on the shores of Manila Bay.

Philippine politics complicated the work of the military leadership. Manuel

L. Quezon, president of the Philippines, helped influence MacArthur's response to the outbreak of hostilities. When Quezon first heard about Pearl Harbor he dismissed the report as nonsense, for he fantasized that the Japanese would not attack the Philippines. Nor was he unique among Filipinos in believing that the islands were not crucial to Japan's projected "Greater East Asia Co-Prosperity Sphere." The Philippines, these people conceded, had military value to the United States, but they convinced themselves that Japan would gain no economic or decisive military advantage by taking the islands and therefore might bypass them entirely. Indeed, Japan might become involved in seizing and exploiting the riches of the Netherlands East Indies and Malaya and simply ignore the Philippines, at least for a while. Quezon believed it important, therefore, to don the mantle of neutrality and avoid provoking the Japanese, so that the Philippines could continue to build a suitable defensive force. His hopes and fears for his unprepared commonwealth persuaded Quezon to plead for neutrality even though the disaster at Pearl Harbor had shattered the substance of his dream.

The sudden coming of war, which numbed Quezon's political instincts, jolted the military decision-making apparatus, and the resulting indecision turned out to be especially critical when it came to the use of the Far East Air Forces, which formed a significant element in MacArthur's defensive plans. For years war planners at Washington believed that the United States could not stop a truly determined Japanese attack. Manila lay over 6,000 miles (9,600km) from San Francisco and nearly 5,000 miles (8,000km) from Hawaii by way of Guam, while the Japanese mandates formed a barrier east of the Philippines, through which an American naval expedition would have to fight island by island. The big Japanese air base at Takao on Formosa, lay less than 300 miles (480km) from Aparri, the northernmost air base in the Philippines, but despite Japan's control of the seas, and its deployment of aircraft to Formosa, concern about air forces did not become a major factor in military thinking about the Philippines until the very eve of war.

According to both War Plan Orange — the old "color" plan for a war with Orange or Japan — and the new Rainbow War Plans directed against a spectrum of enemies, if Japan attacked the Philippines, the American and Filipino defenders could not expect to prevent a landing. The naval forces, too small to offer serious oppostion, would play an ancillary role in defending the islands. Fighting a delaying action, the ground forces would fall back on previously stocked supply depots, eventually withdrawing into the Bataan Peninsula, from which they could hold the entrance to Manila Bay until the Navy came to the rescue. Theoretically, the American

Above: A key figure in the American military effort was Gen. George Catlett Marshall, who had been US Army Chief of Staff since September 1, 1939. Marshall was a strategic thinker of great talent, and proved himself a superb administrator throughout the war.

forces in the Philippines were not expendable, but, given the ominous presence of the Japanese mandates, years rather than months might pass before a relief expedition made landfall at Bataan.

Natural optimism and long experience as military adviser to the Commonwealth of the Philippines encouraged MacArthur to believe that a small, well-trained Philippine army, navy, and air arm, backed by American strength, could stop an invasion. The War Department did not immediately accept MacArthur's scenario, clinging to the old concept until 1941, when something happened to change the minds of American policy makers. In the summer of that year, MacArthur persuaded Gen. George C. Marshall, the Army Chief of Staff, and Secretary of War Henry L. Stimson that he could hold out with the help of air power, particularly if he had more B-17s to attack the Japanese fleet. MacArthur argued that additional B-17s and a ground force of 200,000, mostly Filipinos, could deter the Japanese. Won over by MacArthur's reasoning, Marshall urged that the Department of State and President Roosevelt play for time so that the necessary air force could be in place by April 1942, when MacArthur expected the Japanese to attack.

Although committed to a strategy of Germany first, the Roosevelt administration was willing to do essentially what MacArthur wanted. In late 1941, a good share of the modern American fighters and bombers, including the B-17s, and a majority of capital ships were in the Pacific, mostly in Hawaii and the Philippines. Gen. MacArthur, confident and proud of the equipment he had received, including the celebrated B-17 Flying Fortress, assured Washington political leaders that he could defend the

Philippines against Japan. He insisted that his mixed force of Americans and Filipinos, which was increasing in size and learning to use its new weapons, would be ready by April 1942. He did not expect an invasion before that date and had no realistic plan to defend the islands if the attack came early.

In October 1941, Maj. Gen. Lewis H. Brereton took command of the Philippines-based Far East Air Forces. Brereton arrived under a full head of steam, eager to get the air component ready for its important defensive role by the deadline of April 1942. Although pleased to have MacArthur's interest and support, Brereton did not share the assumption that the islands could easily be made safe from Japanese aggression. Short of manpower, aircraft, spare parts, and funds, Brereton realized he led a weak, improvised air force far from ready for combat. As the overall commander, it was MacArthur who controlled the disposition of air units even though he did not fully understand the limits and potential of air power; furthermore MacArthur gave Brereton little time to organize, train, equip, and find bases for his growing forces. Instead, in November he sent him off on a three-week visit to possible future allies — the British in Malaya and the Dutch in the East Indies. Brereton was sorely missed in the Philippines, for he could not take an active hand in organizing the air defenses of Luzon.

An air of unreality pervaded MacArthur's headquarters in the last days of peace. On November 21, waiting for orders to go on yet another trip, Brereton urged MacArthur to transfer the B-17s south to Del Monte on Mindanao. MacArthur agreed and ordered his chief of staff, Col. Richard K. Sutherland, to

Above: Marshall's political master was Henry L. Stimson, who was appointed Secretary of War in June 1940 at the age of 73. Stimson was supported by an able team of civilian administrators, and emphasized the need for scientific research in a modern war.

Map A
December 10 1941—January 6 1942

14TH ARMY
Homma

December 10

December 10

December 10 Vigan

Aparri

48TH DIV
Tsuchibashi

LUZON

December 22

Lingayen
Gulf

Clark
Field

16TH DIV
Morioka
From Ryukyus

Bataan
Peninsula

Manila
January 2

Lamon
Bay

December 24

**US ARMY FORCES
FAR EAST**
MacArthur

MINDORO

December 12

| 0 | Miles | 100 |
| 0 | Km | 150 |

Map B
January 14—April 9 1942

BATAAN PENINSULA

January 26

April 3

April 6-9

American and Filipino
forces on Bataan
surrender April 9

January 26-27
February 1-2

Failed Japanese landings

January 22-23

CORREGIDOR

USAFFE HQ
Wainwright

MacArthur to
Australia March 11

| 0 | Miles | 20 |
| 0 | Km | 30 |

Japanese attacks began on January 14, 1942
and continued until April 9, when the
remaining forces on Bataan were forced to
surrender themselves to a cruel captivity.

Map C
Corregidor still held, however, but it was only
a matter of time. Day after day for nearly a
month the defenders were subjected to an
overwhelming Japanese bombardment. On
May 5, a force of some 2,000 Japanese
managed to get ashore under heavy fire and
begin their move towards the Malinta Tunnel,
the last American stronghold. Gen.
Wainwright now accepted the inevitable and
surrendered the garrison on May 6.

THE DEFEAT IN THE PHILIPPINES

Map A
The Japanese assault on the Philippines began
on December 8 when carrier-borne aircraft
and aircraft from Formosa began attacks on
American airfields. Air-superiority was
achieved within days, and the Japanese
swiftly moved on to the next stage in their
plan. This was a series of amphibious landings
by elements of Lt. Gen. Homma's Fourteenth
Army. Initial landings in northern Luzon were
designed to seize airfields. The main drive,
however, came towards the south, when over
43,000 Japanese landed at Lingayen Gulf and
together with forces from the Lamon Bay
began a drive towards Manila.

Map B
His defense plan in ruins, Gen. MacArthur
ordered his forces to fall back onto the Bataan
Peninsula, abandoning Manila to the Japanese
in the process. With Bataan and the island
fortress of Corregidor in American hands,
however, Manila Bay was still denied to the
Japanese. A period of siege now began. The
Americans were in an excellent defensive
position, but they were suffering with disease
and surviving on starvation rations.

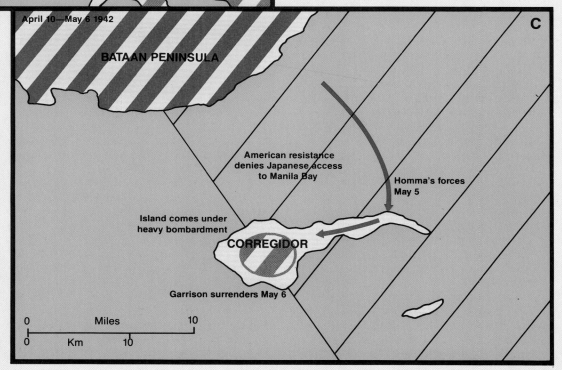

Map C
April 10—May 6 1942

BATAAN PENINSULA

American resistance
denies Japanese access
to Manila Bay

Homma's forces
May 5

Island comes under
heavy bombardment

CORREGIDOR

Garrison surrenders May 6

| 0 | Miles | 10 |
| 0 | Km | 10 |

Japanese Army Uniforms and Equipment

1 Model 1932 steel helmet with canvas cover
2 Wooden chest
3 Standard early Type 30 bayonet
4 Summer tunic with insignia of a superior private on the collar
5 KINSHI brand cigarettes
6 Cloth-covered army 'pocket book', and razor blades
7 Field rations of crackers, rice, sugar, dried plums
8 Officer's water bottle with cup and canvas cover
9 Aluminium mess tin
10 Enlisted man's water bottle
11 Service tropical shirt
12 Arisaka Type 99 rifle, 7.7m caliber
13 Rifle grenade discharger of the cup type, with a Type 99 (1939) grenade
14 Type 2 grenade launcher with grenade
15 Service tropical shirt
16 Service tropical tunic
17 Tags for wounded personnel
18 Wooden identity tags
19 Pair of rush sandals
20 Army gas respirator
21 Ammunition pouches
22 Body armor vest
23 Model 92 steel helmet
24 Aviator's parachute
25 One piece Army aviator's winter flying suit
26 Leather flying boots
27 Silk scarf
28 Felt over-gloves
29 M94 8mm automatic pistol

War Memorial Museum of Virginia

The items on the left hand side consist mainly of the standard enlisted man's M98 uniform and equipment. Most of this equipment dates from around 1944. The rank insignia is found on the collar of the tunic, but could as easily be on the shirt collar. Both items were worn open at the neck, usually with the shirt collar on top. The Type 30 bayonet is distinguished from later models by its bird head pommel and hooked quillon. The scabbard is metal, and the weapon sits in a single loop leather frog. This would have been worn on the soldier's belt with his ammunition pouches (21).

The Army aviator's flying suit (25) is lined and has a fur collar. There appears to be no rank insignia visible. The parachute harness and parachute (24) are standard issue, as are the felt overgloves, which are of a mitten type with a separate 'trigger finger'.

issue the orders, but either Sutherland failed to do so or Brereton never carried them out. Seventeen of the 35 bombers available to the Far East Air Forces remained at Clark Field on Luzon. Instead of acting promptly to move the bombers out of range of the Japanese airfields on Formosa, the military leadership at Manila worried about possible sabotage, increased the guard, and bunched the aircraft together to make it easier to protect them from enemy agents. Neither Brereton nor MacArthur paid enough heed to warnings of possible Japanese attack to cancel a Saturday night party in the ballroom of the hotel where

MacArthur lived. Crewmen of the B-17s still at Clark Field attended the affair, which lasted until 2:00 A.M. on December 8, just about the time the first Japanese aircraft attacked Pearl Harbor. Revelers from the bomber squadron carried in their pockets orders to fly to Del Monte on the day after the party.

Awakened before dawn on December 8, the military and political leaders at Manila realized that the disaster of Pearl Harbor might prevent the reinforcement of the islands. The shock of the Japanese attack on American territory, and the lingering hope that Japan might somehow ignore the Philippines, confused and paralyzed MacArthur and other decision-makers. With Quezon urging neutrality, Hart hoping to regroup to the south, and Brereton calling for a strike against Formosa by his ill-prepared bomber squadrons, MacArthur's command post sank in a positive quagmire of indecision.

The time factor was critical; the Japanese had a reputation for surprise attacks delivered at dawn. Brereton arrived at MacArthur's office at 5:00 A.M., asking to see the chief. Sutherland refused, since MacArthur already was conferring with Hart, so Brereton and the chief of staff discussed missions for the Far East Air Forces. Should Brereton conduct reconnaissance flights over Formosa in preparation for bombing attacks, or should he locate and attack enemy troop transports? As Brereton remembered it, Sutherland told him to stand by until MacArthur gave the order.

At dawn Japanese carrier aircraft attacked Malag on Mindanao, 550 miles (880km) south of Manila. Shortly after 7:00 A.M., two hours after Brereton's first visit to the headquarters, the airman returned and saw Sutherland, who again told him to wait. Radar indications of aircraft headed for Clark Field and Manila

Above: American bomber strength in the Pacific was limited to a small number of B-17C Flying Fortresses. These had little chance to serve as strategic bombers, but instead performed most usefully for long-range reconnaissance and interdiction.

caused Brereton to scramble 36 fighters to intercept. The B-17s at Clark Field took off without bombs to avoid being caught on the ground. The radar lost contact with the unidentified aircraft, however, and the frustrated fighter pilots returned to base, while the B-17s remained aloft. Brereton asked Sutherland's permission to bomb Formosa but was refused. Shortly after 9:00 A.M., Brereton learned of a Japanese air attack in southern Luzon, but Sutherland still refused to permit retaliation against Formosa. At 10:00 A.M. Sutherland agreed to a reconnaissance flight over Formosa, but another hour passed before MacArthur's headquarters approved a bombing mission. In the meantime, Brereton ordered his bombers to land and load up with bombs and fuel, but the timing turned out to be a grievous mistake, for the bombers and fighters were on the ground at the same time, presenting unbelievable opportunity to the Japanese.

A formation of nearly 200 enemy

Above: The Mitsubishi Ki-30 was a two-seat light bomber, and though obsolescent by 1942 played a significant part in Japan's conquest of the Philippines, where its fixed but sturdy landing gear allowed it to use extemporized airfields without difficulty.

bombers and fighters approached Clark Field. Fog over the Formosan airfields had prevented the Japanese airmen from making the traditional dawn raid, and they were immensely anxious that the B-17s might strike first. Fortunately for the attackers the indecision gripping the high command at Manila kept the bombers out of action. Moreover, primitive attempts at electronic jamming may have drowned out the reports of observers on the ground that Japanese aircraft had crossed the coast of northern Luzon. The first air raid hit Baguio, the summer capital, 125 miles (200km) due north of Manila, but word of the attack did not reach Clark Field. The radar officers at the Iba Field control center, on the coast 35 miles (56km) west of Clark, picked up the scent and teletyped a warning, but the operator at Clark Field had gone to lunch. A telephone call raised a young lieutenant at the air base, who promised to spread the word, but the news never reached the flight line.

At about noon, the Japanese attacked Clark Field. A few P-40 pilots, who had finished lunch and were lounging beside their airplanes, managed to take off, but the Japanese numbers overwhelmed them. In a little over an hour, three waves of Japanese aircraft destroyed most of the fighters, bombers, supplies, and facilities at Clark Field. Only one of the B-17s based there survived the attack; it had been on a reconnaissance mission when the enemy struck. Rising smoke from fires started by the Japanese was visible from Manila 75 miles (120km) to the south. The Japanese also attacked the airfield at Iba, destroying the radar and most of the fighters stationed there. American squadrons from some other

Left: The American fighter strength in the Philippines was completely inadequate to the task of checking the air power used by the Japanese to support their ground operations. This is a Seversky P-35 destroyed in an air attack on Nichols Field near Manila.

airfields heard a distress call from Clark, and although radar was no longer available for centralized control, a few fighters took off and gave battle. In all, seven Japanese fighters were shot down, but the high-flying bombers returned unscathed to Formosa. Besides losing their hangars, radar, and control centers, in the first day's raids the Americans lost half their aircraft — 18 B-17s and over 50 fighters that fell victim to enemy bombs and gunfire or were destroyed as a result of accidents.

The air battle was not yet finished, but the surviving American and Philippine aircraft were doomed. The overpowering Japanese air forces had gained control of the skies over Luzon and put an end to the danger of a B-17 attack on Formosa. The defense of the Philippines depended on air power which was meant to beat off enemy fighters and bombers, attack naval and amphibious forces, and hostile troops ashore; but American air power no longer existed in the islands.

Historians have long speculated about the devastation at Clark Field, where so many of Brereton's aircraft perished, at Iba, and elsewhere on Luzon. A number of factors contributed to the defeat. The Americans from MacArthur down tended to underestimate the enemy; indeed, many a soldier or sailor may have gone to his death believing that the Japanese lived on fish-heads and rice and, because of this diet, could not see well enough to fly a modern airplane. Moreover, the American political and military leaders avoided asking tough questions of themselves. Stimson and Marshall accepted MacArthur's assurances, and Sutherland shielded his commander from bad news. Although Brereton and others made mistakes, MacArthur must take much of the blame for not making

Below: Seated in the center of this group of American commanders after their surrender is Maj. Gen. Edward P. King, who commanded Luzon Force during the last desperate days of American resistance to the Japanese Fourteenth Army on the Bataan peninsula.

Above: After Pearl Harbor, the Japanese carrier force divided into detachments for many of the major landings across central and south Pacific. Aircraft such as these Aichi D3As provided close support.

sure the Far East Air Forces could do what he expected of it.

Having won air superiority with their first strikes, the Japanese followed up with other air operations, amphibious landings, and a ground campaign. A small air strike hit a radio station and Nichols Field, both near Manila, on the evening of December 8, but bad weather grounded the enemy the next day. Brereton attempted to mass his surviving B-17s at Del Monte, to stage through Clark for a strike against airfields on Formosa, but he no longer had the aircraft for such a venture. Since Japanese expeditionary forces were steaming toward Luzon, MacArthur threw every-

thing he had against the threatened invasion. On December 10 Brereton sent small formations of from two to five B-17s against Japanese convoys along the north and northwest coast of Luzon. During one of these missions, Japanese fighters swarmed over a B-17 flown by Capt. Colin P. Kelly, shooting the bomber to pieces. Kelly somehow kept the Flying Fortress in the air until the surviving members of the crew had parachuted to safety, then died when the aircraft crashed. Eyewitness reports — affected by danger, excitement, and a lack of training in ship identification — credited Kelly's bombardier, Cpl. Meyer Levin, with sinking a battleship, but at best he scored a near-miss on a transport. While some of the remaining fighters strafed the invasion convoys, other fighters tried to defend Manila, Nichols Field, and Cavite Naval Base from a massive Japanese bombing attack that all but destroyed Cavite. On December 10, as on the 8th, enemy aircraft suffered few losses from outclassed American and Filipino pilots, like Jesus Villamor of the Philippine air force, who managed to down a Japanese aircraft even though he flew an old P-26, the Army's first monoplane fighter.

By the evening of December 10, Brereton had but 22 P-40s, not enough to escort even his handful of B-17s. He chose to conserve the fighters for essential reconnaissance missions, and he again sent his remaining bombers, which had just come north to Luzon, back to Del Monte Field on Mindanao. Japanese bombing raids, which enjoyed a fighter escort that overwhelmed the dwindling number of American aircraft trying to oppose them, continued for a week, until only a few fighters and Navy patrol planes survived. MacArthur, recognizing the vulnerability of the B-17s even at

US Army Uniforms and Equipment

1. Enlisted man's khaki shirt
2. Denim dungaree fatigue blouse
3. Tropical pith helmet
4. Revolver ammunition pouch with half-moon .45 caliber clips
5. Blucher pattern shoes
6. Waist belt
7. Model 1917 Colt revolver, .45 caliber, in leather holster
8. Model 1903 A1 rifle
9. Model 1914 cartridge belt with canteen, first aid pouch and five round, .30 caliber clips
10. Enlisted man's khaki trousers
11. Enlisted man's cotton khaki trousers
12. Model 1938 canvas leggings
13. Enlisted man's cotton khaki shirt
14. Model 1917 A1 steel helmet
15. Model 1941 field jacket
16. Model 1944 cold weather boots
17. Wool overcoat
18. M1 steel helmet
19. Enlisted man's wool shirt
20. Wool olive drab scarf
21. Field trousers
22. M1 carbine
23. Model 1936 pistol belt with carbine magazine, first aid, canteen and compass pouches
24. Winter weight undershirt
25. Winter long underpants
26. Wool olive drab blanket

Dale E. Biever; 2-7, 9, 11, 12, 14: Pritchard: 8; Howard Hendricks: 1, 10, 13, 15-26

This spread of uniforms, weapons and equipment shows the adaptability necessary to clothe and equip a soldier operating in the two opposite extremes of climatic conditions. It also reveals how unprepared the United States was to wage war on such a global scale.

Items *1-14* are early war items, all tropical, which would have been common kit components during the years 1941-2. Many pieces of equipment were of obsolete design, still in service from the period of World War I, but maintained with slight modifications.

Items *15-26* are pieces of winter service kit. Many were of unproved patterns at the time of their initial use. Such equipment was standard in the northern campaigns to recapture the Aleutian islands of Attu and Kiska, and were subsequently worn by garrisons in those cold climates.

Del Monte, ordered Brereton and his staff to take the bombers to the safety of Port Darwin, Australia. On December 14, MacArthur forwarded to the War Department Brereton's request for 200 fighters and 50 dive bombers, in addition to those already on route. In the desperate hope that the aircraft could somehow be delivered, the Army made arrangements to send hundreds of fighters and 80 bombers to the Philippines by way of Australia.

Meanwhile, Adm. Hart recognized that he could not engage the enemy amphibious forces without aircraft to protect his ships, and executed his plan to

send the rest of his fleet southward to safety. Only the inshore patrol craft and 29 submarines with a tender remained available to defend the Philippines. Hart's announced intention to follow his ships southward, moving his headquarters to the Netherlands East Indies, shocked MacArthur. Without air and now naval support, his lines of communication severed by the crippling of the Pacific Fleet, Hart had no hope of preventing the landings.

The Japanese came ashore at Vigan and Aparri in northern Luzon on December 10 and two days later at Legaspi in the southern part of the island, largely to obtain advance fighter bases. The destruction of the Far East Air Force, however, eliminated the need for these airfields and freed the invaders to exploit the landings at the expense of the poorly trained Filipino defenders. The Japanese attacks revealed the absurdity of MacArthur's plan to defend Luzon at the beaches, for the enemy easily established himself ashore, even though the main attack was yet to come. As MacArthur expected, the Japanese struck their hardest blow in the Lingayen Gulf, some 125 miles (200km) northwest of Manila on the South China Sea.

On December 22 Lt. Gen. Masaharu Homma, commander of Japan's Fourteenth Army, sent a reinforced division ashore at three locations in Lingayen Gulf. MacArthur had five divisions in northern Luzon, numbering over 100,000 men, and two other divisions in southern Luzon, compared to 43,000 troops that Homma brought ashore. Neither the poorly trained and equipped Filipinos, the American regulars, nor the skilled and highly motivated Philippine Scouts could stop Homma's forces, even though the enemy encountered problems from the outset. Bad weather raised an obstacle, American submarines and a few aircraft harried the troop convoy, and the landings were poorly executed, but the well-trained Japanese troops got ashore, along with tanks and artillery. The column from Lingayen Gulf joined forces with the regiment that had landed at Vigan and advanced toward Manila. Homma also brought troops ashore at Lamon Bay in the south of Luzon and ordered them, along with the regiment at Legaspi, to form the southern jaws of a pincer closing on the Philippine capital.

When Homma's troops surged forward, MacArthur's ground forces could do little more than fight a delaying action. Lt. Gen. Jonathan M. Wainwright, commander of the North Luzon force, kept his Filipinos from being cut off but could do little more, as his commander soon realized. When Wainwright asked for one of the reserve divisions to mount a counterattack, MacArthur refused; the time had arrived for a change of plan.

On December 23, MacArthur abandoned his original scheme for the defense of all Luzon. He ordered his forces to retreat to the Bataan Peninsula, a 30-by-15-mile (48-by-24km) thumb-like projection bounded by Manila Bay on the east and the South China Sea on the west. MacArthur thus reverted to the concept in the old Orange Plan, but with one fatal difference — as a result of the attack on Pearl Harbor and the Japanese conquest of Wake and Guam, there was no chance that a naval expedition could fight its way across the Pacific in time to save the Philippine garrison. MacArthur engineered a withdrawal to the peninsula that took over a week, in the process evacuating all forces from Manila and declaring it an open city. Homma could occupy Manila but the American grip on Bataan and the fortress at Corregidor would prevent use of Manila Bay by the Japanese Navy.

With the Imperial Japanese Navy dominant in the western Pacific, the China Sea, and the Indian Ocean, help could not reach MacArthur except by way of the Fiji Islands, New Caledonia, and Australia; already the enemy was attacking the Netherlands East Indies, whose fall would isolate the Philippines. The War Department told MacArthur not to expect delivery of aircraft, not even the dive bombers en route by ship when the war began. Even so, he

Above: The Japanese army was less mechanized than the American forces it was fighting, but was used to this fact and was therefore content with the manual effort of hauling barges of supplies to the shore during amphibious operations in the Philippines.

continued building airfields throughout the islands. His engineers constructed as many as 53 airstrips in Mindanao and elsewhere by the beginning of January 1942. For a long time MacArthur expected blockade runners, in ships chartered by the American government, to bring war materials and supplies to Bataan, but the Japanese control was such that only three of these ships reached the Philippines from Australia.

As Wainwright's troops fell back onto the Bataan Peninsula, logistics became critical. Supplies that should have been stockpiled behind a succession of defensive lines never arrived. When MacArthur decided to fight for the beaches, he sent supplies to dumps in the forward areas, not to Bataan. As Homma advanced, transportation collapsed, as did the structure of command. Left to their own devices, individuals headed for Bataan or Corregidor, or simply vanished in the hinterlands. In addition, MacArthur neglected to suspend, because of the emergency, a peacetime regulation that forbade moving foodstuffs from one province to another. Invaluable food and

Above: US Model 1902 officer's sword belonging to Gen. Wainwright. Taken from him when the Philippines surrendered, the sword was recovered from the body of a Japanese officer in 1945. From left to right: Gen. Wainwright's Colt revolver, lost in a plane crash on Mindanao in 1942, but recovered in 1945. Pen used in the Japanese surrender ceremonies aboard USS *Missouri*, September 2, 1945. Medal of Honor presented to Gen. Jonathan M. Wainwright for his defense of the Philippines.
West Point Museum.

medicine went astray in the confusion. As early as the end of their first week on Bataan, defenders lived on half rations because of food shortages.

Confident that MacArthur would defend Manila, Homma was surprised when the defensive line formed at the northern end of Bataan. Wainwright's I Corps held the western half of the peninsula neck. Maj. Gen. George M. Parker, who had commanded troops in southern Luzon before the retreat to Bataan, led II Corps on the eastern side of the peninsula. With water on their flanks and a towering and inaccessible volcano, Mt Natib, anchoring the center, the two corps manned a strong defensive position. A second line took shape eight miles (13km) farther south. Army service forces, along with sailors and airmen hastily trained as infantry, defended the tip of the peninsula, three miles (5km) across the bay from Corregidor, against a possible amphibious attack. As it turned out, starvation and disease eroded the formidable position, for the shortage of food and medicine weakened or incapacitated the defending troops.

Establishing his headquarters in Manila on January 2, 1942, shortly after MacArthur abandoned the city for Corregidor, Homma waited. He did not complain when his best division received orders to take part in the attack on the Netherlands East Indies, for the supply situation on Luzon was rapidly improving, and he believed he faced nothing more than a simple mopping-up operation. The American and Filipino soldiers on Bataan thought otherwise.

In his one visit to Bataan, arriving by PT boat from Corregidor on January 10, MacArthur saw that his troops were still in reasonable health, despite half-rations, and that the two army corps clung to a good defensive position. These defenses held for three weeks until the Japanese, finding a trail over Mt Natib, got into the American rear, forcing a retreat to the second defensive line midway down the peninsula. In the midst of the retreat to this fall-back position, MacArthur sent a message from Corregidor to the troops on Bataan. He told them that help was on the way, including thousands of troops and hundreds of airplanes. He assured them they had supplies enough to hold out until help came, that a determined defense would save the day. Nothing he said was true even if, in defiance of the facts, he somehow believed it to be so. Whether because of their general's inspirational words, or simply as a result of discipline and a sense of duty, the defenders of Bataan fought on for weeks.

Later, some survivors of Bataan criticized MacArthur for what they had come to believe was a cruel and dishonest message; not only was there no relief in sight, tying down Homma's comparatively small force could achieve no larger strategic purpose. The Japanese, triumphant from Pearl Harbor

Above: The poor communications of many areas in the Philippines were less of a hindrance to the Japanese than the Americans. These Japanese soldiers are carrying a dismantled 75-mm gun, either a Tpe 41 or Type 94 weapon, in Bataan.

to Burma, considered the Philippines a sideshow. MacArthur's heroic image lost some of its gloss because he did not spend time on Bataan sharing, to some extent, the suffering of his troops and encouraging them for the impending ordeal of capture and confinement. After the war, his reputation was further tarnished when it was discovered that President Quezon, to bind MacArthur all the more tightly to the fate of the Philippines, had given the general $500,000 and made similar grants to other American officers in the islands.

The unexpectedly stout defense slowed Homma's army; battle casualties and a lengthening sick list forced the Japanese commander to pause and await reinforcements, but the defenders of Bataan, ill and starving, lacked the physical strength to take advantage of the lull and counterattack. Washington recognized the inevitability of defeat in the Philippines and wanted MacArthur, who had become a national hero, to escape from Corregidor and renew the fight

Below: Japanese tanks parade through downtown Manila after the fall of Corregidor in May 1942. The Japanese were in general poor exponents of armored warfare, and usually deployed their indifferent tanks in the infantry support role.

elsewhere. He refused at first, but on March 11 he left as ordered, taking along his wife and child and a few staff officers. Many of the troops grimly holding out on the Bataan Peninsula came to detest the general, whom they called "Dugout Doug" because of his preference for the fortress of Corregidor. Brig. Gen. William E. Brougher summarized the view of many of those MacArthur left behind when he asked: "Who had the right to say that 20,000 Americans should be sentenced without their consent and for no fault of their own to an enterprise that would involve for them endless suffering, cruel handicap, death or a hopeless future?"

While Homma was reviving his troop strength for another attack on Bataan's defenders, Japanese forces took over Hong Kong, British Borneo, Malaya, Singapore, and the Netherlands East Indies. Wainwright, given command over all Philippine troops when MacArthur departed, assumed responsibility for the last troops opposing Japan in the southwest Pacific. By the end of March, Wainwright's forces were surviving on 1,000 calories a day, barely enough to sustain life, let alone enable them to fight. Nearly 80 per cent of the troops on Bataan had malaria, and over 12,000 were in field hospitals when the end came. The final defensive line on the peninsula cracked quickly when Homma returned to the attack on April 3, and six days later the forces on Bataan surrendered. Wainwright was left on Corregidor, the last redoubt on Luzon to remain out of Japanese hands.

Designed to defend Manila from Naval attack, Corregidor mounted a variety of coastal defense batteries, including 12-inch weapons; miles of tunnels and galleries penetrated the rocky soil, and a thick layer of earth and concrete protected most of the vital installations. Food, medicine, and ammunition were available, though in quantities that could not for long support a garrison that now included elements of the 4th Marines, the marines from China who had been transferred from the international settlement at Shanghai on the very eve of

war. Japanese bombers pounded Corregidor, joined in April, after the capture of Bataan, by artillery batteries emplaced at the tip of the peninsula. The preparations for an assault reached a climax on May 4, when over 16,000 shells crashed onto the island, destroying the remaining above-ground facilities, while the defenders within the tunnels suffered from hemorrhaging eardrums. For a time the garrison held off enemy attempts at a landing on May 5, but when the Japanese attackers gained a toehold and then brought a few tanks ashore, a slaughter seemed inevitable. At 10:00 on the morning of May 6, Wainwright surrendered the island and its 11,000 defenders.

The fight continued sporadically on Panay, Mindanao, and other southern islands, until Wainwright convinced subordinate commanders that Homma might well make good his threat to kill captured Americans. Even so, it took almost a month for the word to reach isolated commands, and for all the organized forces to lay down their arms. A number of Americans and Filipinos fled into the jungle, however, and launched a guerrilla war that lasted until American forces returned to the islands late in 1944. The Japanese lost some 12,000 wounded and killed in the conquest of Luzon, defeating an army of 140,000 Filipinos and Americans. The victory secured for Japan the best harbor in the Orient, Manila Bay, and an excellent transshipment point for supplies and reinforcements destined for the defense of the southern portion of the outer defensive perimeter. The American and Filipino troops, fighting on long after they had despaired of reinforcements, held out against the Japanese forces for months. The stubborn fight for Bataan and Corregidor forced Japan to commit more resources than planned to gain an objective far less

Below: Souvenirs of Gen. MacArthur's escape from the Philippines. Model of PT 41, the vessel on which the escape was made; the flag of PT 41; fragment of the Malinta Tunnel; Bible carried by Mrs MacArthur. *MacArthur Memorial Collection.*

Above: A reproduction of the flag of the Philippines Division, US Army. The division was activated in 1921. In December 1941, it covered the Bataan withdrawal. The division surrendered on Bataan in April, 1942. *MacArthur Memorial Collection.*

important to the Greater East Asia Co-Prosperity Sphere than Malaya or the Netherlands East Indies.

The heroic defense of Bataan served as prelude to the "Death March" and cruel imprisonment that followed. Japan's treatment of the Americans and Filipinos who surrendered there varied from callous indifference to torture and even murder. An escaped prisoner, Capt. William E. Dyess of the Army Air Forces, wrote an account of his treatment which aroused cries for vengeance in the United States. Dyess, who surrendered on Bataan, was one of some 20,000 Americans captured in the Philippines, about half of whom died before the war ended. For many the ordeal began during the death march from Bataan to Camp O'Donnell north of Manila, when guards deprived the prisoners of food and water and routinely murdered stragglers. The cruel treatment reflected the attitudes of persons assigned to the lowly job of guarding prisoners; these individuals tended to believe that soldiers should fight to the death and that those who surrendered dishonored themselves and forfeited any right to humane treatment. The health of the captives, who had subsisted for months on partial rations, contributed to the death rate. The Army Surgeon General insisted that the loss of Bataan was "a true medical defeat." Malnutrition, malaria, and intestinal infection left the prisoners incapable of the physical effort needed to endure an overland march and survive harsh captivity. The captors underestimated the number and ignored the fragile health of the prisoners and kept to a travel schedule that fewer captives in much better health would have been hard pressed to maintain. Some of those captured on Luzon received better treatment than the participants in the death march; a few traveled in trucks or were allowed to accept food and water offered by Filipino peasants.

The death march marked just the beginning of the ordeal. The treatment in Japanese prison camps proved as cruel as on the march itself. The captives could take scant consolation from the

Above: On May 5, 1942, one battalion of the Japanese 61st Regiment landed at Cavalry Point on Corregidor (top), and was soon reinforced by another battalion. The Americans were almost out of water, and surrendered on May 6 (above).

Below: American and Filipino prisoners of war under Japanese guard during their desperate march from Bataan to the prison camp at Cabanatuan. The treatment meted out to their prisoners by the Japanese was almost invariably appalling.

Above: Isolated since the surrender of Luzon Force on April 9, Corregidor could not hold out for long. Here the American flag is hauled down at Fort Mills, the headquarters of the US Forces in the Philippines, after the island's surrender during May 1942.

fact that Japanese noncommissioned officers routinely beat or otherwise mistreated the guards, much as the guards did the prisoners. As time passed many prisoners were moved north to Japan, China, and Formosa; some of these were worked to death in mines or elsewhere, perished when packed into the sealed holds of merchantmen, or died when American submarines torpedoed the ships carrying them.

The defense of the Philippines served the American public as an inspiring example of gallantry in a hopeless cause, and the death march and imprisonment that followed presented a picture of Japanese cruelty that heightened the desire for revenge. The fighting also raised questions, largely ignored at the time, about MacArthur's ability to react to the unexpected, his understanding of logistics, and his concern for those he commanded. In short, was the defense of Luzon a masterful delaying action or, in the words of Gen. Brougher, "A foul trick of deception . . . played on a large group of Americans by a commander-in-chief and small staff that is now eating steak and eggs in Australia."

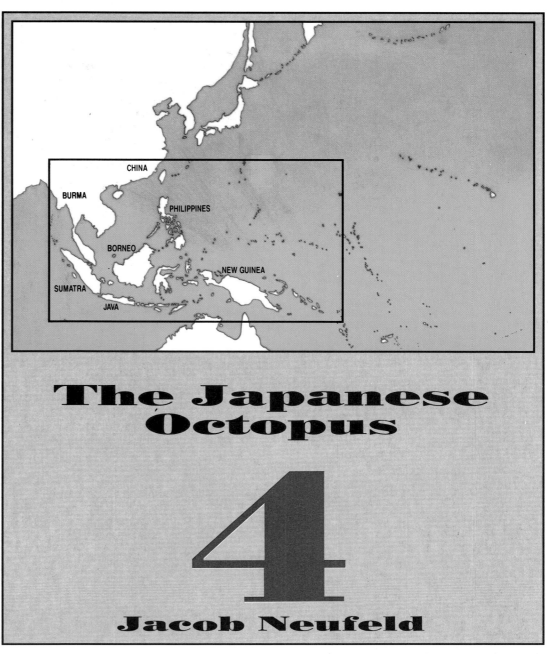

The Japanese Octopus

4

Jacob Neufeld

Propagandists seeking to alert the American public to the danger of Japanese aggression easily found an appropriately dramatic image — the octopus. With its head at the Home Islands and its tentacles stretching to Guam, Wake, Malaya, the Netherlands East Indies, and Burma, the octopus symbolized Japan's success in the early months of World War II. This image appeared on posters and in magazine advertising for as long as Japanese forces were on the move.

On December 7, 1941 without a declaration of war, the Japanese suddenly attacked the American naval base at Pearl Harbor, Hawaii; within hours Japanese planes from Formosa (Taiwan) bombarded Clark Field, near Manila in the Philippines. Most of the American planes, parked in rows, wing to wing, as they had been at Pearl Harbor, were caught on the ground. All the Flying Fortresses there and many of the pursuit planes were destroyed or severely damaged. Two days later Japan's air force further strengthened her hold on the sea by sinking the British warships *Repulse* and *Prince of Wales*. For some time after this

crippling onslaught, neither the United States nor Great Britain had naval or air power in the Far East capable of successfully challenging the Japanese. The two Allies had been thrown back on their bases at Hawaii and Singapore, some 4,000 miles (6,400km) apart.

Early on December 8, 1941, Vice Adm. Sir Tom Phillips, Commander-in-Chief of the British Far Eastern Fleet, received reports of Japanese landings in northern Malaya. Like the United States Navy in the Pacific, Britain had intended to build up its Singapore-based fleet to deter Japan's imperialistic ambitions. Now, according to a fellow officer, Adm. Phillips found it "inacceptable [sic] to retain a powerful naval force at Singapore in a state of inaction" and he "judged it his duty to strike at the enemy while they were disembarking." Phillips assembled a force that included the new 35,000-ton battleship *Prince of Wales*, the older 32,000-ton battle cruiser *Repulse*, and four destroyers — *Electra*, *Express*, *Tenedos*, and *Vampire*. Late that afternoon Force Z, as it was called, sailed northward to intercept the Japanese transports in the Gulf of Siam.

Japanese Airborne Unit Small Arms

1 Test Type 1, paratroop rifle with folding stock extended. The weapon has a caliber of 6.5mm and is believed to have been modified at the Nagoya Arsenal
2 Test Type 1, paratroop rifle with stock folded in the jump position
3 Type 100 paratroop rifle, with folded monopod and barrel detached
4 Type 2 paratroop rifle, of 7.7mm caliber, with barrel detached. Production of this weapon began in late 1943. This is the most frequently encountered arm of Japanese airborne troops
5 Type 100/40 submachine gun, with folding stock; caliber 8mm. This weapon was specifically developed in the early 1940s for airborne operations
6 Thirty round box magazine for Types 100/40 and 100/44 submachine guns
7 Type 100/44 submachine gun 8mm caliber.
8 Type 99 paratroop light machine gun, caliber 7.7mm with stock detached
9 Thirty round box magazine for Type 99 light machine gun
10 Special short bayonet and scabbard issued to airborne troops

US Army Ordnance Museum, 2-10; Laurence J. Beyer Collection, 1

The Type 2 paratroop rifle (*4*), was a bolt-action weapon, fed by a five round, non-detachable magazine. To lock the two halves of the weapon together, the receiver and barrel were put together, and a locking key inserted through the receiver to engage a slot in the barrel section. The Type 99 light machine gun was gas operated. It could fire 850 rounds per minute, and was automatic only. The type 100 submachine gun (*6* and *7*) carried a 30-round magazine and had a cyclic rate of 350 rounds per minute.

The mission involved considerable risk, as the planned area of operations would be within striking range of Japanese aircraft based in French Indochina. Unfortunately for the British, the aircraft carrier assigned to the Far Eastern Fleet was laid up for repairs in the United States after running aground at Kingston, Jamaica. Anticipating the Japanese threat, Phillips had requested that air reconnaissance be provided on December 9 and fighter protection on the 10th. The Far East's Royal Air Force commander, Air-Vice Marshal Conway Pulford, however, had thinned out his forces in meeting multiple Japanese

assaults and could not guarantee the requested air support. Moreover, British airfields throughout Malaya had sustained heavy bombardment. Consequently, Phillips was compelled to sail under the cloak of prevailing bad weather, hoping both to surprise the enemy and protect his own ships from air attack.

Shielded by low clouds and heavy rains, Force Z escaped detection for some 24 hours. But their luck ran out in late afternoon of the 9th when the sky cleared briefly and revealed the presence of three Japanese reconnaissance aircraft. With surprise gone, the admiral calculated it was dangerous to proceed

and subsequently directed Force Z south to home port. However, a message received at midnight, reporting Japanese landings at Kuantan, changed Phillips's plans once more. Since the area in question lay slightly off his return track. Phillips decided to investigate. Force Z advanced toward Kuantan, ignoring the appearance of yet another Japanese aircraft on the morning of the 10th. The destroyer *Express* was dispatched to survey the harbor, while the *Prince of Wales* launched a small plane for air reconnaissance and to look out for enemy submarines. All of the searches returned with reports of "complete peace'' at Kuantan, discrediting the news of Japanese landings there. Having passed some small vessels earlier, Phillips now steered eastward for a closer look.

Japan's Malaya invasion force regarded the *Prince of Wales* and *Repulse* as a grave threat to its plans. Therefore, on December 8 and 9 the Japanese had launched aerial reconnaissance to locate the British fleet. Search planes of the 22d *Koku Sentai* (Air Flotilla) reported two battleships, four cruisers, and four destroyers at anchor in Singapore. But on the afternoon of the 9th a Japanese submarine contradicted the information when it radioed in the report of sighting two battleships ''on a course of 310 [degrees] at a speed of 14 knots, bearing 196 [degrees], distance 225 nautical miles (405km) from Paulo Condore Island.'' By this time the initial invasion of Malaya had been completed and the Japanese fleet was retiring to Cam Ranh Bay. Alerted to the presence of the British, the Japanese detached their transports from the warships in anticipation of the upcoming sea battle. The Japanese naval task force commander sent non-combat ships to seek refuge in the Gulf of Siam. He also launched float planes for reconnaissance and ordered submarine patrols to seek out the British. On the night of the 9th both the Japanese planes and submarines spotted the British, but lost contact because of heavy rainstorms. Subsequently, the Japanese surface fleet decided against engaging the British, instead turning over the task to their submarines and land-based naval aircraft.

Meanwhile, the Japanese 22d Air Flotilla had been extremely busy. Besides the reconnaissance sorties flown, 16 of its aircraft had plastered British airfields at Singapore on December 8 and at Kuantan on the 9th. The submarine sighting of the British fleet, also reported on the 9th, stirred up activity at Japanese airfields in Indochina. Shortly, 95 medium bombers and two reconnaissance planes took off from bases near Saigon and Thu Do Mot. The force included three or four squadrons (numbering nine aircraft each) of G4M1 torpedo planes of the *Kanoya Kokutai* Group, and some seven squadrons of G3M2 bombers, which might double as torpedo carriers of the *Mihoro* and *Genzan* Groups. Darkness foiled the airplanes' attempt to locate the British ships, and the Japanese air units had to return to their bases. They had little rest, however, as a submarine reported sighting the British at 3:40 A.M. on December 10. The planes took off once more.

Shortly after 11:00 A.M. that day, at a point 60 nautical miles (108km) east of Kuantan, the Japanese planes engaged the pride of the Royal Navy's Eastern Fleet. Capt. W.G. Tennant, skipper of the *Repulse*, recorded the battle from his bridge. As a high-level bomber squadron appeared, the ships executed evasive maneuvers and opened antiaircraft fire. The attackers, flying at 10,000 feet

Above: Seen on arrival in Singapore from Europe, the battleship *Prince of Wales* was one of two British capital ships sunk by Japanese air power in Malayan waters on December 10, 1941. After this there was no effective naval resistance to the Japanese invasion.

Below: Survivors of the Japanese attack scramble from the sinking *Prince of Wales* onto one of the escorting destroyers. Between them, the *Electra*, *Express* and *Vampire* rescued 1,285 of the *Prince of Wales'* 1,612-man complement.

(3,000m) in close line abreast formation, concentrated first on the *Repulse*. Each plane dropped a 250-pound bomb, scoring several near misses and one hit on the armored deck. But damage was light and a fire ignited by the blast was quickly controlled. A 25-minute respite was followed by a nine-aircraft torpedo-bomber strike. This time it was the *Prince of Wales'* turn. Launched from between 3,000 (900) and 6,000-feet (1,800m) range at 300 (90) to 400-feet (120m) altitudes, two of the torpedoes hit the battleship. The *Prince of Wales* lost steering control, began to list, and her speed dropped from 25 to 15 knots. The

The Strategy of Germany First

Even before Japan attacked Pearl Harbor and Germany and Italy declared war on the United States, American war planners were thinking in terms of a campaign against the three Axis partners, in which the defeat of Germany would receive the highest priority. As the danger of Axis aggression grew more acute, the old series of joint Army-Navy "color" plans — Red for a war with Great Britain, Black for Germany, or Orange for Japan — were blended into "Rainbow" plans for a war against a coalition of enemies. The Joint Board of the Army and Navy proposed five possible Rainbow plans, each based on a different assumption. Rainbow 1, for example, dealt with the defense of the Western Hemisphere and America's outlying possessions, without the assistance of allies. Rainbow 2 pitted the United States against Japan while the American allies, France and Great Britain, battled Germany and Italy. After the fall of France in 1940, Rainbow 5 took precedence, for it proposed that the United States join forces with Britain to defeat Germany, while containing the Japanese in the western Pacific; once Germany had been beaten, the two allies would direct their combined might against Japan.

Germany was considered to be the main enemy. In the words of Adm. Harold R. Stark, the Chief of Naval Operations, "if Britain wins decisively against Germany, we could win everywhere, but if she loses the problems facing us would be very great, and while we might not *lose everywhere*, we might, possibly, not *win* anywhere." Since the triumph of Great Britain seemed essential to assure an American victory in the event of a war against the Axis, the

greatest threat to British survival had to be eliminated first. This belief, which lay at the heart of Rainbow 5, was adopted by Anglo-American staff planners, who met at Washington from January through March 1941. Although never formally ratified by President Franklin D. Roosevelt and Prime Minister Winston Churchill, Germany first became the unofficial policy of the two nations, should they become allies in a war

Above: Because German troops already occupied most of western Europe and German industrial muscle was greater than than of Japan, the Allies rightly felt that Germany offered the greater strategic threat.

against the Axis. When the United States entered the war, events ratified the plan, for any possibility of an immediate offensive against Japan vanished amid the flames and smoke along Battleship Row at Pearl Harbor.

Repulse, "combing the tracks" — maneuvering parallel to the direction of the incoming torpedoes — managed to avoid being hit. In the attack, Capt. Tennant claimed to have downed two Japanese planes. Twelve minutes later the Japanese torpedo planes returned and two minutes after that came more high-level bombers. But the *Repulse* evaded and escaped both attempts. At noon Tennant informed Singapore of the action.

A third torpedo-bomber strike by nine aircraft began at 12:22. Six of the planes went after the battleship, while three attacked the *Repulse*. As three torpedoes crashed into the battleship, its speed dropped to eight knots. One torpedo found the *Repulse* amidships. The Japanese lost one aircraft. Three minutes later another formation of nine torpedo-bombers entered the fray, swarming in on the *Repulse* from all sides. Two Japanese planes were destroyed, but the ship took four torpedoes, one of which disabled her rudder. Sensing the end, Capt. Tennant ordered his crew topside.

At 12:35 *Repulse* rolled to port, capsized, and sank. The final assault on the *Prince of Wales* began at 12:46. Attacked by a squadron of high-level bombers, the ship sustained a devastating hit which tore through the main deck and sank the ship at 1:20. By the time the British relief planes — six Brewster Buffaloes — arrived on the scene, the Japanese had departed and the destroyers were busy picking up survivors.

Tsutae Murakami, a pilot of the 22d *Koku Sentai* "Wild Eagles," recalled the *Prince of Wales'* "three . . . 20 mm. pom-pom firing 60,000 rounds per minute . . . four . . . 40 mm. high-angle guns, and 16 secondary armament 5.25 inch guns," firing at him. Braving this blistering barrage, the Japanese bombers pressed on using 14 1,110-pound bombs against the *Prince of Wales*. A wave of torpedo-bombers came next, followed by Murakami and his mates on a strafing run. One plane had launched its torpedo into *Repulse*'s middle just before it succumbed to anti-aircraft fire. As the British cruiser began

to list, the Japanese airmen spotted bodies scattered on her deck. Next, launching their payloads from a height of only 75 feet (22m), the torpedo-bombers crippled the *Prince of Wales* and sank a destroyer. As the high-level bombers moved in for the kill, the bombardiers shouted "Banzai" and tears of joy streamed down Murakami's face.

The British lost two irreplaceable capital ships and had 840 men killed; Japanese losses numbered three aircraft and 21 crewmen. Among the British casualties were Adm. Phillips and Capt. John C. Leach, commander of the *Prince of Wales* who — true to naval tradition — went down with their ship. The figures, however, belie the more significant effect on British morale; as Prime Minister Winston Churchill observed: "In all of the war I never received a more direct shock . . . Over this vast expanse of waters (the Indian and Pacific Oceans) Japan was supreme, and we everywhere weak and naked." On the other hand, Japanese spirits soared. They would no longer fear to send their ships "in an area

Commonwealth Small Arms

1 British Pattern 14 (rifle No.3 Mk 1) .303 caliber
2 British Pattern 1907 sword bayonet and scabbard
3 British grenade Model No.36
4 British rifle No.5, Mk 1
5 British Mk VI Webley revolver, .455 caliber
6 Pattern 1937 web ammunition pouch
7 Canadian No.1, Mk 1 Inglis-Browning 9mm semi-automatic pistol
8 British bayonet No.5, Mk 1, with scabbard and web belt frog, for 4
9 Indian bayonet No.1, Mk III, for rifle No.1
10 Australian machete bayonet Mk 1
11 British rifle No.1, Mk III
12 Grenade cup discharger

and Model 1936 grenade
13 British rifle No.1, Mk III
14 Canvas cover for 13
15 British Pattern 1907 sword bayonet and scabbard
16 Ammunition clip, five rounds of .303 caliber
17 British rifle No.4 Mk 1
18 British bayonet No.4, Mk 1
19 British bayonet No.4 Mk 2. A simpler spike version of 18, with belt frog
20 As 19, but with experimental frog
21-24 Components of cleaning kit for Commonwealth rifles
25 Issue bandolier of .303 ammunition, see 16

Allan D. Cors Collection: 3, 4, 6-18, 20, 21, 23-25; Laurence J. Beyer Collection: 1, 2, 5; Russ Pritchard Collection: 19, 22

Rifle *1*, the British Pattern 14, was first manufactured during World War I for service with British forces, by Remington and Winchester in the United States. The arm was reissued during World War II. Grenade *3*, was better known as the Mills Bomb, and was the standard British grenade after its introduction in 1932. The machete bayonet *10*, was introduced in 1944 for airborne operations.

in which the big guns of the British warships might destroy them.'' Most significantly, Japan's unprecedented action demonstrated that ships lacking air cover could be attacked by aircraft based as far away as 40 nautical miles (72km). This episode exploded a universally held tenet which had denied that ''battleships in the open sea could . . . [be] sunk by planes.'' In its place, the jubilant advocates of long-range bombing heralded the warning: ''Capital ships cannot withstand land-based air power.''

With their control of the sea and the air the Japanese were able for a time to strike where and when they pleased.

The isolated Allied forces fought bravely, but were overwhelmed by naval, air, and ground forces which the Japanese concentrated at will. Only hours after the attack on Pearl Harbor the Japanese moved quickly to complete the first phase of their plan to capture Guam and Wake. Guam — where a few hundred American and Chamorro defenders had no weapon larger than a .30 caliber machine gun — fell quickly, but at Wake the Japanese received their first surprise of the war.

Wake's 2,600-acre (1,040-hectare), V-shaped atoll made up of three long islands figured importantly in American

military plans as a way station for aircraft en route to the Philippines and as a reconnaissance base for observing the Japanese-held Marshall Islands. Since the beginning of 1941, more than one thousand construction workers had worked tirelessly to transform the atoll into a military base. On Wake, the largest island, they had built a 5,000-foot (1,500m) runway; on Peale Island a seaplane base was under construction; and on Wilkes Island plans called for a submarine base.

Commanded at the time by Navy commander Winfield Scott Cunningham, the island was defended by a 450-man

Commonwealth Uniforms

1 Temperate climate, double-breasted service jacket, regulation white shirt and black tie of Cdr. W.H.N. Martin. Martin served in HMS *Ark Royal*, and was commanding officer of 814 Squadron — a squadron of Swordfish torpedo planes — aboard the carrier HMS *Hermes*, until spring 1942. He was posted off the ship shortly before she was attacked off the coast of Ceylon by Japanese carrier-borne aircraft and sunk — April 9, 1942.
2 Service cap of Cdr. Martin. Note the white cover on the cap and visor insignia indicating the rank of commander
3 Service cap of Maj. L. Gordon Darling, 9th Division, Australian Army. The 9th was transferred from the Middle East to the Southwest Pacific theater after the battle of El Alamein
4 Service jacket of Maj. Darling. Note the Australian general service badge on the lapels, and the distinctive national device on the buttons. The major served in both New Guinea and Borneo

War Memorial Museum of Virginia

Cdr. Martin's service jacket bears the winged insignia of a Royal Navy officer pilot on the left sleeve, above the rank stripes. These are the three bars indicating the rank of commander. This particular jacket does not possess shoulder straps, though these were worn by Royal Navy personnel, and up to the rank of commodore were the same pattern insignia as that worn on the sleeve. In an aviator's case, they would have featured an 'A' within the bar loop. The medal ribbons include some awards that were earned during Cdr. Martin's postwar career.

Major Darling's jacket is of the khaki drill service dress type. The buttons and the insignia both on the jacket and the service cap are specific to Australian forces. Insignia are also in evidence on the major's shoulder straps.

detachment of the First Marine Defense Battalion, under Maj. James P. S. Devereux, and a Marine fighter squadron, VMF-211, under Maj. Paul A. Putnam. The defenders were terribly under strength, possessing only a dozen anti-aircraft guns and no radar for fire control or early warning. Their 12 F4F-3 Wildcat fighters were obsolete and the pilots barely trained to fly them. The Japanese fighters struck at noon on December 8, 1941.

The mission of capturing Wake was assigned to Vice Adm. Shigeyoshi Inoue's Fourth Fleet, which was responsible for the defense of the Japanese possessions in the southwest and central Pacific. Indeed, planes from Inoue's base at Kwajalein were on their way to bomb Wake by the time the attack on Pearl Harbor began.

Some of the Wildcats from Wake were on patrol as the Japanese bombers approached, but missed them because of the weather. The remaining fighters were destroyed on the ground along with much of the aviation gasoline stored near the field. Subsequent air raids destroyed the hospital and fire control systems on some coastal defense guns — but the guns remained intact, as the Japanese invaders learned when they made their first attempt to land on December 11. Three cruisers and six destroyers escorted a 450-man Japanese invasion force. When the ships came within 5,000 yards (4,500m) of the island, the 5-inch batteries on Wake opened a blistering barrage which turned back the light cruiser *Yubari* and blew the destroyer *Hayate* out of the water. Soon another three destroyers and a transport sustained hits and broke off the action. Four surviving Wildcats pursued the fleeing Japanese, sinking a destroyer, and damaging two light cruisers and a transport. However, they had all succumbed by December.

As the courageous defense of Wake was bolstering American morale, Adm. Kimmel in Hawaii made plans for the relief of Wake Island by committing his three carriers, the *Lexington, Saratoga,* and *Enterprise.* But delay and hesitiation frustrated the relief. Marine reinforcements, aboard the seaplane tender *Tangier*, waited two days at Pearl Harbor waiting for the *Saratoga*, which had been rerouted because of a submarine scare. The task force, under Rear Adm. Frank Jack Fletcher, did not finally sail until December 16th. Moreover, because the task force had to fuel en route, the entire fleet was limited to 13 knots, the top speed of the accompanying oiler.

Meanwhile at Pearl Harbor, Vice Adm. William S. Pye had replaced Kimmel as commander of the Pacific Fleet, until the new commander, Adm. Chester W. Nimitz, arrived. The Chief of Naval Operations and the Secretary of the Navy informed Pye that they considered Wake a liability. Aware that the Japanese could muster greater strength, Adm. Pye ordered the *Lexington* task force under Vice Adm. Wilson E. Brown to join Fletcher, causing further delay. Fletcher took so much time to fuel that he was 600 miles (960km) from Wake on December 23d when the Marine defenders reported a second Japanese landing.

The second Japanese landing was considerably stronger than the first, including four heavy cruisers and about 2,000 men. Two carriers detached from the fleet returning from the attack on Pearl Harbor, the *Soryu* and *Hiryu*, provided long-range air support against Wake. Keeping out of range of the Marine batteries, the Japanese shelled the island while 1,000 troops in assault barges and patrol boats landed on nearby Wilkes Island and on Wake itself. With many of the defenders operating the 5-inch guns and machine gun positions, Maj. Devereux had only 85 men available as infantry to oppose the invaders. By dawn the Japanese were fully established ashore and the Marines were surrounded.

While Adm. Fletcher's forces still labored through heavy seas 450 miles (702km) from Wake. Pye and his chief of staff, Rear Adm. Milo F. Draemel, were having second thoughts, after receiving reports of the ''grim'' situation at Wake. Moreover, on the morning of December

23d Commander Cunningham informed Pacific Fleet Headquarters that the enemy had apparently landed. Two hours later, while the headquarters staff debated what course of action to take, Cunningham reported that the Japanese had seized a foothold on the island. At 9:00 A.M. Pye ordered Fletcher to return to Pearl Harbor. With help no longer expected, Cunningham and Devereux had no choice but surrender.

With the capture of Wake and Guam, Japan gained absolute control of the lines of communications across the central Pacific. The Philippines were now isolated and the Japanese conquest of the archipelago was a foregone conclusion. In December, coincident with the fall of Guam and Wake, Japan accepted the surrender of Thailand and captured Hong Kong.

The Japanese now struck Singapore from the landward direction via Thailand's Kra Isthmus. Using bases in Indochina and Thailand, their planes systematically destroyed the few British aircraft remaining in northern Malaya and by neutralizing the airfields in that region forestalled the possibility of British aerial reinforcement. Although the British fought valiantly and repeatedly tried to establish and hold a line across the Malay Peninsula, the Japanese controlled the sea and were able to mount an amphibious campaign. The Japanese, under the leadership of Gen. Tomoyuki Yamashita, repeatedly forced the British to retreat by landing forces behind the British lines. The British fought a hopeless rearguard action over some 400 miles (640km). Finally, on January 30, 1942, they fell back on

Above: Japanese infantry manhandle a 75-mm infantry support gun over a bank in the Malayan jungle. Operating with lighter equipment scales and a smaller logistic tail, the Japanese constantly outmaneuvered their Allied opponents in such terrain.

Below: Meeting negligible aerial opposition, Japanese air power was able to dominate at the tactical and strategic levels. This is a casualty being rushed to hospital in Singapore after yet another of a whole series of Japanese bombing raids.

THE FALL OF MALAYA, SINGAPORE AND BURMA

Maps A and B
The Japanese attack on Malaya began with amphibious landings by Yamashita's Twenty-Fifth Army, together with a drive south from Thailand. The British, convinced that the terrain made an attack from their rear impossible, were continually outflanked and infiltrated by the fast-moving Japanese forces.

British and Australian forces were finally driven into Singapore, where they set up a static defense. This, however, did not hold when the Japanese attacked on February 9. Faced with the possibility of many civilian casualties and a water shortage, Lt. Gen. Percival surrendered on February 16.

Maps C and D
Gen. Iida's aims in the Burma attack included defense of the attack on Malaya, and the severing of the Burma Road to China. The port of Rangoon fell on March 8 cutting off Allied forces from their supplies. Iida then pushed his forces forward separating the British and Chinese armies and cutting the Burma Road at Lashio. Only the monsoon and the Salween River prevented an attack on India.

JAPANESE NAVAL PARATROOPER

At the beginning of the war, the Japanese Navy had two units of airborne troops, each with about 1,000 men. Their role was to capture airfields for the use of naval aircraft. They saw most action during the capture of the Netherlands East Indies. This trooper wears the silk/cotton uniform of his service and carries the Type 100/40 submachine gun. Its stock is hinged so that it can be folded over during a jump.

Above: Japanese tanks move into the center of Singapore city. The British had not anticipated an attack on the island from the north, and therefore were poorly placed to cope with the Japanese offensive across the Johore Strait on February 8-10, 1942.

Below: Lt. Gen. A.E. Percival (far right) surrenders the British forces in Malaya on February 15. The Japanese had suffered only 9.824 casualties but the British had some 138,700 (about 9,000 killed and wounded, and the rest taken prisoner).

Left: Lt. Gen. Tomoyuki Yamashita (seated on the left) meets Gen. Percival at the conference that ended British resistance on Singapore, at the end of a campaign characterized by the very high quality of Japanese planning and leadership.

Singapore. There Yamashita demonstrated that the £100-million ($400-million) British naval base could not hold off a land attack, and on February 15th a British force of 100,000 men surrendered. Thus did the Japanese general earn the nickname "Tiger of Malaya." The conquest of Singapore gave the Japanese passage from the Pacific to the Indian Ocean. It also gave them control of what had been regarded as the main area of defense for Sumatra and Java and released men and planes for use on other battlefields.

Even as one Japanese force was driving southward toward Singapore, another operating from Thailand advanced westward into Burma (Myanmar). Burma had recently been separated from India, but the British-backed political regime proved unpopular to many Burmese. Consequently, in many places the local population collaborated with the Japanese by guiding them through hidden jungle paths to outflank the British and to destroy British supplies and communications. At best, only about two British contingents were available to defend the region when the Japanese launched their attack into Burma in January 1942. On March 9 the Japanese captured Rangoon, the capital, and secured a major port of entry for supplies and reinforcements.

During the succeeding weeks the Japanese advanced northward up the Irrawaddy, Sittang, and Salween rivers. In this period the British fought in conjunction with two Chinese armies, led by the American military adviser to Generalissimo Chiang Kai-shek, Lt. Gen. Joseph W. Stilwell, to whom was entrusted the defense of eastern Burma. But the ensuing developments were very much like those in Malaya. Repeatedly outflanked by the Japanese, the defenders were compelled to fall back. In April the Japanese launched a surprise attack northward from Thailand, which cut behind the Chinese defenders and captured Lashio, the southern terminus of the Burma Road. At the same time a frontal attack from the south up the Irrawaddy Valley split the Chinese forces, and on May 1, 1942 the Japanese captured Mandalay. Some of the British managed to reach safety in India, and Stilwell extricated some of his forces. Burma was lost, however, and with it the last effective route for sending American and British supplies to Chiang Kai-shek and the Nationalist Chinese.

By Christmas 1941, Allied prospects throughout the region were desperate indeed. On that very day, Hong Kong fell after a gallant but hopeless defense by a small garrison of British and Commonwealth troops. The Japanese, moreover,

Above: Issue 1911 campaign hat and service boots worn by General Stilwell during his 140-mile (224-km) march from China into India, May 5-14 1942. *West Point Museum.*

controlled the Celebes Sea between the Philippines and the Netherlands East Indies and dominated the Makassar Strait. Besides conquering Hong Kong and advancing in Malaya and Burma, the Japanese invaded the Dutch colony to acquire the oil needed to prosecute the war.

During this bleak December, the Anglo-American military and political leaders met at Washington. The so-called Arcadia Conference resulted in an agreement to establish a single unified area command known as AB-DACOM — for American, British, Dutch, and Australian Command — to counter the Japanese advance along the crescent from Burma to western New Guinea. The forces which the Allies could marshal to meet the anticipated invasion were none too formidable. The Dutch had an inexperienced colonial army of 100,000 natives, built up from a nucleus of some 30,000 professional soldiers, which was largely concentrated

Below: The assault on Hong Kong by the Japanese 38th Division on December 8, 1941 was greatly facilitated by the efforts of naval bombers such as these Mitsubishi G3M "Nells" that destroyed the limited British air strength at Kai Tak Airport.

in Java. They also had some 400 airplanes, a few cruisers, and a number of destroyers and submarines. The American Asiatic fleet — consisting of the heavy cruiser *Houston*, the light cruisers *Boise* and *Marblehead* and a number of destroyers and submarines — had also sailed to the Netherlands East Indies, where it joined a British cruiser, an Australian cruiser, some smaller British ships, and the Netherlands naval foces. The ABDACOM area included Burma, Malaya, the Dutch East Indies, Western New Guinea, Northwest Australia, and the Philippines. All the territories, except Australia, were to fall to Japan within a matter of months.

Neither the British nor the Americans sought command of ABDACOM, for it was obvious that the area was untenable. The British finally named Gen. Sir Archibald Wavell for the thankless and unwanted job. By the time he arrived on Java in January 1942, the Japanese had nearly completed their conquest of Southeast Asia. Adm. Thomas C. Hart of the US Navy headed the ABDACOM naval forces; a Dutch officer, Lt. Gen. Hein ter Poorten, led the ground troops; while British Air Chief Marshal Sir Richard E.C. Pierse commanded the air forces.

Most of the ABDACOM commanders (except the Americans, who had no local territory to protect) devoted their attention to safeguarding their own nation's individual colonies, rather than devising a coordinated defense. The American and Australian governments worried most about protecting the approaches to Australia and the southwest Pacific. Wavell and Hart concentrated on saving Malaya, already a lost cause.

On January 21, 1942, three weeks before Singapore surrendered, the Japanese invaded oil-rich Balikpapan, Borneo. Two American light cruisers *Marblehead* and *Boise*, and four destroyers patrolled to the southeast, but *Marblehead* experienced engine trouble, and *Boise* struck a rock and had to head for Java for repairs. The American destroyers steamed to the Makassar

Strait, for the first surface battle of the war involving American warships. In the Battle of Balikpapan that ensued four destroyers — built to patrol the Atlantic in World War I and with ventilation systems ill-suited for the tropics — sank four Japanese transports and, except for malfunctioning torpedoes, might have wreaked additional havoc. The elderly American ships momentarily checked, but could not stop, the Japanese advance. Subsequently, enemy air attacks frustrated a combined American, British, and Dutch fleet trying to stop the Japanese invasion of Celebes; *Houston* sustained a hit that knocked out the after turret, and *Marblehead* suffered damage that forced her to steam half-way round the world, at times steering with engines when the rudder failed, to undergo repairs at the Brooklyn Navy Yard. Then, in a nighttime battle of the Badung Strait two Japanese destroyers defeated a vastly superior Allied fleet.

The Japanese continued on toward Java, occupying Bali on February 19, and on the same day Adm. Nagumo's carrier aircraft attacked Darwin in northwest Australia, sinking a dozen ships and cutting the supply lines between Australia and Java. Wavell concluded that it was futile to defend the Netherlands East Indies, but the Dutch disagreed, insisting on protecting Java. Complaints by the Dutch led to the relief of Adm. Hart and his replacement by Vice Adm. Conrad E.H. Helfrich, Commander-in-Chief of the Royal Netherlands East Indian Navy. On February 25 the British Combined Chiefs of Staff agreed to close Gen. Wavell's headquarters and turn over command to the Dutch. Most of the British and Americans left with Wavell, but the Asiatic Fleet remained behind to defend Java.

On the 24th a large Japanese convoy was spotted in the Karimata Channel, between Borneo and Sumatra, near Bawean Island in the Java Sea. A combined Allied force of five cruisers and 12 destroyers sortied to intercept the Japanese, and on the 27th sighted four

Above: The Allied flagship in the Battle of the Java Sea was the Dutch cruiser *De Ruyter.* Outgunned by her Japanese opponents, the ship was damaged by gunfire and was then torpedoed, sinking with the loss of Adm. Doorman and 344 other men.

Above: An American destroyer races toward an Australian transport (left) heavily on fire after being hit by Japanese bombs during an air raid on the strategically vital northern Australian port of Darwin. A British ship (right) was also set on fire.

Japanese cruisers, with 16 destroyers, covering a large convoy. In the Battle of the Java Sea, the Japanese again demonstrated their superiority in night fighting and torpedo warfare, sinking half the ABDACOM squadron at the cost of one destroyer damaged. In trying to escape, the American cruiser *Houston* and the Australian cruiser *Perth* ran into 50 Japanese transports unloading at Banten Bay, together with their escorting cruisers and destroyers. In the ensuing fight the two Allied cruisers managed to sink or damage about a dozen of the enemy ships before going down themselves. The *Houston* ran out of ammunition and was firing flares at the Japanese when the end came. About a third of *Houston*'s crew lived to join the survivors of the *Perth* in a brutal imprisonment lasting more than three years. The Japanese landed on Java on March 1st, and Batavia fell the next day. A week later the Dutch surrendered, officially ending the existence of ABDACOM. With the conquest of the rich Netherlands East Indies, the Japanese gained

access to the oil that had been one of their chief objectives in going to war.

The conquest of the Netherlands East Indies had followed a careful plan. In January 1942, after capturing a few bases on islands to the north of Java, the Japanese marshaled a fleet of more than 100 transports and warships. In Makassar Strait, off Balikpapan, the four American destroyers momentarily disrupted the enemy's timetable, but overwhelming numbers and an uncanny skill in night warfare put the conquest back on schedule. Temporarily checked in their drive on Java, the Japanese next approached in an indirect way. Immediately after the fall of Singapore they captured Sumatra to the northwest of Java and then, coming from the other direction, they seized the islands of Timor and Bali off the eastern tip of Java. Later in February, the Japanese navy again advanced on Java and the Allied fleet once more challenged the Japanese, this time unsuccessfully. Thus did Japan gain possession of an empire rich in foodstuffs, minerals, oil, and

Below: Celebrations in Tokyo marked several phases in Japan's seizure of the "Southern Resources Area" in the creation of the "Greater East Asia Co-Prosperity Sphere". This meeting celebrated the sinking of the two British capital ships on December 10, 1941.

rubber, the commodities which she greatly coveted and vitally needed.

As one tentacle of the Japanese octopus wrapped itself around the Netherlands East Indies, others enveloped the Philippines and probed the Indian Ocean. Adm. Chuichi Nagumo, after bombing Pearl Harbor and Darwin, steamed toward the British base at Colombo, Ceylon (Sri Lanka). Communications intercepts alerted the British fleet that had gathered there, but the commander, Adm. Sir James Somerville, whose force included five battleships and three aircraft carriers, chose to head for the Maldive Islands to take on fuel and water before attempting to give battle. On April 5, Easter Sunday, Nagumo's airmen found Colombo harbor largely empty, but they sank two small warships, inflicted heavy damage on docks and workshops, and caught two cruisers that had fled to the open sea, sinking both of them. The Japanese bombed the second major naval base on Ceylon, Trincomalee, on April 8, and lost perhaps two dozen aircraft to defending fighters. Again, Nagumo's aviators caught British warships at sea, sinking the aircraft carrier *Hermes*, the destroyer escorting it, and three lesser ships.

Not until May 1942, as the octopus sought to embrace Australia, did Japan overrreach itself. The Imperial Japanese Navy suffered its first real setback, when an American task force located an invasion fleet headed for Port Moresby in New Guinea to cut off the Australian supply line. The ensuing Battle of the Coral Sea — fought entirely between carrier-based planes — was the first sea battle in history where surface ships did not exchange a single shot. The Japanese lost one carrier and had another damaged. The Americans lost the *Lexington*, and the *Yorktown* was badly damaged, but the Japanese were held back, for the first time in the Pacific War.

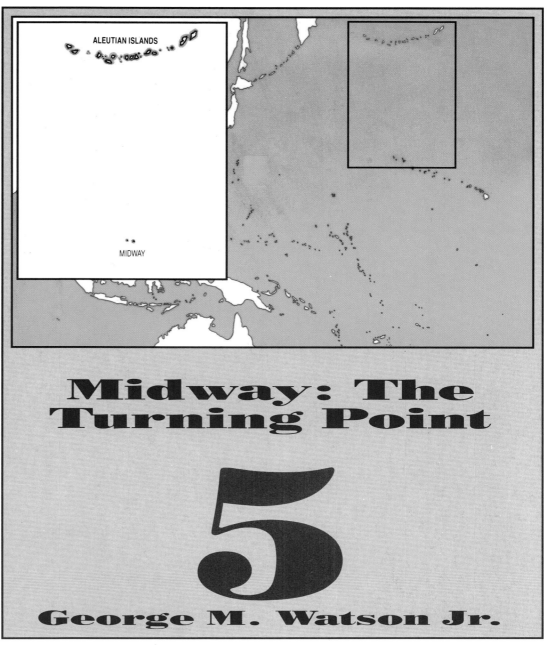

Midway: The Turning Point

5

George M. Watson Jr.

Still suffering from the shock and humiliation of Pearl Harbor, and the continuing succession of Japanese victories, the United States seemed unable to stem the onslaught. An American victory of sorts had been won in April 1942 when Adm. William F. Halsey and Lt. Col. James H. Doolittle raided the Japanese mainland; even though the attack inflicted very little damage, it shattered the Japanese belief in the invulnerability of their homeland to air attack. In part a consequence of the raid on Japan, the Battle of Midway, in June of that year, marked a turning point in the war, destroying the Japanese carrier force even as it spawned an inconsequential campaign in the northern Pacific.

The raid by Halsey and Doolittle was inspired by two Navy captains, Francis S. Low and Donald B. Duncan, who convinced Adm. Ernest J. King, Chief of Naval Operations, and Gen. Henry "Hap" Arnold, the Commanding General, Army Air Forces, that Army bombers could take off from the deck of an aircraft carrier. As a result of the cooperation between Arnold and King, the aircraft carrier USS *Hornet* loaded 16

Army B-25s onto its flight deck and steamed through San Francisco's Golden Gate. To lead the air strike, Arnold chose Doolittle, a distinguished aviator and aeronautical engineer, who set about supervising the training of his volunteer crews and the modification of their B-25s to obtain maximum range. The crew members knew nothing about their mission until they were far out to sea, nor had they ever practiced taking off from the deck of an actual carrier. On the morning of April 18, the radar of the carrier *Enterprise*, escorting the *Hornet*, picked up one of the Japanese picket boats that formed a warning line extending some seven hundred miles east of the Japanese Home Islands. Assuming the task force had been spotted, Halsey chose not to risk *Hornet* and *Enterprise*, half the carrier strength of the Pacific Fleet, and instead launched the bombers 150 miles (240km) further from Japan than planned. Halsey's decision, with which Doolittle agreed, greatly reduced the likelihood that the bombers could reach their destination in China after bombing Japan. All 16 planes dropped their bombs, and all but one, which

Japanese Army Aviator's Equipment

1 Army intermediate weight aviator's flying jacket, without lining
2 Army pilot sweater
3 Army intermediate weight flight trousers without lining
4 Army leather flying helmet with fur lining for cold weather
5 Army flying goggles
6 Cardboard storage box with lens wiping cloth, for flying goggles
7 Army flying gloves with fur lining for cold weather
8 Japanese National Flag. Made of silk, this was folded and carried in a pocket of the aviator's flying jacket
9 Type 14 (1925) semi-automatic pistol of 8mm caliber. The weapon is complete with a tropical-issue rubberized canvas shoulder holster, securing straps, and a spare magazine of pistol ammunition
10 A 1000 stitch belt. Worn usually around the waist or carried in a jacket pocket, these belts were kept by aviators as good luck charms
11 Army intermediate weight flying helmet, without lining

Eugene C. Gibson Collection

landed in the Soviet Union, ran out of fuel and went down in Japanese-occupied China. Of the 80 crewmen, 71 survived, one died, and eight were captured. The Japanese executed four of the prisoners as war criminals, but the others survived cruel treatment and were freed when the war ended. Most of the pilots who found their way to friendly lines were aided by Chinese peasants, many of whom the Japanese killed in retaliation. While the actual damage of the Doolittle raid was slight, it had a psychological effect on the Japanese whose Army and Navy had failed to protect the homeland.

Until the Halsey-Doolittle raid, Japanese army and navy planners disagreed about the need to push the defensive perimeter further eastward by capturing Midway Island. Both factions recognized Midway as an important forward fueling station for American submarines. Located in the central Pacific, Midway lay 2,250 miles (3,600km) from Japan but only 1,100 miles (1,760km) from Oahu, at the apex of a triangle formed by Hawaii, Johnston Island and Midway. Whereas some Japanese opposed a Midway campaign — including Adm. Osami Nagamo, the Chief of Naval General Staff, who preferred an invasion of

Australia — Adm. Isoroku Yamamoto, the Commander-in-Chief, Combined Fleet, supported the operation, reasoning that it would enable him to draw out and destroy *Hornet, Enterprise,* and the other American carriers. Yamamoto also believed that if the US Navy chose to avoid a fight, the Japanese would profit from advancing their defensive perimeter to Midway and the western Aleutians.

The Doolittle raid ended the opposition among Japanese strategists to a Midway attack. To prevent another air strike like the April raid, Yamamoto approved an assault plan later that same month

All the objects in this photograph, with the exception of the flying goggles, were worn by a Japanese Army aviator who in 1945 flew into the American-held island of Okinawa to surrender. These artifacts were collected by an enlisted member of a US Construction Battalion stationed on the island at the time.

Left: Photographed from a North American B-25 Mitchell bomber, the naval base at Yokosuka was one of the targets for the "Doolittle Raid" of April 1942. This secured no worthwhile military success but was an enormous propaganda and morale coup.

and submitted it to Adm. Nagamo, who subsequently issued orders for the Commander-in-Chief, Combined Fleet, to seize and occupy Midway Island and key points in the western Aleutians, in cooperation with the Japanese Army.

The Japanese forces for the Midway operation were divided into 16 groups of warships, which had to cooperate flawlessly in executing a complicated plan. Capt. Kameto Kuroshima, Yamamoto's senior operations officer, prepared a battle plan calling for air attacks on Dutch Harbor in the Aleutians from two carriers under Vice Adm. Boshiro Hosogaya's Northern Area Force, and the occupation of two islands of the western Aleutians. This attack would divert attention from Midway, where the four big carriers of Adm. Chuichi Nagumo's Mobile Force would attack on the next day from the northwest. An invasion force — including two battleships, a small aircraft carrier, and a half dozen heavy cruisers — would then close in from the southwest. Yamamoto chose to remain 300 miles (480km) to the west, with his own force of three powerful battleships and a small carrier, to thwart any counterattack.

Since the loss of Guam and Wake Island, the United States had no outpost west of Midway. In the absence of outlying bases, American planners had to rely on cryptanalysts, who succeeded in intercepting and decoding nearly 90 per cent of Japanese message traffic dealing with the Midway operation. By May 22 Adm. Chester W. Nimitz, the Commander-in-Chief, Pacific Ocean Areas, was certain of a Japanese attack on Midway, but Adm. King wanted some irrefutable evidence, fearing it might be a feint and that the South Pacific could be the real objective. In order to make the enemy provide the conclusive evidence, Midway sent an uncoded message that the fresh water distilling plant had broken down; Pearl Harbor replied that a fresh water barge was on its way. All intercept stations were instructed to listen and very soon were rewarded with a Japanese message reporting a shortage of water at the objective. Adm. Nimitz knew then for certain that the Japanese planned to attack Midway.

Nimitz now faced the challenge of defending Midway while keeping open the line of communication between the west coast of the United States and Australia. To defend Midway, he organized Task Force 16, consisting of the carriers *Enterprise* and *Hornet* supported by 6 cruisers and 9 destroyers. The *Saratoga* had been torpedoed 500 miles (800km) southwest of Oahu on January 11, and would not be ready for the approaching battle. Nimitz therefore needed the aircraft carrier *Yorktown*, under repair at Pearl Harbor from damage sustained in the Battle of the Coral Sea. Hundreds of electricians, fitters, machinists and welders swarmed over the ship, and many of them remained on board when the *Yorktown* set sail for Midway at the end of May. At the same time Nimitz and the senior Army commanders were reinforcing the defenses of Midway Island.

The carriers *Hornet* and *Enterprise* steamed for Midway but without their commander, Adm. Halsey, hospitalized with a skin infection. Halsey recommended Rear Adm. Raymond A. Spruance to replace him. Spruance, a 1906 graduate of the Naval Academy,

Right: Seen here in November 1941 with Sand Island behind Eastern Island, Midway atoll was the most western American base in the central Pacific during mid-1942. As such, it was a magnet for decisive events.

advanced through the ranks to become rear admiral in 1941. As commander of Cruiser Division Five, based at Pearl Harbor, he was 200 miles (320km) at sea when the Japanese attacked Hawaii. The appointment surprised Spruance, since he was comparatively junior, had never served on a carrier, and was not a pilot. Unlike the impulsive, publicity-seeking Halsey, Spruance remained an introvert, quiet and methodical, who knew how to use the knowledge and experience of the staff he had inherited. Adm. Frank Jack Fletcher in the *Yorktown*, commanding Task Force 17, was named the overall commander of the Carrier Striking Force on May 28.

Nimitz instructed his commanders to take a position northeast of Midway, hoping to avoid Japanese reconnaissance flights. Meanwhile, American search planes from the island would be looking for the enemy. While the marines at Midway worked frantically on the defenses, Navy PBY Catalina flying boats and Army B-17 bombers searched for the Japanese.

Yamamoto in the meantime had been monitoring American radio traffic and knew of the Midway activity, but he did not pass the information to Nagumo in order to preserve radio silence. Nagumo might have welcomed the intelligence, for mist and fog on June 2 and 3 impeded his own reconnaissance. Yet the fog helped screen Nagumo from American aircraft even though it hampered his own operations.

On June 3, a PBY from Midway reported sighting enemy transports and destroyers heading for Midway which erased any remaining doubt that the Japanese were converging on the island. But the location of Nagumo's carriers, the critical element in the enemy's plan, remained unknown.

In the meantime, Nagumo's fleet endured another day of foul weather accompanied by false sightings of enemy aircraft. Nagumo believed that the

American fleet, which he had not yet located, would probably engage when the landings commenced. Thus, when Nagumo launched his attack on Midway at 4:30 A.M. on June 4, he held back half his planes to deal with the American carriers, and sent cruiser scout planes to hunt for Spruance and Fletcher. A scout from the cruiser *Tone* was late getting off, a delay that proved costly.

As the Japanese aircraft headed for Midway, a Navy PBY spotted the large formation and radioed a warning. At about the same time a Midway-based search plane piloted by Lt. Howard P. Ady reported two carriers and two battleships 180 miles (288km) northwest of the island. Adm. Fletcher, the overall commander of the carrier forces, ordered Adm. Spruance to head southward to attack the Japanese carriers. While Spruance prepared to strike, squadrons at Midway tried to intercept the approaching Japanese aircraft while at the same time going after the carriers.

The fighters defending Midway, many of them obsolete Brewster Buffaloes, could not prevent the Japanese bombers from starting fires, but the damage remained confined to buildings and fuel dumps. The runways could still be used. This initial strike cost Nagumo 38 aircraft, and another 30 were damaged too badly to fly again. Nagumo now had fewer aircraft on his four carriers than the Americans had on their three.

Japanese fighters in the meantime easily broke up the first attack from Midway by six torpedo planes and four Army B-26 bombers rigged to carry torpedoes. Upon learning that the airfield at Midway remained operational, Nagumo faced a key decision: to launch a second attack as soon as possible, which involved tying up his flight decks for an hour or more to replace the torpedoes and armor piercing bombs with general purpose bombs, or to continue waiting for the American carriers to appear. He chose the former. While he rearmed for another strike against Midway, the scout plane from the cruiser *Tone*, which had been slow to start its search, reported the whereabouts of the American carriers. Nagumo immediately ordered the armorers to stop the changeover and stand by for orders.

A second wave of Midway-based planes bore down on Nagumo's carriers. Marine major Lofton Henderson, for whom Henderson Field on Guadalcanal would be later named, led 16 SBD-2 dive bombers, only half of which survived the swarming fighters — Nakajima type 97s and Mitsubishi Zeroes — and bursting antiaircraft shells. Henderson died leading the attack, and the Marine airmen did not score a single hit. Lt. Col. Walter C. Sweeney, leading 15 B-17s,

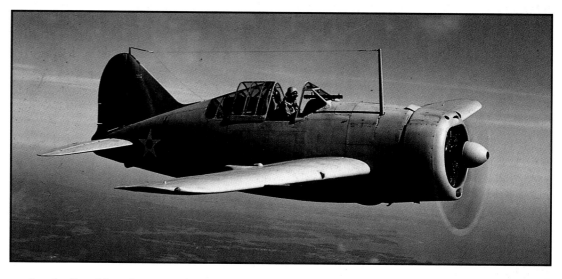

arrived after Henderson; the Army aircraft dropped their bombs, hit nothing, and escaped without loss. After Sweeney, a flight of 11 ancient Vultee Vindicator dive bombers, which started out with Henderson but fell behind, attacked, losing three aircraft, but inflicted no damage.

Adm. Spruance, to the northwest of Nagumo, initially planned to close the range to 100 miles (160km) and launch his aircraft at about 9:00 A.M. After hearing that the Japanese had hit Midway at 7:00 A.M., he decided that if he struck early he could catch Nagumo's first wave as it was on deck refueling. His squadrons took off while about 155 miles (248km) from the enemy, a calculated risk since the aircraft had a radius of action of about 175 miles (280km).

At about 9:20 that morning, Torpedo Squadron 8 led by Lt. Cdr. John C. Waldron from the *Hornet* made contact with the Japanese. Low on fuel, and without fighter cover, Waldron's squadron attacked, but not one of the 15 planes got close enough to launch a torpedo before being shot down by enemy fighters. Only one pilot survived, Ens. George H. Gay. He managed to escape from his TBD, bringing with him

Above: The Brewster F3A (seen here in the form of an early F3A-1) was obsolescent as a naval fighter even as it entered service, but the 21 land-based F3A-3s of the US Marine Corps' VFM-221 performed heroically against Japanese aircraft at Midway.

a bag holding his life raft and also a black rubber seat cushion, under which he hid until the battle passed him by and he could safely inflate the raft. A Navy PBY picked him up the next day.

The *Enterprise* torpedo planes, led by Lt. Cdr. Eugene E. Lindsey, also attacked, causing no damage and losing 10 of their 14 aircraft. Torpedo bombers from *Yorktown* did no better at the cost of 10 of 12 aircraft. Nevertheless, these initial torpedo attacks did accomplish something. They caused the Japanese to maneuver radically, which prevented the carriers from launching additional aircraft, and drew the Japanese fighters already in the air down to wave-top height. The diversion enabled the dive bombers, at medium altitude, to have almost unchallenged access to the critical targets — the four carriers. Dive bombers from the *Yorktown* and the *Enterprise* attacked the Japanese carriers untouched, and caught them as their aircraft took on bombs and fuel for

Right: Considerable damage was caused to Midway's installations by Japanese carrier-borne attackers in June 1942, but this was secondary to the naval maneuvering that gave the outnumbered American carriers the edge over their Japanese opponents.

US Navy Uniforms and Equipment

1 Navy enlisted man's wool pullover blouse. Note the distinctive collar and silk neckerchief. Belt plate is private purchase
2 White duck enlisted man's cap
3 Naval gun crew or 'talker' helmet. The interior of this broad helmet is constructed so as to allow ear phones and microphones to be worn underneath. These helmets were worn by personnel posted to the communications link between fire control and individual anti-aircraft gun chiefs
4 Inflatable canvas life belt
5 Naval aviator's jacket
6 Light-weight khaki drill aviator's flying helmet
7 Paper flight maps
8 Aviator's flight goggles
9 Emergency/survival all-purpose fishing pack carried in life rafts and by flight personnel. Pack contains various types of lines, hooks and lures
10 Aviator's instruction manuals
11 USN medical corpsman supply bag

Andrew L. Chernak: 1, 2;
Dale E. Biever: 3, 4, 9;
Andrew W. Xaras: 5-8;
Pritchard Collection: 11

The insignia on the enlisted man's wool pullover blouse (1), is that of a Petty Officer (Gunnery), Third Class. The insignia on the lower sleeve is that of the submarine service. The blouse also carries three good conduct stripes on the cuffs. This type of blouse with full insignia and medal ribbons would have been worn during shore leave.

The aviator's flight map (7) is of Mindoro Island in the Philippines. Should he run into trouble while he is over there, and have to land his plane in the sea or bale out, the all-purpose fishing kit (9) contains, as well as a wide variety of equipment, a full instruction leaflet. This tells the downed airman how to use the fishing gear, and about the preparation of the fish once caught. It also lists the Pacific Ocean's poisonous fish, eels and sea snakes to avoid.

future strikes. Fliers from *Enterprise* dropped a bomb that penetrated the flight deck of the carrier *Akagi*, exploding on the hangar deck and triggering, in domino fashion, a succession of blasts among the bombs and torpedoes being used to rearm aircraft. Within minutes flames encompassed the *Akagi*, but the burned hulk remained afloat until the next morning when destroyers scuttled it with three torpedoes.

The carrier *Kaga* took four bombs which shattered the island superstructure, caused chain reaction explosions among the munitions on the flight deck, and killed almost everyone on the

bridge. Fire crews fought desperately but unsuccessfully to put out the spreading flames, and soon the entire ship was ablaze. *Kaga* sank later that evening with a loss of 800 crewmen. Two bombs also hit the carrier *Soryu* and within 20 minutes the ship was aflame and had to be abandoned. The fourth carrier, *Hiryu*, had become separated from the others. At 11:00 A.M. it launched two waves of dive bombers and torpedo planes against *Yorktown*. Aircraft in the first wave penetrated the American carrier's fighter screen and antiaircraft barrage to drop bombs on the flight deck. Two torpedoes from the second wave also found their mark. The *Yorktown* was out of action; the crew soon abandoned ship, and before the carrier could be taken in tow, an enemy submarine delivered the *coup de grace*.

Very few of the airmen who crippled *Yorktown* made it back to the *Hiryu*, and within a few hours that carrier paid in kind for the destruction of the *Yorktown*. Fourteen dive bombers from the *Enterprise* and ten more from the *Yorktown* pounced on the *Hiryu* and reduced the proud ship to a burning derelict that had to be scuttled the following day.

By nightfall Adm. Fletcher had transferred from the mortally wounded *Yorktown* to the cruiser *Astoria*, and had, in effect, yielded command to Adm. Spruance. According to Gordon Prange, the author of *Miracle at Midway*, Fletcher's decision was an act of selfless integrity and patriotism since Fletcher understood that the man who provided the United States with its first major sea victory in World War II would become a popular hero. Fletcher stepped aside, and Spruance took his place in the hall of American naval heroes. Fletcher, according to Prange, was "a man of talent who had the brains to give a free hand to a man of genius."

Responsibility for exploiting the sinking of the carriers now rested upon Spruance, who chose to exercise caution. He did not know the strength and location of the surviving Japanese ships, and he realized the enemy battleships outgunned his cruisers and would have an advantage in a night action, when darkness would neutralize American air power. He therefore decided to retire to the east and did not turn westward again until after midnight.

Right: Just after midday on June 4, the *Yorktown* was damaged by the explosions of three bombs on the flight deck, by the funnel, and deep in the ship. The crisis was brought under control, but later two torpedo hits led to the ship's abandonment.

Above: A Japanese map of the military situation in the Pacific — early war. In translation the title reads: "Emergency national defense at a glance. Map of East Asia and the Pacific. Supplement to 'King', Volume 11, No.1". *Russ Pritchard Collection.*

The Japanese, however, still hoped to capture Midway. Yamamoto steamed toward Nagumo and requested four heavy cruisers to join them. At 7:15 P.M., Adm. Nagumo and his two battleships were only 100 miles (160km) from Spruance, and the cruisers 150 miles (240km). But at this stage Yamamoto changed his mind. Knowing that he could not recall the Aleutian diversionary force in time to renew the battle, he called off the Midway operation at about 3:00 A.M. on June 5.

Two of the four cruisers Yamamoto had ordered to join him were less than a hundred miles (160km) from Midway when they spotted the U.S. submarine *Tambor*. Swerving to avoid a submarine attack, the cruiser *Mogami* collided with the *Mikuma*. As a result, the *Mogami* lost the bow section forward of the first turret and was forced to stop for repair. By shoring up damaged bulkheads, the crew managed a speed of 12 knots, but at daylight on 5 June planes from the *Enterprise* and the *Hornet* spotted the two damaged cruisers, sank the *Mikuma*, and so damaged the already limping *Mogami* that it was out of action for a year. Adm. Spruance gave chase for a while, but low on fuel and determined to keep out of range of aircraft on Wake Island, he decided to head eastward for Pearl Harbor on the morning of June 6.

The losses for the Japanese were substantial. Four large carriers and one

Left: Listing and with her watertight integrity not fully restored by the emergency repairs after the Battle of the Coral Sea, the *Yorktown* was abandoned at 3.00 P.M. Some 2,270 of her crew were rescued by destroyers.

cruiser sunk, severe damage to another cruiser, and the loss of 322 aircraft. The United States lost one carrier and one destroyer, both victims of the same submarine, and 147 planes, and sustained substantial damage to shore installations at Midway. Some 2,500 Japanese perished, along with 307 Americans. At least three of the American dead were airmen whom the Japanese had plucked from the sea, interrogated, and then murdered, one of them even though he had provided information on the number of American carriers.

Midway marked the end of a succession of Japanese victories extending from Pearl Harbor to the Java Sea, and westward to Ceylon in the Indian Ocean. The United States in consequence went on the offensive, forcing the Japanese to reinforce their defensive perimeter. Midway also established the carrier as a truly decisive weapon of naval warfare. The public, however, was slow to grasp the importance of the aircraft carrier. Indeed, Marine Corps and Army aircraft stationed at Midway had initially received much of the credit for sinking the four Japanese carriers. The Army heavy bombers had flown over 50 sorties and delivered over 92 tons of bombs, while Navy and Marine Corps aircraft from Midway dropped another 25 tons. Newspaper accounts at first gave them a lion's share of credit for the victory at Midway but, with the exception of a Marine pilot, Richard Fleming, who crashed his damaged aircraft into the cruiser *Mikuma*, the land-based aircraft did no damage to the Japanese fleet. For the moment, however, the carrier-based airmen had to share the spotlight with the fliers who operated from Midway.

More serious than the erroneous descriptions of the battle was another newspaper account that nearly compromised the American code-breaking operation. On June 7, 1942, *The Chicago Tribune* headlined, "Navy Had Word of Japanese Plan to Strike at Sea." The newspaper thus revealed that Nimitz knew in advance of the Japanese order of battle and the plan for the Aleutian diversion. The Navy was furious and considered an indictment against the paper for violating security regulations, but to have done so would have revealed additional classified information. Legal action would have been self-defeating.

On June 3 the Japanese launched the diversionary attack against the Aleutians. They bombed Dutch Harbor and within 20 minutes killed about 25 soldiers and sailors, damaging the tank farm, radio station, barracks, and some seaplanes riding at anchor. The next day bad weather forced cancellation of an attack on Adak, but clear skies over Dutch Harbor permitted another strike there, which destroyed four new fuel storage tanks, demolished a hospital wing, damaged an uncompleted hangar and a barracks ship, and killed another 18 soldiers. Strategically, the Japanese

JAPANESE ARMY PILOT

The Japanese air arm was divided between the Army and Navy; there was no independent air service. As such Japanese Army Air Service personnel wore army uniforms with specific arm-of-service insignia: sky-blue breast chevron and collar patches. This pilot wears the one-piece winter flying suit of fur-lined rubberized fabric. He carries a short, largely symbolic, sword and is armed with an 8mm automatic pistol.

Japanese Naval Uniforms and Equipment

1 Rear admiral's designating flag, from the heavy cruiser *Aoba*, sunk in the Inland Sea in the final weeks of the war
2 Naval officer's fur-lined overcoat
3 Naval enlisted personnel field cap
4 Naval landing forces steel helmet
5 Naval officer's fur-lined cap
6 Naval officer's fur mittens for winter wear
7 Officer's heavy-duty sea boots
8 Navy Model 93 gas mask respirator
9 Naval personnel life jacket with securing straps
10 Naval personnel life jacket, variant form
11 Naval china mess bowl. On the side of the bowl is displayed the Imperial Japanese Navy insignia
12 Naval enlisted man's black silk cap band (tally)
13 Abacus taken from the battleship *Nagato*, in Yokosuka Harbor
14 Naval commissioned officer's two-piece belt plate, post 1914
15 Assorted naval officers/enlisted mens' rank and rating insignia

War Memorial Museum of Virginia

The Imperial Japanese Navy adopted khaki uniforms as the war progressed. The field cap (3), is evidence of this. The Navy's commitment to land warfare, both in the offensive and defensive operations accentuated its adoption as a service color. The collection of Imperial Japanese Navy insignia (15), includes officer's shoulder boards (top), collar badges (left), and officer's cap badges (far right); the remaining badges are cap and arm insignia of ratings. The shoulder board on the right is that of a captain of aviation, (note the blue colored piping). The black silk tally (cap band), was worn by ratings on their round caps. The round cap (and tally) was replaced as service dress by the Army pattern peaked cap (3). The naval service steel helmet (4), was also replaced by the Army pattern version as the war went on.

diversion effort proved useless because code-breaking had already told the Americans that the Japanese were aiming at Midway.

On June 7, about 1,800 Japanese troops occupied two islands at the far western end of the Aleutians, Kiska and Attu. Because of poor weather it took a week for the Americans to discover the presence of the enemy, who had seized the islands to forestall an invasion of Japan — an unlikely possibility. Japan did not plan to advance along the Aleutians and invade Alaska. Merely holding Attu and Kiska proved difficult enough, since the Japanese had to supply them

from the naval base at Paramushiro in the Kuriles, some 650 miles (1,040km) west of Attu.

The United States intended to prevent a Japanese build-up in the Aleutians, to cut sea communications to Japan, and to create a force strong enough to reconquer the islands. Such a force was ready in the spring of 1943; but Alaska remained a secondary theater. Indeed, Gen. Arnold did not want to commit any more aircraft than absolutely necessary. He believed that the poor weather conditions made combat in the theater primarily a job for naval surface craft, supported by long-range bombers when

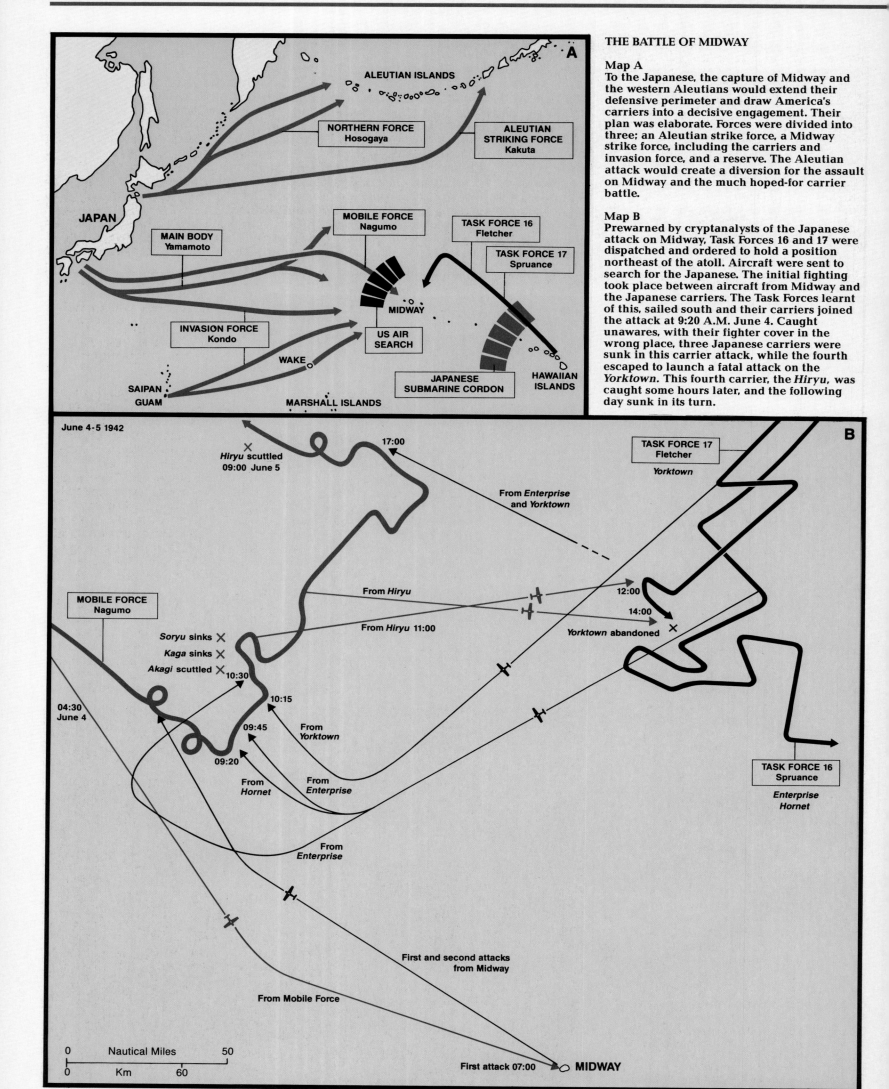

A

ALEUTIAN ISLANDS

| NORTHERN FORCE Hosogaya | | ALEUTIAN STRIKING FORCE Kakuta |

JAPAN

| MAIN BODY Yamamoto |

| MOBILE FORCE Nagumo |

| TASK FORCE 16 Fletcher |

| TASK FORCE 17 Spruance |

MIDWAY

| INVASION FORCE Kondo |

US AIR SEARCH

WAKE

SAIPAN GUAM

| JAPANESE SUBMARINE CORDON |

HAWAIIAN ISLANDS

MARSHALL ISLANDS

THE BATTLE OF MIDWAY

Map A
To the Japanese, the capture of Midway and the western Aleutians would extend their defensive perimeter and draw America's carriers into a decisive engagement. Their plan was elaborate. Forces were divided into three; an Aleutian strike force, a Midway strike force, including the carriers and invasion force, and a reserve. The Aleutian attack would create a diversion for the assault on Midway and the much hoped-for carrier battle.

Map B
Prewarned by cryptanalysts of the Japanese attack on Midway, Task Forces 16 and 17 were dispatched and ordered to hold a position northeast of the atoll. Aircraft were sent to search for the Japanese. The initial fighting took place between aircraft from Midway and the Japanese carriers. The Task Forces learnt of this, sailed south and their carriers joined the attack at 9:20 A.M. June 4. Caught unawares, with their fighter cover in the wrong place, three Japanese carriers were sunk in this carrier attack, while the fourth escaped to launch a fatal attack on the *Yorktown*. This fourth carrier, the *Hiryu*, was caught some hours later, and the following day sunk in its turn.

B

June 4-5 1942

Hiryu scuttled
09:00 June 5

17:00

From *Enterprise* and *Yorktown*

| TASK FORCE 17 Fletcher |

Yorktown

| MOBILE FORCE Nagumo |

From *Hiryu*

12:00

From *Hiryu* 11:00

14:00

Yorktown abandoned

Soryu sinks
Kaga sinks
Akagi scuttled 10:30

10:15

09:45

09:20

From *Yorktown*

04:30 June 4

From *Hornet*

From *Enterprise*

| TASK FORCE 16 Spruance |

Enterprise *Hornet*

From *Enterprise*

First and second attacks from Midway

From Mobile Force

| 0 | Nautical Miles | 50 |
| 0 | Km | 60 |

First attack 07:00   MIDWAY

Above: Marines on the alert in the Aleutians. The Japanese offensive against these islands was pointless, for without significant advantage it diverted the Japanese resources that might have turned Midway into a decisive Japanese victory.

cloud cover permitted. No aircraft needed elsewhere should be sent to Alaska, and for months all the Army Air Forces did was occasionally to bomb the islands, a task carried out by the Eleventh Air Force under Brig. Gen. William O. Butler.

On the Navy side, Rear Adm. Robert A. Theobald, Commander, North Pacific Area, failed in his first attempt to bomb Kiska because bad weather prevented his pilots from finding it. A second mission found the island but merely blasted holes in the tundra. In December 1942 Theobald was replaced by Rear Adm. Thomas C. Kinkaid who had seen combat in the South Pacific. Kinkaid immediately blockaded.

On March 26, 1943, the old light cruiser *Richmond*, the heavy cruiser *Salt Lake City*, and four destroyers commanded by Rear Adm. Charles H. McMorris encountered a Japanese force, commanded by Adm. Hosogaya, that included two heavy cruisers and was escorting merchant ships carrying reinforcements to Attu. For an hour the *Salt Lake City* punched it out at long range with the heavy cruisers *Nachi* and *Maya*. The *Nachi* sustained several hits, and the *Salt Lake City's* hydraulic steering system was damaged by the shock of its own guns. Maneuvering became difficult, causing the *Salt Lake City* to take a hit that left the ship dead in the water. Although the American cruiser kept firing from the after turrets, the *Nachi* and the *Maya* closed in for the kill. In desperation, McMorris ordered his destroyers to attack with torpedoes, but before they could close the range, Hosogaya directed salvoes of eight-inch shells at them. With victory in hand, the Japanese did the unexpected and broke off the action. The enemy commander

Right: Men of the 7th Infantry Division board their landing craft for the southern part of the Attu invasion on May 11, 1943. This involved a landing at Massacre Bay and then a slow slog as the men of the southern and northern assaults tried to link up.

explained his decision by claiming that he was low on ammunition and fuel and expected an air attack at any moment. The Japanese high command did not believe him, however; Adm. Hosogaya was dismissed.

The crew of the *Salt Lake City* restored power, and McMorris became a hero when he returned to Dutch Harbor, the victor by default in what has been called the Battle of Komandorski Islands.

Once the assault force was ready, Adm. Kinkaid proposed attacking Attu, believed to be the less defended of the two islands. The Joint Chiefs of Staff agreed to May 7, 1943 as D-day for the landing — Operation Landgrab. Army bombers pounded Attu for weeks prior to the attacks, and Adm. Nimitz sent an escort carrier and three aging battleships — *Pennsylvania, Idaho,* and *Nevada* — for additional naval support.

Two major landings were planned, one at Holtz Bay on the northern side of the island and the other at Massacre Bay to the south. Initial landings of 100 scouts from two submarines were made early on the morning of May 11. These men

Above: Japanese naval aircrew pose for the camera after the occupation of Attu at the extreme western end of the Aleutians. Airfields were built on the two occupied islands as much for supply aircraft as for offensive air operations.

joined up with about 400 soldiers put ashore from the destroyer transport *Kane* and met no resistance. That evening about 2,000 American troops had established two beachheads extending a mile (1.6km) inland, set up command posts, and encountered only light opposition. The Japanese, commanded by Col. Yasuyo Yamasake, had only 2,630 men to defend Attu. Yamasake realized he could not possibly defend both beaches, so he decided on a delaying action, blockading Massacre Valley which connected the northern and southern beachheads.

Five days of attacks on Jarmin Pass in the Massacre Valley barely dented the Japanese line. Maj. Gen. Albert E. Brown, commanding the southern force blamed the terrain, the weather, and the unanticipated strength of the enemy. He wanted reinforcements and was

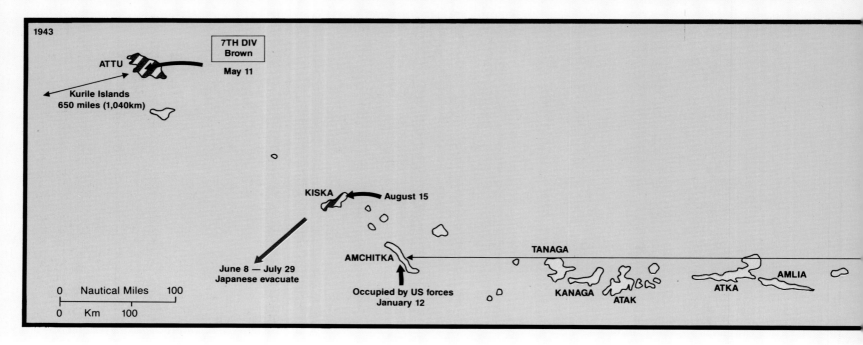

1943

ATTU

Kurile Islands
650 miles (1,040km)

7TH DIV
Brown

May 11

KISKA ← August 15

June 8 — July 29
Japanese evacuate

AMCHITKA

TANAGA

Occupied by US forces
January 12

KANAGA   ATAK   ATKA   AMLIA

0   Nautical Miles   100
0   Km   100

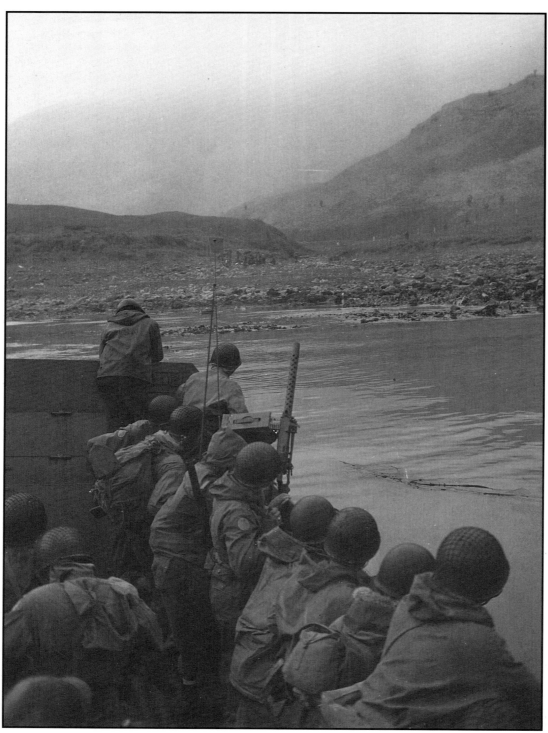

overheard saying that it would take six months to clear the enemy out of Attu. This statement supposedly got back to Adm. Kinkaid who promptly relieved Brown on May 16, replacing him with Maj. Gen. Eugene M. Landrum.

The Northern Force had an easier time clearing the high ground around their beachhead, and forcing the enemy to withdraw. Fearing that the northern group would attack from the rear, the Japanese decided to pull back from their hitherto impregnable position. Two days later on May 18, the northern and southern forces made contact.

The Americans renewed their naval and aerial bombardment, and the Japanese aircraft retaliated on May 22 and 23 but did little damage while losing a few bombers. The invading troops gradually forced the enemy into a confined area, so that by May 28 Gen. Landrum was confident he could wind up the campaign the next day with a full-scale attack. That evening a Navy PBY dropped surrender leaflets on the Japanese position.

Yamasake had other plans, however. He launched a desperate counterattack to overwhelm the American lines, destroy the base at Massacre Bay, and drive the invaders into the sea. At first light on the morning of May 29, the Japanese ran screaming at the American foxholes, breaking through the surprised infantry and heading towards Massacre Bay until fought to a standstill by hastily organized engineers and service troops. Within 48 hours all the Japanese except for isolated groups had been killed or committed suicide. The Japanese suffered appalling losses: 2,351 killed, and only 28 taken prisoner; but their suicide charge took a heavy toll, killing 600 and wounding

Left: American troops approach their assault beach on the Aleutian island of Kiska at the beginning of a massive invasion on August 15, 1943. This considerable effort was wasted as the Japanese had evacuated their garrison almost three weeks earlier.

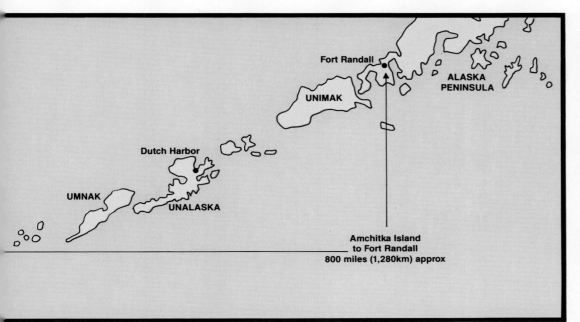

THE ALEUTIANS CAMPAIGN

Because of the failure of the attack on Midway, the Japanese capture of Kiska and Attu in June 1942 never held strategic importance. From the beginning, the Japanese garrisons suffered irregular supply and bombardment from American forces. Because of the shortage of resources on the Allied side, a plan to retake Attu was not put into effect until May 1943. Landings were made at two positions and a bitter series of fights developed, with Japanese defenders caught between the two lines of advance. The defense ended with a mass *banzai* charge and the deaths of 600 Americans and all but 28 of the Japanese.

The attack on the larger Japanese garrison on Kiska became the next objective. More men and greater resources were set aside for the assault, planned for August, 1943. A prolonged naval and air bombardment softened up the target. When the assault force of Americans and Canadians hit the beaches, however, the entire island was devoid of the enemy. The Japanese, their position untenable, had already evacuated.

twice that number in penetrating as far as the base camp, where the attackers bayoneted patients in a field hospital and a chaplain on duty there.

Operation Cottage, the invasion of Kiska, seemed a more difficult undertaking than Attu because the Japanese garrison was larger, numbering between 7,000 and 8,000 troops. The target date was set for August 15, 1943, and the assault force included 34,000 ground troops. Again, aerial and naval bombardment softened up enemy defenses, as the Eleventh Air Force, with more than 350 aircraft, concentrated on artillery positions and the Kiska airstrip. On occasion, Navy Venturas equipped with radar guided the Eleventh Air Force bombers through bad weather to the targets. The real surprise came on D-Day when the invaders discovered that the Japanese had

disappeared from Kiska. Under the cover of bad weather more than 7,000 troops had evacuated by surface ship in just two hours on July 28. The withdrawal proved somewhat of an embarrassment to the Americans who had bombed Kiska consistently for two weeks after the Japanese had departed. Thus did the United States regain the Aleutians and the Japanese abandon their last foothold on American soil.

During the remaining months of the war, American planners seldom gave serious consideration to launching an invasion from the Aleutians against the

Below: After a two-day sweep, the Americans had discovered four abandoned dogs as the only living evidence of the Japanese occupation of Kiska. This is a Shinto shrine in the main camp of the island's departed Japanese garrison.

Japanese base at Paramushiro and other points in the Kurile Islands. On September 18, 1943, the Joint Chiefs of Staff rejected such an operation on the grounds that forces could not be spared from the projected invasions of the Gilberts in the Central Pacific and Bougainville in the northern Solomons. The Chiefs also reasoned that an invasion of the Kuriles had no value except as a springboard for a further attack on Hokkaido, which simply was not on the cards. The American stategists therefore concluded that Paramushiro was not a worthwhile objective.

Later, an assault from the Aleutians seemed useful as a means of encouraging the Soviet Union to enter the war against Japan, but the Joint Chiefs recommended against mounting such an attack unless the possibility of intervention became a reality. Throughout the war, aircraft from the Aleutians raided Paramushiro, but the western Aleutians never had more than a nuisance value, forcing the Japanese to maintain a sizeable force in the Kuriles in case of an invasion. Besides manpower, the Japanese also had to keep in the area more than 400 army and navy aircraft, which could have been better used in another theater. When the war ended, there had been no invasion of the Kuriles by forces gathered in the Aleutians, but the threat had persisted for nearly two years.

The Japanese never recovered from the defeat at Midway. They lacked the raw materials and the industrial base to replace the four carriers sunk or scuttled there. Nor did they have the fuel and training facilities to replace quickly the experienced pilots who died there. Whereas Midway proved decisive, the Aleutians campaign did not. Despite the prewar predictions of Billy Mitchell, who saw the islands as a dagger aimed at Japan, Alaska proved a dead-end strategically, largely because of the consistently foul weather and the long and tenuous supply line.

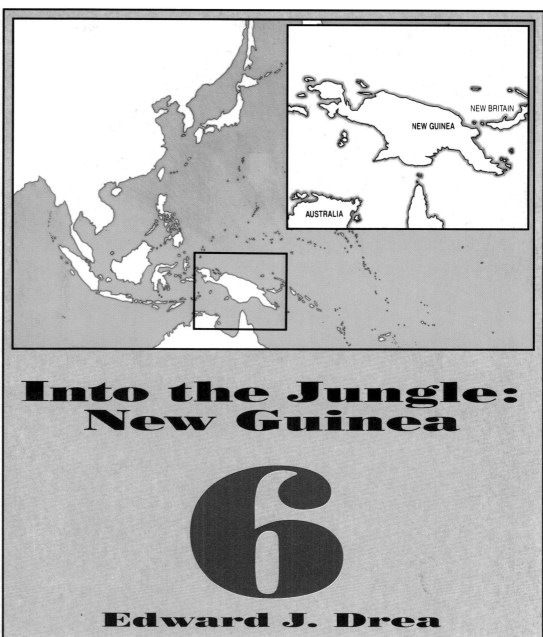

Into the Jungle: New Guinea

6

Edward J. Drea

New Guinea's lush tropical jungle imposed cruel demands on the soldiers who fought there during World War II. New Guinea is the second largest island in the world, and its north coastline extends nearly 1,500 miles (2,400km) stretching from 12 degrees South latitude to just south of the Equator. A major mountain range cuts across the island's center from its eastern tip to Geelvink Bay on the west. The high mountain peaks and deep gorges, covered with thick jungle vegetation, make passage overland through the mountains by large units nearly impossible. The lee of the mountainous spine, around the Port Moresby area, is wet from January to April but otherwise dry. On the windward side, scene of most of the ground fighting during 1942-5, rainfall runs as high as 150, 200, or even 300 inches (3, 5 or 7m) per year. As one veteran recalled, "It rains daily for nine months and then the monsoon starts."

Beyond scattered, tiny coastal settlements along the flat malarial north or south coastlines, the deadly landscape remained untouched when war came to New Guinea. The north shore was a tangled morass of large mangrove swamps and vast patches of razor-sharp kunai grass growing to heights of seven feet (2m). Inland, the towering rain forest, nourished by frequent deluges, was so thick that it blocked out the light of the sun. Numerous streams and rivers cut the area into swampy and muddy bogs. Roads or railways did not exist. A commander at most had a so-called "unimproved native track," usually a dirt trail a yard or so wide tramped out over the centuries through the gloomy jungle growth. Downpours quickly dissolved such tracks into calf-deep mud that left a soldier exhausted by fatigue after wallowing a few hundred yards through the glue-like soil. Monsoon rains of eight or ten inches (20 or 25cm) a day turned torpid streams into raging rivers. Steaming humidity reinforced the equatorial heat — temperatures in the mid-90s. On New Guinea man was at the mercy of the elements.

Disease thrived in this pesthole, malaria being the most deadly and debilitating to the opposing armies, but dengue fever, dysentery, and a host of other sicknesses awaited soldiers in the

Allied Sub-Machine Guns

1 British Sten Mk II 9mm sub-machine gun. The name STEN is derived from the first letters of the names of the men who developed it, R.V. Sheppard (S), and H.J. Turpin (T), and the company who fabricated it: Enfield (EN)
2 French MAS Model 38 sub-machine gun. Fabricated at the St. Etienne Arsenal, this weapon was the standard French sub-machine gun from 1938-49
3 Australian Owen Mk 1 9mm sub-machinegun. Over 40,000 of these awkward-looking weapons were fabricated during the war and proved successful in jungle warfare
4 US M1 Thompson sub-machine gun, .45 caliber. This simplification of an early design, although slow and heavy, proved an excellent weapon
5 US M3 sub-machine gun, .45 caliber; first introduced in December 1942
6 US Reisling Model 55 sub-machine gun
7 US Reisling Model 50 sub-machine gun
8 US Model 1928 A1 Thompson sub-machine gun

West Point Museum

The US M3 sub-machine gun, known as the 'Grease Gun', was introduced to replace the more costly Thompson and utilized the same .45 ammunition. The Reisling Model 55, of .45 caliber, was manufactured by Harrington and Richardson, primarily for Marine airborne units; unfortunately it was unreliable. The Reisling Model 50, of .45 caliber, was no more successful than the Model 55, and was often discarded by the troops. The Model 1928 A1 Thompson is shown with both a 30-round box magazine and a 50-round drum magazine.

jungle. Disease-carrying insects were everywhere, and men ate their rations with one hand, using the other to flick away clouds of black flies that swarmed to the food. Malaria-bearing mosquitoes made nights miserable, and chiggers, leeches, and other parasites drained men's physical health just as the rigors of surviving in the jungle climate sapped their spirits. This was life in the New Guinea jungles during World War II.

In December 1941, the eastern half of New Guinea including the Papuan Peninsula, along with the Bismarck Archipelago — that is New Britain, New Ireland, and the Admiralty Islands —

were Australian protectorates; the western half was Netherlands New Guinea, a part of the Dutch colonial empire. Bordering the vast Geelvink Bay on the north were three smaller islands: Japen, Biak, and Noemfoor. From the western side of the Bay the Vogelkop Peninsula reached out for the Halmahera Islands and the Philippines.

Following Japan's attack on Pearl Harbor, the Rising Sun cast its rays over a tremendous empire, rich in raw materials and manpower. In late January 1942, Japanese troops, covered by naval gunfire, stormed ashore near the major anchorage at Rabaul, New Britain. The

Australian Chiefs of Staff had earlier determined that forward bases like Rabaul were indefensible, so they concentrated their limited forces to protect mainland Australia. Maj. Gen. Tomitaro Horii's 5,000-man South Seas Detachment quickly overwhelmed the 1,400 poorly equipped and isolated Australian defenders, killing about 300 and taking more than 800 into a cruel captivity.

While the Imperial Army wanted to consolidate its gains, the Imperial Navy hoped to push southward to sever Allied lines of communication with Australia. Japan's admirals aimed to seize Port Moresby as well as forward air bases

Above: The climate and other conditions on New Guinea were ideal for a host of diseases and infections. In these circumstances, the rapid and effective treatment of the wounded and sick was of paramount importance to the Allies in this theater.

in the Solomon Islands. The former would isolate Australia from the north and the latter cut its lifeline to the United States. These formed the two prongs of the so-called FS operation.

Step one was to capture airstrips and port facilities at Lae and nearby Salamaua on Papua's north coast. Three thousand Japanese troops landed unopposed at Lae on March 8, because weak Australian ground forces had already withdrawn inland to Wau in the Bulolo Valley. But the consolidation of the landing areas still cost the Japanese dearly when more than 100 carrier aircraft from the USS *Lexington* and *Yorktown* swooped down on the landing beaches of the unsuspecting Japanese. For the loss of one plane and its two-man crew, the carrier pilots' torpedoes and bombs sank or damaged 11 transports or warships and left nearly 400 Japanese troops dead or wounded.

Otherwise in early 1942 the Allies posed little threat to Japan's latest territorial acquisitions because the Australians and Americans were still gathering their resources for the fight. The Australian government had recalled its 6th and 7th divisions from the Middle East, while in February the American Joint Chiefs of Staff dispatched the US 41st and 32d Infantry Divisions plus additional support troops to Australia.

In March, the Joint Chiefs of Staff reorganized the Pacific into two main zones: Pacific Ocean Areas, including North, Central, and South Pacific areas; and Southwest Pacific Area, including Australia, the Philippines, and a portion of the Netherlands East Indies. The same month Gen. Douglas MacArthur fled in defeat from the Philippines to Australia where he would transform the continent into a staging area to support his famous declaration: "I shall return."

For MacArthur the liberation of the Philippines was an unwavering beacon that guided his strategic course. New Guinea's pivotal location was the lure

that attracted hundreds of thousands of American, Australian, and Japanese troops to its otherwise uninviting shores. In Allied hands, it blocked a Japanese invasion of Australia and was a springboard to liberate the Philippines. In Japanese hands, it threatened Australia and protected the southern approaches to the Philippines.

The day that Southwest Pacific headquarters opened, April 18, 1942, plans were already in motion for a counteroffensive against the Japanese on New Guinea. The critical point was Port Moresby, which had to be held in order to protect the vital north coast of Australia and support offensive operations on New Guinea. From decrypted Japanese naval signals, however, the Allies had already uncovered an imminent enemy amphibious operation directed against Port Moresby. Forewarned of enemy intentions, a naval task force organized around the carriers

Lexington and *Yorktown* intercepted the Japanese invasion fleet. The resulting Battle of the Coral Sea was a revolution in naval warfare, a tactical draw, and an Allied strategic victory. For the first time in history a naval battle had been fought entirely between carrier aircraft by opposing fleets that never came within 100 miles (160km) of each other. At the tactical level, Japanese carrier pilots sank *Lexington* and damaged *Yorktown*, but American airmen sank the carrier *Shoho* and severely damaged *Shokaku*. Realizing that without air cover an invasion was impossible, the Japanese recalled their armada to Rabaul.

The Japanese then shifted their axis of advance to Guadalcanal in the southern Solomons where they expected to complete an airfield by August to support the FS operation. Japan's crushing naval defeat at Midway ended the FS scheme, but Imperial Navy officers deliberately concealed the extent of the Midway losses from their army counterparts, so the General Staff launched an overland attack against Port Moresby. The Japanese landing at Buna on July 22 caught MacArthur off-guard.

Neither MacArthur nor Gen. Sir Thomas Blamey, the Australian commander of Allied Land Forces, paid much attention to the Japanese threat against the north coast. Blamey believed that the difficult terrain sheltered Port Moresby from a Japanese advance in strength overland. MacArthur was absorbed with his own optimistic Tulsa Plan to capture Rabaul in just 18 days.

In Washington US Army Chief of Staff, Gen. George C. Marshall, and Chief of Naval Operations, Adm. Ernest J. King, worked out a compromise scheme that the Joint Chiefs of Staff approved on July 2. The resulting directive divided the counteroffensive into three parts. The US Navy, led by Adm. Chester W. Nimitz, would retake the southern Solomons. Next, MacArthur would capture Lae,

Below: First indications were that the *Lexington* would survive her damage in the Battle of the Coral Sea. Later, however, she was racked by internal explosions and abandoned. The destroyer *Phelps* finally torpedoed the crippled wreck.

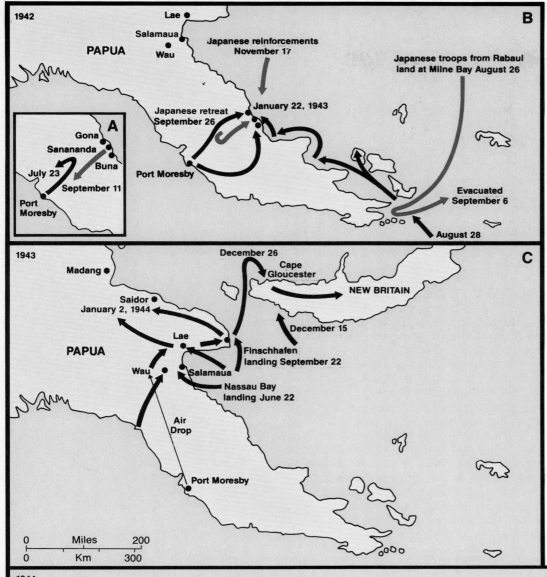

THE NEW GUINEA CAMPAIGN

Maps A (inset) and B
The struggle for New Guinea arose from the strategic imperatives of both sides. For the Japanese, bases in New Guinea could effectively cut Australia off from its lines of communications with the United States, while for the Allies, it held the key to a southern approach to the Philippines, and was essential to the defense of their southwest Pacific build-up.

The Japanese began with an attack on Port Moresby. Landing on the northern coast at Buna, the Japanese advanced inland to the Owen Stanley Range (Map A — inset), forcing the Australian defenders back. At the same time the Japanese made an amphibious assault on Milne Bay to the southeast. Both attacks were thrown back, however, and now Allied troops attacked the retreating Japanese at the villages of Gona, Sanananda and Buna. After much heavy fighting these positions were taken.

Map C
The Japanese next moved against the Australian airstrip at Wae, but were severely beaten and driven back to Lae. An attempt to reinforce them by sea was destroyed at the Battle of the Bismarck Sea. The Allies now landed troops of their own at Nassau Bay and began a pincer movement towards Lae with troops from Wau. Lau held out until finally outflanked, the Japanese then withdrew to Finschhafen. The Allies followed with an amphibious landing there. The next objective was New Britain, but conditions prevented a drive on Rabaul.

Map D
The campaign now developed into a series of amphibious assaults by the Allies, outflanking Japanese positions on the coast and driving their defenders into the unforgiving interior. The landings were supported by aircraft flying from country captured in the previous landings.

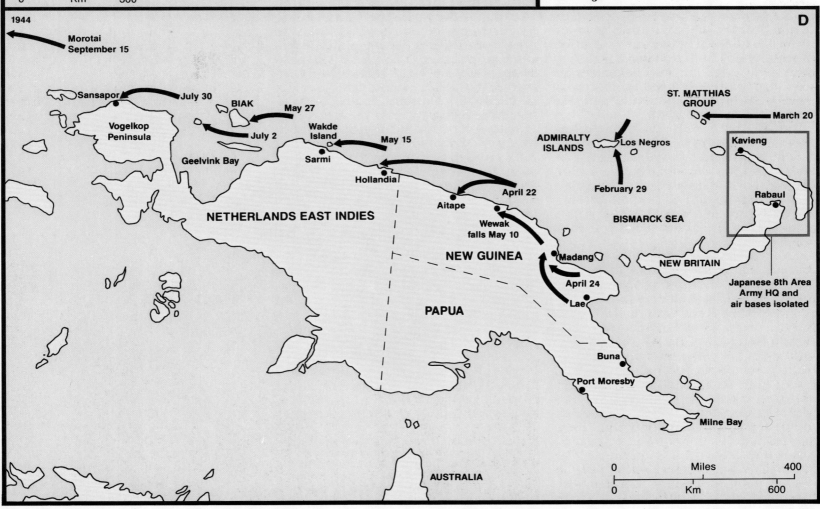

Salamaua, and the northeast coast of New Guinea while the Navy seized the rest of the Solomons. Both wings of the advance would then converge on Rabaul. MacArthur expected to deploy troops to Buna where they would construct a forward airbase to support his offensive against Lae. Simultaneously Southwest Pacific forces were building an airfield at Milne Bay to prevent the Japanese from turning the strategic flank of southwest New Guinea by another seaborne invasion of Port Moresby.

South Seas Detachment veterans again found themselves loading aboard troop transports, this time bound for Buna, site of an Australian mission, a small port and corduroy road running inland, and a government station. With Buna as a resupply point and forward air base, Horii's men were expected to follow the road into the interior, cross the Owen Stanley Range, and take Moresby from the rear. On maps pinned to the walls of Imperial Headquarters in Tokyo it looked deceptively simple, especially since terrain details and contour lines ended just inland of the coastline.

MacArthur reacted slowly to the latest Japanese invasion believing that what the enemy intended was to build a forward air base at Buna. As Horii's veterans spread underneath the jungle canopy and drove the Australian militia units steadily backward toward Moresby, MacArthur became convinced that the Australians were poor fighters who gave ground to inferior numbers of Japanese. Certain that American soldiers would do better, he never wavered in his mistaken first impression of the Australians which proved a source of considerable friction between himself and Blamey.

Horii's troops cut and hacked their way through the rain forest, overcame small units of Australian militia to capture Kokoda, and then climbed the Owen Stanley mountains, A seemingly remorseless advance on Port Moresby impended. In truth, the Japanese troops were reaching the end of their tether, broken as much by the unforgiving climate and terrain as by the fighting.

It was now late August. The Allied situation in the South Pacific turned desperate. US Marines had landed on Guadalcanal on August 7, but the ferocious Japanese reaction forced the US Navy to withdraw its support to the marines just as the Japanese were rushing army reinforcements to the island. A savage battle of grinding attrition ensued on Guadalcanal. Simultaneously the Japanese pushed stubbornly ahead with their two-pronged New Guinea offensive. Horii's troops launched a last, desperate push on Port Moresby on August 24-25. That same night about 2,500 men of the Kure Special Naval Landing Force invaded Milne Bay.

Landing on the eastern side of 20-mile (32-km) long Milne Bay, the Japanese naval infantry stumbled along a narrow muddy track enclosed by the sea on one flank and mangrove swamps on the other. The downpours reduced visibility to a few feet as the landing force groped through the thick, tangled overgrowth. Japanese night attacks employed light tanks, machine guns, grenade launchers, and bayonets. Red and green tracers flashed while Japanese tanks, headlights blazing, drove into and through the Australian positions. Restricted to the mud track, the Japanese sent in attack after attack on a narrow front but made little headway. After several days of tough, close-in fighting, the Japanese navy evacuated the survivors.

This fighting marked the introduction of new Allied Air Forces commander Maj. Gen. George C. Kenney to jungle warfare. Although his airmen had accomplished little against the Japanese landing force at Milne Bay — they mistakenly bombed Australian troops — Kenney learned quickly. His adaptability and innovativeness were the ideal attributes for aerial warfare in a theater where the few airstrips were primitive, maintenance problems severe, and pilots and planes stretched to the limit.

With Milne Bay secure, more good news arrived from the Owen Stanleys where Australian counterattacks on September 26 sent Horii's men into full retreat. Horii himself drowned when his log raft overturned in a swift river current. MacArthur now struck at Buna to cut off the remainder of Horii's beaten force. The I Corps commander, Maj. Gen. Robert Eichelberger, tapped the 32d Infantry Division for the Buna campaign. Everyone from MacArthur to the greenest riflemen expected little more than mopping up dispirited Japanese stragglers. Certainly this attitude infected the division commander, Maj. Gen. Edwin F. Harding, and his staff expected a walkover.

Instead officers and men of the 128th Infantry, 32d Infantry Division, walked into a jungle nightmare. Strengthened with fresh Japanese reinforcements, Buna, and the nearby villages of Sanananda and Gona, rested on the sea immune to encirclement. The villages were sited on high ground so the GIs had to advance through swampy malaria-infested marshes to attack. Japanese machine gunners in well-camouflaged bunkers of coconut logs, with good lateral communications along the beach, covered the only avenues of approach to the villages. Japanese infantrymen might lurk in their foxholes until the Americans passed, and then rise up to fire at them from the rear. Skilfully concealed Japanese machine gun teams and riflemen peppered the Americans' ragged assault line. The attackers halted,

Right: Australian troops use a makeshift bridge to cross the fast-flowing Girua river near Buna. Here the Allies scored their first land victory over the previously invincible Japanese army, learning many invaluable tactical lessons in the process.

MacArthur summoned Eichelberger and dramatically ordered him "to take Buna or not come back alive." Eichelberger flew to Buna and soon relieved Harding. With additional artillery and tanks, unavailable to the luckless Harding, the division, led by a corps commander who could be found leading patrols, finally took Buna on January 2, 1943. Sanananda held out for another 20 days. Perhaps 13,000 Japanese troops perished in the stinking muck and rotting jungle vegetation, but Allied casualties were severe; 8,500 men fell in battle (5,698 of them Australians) and 27,000 cases of malaria, mainly because of shortages of medical supplies, were reported. Three months of unimaginative attrition warfare gave MacArthur his airstrip at Buna, but had ruined two infantry divisions and exhausted two others. The Americans needed six months to reconstitute for their next operation. The Japanese did not allow the battered Australians such a luxury.

In response to the Allied drives on New Guinea and in the Solomons, Tokyo dispatched reinforcements and created new headquarters. On November 9, 1942, Eighth Area Army, commanded by Lt. Gen. Hitoshi Imamura, opened on Rabaul. Eighteenth Army, commanded by Lt. Gen. Hatazo Adachi, was organized the same day and subordinated to Imamura. Adachi took charge of operations on New Guinea.

Imamura saw eastern New Guinea as a citadel guarding the build-up of Japanese air and supply bases on the western half of the great island. Lae was the stronghold from which Japanese troops could sortie under air cover to capture a forward air base at Wau, located about 150 miles west-northwest of Buna. Isolated and weakly protected, the Australian airstrip at Wau in the malarious Bulolo Valley seemed ripe for Eighteenth Army's picking.

In January 1943, Imamura chose the fresh 102d Infantry, 51st Division, for the Wau operation. Here the jungle forced his hand. Lae was within range of Allied aircraft, but if Imamura landed the 102d at a safer port farther west, it faced the daunting prospect of moving overland through a rugged, uncharted jungle landscape and delaying its attack on Wau. Imamura cast the dice for Lae and lost.

Kenney's air forces repeatedly struck the hapless Japanese convoy, sinking two troop transports, damaging another, and killing 600 Japanese soldiers. Under air attack in Lae Harbor, only one-third of the Japanese got ashore and these survivors salvaged only half of their equipment. With the blind determination to follow orders, they struck for Wau and almost made it. On January 30, 1943, the last-ditch Japanese charge carried them to the edge of the Wau airstrip. The Australian defenders, augmented by reinforcements who literally ran out of the of transport aircraft firing into the Japanese, stopped them dead.

Above: Tactical air transport was very important to the Allies in New Guinea. These are Douglas C-47 transports of the 6th Troop Carrier Squadron on Wau airfield during April 1943. Allied possession of Wau was vital to the capture of Lae and Salamaua.

confused and bewildered by a form of combat they neither trained for nor expected. Besieged by insects, pelted by tropical downpours, staring at jungle thicket that seemed impassable, and in terror of the new and unknown, the 128th Infantry stopped. Reports of cowardice, malingering, and inaction filtered back to MacArthur's headquarters.

Such charges were all the harder for MacArthur to bear because troops of the Australian 7th Division at Buna pressed home their assaults regardless of physical hardships. The jungle and swamp terrain fragmented units, rendered battalion maneuver impossible, and shifted the burden of the fight to rifle and weapons squads. Small parties of Australian infantrymen crawled through the slime searching for well-concealed enemy strongpoints. Riflemen destroyed each bunker complex in turn, all the while living in vile conditions. In such close-in fighting, the Japanese exacted a terrible toll on the Australians, who hammered away at each enemy pocket and seized Gona, ten miles (16km) west of Buna, on December 9. Heavy battle casualties and malaria, however, wrecked the 7th Division as an effective fighting force.

In contrast, the American 32d Infantry Division, ravaged by disease and severe casualties, was mired in the swampy morass that formed an arc around the land approaches to Buna and Sanananda. Dissatisfied with the division's lackluster effort, on November 29

AUSTRALIAN INFANTRY, NEW GUINEA, 1943

As the war went on in the jungles of New Guinea, uniforms and equipment developed to take into account the appalling conditions. The felt bush hats that these two men wear, for example, were replaced in 1944-45 by a simpler beret. The figure on the left carries a Bren light machine gun, while the man to the right is armed with the Short Magazine Lee Enfield Mk III, with its characteristic sword bayonet.

The battered remnants fell back into the jungle slowly giving ground toward Lae.

Defeated at Wau and pressed by the Australians, Japanese forces on New Guinea desperately needed reinforcements. On February 19, 1943 US Navy cryptanalysts handed MacArthur solid intelligence that the enemy was planning a major landing at Lae in early March. With this alert, Kenney and his newly arrived deputy, Brig. Gen. Ennis C. Whitehead, systematically plotted the destruction of Convoy 81, the Japanese designation for the Lae shipment. Greatly reinforced with B-25 medium bombers, Kenney ordered his airmen to rehearse new, low-level, bombing tactics and husbanded his force for a total effort against the convoy. Every aircraft was thrown into a three-day struggle, from March 2-5, known as the Battle of the Bismarck Sea. High altitude attacks by B-17s and B-24s on March 2 sank one and damaged two of the slow moving transports. As the survivors neared Lae they came within range of Kenney's B-25 medium bombers which roared in on the transports and their escorting destroyers at mast-top level. Japanese airmen flying at 7,000 feet (2,100m) above the convoy to intercept the enemy planes were caught completely off-guard by the low-level attackers.

The Japanese lost eight transports and four destroyers. Of the 6,912 51st Division troops, about 3,900 survived, but only 1,000 soaked, oil-stained, and dispirited officers and men reached Lae. Allied fighters strafed helpless Japanese in the water who were clinging to debris or in lifeboats. The sea turned into a bloody pink froth and pilots vomited at the horrible sight of hundreds of shattered corpses bobbing like broken dolls in the red swells. Kenney smashed the 51st Division and condemned the Japanese to the strategic defensive on New Guinea.

Below: The New Guinea campaign became a Japanese Army priority after initial naval failures, and considerable resources were pushed forward. But soon Allied air power became a decisive with raids on airfields such as this at Wewak in July 1943.

The destruction of the 51st Division critically weakened the southeastern approach to Rabaul and demanded a hurried revision of Japanese joint policy. The Army-Navy Central Agreement on Southeast Area Operations of March 25 shifted priority from the Solomons to protect the endangered New Guinea flank. It was in these circumstances that the diminutive Commander-in-Chief, Combined Fleet Adm. Isoroku Yamamoto, launched the *I* Operation.

This massed aerial onslaught against Allied air and shipping in the Solomons offered Japan the best opportunity to retard the swelling enemy counteroffensive. Yamamoto hurled 350 naval aircraft into a four-stage aerial blitz against Guadalcanal and New Guinea targets. Inexperienced Japanese aircrews reported sinking 28 transports or warships and destroying 150 Allied aircraft, with only 49 Japanese aircraft lost. (Actual Allied losses amounted to four small ships and 12 aircraft.) A jubilant Yamamoto scheduled a morale-raising visit to his front-line pilots. His itinerary to Ballale in the Shortland Islands was learned from a deciphered message three days in advance of the trip. Decisions at the highest level of the Navy Department culminated in American P-38 pilots intercepting and shooting down the bomber carrying the admiral who planned the attack on Pearl Harbor. Perhaps fittingly his death came at the conclusion of the last great Japanese aerial offensive in Southwest Pacific Area.

MacArthur's counteroffensive was gaining momentum, and his headquarters had a new timetable for the return to the Philippines. Codenamed Reno, it became the basis for operations against Japan from February 1943 through August 1944. During that time, Reno underwent five modifications to keep pace with changing operational and strategic requirements. Reno I envisaged leapfrogging past Japanese strongholds in New Guinea and the use of paratroops to seize key bases en route to Mindanao in the southern Philippines. The Japanese roadblock to MacArthur's

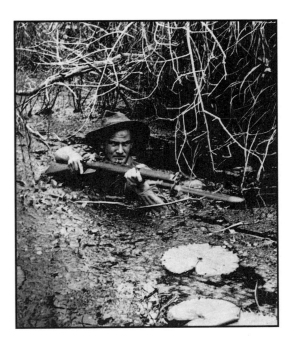

Above: An Australian infantryman wades through a less-than-salubrious swamp, typical of conditions in New Guinea. Here the combination of tropical insects and disease was often a considerably greater threat than the Japanese enemy.

scheme was the so-called Bismarck Barrier consisting of New Britain, with its naval and air bases at Rabaul, and the series of Japanese air enclaves dotting the northern New Guinea coastline.

The Joint Chiefs directive of March 28, 1943 described Southwest Pacific objectives as a line running across the Vitiaz and Dampier straits from Finschhafen, New Guinea, to western New Britain. Meantime, the US Navy and Marine Corps would clear the Solomons to southern Bougainville. From these decisions grew the Cartwheel Operation which kicked off on the night of 29-30 June when Adm. William F. Halsey, commander, South Pacific Area, invaded New Georgia, Solomon Islands, while MacArthur struck at Nassau Bay.

For Cartwheel MacArthur created Alamo Force, an independent operational command, but in reality almost identical to Southwest Pacific's newly created US Sixth Army. MacArthur personally selected Lt. Gen. Walter Krueger to command Sixth Army. Krueger was a deliberate and methodical leader, accused by some of being too conservative, but talented enough to implement his chief's wishes and patient enough to endure MacArthur's slights. Another American, Vice Adm. Arthur S. Carpender, commanded Allied Naval Forces which included the US Seventh Fleet. His aggressive assistant was Rear Adm. Daniel E. Barbey who commanded VII Amphibious Force, the ships that would carry the ground forces, their equipment, and supplies forward into battle against the Japanese during Cartwheel.

The Nassau Bay landing was a minor affair that involved an American infantry battalion assaulting a much understrength Japanese battalion. After confused nighttime skirmishes in a

Japanese Equipment and Personal Items

1 Japanese officer's leather document case
2 Japanese officer's leather map case, worn on a shoulder strap
3 Japanese officer's canteen. The canteen has its cover and attached strap, but the cup is missing
4 Clear plastic map holder carried in officer's map case 2
5 Writing tablet and pencils, also carried in map case 2
6 Personal, patriotic good-luck flag inscribed to the soldier by friends, family or associates, with prayers

for good fortune, honor and the emperor
7 Hand fan bearing the Japanese national emblem: a personal item
8 Canvas haversack carried slung over the shoulder, used for rations or personal items
9 Rubber-soled, canvas-upper shoes with separate big toe; known as *Tabi*
10 One of three ammunition boxes carried by the Japanese soldier
11 Japanese entrenching tool
12-16 Rifle cleaning components and carrying bag

US Marine Corps Air-Ground Museum

The ammunition box (*10*), was one of three carried by the Japanese soldier on his waist belt. A box of the type shown was worn on the small of the back, and contained 60 rounds of rifle ammunition, together with rifle cleaning equipment. Two smaller pouches, carrying ammunition, were worn on the front of the belt. These pouches were made of leather at the beginning of the war, but as the conflict progressed, they were more frequently manufactured from rubberized canvas or layers of stitched cotton.

tropical downpour, the Japanese fled into the thick jungle. About 40 miles (64km) from Lae, Nassau Bay could serve as a staging base and put pressure on Japanese defenders at Salamaua, a village about 20 miles (32km) to the north that guarded the overland approach to Lae. Adachi had to siphon troops from Lae to protect Salamaua thereby leaving the understrength Lae garrison vulnerable to a flanking attack by sea and air.

An Allied pincer closed on Lae, as the American 162d Infantry, 41st Infantry Division, pushed slowly north along the coast from Nassau Bay, and Australian troops advanced on a western axis from Wau. The mainstay of the Japanese defense was a lone infantry regiment. In such rugged terrain, however, a few determined men could slow down ten times their number. Numerous streams cutting the coastline also impeded the American push. With but a few jungle trails capable of bearing basic logistic support, the direction of the Australian overland thrust was predictable, and Lt. Gen. Hidemitsu Nakano's infantrymen dug in along key terrain dominating the likely approaches. A grueling 75-day ordeal followed in the jungle wilds under appalling conditions. Patrol-size probes lurching through overgrown and tangled vegetation became the maneuver elements. Ambush and sudden death awaited the careless or unlucky because it was often impossible to see more than a few feet into the undergrowth. In the Southwest Pacific, small arms claimed 32 percent of Americans killed in action during the war, and artillery 17 percent — a marked distinction contrasted to the overall rates of 19.7 and 57.5 percent respectively. In part the aberration stems from the relative paucity of Japanese artillery compared to their Axis allies; in part it reflects the close-in combat characteristic of jungle fighting.

Australian Uniforms and Equipment

1 Officer's peaked cap, wool with leather visor and Australian insignia. Dated 1943
2 Officer's service dress jacket with rank insignia of captain
3 Brown leather ankle combat boots complete with brass cleats on the sole. Dated 1944
4 Enfield pistol No.2, .38 caliber, together with pattern 1937 web, flap holster
5 Webley pistol No.1, Mk VI, .455 caliber with box of ammunition
6 Tropical field trousers of olive drab denim c. 1944
7 Tropical field shirt, dated c. 1944
8 Mk 1 steel helmet with camouflage net
9 Pattern 1937 web gear including waist belt, combat harness, bayonet frog, and two universal pouches each capable of holding 50 rounds of .303 ammunition or two grenades
10 Pattern 1937 sword bayonet
11 Pattern 1908 canteen
12 Webbing gaiters
13 Rifle No.1 Mk 3, short magazine Lee Enfield (SMLE), .303 caliber. This particular arm was manufactured in Australia at Lithgow, New South Wales

MacArthur Memorial: 1-3, 6-13; Eugene C. Gibson Collection: 4, 5

The Australians served in Malaya at the beginning of the war, but their main contribution was to be in the southwest Pacific. They fought through New Guinea and into Bougainville and New Britain, and ended the war in an invasion of Borneo by two divisions of their I Corps.

The medal ribbons on the captain's service dress jacket (2) include those of the 1939-45 Star, Pacific Star and Defense Medal. The leather ankle boots, known as 'ammunition' boots were replaced towards the end of the war by a specially-designed jungle boot. Like so much kit from the early years of the conflict, it was found to be inadequate against the terrible jungle conditions. The Pattern 1907 sword bayonet (10) is shown with its metal mounted leather scabbard. This weapon was also known as Bayonet No.1 Mk II.

American losses between the end of June until September 12, when Sala-maua fell, were 81 killed and 396 wounded while the Australian 15th Brigade suffered 112 killed, 346 wounded, and 12 missing. Japanese losses were well over 1,000 men. Battle casualties tell only part of the struggle fought out against nature in the jungle wilds. Men on both sides of the fighting collapsed, exhausted from the debilitating tropical heat and humidity; soldiers shook violently from malaria chills or from being drenched in tropical downpours. Others simply went mad. The neuropsychiatric rate for American soldiers was the

highest in the Southwest Pacific theater (43.94 per 1,000 men). The Japanese foot soldier survived on millet and hard-tack. Malnutrition, amoebic dysentery, beri-beri, and malaria plagued him. Rice was an undreamed-of pleasure. The same monotonous field ration — bully beef and biscuits for the Australians, C-Rations for the Americans — left soldiers undernourished and susceptible to the uncountable tropical diseases that flourished in the warm, moist jungle.

For his part, Gen. Adachi expected the newly organized Fourth Air Army to protect Lae's flanks against possible allied airborne or seaborne assaults.

Faced with Japanese air power on two fronts — Rabaul and now Wewak — Kenney concentrated all his might against the latter. Wewak, however, lay beyond the effective range of Allied fighters and ordering unescorted heavy bombers to make the raid risked unacceptable losses. Kenney improvised by building a secret staging base 60 miles (96km) southeast of Lae from where he would strike Wewak.

The scarcity of airfields in eastern New Guinea forced the Japanese to concentrate two air divisions at Wewak. By the time of his August 17, 1943 raid, Kenney already identified at least ten flying regiments at Wewak from decrypted Japanese radio message traffic. Kenney's airmen left 100 parked airplanes destroyed on taxiways or damaged in earthen revetments. A follow-up strike the next morning wrecked 28 more Japanese planes. In two days Fourth Air Army lost three-quarters of its aircraft.

Two weeks later, when Allied troops landed north of Lae, a few twin-engine Japanese bombers from Wewak attacked the beachhead and inflicted some damage. The next day, September 5, unchallenged by Japanese airpower, American paratroopers dropped on Nadzab, 20 miles (32km) west of Lae, cutting off the 51st Division from the rest of Eighteenth Army. Adachi ordered a withdrawal to Finschhafen 50 miles (80km) east of Lae. In retreat the unfortunate Japanese had to detour over rugged, 12,000-foot (3,600-m) high mountains to reach the north coast. About 8,000 officers and men trekked into the forbidding mountains. Discipline collapsed, and only the strong survived. More than 2,000 Japanese never came out of the unforgiving mountains, most victims of starvation.

Finschhafen now became the strong point that guarded the western side of the 60-mile (96-km) wide straits separating New Guinea and New Britain. Lt. Gen. Eizo Yamada, Commander, 1st Shipping Engineer Group, assembled about 3,000 soldiers. Yamada used his engineer's eye and his men's training to fortify Satelberg Ridge, which overlooked the entire coastline about Finschhafen and blocked any further ground push north toward Sio. They perched on the jungle covered ridgeline waiting for the inevitable Allied landing.

Australian troops landed at Finschhafen on September 22 and quickly cleared the narrow coastal enclave encompassing the port. They then started up the Satelberg ridgeline and the fighting degenerated into a series of deadly small unit combats against a well-entrenched and fanatically stubborn opponent. By the end of September, 2,400 more men from the 20th Division had reinforced Yamada's battle-depleted numbers and they fought on for two more months. Australians of the 9th Division attacked the ridgeline again and again, isolating and destroying pockets of Japanese resistance one at a

Above: In jungle conditions, the mortar can be a very effective weapon. This American 81mm mortar is in action near Maffin airstrip on Wakde Island, which American forces took on May 17, 1944, in an effort to secure land suitable for bomber airfields.

time. At least 5,500 Japanese perished, but they held their ground until late November. MacArthur found himself bogged down at Finschhafen, where he had expected a walkover.

While the Australians were doing most of the fighting in Papua from Nassau Bay to Finschhafen, Gen. Krueger was training his increasing number of American divisions to fight as amphibious task forces. Adm. Barbey had responsibility for the amphibious portion of the training designed to take full advantage of Southwest Pacific's domination of the air and sea by moving infantrymen over water to strike at their objectives unhindered by enemy or terrain.

Southwest Pacific Area had expanded dramatically. From two infantry divisions, the 32d and 41st, in December 1942, the American contingent numbered five divisions (those two plus the 1st Cavalry Division and the 6th and 24th Infantry Divisions) by January 31, 1944. MacArthur also had three regimental combat teams (formed by attaching a field artillery battalion to the 503d Parachute Infantry, 112th Cavalry, and 158th Infantry regiments), three engineer special brigades, and five Australian infantry divisions. Three more US infantry divisions — the 31st, 33d, and 40th — were on the way. Kenney had about 1,000 combat aircraft at his command. The new Seventh Fleet commander, Vice Adm. Thomas C. Kinkaid, had about the same number of warships as his predecessor, but Barbey's amphibious fleet had grown with transports, and landing craft.

The Japanese, in contrast, could not replace their losses in aircraft, shipping, and skilled manpower. Japan may have lost more than 3,000 aircraft on the New Guinea and Solomons fronts. On the ground, Eighteenth Army had suffered

around 35,000 casualties. Of the three Japanese divisions in eastern New Guinea — the 20th, 41st, and 51st — only the 41st was near full strength. Airfield, shipping regiments, engineer construction units, and assorted service outfits brought Japanese strength in the eastern half of the island to around 60,000 troops. A dangerous 350-mile (560-km) gap separated maneuver elements of the 41st Division at Wewak from those of the 36th Division at Sarmi, Netherlands New Guinea. The 36th was part of a frenetic Japanese effort to strengthen the western half of the island through the construction of a web of interlocking airdromes. Until the build-up in the west was completed, Imamura and Adachi were locked in a desperate battle of attrition against a foe with a crushing superiority in resources.

Paradoxically the jungle that had claimed so many Japanese lives now sheltered them from a concentrated Allied ground offensive. The jungle prevented large units from maneuvering, so the Allies could not mass their overwhelming firepower, manpower, and material resources against a particular Japanese stronghold. To sustain an infantry regiment in combat required the services of the equivalent of two divisions. Every Allied operation depended on an extensive logistics infrastructure, painstakingly scratched out of the wilds, that stretched from engineers developing a coastal enclave and port, back through the ships that were the umbilical cord between the advance base and the staging areas. Few soldiers actually fought the Japanese. The majority, maybe seven of every eight, served in support roles — unloading ships, building roads, hauling supplies, preventing malaria, and constructing airfields.

In such circumstances, MacArthur's forces crossed the Dampier Straits and invaded the southern tip of New Britain in December 1943. On the south side of the island, Japanese gunners shot the first wave of the 112th Cavalry to pieces and repulsed its attack. Its main force did get ashore, but thereafter the cavalrymen were bogged down in the swampy ground and thick mud fed by almost continuous tropical rains. On the north side, the 1st Marine Division found itself in similar circumstances, except on a larger scale. Mud, thick swamp, and dense jungle made an overland advance toward Rabaul impossible.

MacArthur then skilfully employed Barbey's VII Amphibious Fleet to carry the 126th Infantry from Finschhafen through the Dampier Straits 175 miles (280km) to Saidor. This landing cut off the 20th Division then defending Sio against the Australian 9th Division's steady advance. Again the Japanese found themselves forced to flee into the rugged mountains in order to escape encirclement. Starvation and disease again stalked the soldiers who marked their latest line of retreat with the corpses of their comrades.

In late January 1944, an Australian patrol pushing through Sio after the retreating Japanese discovered a half-buried trunk in a stream bed. It held the complete cipher library of the Imperial Japanese Army's 20th Division. The find was immediately returned to Central Bureau, MacArthur's Allied cryptanalytical agency in Brisbane, Australia. Central Bureau used the captured code books to break into the Japanese Army's ciphers exactly when MacArthur most needed the advantage.

In January 1944 MacArthur and his staff were searching for ways to accelerate the final phases of the campaign against Rabaul. Around this time, Fifth Air Force pilots consistently reported the absence of any signs of Japanese activity on Los Negros, largest of the Admiralty group which lay about 360 miles (576km) west of Rabaul. Kenney was convinced that his airmen had driven the Japanese from the island and recommended the immediate seizure of the supposedly undefended island and its valuable airstrips.

MacArthur dispatched a reconnaissance-in-force, about 1,000 officers and men from the reinforced 5th Cavalry Regiment, 1st Cavalry Division, against Los Negros on February 29. Since the Japanese defenders expected an attack from the opposite direction, by accident rather than design, the 5th Cavalry landed behind the main enemy defenses. Vicious night fighting typified the next five days. Krueger threw sufficient reinforcements into the battle to tip the balance in the cavalrymen's favor. MacArthur's luck and daring, plus the courage of a handful of cavalrymen, had won an impressive victory.

Capture of the Admiralties isolated Rabaul and gave MacArthur a forward air base that extended his fighter range beyond Wewak. Seizing the Admiralties two months ahead of schedule led the Joint Chiefs to re-evaluate Pacific strategy. MacArthur sent his chief of staff, Lt. Gen. Richard K. Sutherland to Washington to brief an operation remarkable in scope, daring in execution, and likely to cut months off the southwest Pacific advance. This was the revised Reno IV plan to jump an unprecedented 400 miles (640km) up the New Guinea coastline to capture the Japanese major air and supply base at Hollandia. Code-named Reckless, the Hollandia operation was a masterpiece of sound planning that took full advantage of extremely accurate intelligence obtained from reading Japanese codes. For MacArthur it proved the decisive operation on New Guinea and was the turning point in his war against the Japanese.

When Allied codebreakers lifted the veil shrouding Japanese defenses, it became evident that MacArthur's next landing, scheduled for April 26 in Hansa Bay, could expect strong ground opposition. Moreover, Japanese aerial reinforcements were filling up the major airbase complex at Hollandia from

where they would support the land defense of Madang. Conversely, Hollandia had almost no ground defenses; the soft Japanese center remained vulnerable to an Allied landing.

Approval of Reckless by the Joint Chiefs of Staff did not automatically ensure success of execution. MacArthur, for instance, needed carrier air support because Hollandia was far beyond the range of his land-based fighter aircraft. Allowed three days of carrier support, General Headquarters planners decided to seize Aitape, about 140 miles (224km) east of Hollandia, and use its airstrips to provide fighter support to the ground troops at Hollandia. The operation now evolved into a herculean effort by 217 ships to transport safely 80,000 men, their equipment and supplies, 1,000 miles (1,600km) to conduct three separate amphibious landings deep in the enemy rear area. Control of the skies along the invasion route was the prerequisite to success.

By late March, Kenney knew from deciphered Japanese communications that about 350 enemy warplanes were concentrated near Hollandia where they believed themselves safely beyond the range of Allied aircraft. Kenney outfitted new-model P-38s with wing tanks to extend their range and used them to escort 60 B-24 heavy bombers that smashed Hollandia on March 30. Follow-up raids demolished nearly all the operational Japanese aircraft at Hollandia. Never again would the enemy contest air superiority over New Guinea.

To bag all of Eighteenth Army it was imperative that Adachi continue to believe that MacArthur's next blow was aimed at the Madang-Hansa area. A well-designed deception effort fed Gen. Adachi and his staff a steady diet of false information about an Allied landing in Hansa Bay that the Japanese were predisposed to believe anyway. The deception was so successful that on April 22, 1944, the 24th and 41st Infantry Divisions landed unopposed 25 miles (40km) apart at Hollandia. The 163d Regimental Combat Team simultaneously waded ashore against no opposition at Aitape. In one swoop MacArthur had split the Japanese defenses on New Guinea, cutting off Eighteenth Army and isolating it in eastern New Guinea.

MacArthur's strategy was to capture forward airfields from which to cover his further advance into Geelvink Bay and thence the Vogelkop Peninsula. Gen. Krueger now had to prevent Adachi's Eighteenth Army from breaking through the envelopment, while his Sixth Army simultaneously advanced rapidly westward, to exploit his Hollandia advantage by not allowing Japanese defenders time to regroup and reorganise their forces. Just five days after the Hollandia-Aitape landings, MacArthur ordered the 41st Infantry Division to seize Wakde Island and airstrips at Sarmi on the adjacent New Guinea coast on May 15.

Left: French-designed Brandt 81mm mortar and 7lb bomb — range 3,200 yards (2,900m). This weapon was also bought by the Japanese. Below: French-designed Brandt 60mm mortar, and 3lb bomb.
US Marine Corps Air-Ground Museum.

Wakde proved a tough nut to crack. It took two days of nasty squad-size fighting to pry almost 800 Japanese defenders from their spider holes, coconut log bunkers, and coral caves. The Sarmi landing, conversely, met little resistance because most of the Japanese defenders had departed from the landing area to counterattack the Allied beachhead at Hollandia. By May 22, Krueger had achieved his objectives at Sarmi. He then enlarged the mission of the task force by ordering an overland advance toward Sarmi village about 18 miles (28km) west of the beachhead. The American push by the 158th Regimental Combat Team and 6th Infantry Division ignited a battle of attrition for a coral lump overgrown with rain forest, forever after known as Lone Tree Hill. The objective was not cleared of the enemy until late June, but at a cost of 2,299 American casualties — 437 killed — as opposed to just over 4,000 Japanese killed. Although the area later supported five invasions, the push toward Sarmi was a significant distraction at a time when Krueger had his hands full juggling four other major operations Aitape, Noemfoor, Sansapor, and Biak.

Biak Island dominates strategic Geelvink Bay. Its coral airstrips, suitable for heavy bombers, were a powerful lure to MacArthur and Kenney. On May 27, 1944, elements of the 41st Infantry Division landed on Biak which lies only 60 miles (96km) south of the Equator. The steaming equatorial heat, thick, 12-foot (3-m)-high scrub growth, and scattered Japanese ambushes combined to slow the American advance inland toward the vital airstrips. A deceptive Japanese defense relying on the numerous caves that pockmarked the dominating cliffs stopped the American push in its tracks. MacArthur dispatched Gen. Eichelberger to the island to get the troops moving. Despite a shake-up of commanders, the fighting continued unabated on Biak through June. The prolonged campaign pinned Barbey's amphibious fleet and Kinkaid's Seventh Fleet close to Biak where they remained vulnerable to Japanese air and surface attack.

On June 3, Japan's powerful 16th Cruiser Division sortied from Davao in the Philippines, escorting a reinforcement convoy destined for Biak, and inaugurating the so-called *Kon* operation. Broken Japanese naval signals foretold the impending effort to the Allies. Long-range B-24 bombers spotted the Japanese fleet, which soon reversed course and returned to Davao. By June 7, deciphered messages pointed to another *Kon* effort. Kinkaid confidently ordered his task force commander to stand off the intended Japanese landing area along Biak's north coast. B-25 medium bombers discovered the second *Kon* convoy during daylight hours and sank one destroyer. The remainder of the convoy and its escorts steamed to Biak only to meet the waiting Allied task force. After an ineffectual exchange of gunfire and torpedoes, the *Kon* forces, thwarted again, withdrew to Davao.

Combined Fleet Headquarters cancelled the third *Kon* attempt in favor of an all-out air and surface attack against the imminent American landings in the Marianas. Only a handful of Japanese reinforcements ever reached Biak. The doomed garrison fought tenaciously, but to a foregone conclusion that left more than 4,800 Japanese dead at the cost of nearly 2,800 American casualties. Because Biak's airfields were not taken as scheduled, MacArthur ordered the capture of the strips on tiny, 15 miles (24km) long by 12 miles (19km) wide, Noemfoor Island situated 60 miles (96km) west of Biak.

Preceded by an intense naval bombardment, more than 13,500 troops of the 158th Regimental Combat Team (Reinforced) stormed ashore on Noemfoor on July 2, 1944 against desultory resistance. One dazed Japanese prisoner announced that recently arrived reinforcements had raised the garrison's strength to nearly 4,500 men. The task force commander immediately requested reinforcements from Sixth Army. In truth no Japanese reinforcements had landed on Noemfoor, but the reserve of 1,500 officers and men of the 503d Parachute Infantry Regiment jumped onto the island using its runway as their drop zone. High winds carried the parachutists to bone-cracking landings in supply dumps, vehicle parks, and amidst wrecked Japanese aircraft. No paratroopers fell to hostile fire, but 128 were injured in the jump, including 59 serious fracture cases. For the entire Noemfoor campaign, the task force incurred a total of 411 battle casualties while killing 1,759 Japanese and capturing another 889, mostly laborers.

Other misperceptions marred the Aitape fighting. After scant opposition following the April 22 landing there, Allied engineers had quickly converted the existing Japanese airdromes into a major fighter base. By early June, the 32d Infantry Division had established an outer defensive perimeter along the western banks of the Driniumor River, about 15 miles (24km) east of the airstrips. Extensive intelligence warnings about a Japanese attack were available to the responsible commanders in sufficient time for them to alter their tactical plans in order to smash Adachi's offensive.

Privy from codebreaking to the unfolding enemy plan, Krueger asked MacArthur for, and received, additional infantry, artillery, and air reinforcements for Aitape bringing the total forces, either present or en route, to two and two-thirds divisions. On June 28, Krueger created XI Corps to oversee the growing Allied force and appointed Maj. Gen. Charles P. Hall its commander. Hall enclosed the vital airstrips with a semicircular, ten-mile (16km) defensive belt whose flanks rested on the sea. Along this line were more than 1,500 mutually protective log bunkers. Barbed wire obstacles and entanglements girded the line. Within that perimeter stood the equivalent of two divisions, including nine infantry battalions. Fifteen miles (24km) east, however, only three infantry battalions and two understrength cavalry squadrons defended the Driniumor River line. They had little barbed wire, few bunkers, poor fields of fire, and miserable jungle tracks for communication.

The Driniumor was an easily fordable 20-foot (6-m)-wide stream. Dense jungle and towering trees on both sides of the wider river bed effectively masked movement on the opposite banks. American riflemen and machine gunners in foxholes, pits, and a few bunkers along the river nervously awaited a Japanese attack. Japanese prisoners-of-war told of such an offensive. American

Right: US Marine Corps artillerymen work with a will as they blast Japanese positions on Cape Gloucester, at the western end of New Britain, at the very end of December 1943. The weapon is a 75-mm pack howitzer, a light but effective piece of artillery.

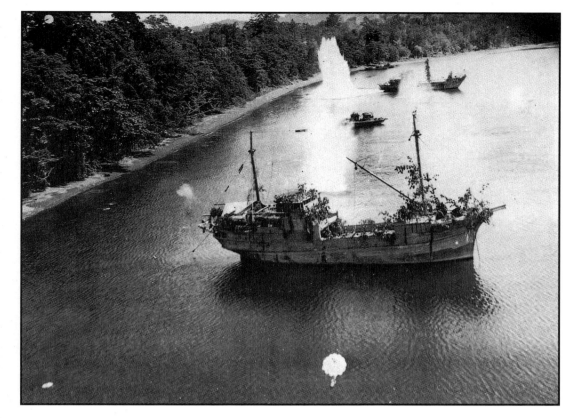

Above: Japanese shipping under attack at Manokwari in June 1944. The raid was made by medium bombers. The parachute retarders allowed the attackers to escape before the bombs detonated.

patrols had encountered stiffening Japanese resistance, and numerous decrypts pointed to an imminent offensive. Rather than wait for the Japanese attack, Hall finally ordered a textbook maneuver, a reconnaissance-in-force along both enemy flanks to commence on July 10.

That morning an American infantry battalion on the north and a cavalry squadron on the south crossed the Driniumor and probed cautiously eastward. The reconnaissance-in-force passed north and south of Eighteenth Army's main assembly areas which were from two to four miles (3-6km) inland from the coast. Only two infantry battalions and a cavalry squadron were left on the Driniumor.

That night 10,000 howling Japanese troops burst across the shallow Driniumor and charged through the center of the badly outnumbered and undermanned covering force. GIs fired their machine guns and automatic rifles until the barrels turned red hot, but the Japanese, eerily visible under the light of flares, surged forward. American artillery shells fell in clusters on the Japanese infantrymen, killing and maiming hundreds or crushing others beneath the tall trees that snapped apart in the unceasing explosions. Japanese numbers proved irresistible. Their breakthrough precipitated a month-long battle of attrition in the New Guinea wilds. GIs moved behind heavy artillery support to close off pockets of Japanese resistance. The jungle restricted movement so the hardest fighting fell to rifle squads or companies. Infantrymen fought a disconnected series of vicious actions that appeared coherent only on headquarters' situation maps. Adachi's men asked no quarter and received none. During July and August 1944

nearly 10,000 Japanese perished. Almost 3,000 Americans fell along the Driniumor, 440 of them killed. In terms of American casualties it was MacArthur's most costly campaign since Buna.

Hall's victory allowed Sixth Army's other ongoing operations to proceed on or ahead of schedule and validated MacArthur's concepts of bypassing the enemy. Adachi's terrible defeat left Eighteenth Army trapped between the Americans in the west and the Australians in the east. In mid-December 1944, Australian forces began a slow, determined drive from the east toward Wewak which finally fell on May 10, 1945. Australian losses were 451 killed, 1,163 wounded, and 3 missing. About 7,200 Japanese fell. Adachi then kept his approximately 13,000 survivors together in the hills and did not surrender until September 1945. During the eastern New Guinea campaigns, 110,000 of the emperor's soldiers and sailors died from enemy action, disease, or starvation in the pestilent jungles, the cold mountains, or the empty seas. Adachi himself was tried for war crimes at Rabaul, but beat the hangman by committing suicide in September 1947.

In the summer of 1944, with the fighting along the Driniumor flickering out, MacArthur's final assault landing on New Guinea took place at Sansapor, a weak point between two known Japanese strongholds on the Vogelkop Peninsula. There were about 15,000 Japanese troops of the 35th Division at Manokwari, 120 miles (192km) east of Sansapor. Sixty miles (96km) to Sansapor's west were 12,500 enemy soldiers

at the major airbase complex of Sorong. Rather than fight on the enemy's terms, MacArthur employed his command's well-tested amphibious capability to leapfrog to Sansapor where, on July 30, 7,300 men of the 6th Infantry Division conducted an unopposed landing. Sixth Army had once again split the Japanese forces in order to seize a coastal enclave that combat engineers quickly transformed from jungle overgrowth into two airfields that provided valuable support during MacArthur's invasion of Morotai, a substitute for Halamaheras. Japan's 35th Division and most of 2d Amphibious Brigade found themselves isolated in western New Guinea. Another 15,000 Japanese perished in western New Guinea fighting while perhaps 30,000 more were isolated there and neutralized. Add to this the 57,000-plus imperial soldiers and 39,000 sailors bypassed on New Britain and the totality of Allied victory in the New Guinea campaign comes into sharp relief.

The Allied casualty toll underscores the nature of the campaign. The struggle for control of the air, the *sine qua non* for the campaign, proved costly. Kenney's Fifth Air Force lost 1,374 aircraft to all causes between September 1942 and September 1944. More than 4,100 American airmen were killed or listed as missing in action. Approximately 2,000 Australian airmen fell in battle. In the attrition warfare characteristic of eastern New Guinea ground operations through the Admiralties, the Allies suffered more than 24,000 battle casualties, about 70 percent (17,107) being Australians. There were 70,000 malaria casualties. all this to advance 900 (1,440km) miles in 20 months. But following the decisive Hollandia envelopment, losses were 9,500 battle casualties, mainly American, to leap 1,500 miles (2,400km) in just 100 days.

MacArthur came to understand that New Guinea's terrain precluded even rudimentary ground maneuver and that it was the sea that offered the avenue to battlefield mobility in his theater. Victory on the ground, in turn, depended on local air superiority which enabled the navy to carry the ground forces safely forward to the next objective. The infantry held the ground and allowed the engineers to construct a forward air base, and the cycle began again.

Tokyo never seemed to grasp that geography determined the New Guinea campaigns. Hardened veterans were asked to do the impossible. Japanese infantry operations, brave, determined, but futile, were swept aside by Allied joint operations relying on the combined air, naval and ground firepower essential for the conduct of modern war. Rather than conquer the New Guinea jungle, MacArthur ultimately bypassed it to seize coastal enclave bases. Isolated in the interior, Japanese were devoured piecemeal in a relentless struggle against the enemy and jungle.

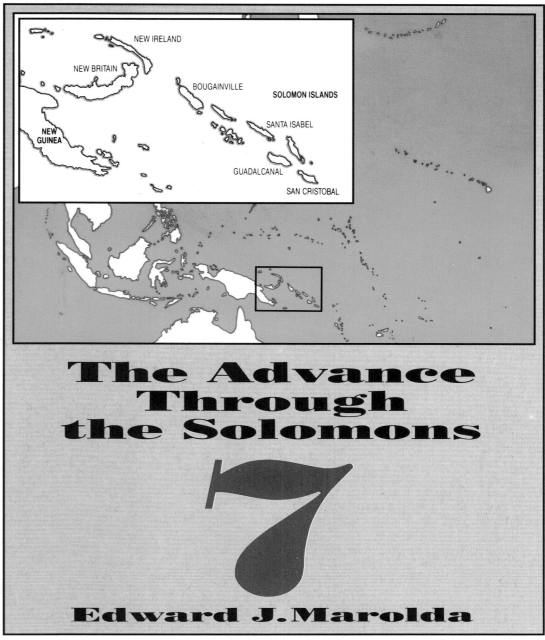

The Advance Through the Solomons

7

Edward J. Marolda

The Allied campaign in the Solomon Islands, with the exception of the Guadalcanal battle, is one of the forgotten campaigns of World War II. It was preceded by the momentous Japanese attack on Pearl Harbor and the pivotal naval battles of Coral Sea and Midway. The operations in the Solomons were followed by the more dramatic assaults on Tarawa, Saipan, Iwo Jima, Okinawa, and the other Japanese island bastions of the Central Pacific.

Many have a vivid picture of marines storming the beaches of countless island atolls, as Navy carrier planes roar overhead and huge battleships blast away at enemy fortifications. Others know the details of the Army's fight to liberate the Philippine Islands. The Army Air Forces' aerial blitz of Japan and the dropping of the atomic bombs on Hiroshima and Nagasaki are familiar to us all.

The advance through the Solomons has not received the attention it warrants primarily because it lacked a dramatic last act. The ultimate strategic prize of the operation — the Japanese stronghold of Rabaul — was never seiz-

ed by Allied forces during the war. Denied this climax, historians and others have quickly surveyed this campaign and pressed on to other, more memorable events.

Yet the offensive through the Southwest Pacific, of which the Solomons operations were part, was significant from many standpoints. It lasted longer than any other Allied campaign of the Pacific war. The Allies slowly fought their way forward for almost two years, from August 1942 to March 1944. Conversely, a period of only 17 months elapsed from the end of the Solomons campaign to the final defeat of Japan in August 1945.

The Solomons were a vital testing ground for the coalition that made up the alliance fighting the Japanese imperium. Americans, New Zealanders, Australians, and Melanesians learned how to work together in the common effort to evict the enemy from the region.

That enemy was armed with the most modern weapons, led by officers skilled in the art of war, and motivated by an ethic of duty and self-sacrifice. In August 1942, the armed forces of the Japanese

US Small Arms and Accoutrements

1 US rifle Model 1903 A1, .30 caliber, with Model 1905 bayonet and early leather, reinforced canvas-covered scabbard
2 Johnson Model 1941 semi-automatic rifle, .30 caliber with Model 1941 spike bayonet
3 US rifle M1 Garand, .30 caliber with Model 1942 bayonet and green plastic scabbard
4 Model 1936 rifle ammunition belt with one pocket open, showing an eight round clip
5 US carbine M1, .30 caliber with two extra ammunition clips, together with two ammunition pouches — obverse and reverse

6 US rifle Model 1903 A1, .30 caliber equipped with M8 8x telescopic sight as used by the United States Marines
7 Winchester Model 1917 trench gun (pump-action shot gun), 12 gauge, with leather military sling and bayonet adaptor
8 Winchester Model 12 trench gun, 12 gauge, with all brass cartridge below
9 Model 1911 semi-automatic pistol, .45 caliber. A box of 50 rounds is nearby. The holster is leather issue and there is a Model 1923 web clip pouch for two clips, one of which is shown

Dale E. Biever: 7; Pritchard Collection: 5, 9; Scott A. Duff: 1-4, 6, 8

Beneath the muzzle of the M1 Garand (*3*), can be seen the separate issue components of the rifle's cleaning kit. These include oil container, brush, pull-through, and combined rifle tool. They were stored inside the butt of the piece, and held secure by a hinged trap in the butt plate. The Model 1917 and Model 12 trench guns, (items *7* and *8*) were both developed from commercial pump-action shotguns and were found to be highly effective close-quarter weapons.

Empire had just completed the conquest of the Far East and the Western Pacific.

The Solomons were a laboratory for the coordinated operation of American armed forces. In contrast to later campaigns when one service often predominated, in the Solomons, Army, Army Air Forces, Navy, and Marine Corps units were dependent on one another not only to succeed, but also to survive.

The Solomons campaign also provided valuable experience for the Allies in the coordination of long-range bombing by land-based and carrier-based aircraft, fighter support, and aerial recon-

naissance; landing beach protection and gunfire support by naval warships; the loading, transportation, landing, and resupply of ground troops by Navy amphibious forces; and the command and control of Army and Marine ground forces on extended land operations. New tactics, weapons, and equipment evolved from the experience of this campaign. Allied soldiers, marines, and airmen learned how to carry on in spite of the extreme heat and humidity and disease characteristic of the tropical Solomon Islands.

While suffering operational setbacks, for the first time in the war Allied forces

mounted a successful offensive against the previously unbeaten Japanese. Clearly, the Solomons campaign foreshadowed the defeat of Japan itself.

An Allied victory in the Pacific war was not a clear vision at the outset of the campaign in mid-1942. At that time, the Allies were focusing on Europe and the defeat of Hitler's Germany. The Allied command, however, decided to keep the pressure on Japan through limited offensive action. Accordingly, the US Joint Chiefs of Staff ordered a three-phase campaign to seize the Japanese South Pacific bastion of Rabaul on the large island of New Britain.

The campaign entailed mutually supporting advances along the western and eastern edges of the Solomon Sea. The forces on the western flank, commanded directly by Army Gen. Douglas MacArthur, the Commander-in-Chief, Southwest Pacific Area, would advance over Papua New Guinea's formidable Owen Stanley mountain range and then proceed northwestward along the coast of New Guinea before crossing to the western tip of New Britain for the final thrust toward Rabaul. American and Australian infantry divisions made up the bulk of this force. The eastern advance would proceed northwestward through the many islands of the Solomon chain and then cross over to the large island of New Britain for the final assault on Rabaul.

The initial phase of this eastern campaign would take place in the Pacific Ocean Areas, the operational responsibility of Adm. Chester W. Nimitz, who also commanded the US Pacific Fleet. For that reason, a naval officer subordinate to Nimitz would direct all assigned Allied forces. Vice Adm. Robert L. Ghormley initially led the South Pacific Command, but his lackluster performance and physical exhaustion led Nimitz to replace him with the dynamic and inspiring Adm. William F. Halsey. He would lead a heterogeneous force of US Navy aircraft carriers, battleships, cruisers, destroyers, and patrol torpedo (PT) boats; US Marine Corps ground and air units; US Army infantry divisions and Army Air Forces fighter, ground attack, bomber, and reconnaissance squadrons; and similar elements of the New Zealand armed forces.

The Allied offensive campaign's first phase, codenamed Watchtower, called for the seizure of the small island of Tulagi by the eastern flank forces of Commander, South Pacific. The existence of a Japanese airfield under construction on nearby Guadalcanal, however, motivated American planners to add that island to the list of objectives.

Meanwhile, beating the Allies in the theater to the punch, the Japanese landed large forces at Buna on New Guinea's north coast and launched a ground offensive south toward Port Moresby.

Despite this unwelcome development, Watchtower went forward. On the 7th and 8th of August, 1942, against minimal opposition from the Japanese, elements of the US 1st Marine Division, under square-jawed Maj. Gen. Alexander A. Vandegrift, disembarked from Rear Adm. Richmond Kelly Turner's ships of the Amphibious Force, South Pacific, and waded ashore on Tulagi and the smaller islands nearby. The marines also landed on Guadalcanal and secured the airstrip, soon named Henderson Field after Lofton Henderson, an officer who was killed leading Marine aircraft in the Battle of Midway.

In an early instance of interservice discord, Rear Adm. Frank Jack Fletcher, commander of the escorting carrier task

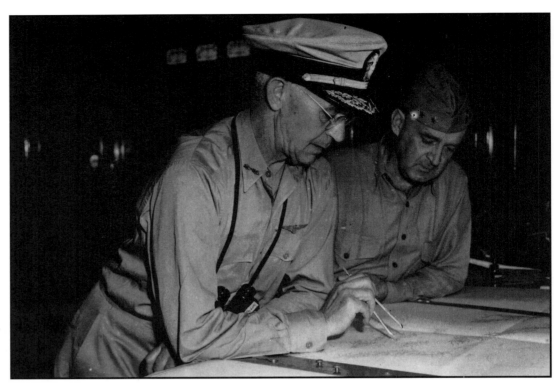

Above: The commanders of the amphibious force for the Guadalcanal operation were Rear Adm. Richmond K. Turner (left) and Maj. Gen. Alexander A. Vandegrift (right) under the overall direction of Vice Adm. Robert L. Ghormley's South Pacific Area.

Below: Marines break off from building a log and dirt shelter to watch the development of a Japanese air attack on Guadalcanal. The growing American air strength on Henderson Field soon reduced the effect of Japanese air attacks on the marines' positions.

force, withdrew his ships from the waters around Guadalcanal, fearing their loss to Japanese land-based aircraft. Henderson Field was not then ready to receive marine aircraft. Bereft of air support, the marines on the ground were at the mercy of the enemy's air and naval forces.

The Japanese reaction to the Marine lodgment on Guadalcanal was not long in coming. On the night of August 9, Vice Adm. Gunichi Mikawa led a force of eight cruisers and destroyers from his Eighth Fleet south through what came to be known as "the Slot" toward Guadalcanal. At 1:36 A.M. on August 9, Mikawa's force fell upon ten unsuspecting American and Australian cruisers and destroyers arrayed to the north and south of the small islet of Savo. In short order, the Japanese launched spreads of their lethal "long lance" torpedoes against the Allied warships, illuminated the battle scene with flares and searchlights, and opened up with naval gunfire. In the ensuing Savo Island debacle, the Australian cruiser *Canberra*, the American cruisers *Quincy*, *Astoria*, and *Vincennes*, and the American destroyer *Jarvis* were sent to the bottom, with the loss of 1,270 sailors. The carnage would have been even worse, but the Japanese admiral, fearing an American daylight air attack on his force, failed to press his advantage.

For the remainder of August, the Americans and Japanese tangled with one another on the ground, in the air, and at sea as both sides reinforced their theater forces. Once they deployed to Henderson, Marine fighter and dive-bomber aircraft joined Army Air Force's bombers based in New Caledonia, Fiji,

and the Santa Cruz Islands to wrest daytime air and naval superiority from the Japanese. This was achieved despite the difficulty the Army Air Force's high-flying bombers had in hitting the enemy's zig-zagging surface vessels. In any event, American ships and aircraft eventually prevailed, forcing the Japanese to restrict their reinforcement and resupply missions to nighttime destroyer dashes, which the Americans labeled the "Tokyo Express."

Sizable Allied and Japanese naval forces were involved, on August 24 and 25, in the Battle of the Eastern Solomons, but the action proved indecisive. Nonetheless, American air units sank the light carrier *Ryujo*, a destroyer, and a troop transport, while Japanese carrier planes damaged the American aircraft carrier *Enterprise*.

The combat intensified in September. On the 13th, 6,000 Japanese troops attacked the thin Marine perimeter on Guadalcanal, at a point thereafter called "Bloody Ridge." The enemy failed to break through Marine lines and lost many men in the process. Five days later, the Japanese exacted retribution, however, when one of their submarines caught the carrier *Wasp* in nearby waters and sank her.

In the seesawing naval war, an American surface force led by Rear Adm. Dan Scott pounced on the Japanese off Cape Esperance on October 11 and sent the heavy cruiser *Furutaka* and one destroyer to the depths of the appropriately nicknamed "Ironbottom Sound." Several nights later the Japanese returned the favor when a force of battleships and cruisers rained hundreds of high-explosive shells on Henderson Field, knocking it out of action for a week and destroying many of the aircraft caught on the ground there.

Reinforced by the 7th Marines and the Army's 164th Infantry, whose troops fought side by side, the defenders of Guadalcanal savaged a Japanese attacking force on October 23 and 24. The enemy left over 3,500 dead in front of the American positions.

Two days later, in the Battle of the Santa Cruz Islands, the contending navies clashed once again. A force of four Japanese carriers fought it out with an American carrier flotilla half that size. As in the battle of the Eastern Solomons, there was no clear victor. The Americans damaged the carriers *Zuiho* and *Shokaku* but the Japanese hit *Enterprise* hard and sank the carrier *Hornet*.

By November 1942, however, the tide was decidedly turning in favor of the Allies. On the 12th and 13th, in the Naval Battle of Guadalcanal, the Americans lost two cruisers and four destroyers but aircraft from Henderson Field and carrier *Enterprise* and the gunfire of battleship *Washington* sank no fewer than two Japanese battleships, a cruiser, and two destroyers. While losses were heavy on both sides, it was clearly an American victory. The Japanese fleet was forced to retire from the scene of the action. Adding to the enemy's increasingly desperate situation, during the remainder of the month, Allied aircraft jumped the enemy's vulnerable troop transports. In one instance, thousands of Japanese soldiers met their end when American aircraft caught four troopships in broad daylight off Tassafaronga on Guadalcanal. Every one of the ships was destroyed from the air.

In contrast to the Japanese plight, American reinforcements poured into Guadalcanal. On December 9, Army Maj. Gen. Alexander M. Patch established his XIV Corps headquarters on the island and took charge of the Army's Americal Division, 25th Infantry Divi-

Above: During the Battle of the Santa Cruz Islands on October 26, 1942, the *Hornet* was caught in the classic pincer attack of naval air power, with torpedo bombers closing at very low level and dive-bombers plummeting from almost directly overhead.

sion, and the 2d Marine Division, which earlier had relieved the 1st Marine Division, much in need of rest.

At the beginning of the new year, Japanese Imperial Headquarters had no choice but to conclude that the battle for Guadalcanal was lost. The Japanese were also faced with the loss of their position on New Guinea's north coast at Buna, then being stormed by the Americans and Australians. Accordingly, on January 4, 1943, the Japanese high command ordered the evacuation of the Buna area and Guadalcanal. During the first week in February, 11,000 Japanese troops evacuated Guadalcanal ahead of Gen. Patch's advancing XIV Corps.

Both victor and vanquished were exhausted from their six-month trial by fire among the islands at the south end of the Solomons chain. A period of resupply, reinforcement, and strategic rethinking

set in. Between February and June 1943, the Allies and the Japanese prepared for the next phase of the campaign for Rabaul.

In March and April, American cryptanalysts helped determine the course of the fighting in the Southwest and South Pacific theaters. Intercepted and decoded radio messages enabled Allied airmen to destroy most of a convoy bringing reinforcements to New Guinea. Shortly afterward, the same kind of intelligence revealed the itinerary of Adm. Isoroku Yamamoto, the principal planner of the attacks on Pearl Harbor and Midway, who was making an inspection of installations in the Solomons. Army Air Force fighters intercepted the bomber carrying the admiral and shot it down.

During this time of rejuvenation in the early months of 1943, the American command further defined plans for the

Below: American soldiers come ashore on Rendova island during June 30, 1943, during a tropical thunderstorm. The island provided sites for the long-range artillery that bombarded the area's main target, the Japanese garrison on New Georgia island.

continued advance on Rabaul, now called Operation Cartwheel. In March the Joint Chiefs of Staff ordered execution, under MacArthur's overall strategic direction, of the next phase of the offensive. As MacArthur's forces continued north along the New Guinea coast, Halsey's would seize New Georgia Island, further up the Solomons' "Slot"

and then gain a lodgment on the southern end of Bougainville Island. In the final phase, MacArthur would carry out an amphibious landing on New Britain's Cape Gloucester while Halsey's forces secured the east coast of Bougainville.

Throughout these moves forward, the ability of Allied fighters to provide air

cover for subsequent landings was a key factor in determining objectives.

The next operation by the eastern flank forces, the seizure of the air strips at Munda Point and Segi Point on New Georgia and at Villa on nearby Kolombangara, was ready for execution in late June. This followed months of preparatory bombing by Air Forces, Solomons

(AIRSOLS) aircraft; bombardment by the Navy's surface combatants, and reconnaissance ashore by American marines and Australian "Coast Watchers." Supporting the New Georgia operation, codenamed "Toenails," was an air fleet of 533 fighters, light bombers, and heavy bombers and a surface force of 2 heavy and 3 light aircraft carriers, 3 battleships, 9 cruisers, 29 destroyers, and numerous other ships.

D-Day was set for June 30, but fears that the enemy would move into one of the planned landing areas prompted Halsey to deploy elements of the 4th Marine Raider Battalion and the Army's 103d Infantry Regiment to Segi Point nine days early. With only light resistance from the Japanese, these forces secured their objective. The main Allied deployments began on June 30, 1943 when Adm. Richmond Kelly Turner's troop and cargo transport ships landed elements of the Army's 43d Infantry Division on Rendova Island, just across the water from Munda airfield. Throughout the battle for Munda,

LOCKHEED P-38 LIGHTNING

Although the exploits of the F4U Corsair, F6F Hellcat and B-29 Superfortress cannot be denied, it is a fact that one of the unsung heroes of the Allied campaign, the Lockheed P-38 Lightning, was responsible for shooting down more enemy aircraft than any other fighter during the Pacific War. With its unusual twin-boom configuration and ferocity in the heat of battle, this "jack of all trades" for the USAAF soon earned itself the nickname of "fork-tailed devil". Just short of 10,000 were built for service on all fronts, but its most famous exploit was undoubtedly on April 18, 1943, when sixteen of these "devils" dispatched Adm. Yamamoto to his death in the skies over the Solomons.

GUADALCANAL AND THE SOLOMONS CAMPAIGN

Map A
The Solomons campaign began as a limited offensive action, aimed at capturing the fortress of Rabaul, on New Britain. In conjunction with troops invading New Britain from New Guinea, a force would fight its way up through the Solomon Islands chain. The first objective of this eastern advance was the capture of Tulagi and the Japanese unfinished airfield on nearby Guadalcanal.

Map B
The initial landings on Guadalcanal were unopposed and marines quickly formed a perimeter. The Japanese, however, responded with both air and naval assaults which forced American naval forces, including carriers, to withdraw. The marines were now on their own. Working without air cover and bombarded by the Japanese, the marines held their ground and completed the airfield — Henderson Field. Supplies and aircraft then began to arrive in their support. The Japanese were also reinforcing, and troops under Colonel Ichiki were landed at Taivu Point.

Maps C and D
Ichiki's force quickly went onto the attack. This was repulsed, and a flanking attack by marines the following day destroyed the threat. The Japanese naval supply route, the "Tokyo Express" was still in operation, and another force was landed to attack the marines. This attack fell mostly on Bloody Ridge but was also repulsed.

The Japanese reinforced a third time, landing troops at Cape Esperance, Bloody Ridge was again the target. The marines again threw the Japanese back. A series of naval battles then closed off the island to Japanese reinforcement, and Marine and Army units began a drive westward. Faced with this, the Japanese ordered a withdrawal.

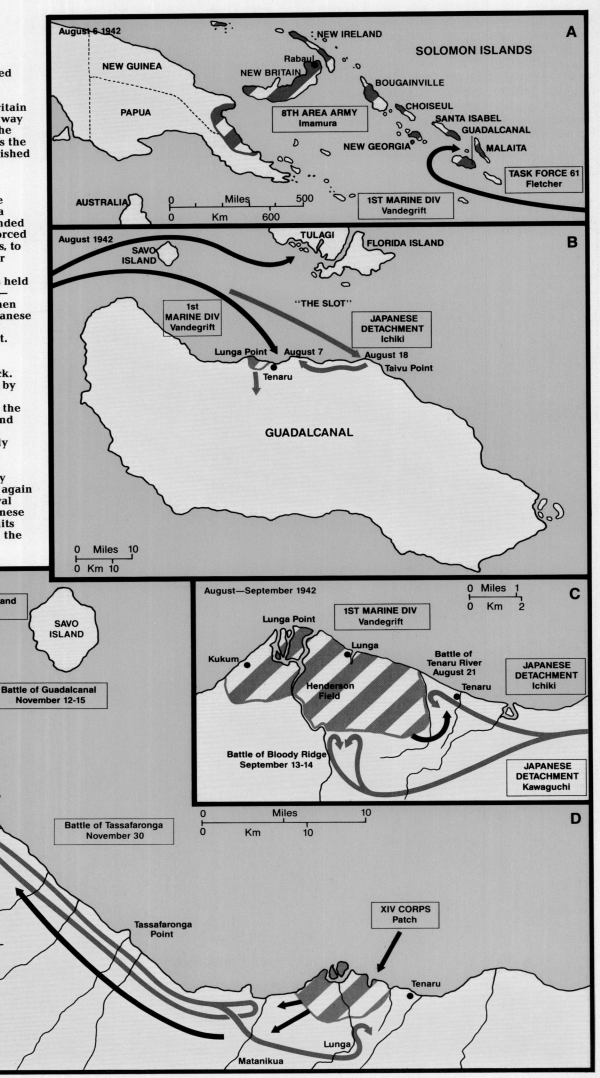

American artillery positioned on Rendova kept up a murderous fire on the enemy.

The swiftness of the Allied move to New Georgia caught the Japanese by surprise. The air response was tardy and piecemeal. Although enemy torpedo bombers sank the *McCawley*, Adm. Turner's flagship, American fighters and Marine and Army antiaircraft guns destroyed nearly all of the 27 enemy aircraft thrown into the first attack.

Within a week of the June 30 landing, American ground forces were firmly positioned ashore on New Georgia and prepared to advance on the enemy's concentrations at Bairoko and Munda Point. Two regiments of the 43d Infantry Division — the 169th and the 172d — moved from their staging point at Zanana westward toward Munda while the 1st Marine Raider Battalion and two battalions of the Army's 37th Infantry Division proceeded southwestward toward Enogai and Bairoko from their beachhead near Rice Anchorage.

Almost immediately, these advances bogged down. Daily tropical downpours turned the primitive jungle trails into quagmires that swallowed jeeps, trucks, and even bulldozers. Even more serious, it soon became clear that the American ground forces on New Georgia lacked the strength to overcome the enemy's resistance quickly.

At the same time, the US Navy was unable to prevent reinforcement of New Georgia from Kolombangara and other islands to the north where Maj. Gen. Noboru Sasaki concentrated a 10,000-man force. On the night of July 5-6, a Japanese naval force of ten destroyers, carrying ground troops, ran into Rear Adm. Walden L. Ainsworth's task group of cruisers and destroyers off the northwestern coast of New Georgia. In the Battle of Kula Gulf, the Americans sank two enemy ships, while losing the cruiser *Helena*. A week later, off the northeastern coast of Kolombangara, the contending naval forces met again. This time, the Americans sank the Japanese light cruiser *Jintsu*, but suffered the loss of destroyer *Gwin* and damage to New Zealand light cruiser *Leander* and two American cruisers. Despite this Allied opposition at sea, the Japanese were able to push ground reinforcements through to their frontline units. In light of later difficulties on New Georgia, it was fortunate for the Americans that the Japanese theater command refused Sasaki's request for even greater reinforcements.

Meanwhile on New Georgia, the 43d Infantry Division found the going rough. The baptism of fire for the division, made up of National Guard troopers from New England, was especially sobering. A patrol of Americans, New Zealanders, and Fijians first ran up against Japanese positions on "Bloody Hill." Soon, both the 169th and 172d Infantry were stopped short by Japanese troops who skillfully defended pillboxes protected by interlocking machine guns and dug-in heavy guns. A general ground attack on July 9, supported by artillery from Rendova, the naval gunfire of Rear Adm. Aaron Merrill's warships, and Rear Adm. Marc A. Mitscher's AIRSOLS dive bombers, made little forward progress. Casualties steadily mounted.

The green troops fought in a maze of hills and valleys crisscrossed with rock-strewn draws and gullies and swampy lowlands that did not appear on any maps held by the Americans. This terrain was covered with almost impenetrable tangles of vines, creepers, and the flora typical of the jungle landscape of the Solomon Islands. The ever-present heat and humidity added to the soldiers' misery.

Sickness and disease felled more of the Americans than did the Japanese. Malaria, beri beri, and other tropical diseases were prevalent. Men suffered from chronic diarrhea that steadily drained them of energy and eventually put them out of action.

The enemy added psychological terror to the physical stresses endured by the American troops. After a year of experience with jungle warfare, the Japanese were masters at it. They were especially adept at spooking their foes by crawling close to them at night, making unsettling noises, shouting death threats, and lobbing grenades around. Panic swept through some of the division's units, especially the 169th Infantry. Soldiers fired blindly into the night or tossed grenades into neighboring foxholes held by their friends. In the darkness, some men knifed fellow Americans whom they believed to be

Japanese. In the words of John Miller, Jr., author of the Army's official account, "on occasion mass hysteria took over."

The days and nights of actual combat, harassment by the enemy, and physical suffering began to take a toll of American soldiers, especially those who were in action from the outset of the operation. Medical personnel reported a disproportionate number of cases that they diagnosed as "war neuroses." A significant number of the men exhibited genuine mental disturbance, but others were misdiagnosed. They simply suffered from physical and emotional exhaustion — combat fatigue.

This exaggerated behavior in units newly tested in combat was sometimes the result of poor leadership. Such was the case with the 43d Infantry Division. To correct the problem, Maj. Gen. Oscar Griswold, the corps commander, replaced officers who had not measured up with subordinates who had. During July new men were placed in the positions of commanding officer, executive officer, and heads of the intelligence and operations staff sections of the 169th Infantry.

A new phase in the battle began in mid-July 1943, when Adm. Turner, as earlier planned, relinquished operational control of ground forces on New Georgia to Griswold and his XIV Corps headquarters. The general beefed up his 43d Infantry Division units ashore with reinforcements and established a new supply base at Laiana, much closer to the front than Zanana. In addition, the Allies improved medical and logistic support. The air drop of supplies to troops fighting deep in the trackless jungle of New Georgia proved to be an especially successful method of delivery.

The GIs in the line got help from other quarters as well. Allied aircraft based on Guadalcanal continually bombed the enemy's rear areas and fended off

Below: During September 1942, the men of the 1st Marine Division fighting on Guadalcanal were kept fully up to date with the local situation by the enterprising "Guadalcanal Gazette," which also covered events at home as well as the sports scores.

US Marine Uniforms and Equipment

1 Herring bone twill field utility cover (cap)
2 Herring bone twill three pocket utility shirt
3 Herring bone twill four pocket utility trousers
4 M1936 pistol belt with M1923 web magazine pouch, M1910 canteen with USMC cover, USMC stiletto with sheath, M1911 A1 semi-automatic pistol, .45 caliber with issue leather holster and M1942 first aid pouch
5 M1 steel helmet with camouflage cover
6 Field maps
7 M1938 dispatch case
8 M1 steel helmet
9 M1944 herring bone twill utility shirt
10 Herring bone twill field utility cap
11 Field shoes, 'rough side out'
12 M1918 A2 Browning Automatic Rifle (BAR), .30 caliber, with 20 round magazine
13 BAR gun tool with extra magazine, loading tool and loose .30 caliber rounds
14 M1938 canvas leggings
15 USMC fighting/utility knife
16 Mk 2 grenade
17 M1937 BAR magazine belt
18 Herring bone twill utility trousers
19 Field compass
20 Identity tags

Dale E. Biever: 11-13, 16-18; Scott A. Duff: 1, 3-7, 14, 15, 19; Richard A. Kos: 8, 20; Elliot R. Laine Jr.: 2, 9, 10

The camouflage helmet cover for the M1 helmet 5, was first introduced in 1943. It was the beginning of the official experiment with jungle camouflage gear that led to the one piece combat overall. Except for the cover on the helmet, the idea was largely unsuccessful. Under the helmet was sometimes worn the field utility cap (10), often seen with the brim turned backwards, to cover the back of the neck. The short lace-up field shoes (11), were worn with the canvas leggings (14), though these were often discarded later on in the war, or the trousers simply worn over them. The advent of the canvas and rubber jungle boot and double buckle combat boot eventually made them obsolete. The M1937 BAR magazine belt (17) held six pouches, each with two 20 round magazines. Seen near the belt is the M1910 canteen and M1942 first aid pouch.

Japanese bombers. On July 15 alone, Allied fighters shot down 45 of 75 enemy aircraft sent over the New Georgia battlefield. This success ended Japanese daylight air operations in the area.

The Navy's surface fleet also added to the enemy's difficulties. On July 25, for instance, Capt. Arleigh Burke, soon to be nicknamed "31-knot Burke" for getting the most speed from the battered destroyers he commanded, brought the seven ships of his task group close inshore and bombarded Japanese positions near Munda with 4,000 rounds of 5-inch shellfire.

That same day, XIV Corps launched a general offensive all along the line. Gains initially were limited, but the combined weight of Allied air, naval, and ground power began to tell. The 26th witnessed the first use on New Georgia of a weapon that would become a fixture of pillbox-busting operations in the Pacific war — the flame thrower. By carefully coordinating artillery and mortar support with the actions of flame thrower, light tank, and infantry teams, the 37th and 43d Infantry Divisions began systematically to reduce the enemy's defenses.

On the first day of August 1943, there was a perceptible lessening of Japanese

Japanese Optics

1 Artillery spotting telescope, 25x magnification. With lens cover and protective case. Made by NIKKO
2 Telescopic gun sight
3 Base Range Finder
4 Heavy Field Range Finder (tripod missing)
5 Stereoscopic Base Range Finder, with tripod
6 Model 93 battery commander's telescope, 8x magnification
7 Brass candle-powered signal lamp, with lenses and carrying case
8 Canvas case for 9
9 Surveying transit, 20x magnification with wooden case. Made by NIKKO
10 Artillery aiming circle, with tripod
11 Teak box for 18
12 Hand signal lamp with canvas container
13 Sunglasses with case
14 Sunglasses with case
15 Sunglasses
16 Leather case for 17
17 Monocular sight
18 Trench periscope
19 Slide rule with case
20 Brass slide rule with case
21 Handheld periscope binocular
22 Sighting device with field case
23 Sighting compass
24 Battery commander's telescope with tripod
25 Magnetic compass
26 Binoculars captured at Guadalcanal
27 Brass magnetic compass

War Memorial of Virginia Collection

Japanese optics are well made, sturdy and versatile. All of the objects in this photograph were designed to withstand prolonged use in tropical climates and in other adverse situations. Such instruments were as well respected then as they are today.

Of particular interest is the artillery spotting telescope (1), which was taken from a gun emplacement overlooking Yokohama Harbor. The artillery aiming circle (10), of 4x magnification, was used by artillery units to measure angles in azimuth and site, and for general topographical work. Other objects of interest are the sunglasses. Number 13 has amber lenses, mesh side screens, elastic headband with a velvet edge and comes with its velvet-lined metal storage case. Number 14 has green lenses and tortoise shell frames with linen-covered, velvet-lined metal storage case. Number 15 has amber-green lenses, leather side screens and spring wire temple bars.

resistance. During the next four days, the XIV Corps troops battled their way forward, destroying die-hard enemy units on Bibilo Hill and Kokengolo Hill before finally crossing the tarmac of Munda airfield. On August 5, the corps reached the sea, where many of the men enjoyed their first bath in a long time. Gen. Griswold radioed Adm. Halsey that Munda was in Allied hands.

The US Navy soon capped this with victory in the Battle of Vella Gulf, which occurred off Kolombangara on the night of August 6-7. An American destroyer force of six ships under Cdr. Frederick Moosbrugger tore a page from the

Japanese naval manual and sank, in a nighttime torpedo attack, three enemy destroyers loaded with troops.

Adm. Halsey allowed the enemy no rest. The Army's 25th Infantry Division, under Maj. Gen. J. Lawton Collins, who would later gain fame as "Lightning Joe" in the Normandy Campaign, landed on the island and pressed an advance to the north. Allied ground forces had secured New Georgia by the end of the month.

The struggle for New Georgia was long and bloody. The two-month battle cost the lives of 1,094 Americans. Another 3,873 men were wounded. Many more were incapacitated from disease and

combat fatigue. At least 2,500 Japanese paid the ultimate price for their brave and determined stand on the island.

Halsey now took advantage of the growing Allied air and naval strength. He decided that his forces would not storm Kolombangara, the next planned operation in the campaign. The Japanese expected him to strike there. The island bristled with newly built fortifications, defensive weapons, and over 10,000 troops. Instead, the admiral set his sights on Vella Lavella Island, which, in addition to being lightly held, was closer to Bougainville and Rabaul, his next objectives.

On August 14, Marine fighter aircraft landed at the new airstrip constructed at Munda by the 73d and 24th Naval Construction Battalions (Seabees). The air units thus were in position to cover the landing on Vella Lavella. One day later, Rear Adm. Theodore S. Wilkinson's troop transports and cargo ships landed the 35th Infantry of Collins' "Tropic Lighting" division at Barakoma on Vella Lavella. In a testament to masterful planning and execution, by the end of the day, all of the regiment's 4,600 troops and their essential supplies were ashore, even though the enemy contested the landing with air attacks.

During late August and early September, the Allies continued to strengthen their hold on the island. On September 18, the 14th New Zealand Brigade Group of the 3d New Zealand Infantry Division deployed to Vella Lavella and immediately moved against the remaining Japanese forces there. At the same time, Allied construction units completed an airfield that eventually could accommodate over 100 aircraft.

A total of 198 Americans and New Zealanders were killed and wounded taking Vella Lavella, but these casualties would have paled in comparison to the probable cost of an Allied assault on heavily defended Kolombangara. Surprised and flanked by the Allied operation, the Japanese had no choice but to give up their positions in the central Solomons. In late September and early October 1943, despite the US Navy's opposition in a nighttime surface action near Vella Lavella, the Japanese command evacuated its forces from both islands and deployed them to Bougainville, the next likely Allied objective in the Solomons offensive.

Allied leaders were indeed planning to seize the island in the next phase of the campaign, as laid out in basic planning directives. During much of 1943, however, Allied civilian and military leaders reconsidered the original objectives of Cartwheel. At the Casablanca Conference in January and the Washington Conference in May, the Combined Chiefs of Staff approved the concept of a drive through the islands of the Central Pacific by Adm. Nimitz' US Pacific Fleet. Key Washington military leaders now felt that Rabaul should be neutralized by air and naval action rather than captured by direct assault.

At the Quadrant Conference, held in Quebec, Canada, during August 1943, the Joint Chiefs of Staff considered the prospect of a direct attack on fortress Rabaul. The Japanese armed forces positioned on New Britain to defend the base consisted of almost 100,000 battle-ready soldiers and sailors. These men were armed with 367 antiaircraft guns, 43 coast defense guns, 475 artillery pieces and howitzers, and 1,762 machine guns. Further, they were protected by hundreds of concrete pillboxes and dug into 350 miles of tunnels and caves. The garrison of Rabaul was amply supplied

with tanks, mines, small arms, and ammunition. Worse, if recent experience was any guide, Allied leaders knew that the Japanese garrison would fight to the death. Bypassing the fortress seemed the wiser course.'

Gen. MacArthur, fearing the loss to Nimitz of scarce Marine and Army ground troops and Navy warships and transports, initially opposed the new operational concept of neutralizing rather than storming Rabaul. Once Gen. George C. Marshall, Army Chief of Staff, and Adm. Ernest J. King, Chief of Naval Operations, told MacArthur that he could begin planning his long-cherished campaign to liberate the Philippines, however, the Southwest Pacific commander agreed to the strategic bypass of Rabaul.

Even as the battle for New Georgia raged during July and August 1943, Adm. Halsey directed preparation for the landing on Bougainville. The initial phase of the operation would be a limited lodgment of forces on the west coast of the island of Choiseul. Allied units there would be in position to threaten the Japanese aircraft, naval vessels, and troops concentrated on the southern end of Bougainville and the nearby Shortland Islands. MacArthur, with responsibility for the overall strategic direction of the campaign, also added capture of the Treasury Islands southwest of Bougainville to the list of preliminary operations.

Meanwhile, there was no let-up in the pressure on Japanese forces in the Southwest Pacific theater. MacArthur's

American, Australian, and New Zealand forces pushed northwestward along the New Guinea coast, seizing Lae and Salamaua from the stoutly resisting enemy. In addition, the Army Air Forces of MacArthur's Southwest Pacific Command brought the war directly to the defenders of New Britain. From October 12 to November 2, 1943, the 349 bombers and fighters of Lt. Gen. George C. Kenney's Fifth Air Force attacked warships and merchant vessels in the harbor at Rabaul, bombed and strafed local airfields, and fought for the skies overhead with Japanese fighter aircraft. During the same period, the units of Air Forces, Solomons, now under Army Air Forces Maj. Gen. Nathan F. Twining, struck at enemy air strips on Bougainville, putting all of them out of operation by the end of October. The Allied air strikes disrupted Japanese preparations for Operation *RO*, a air effort by 546 aircraft to defeat the anticipated landing on Bougainville.

Halsey launched his Bougainville campaign on the night of October 27, when the US destroyer *Conway* and four troop transports landed Col. Victor Krulak's 2d Marine Parachute Battalion on the west coast of Choiseul. Also on the 27th, the 8th New Zealand Brigade Group landed on Treasury Island, which the "Kiwis" secured within a few weeks. These

Below: On August 2, 1944, Marine Corps dive-bombers attacked and destroyed the fuel dump at Simpson Harbor, Rabaul. By this time New Britain and New Ireland had been isolated and their garrisons left to "wither on the vine," under the effect of limited attacks.

moves were primarily feints to fix Japanese attention on southern Bougainville, where the enemy seemed to expect the main landing. Most of the 37,500 soldiers and 20,000 sailors of the Japanese garrison were deployed at this end of the island.

On November 1, 1943, Allied air, naval, and ground forces hit the Japanese on Bougainville with full fury. Planes from the aircraft carriers *Saratoga* and *Princeton* of Rear Adm. Frederick C. Sherman's Task Force 38 attacked enemy airfields at the north end of the island. Then the four light cruisers and eight destroyers of Adm. Merrill's Task Force 39 steamed close inshore and poured 2,700 rounds of

Above: General quarters finds a 20-mm anti-aircraft cannon fully manned on board an LST heading for Bougainville at the beginning of November 1943. Dawn and dusk were the favored times for the steadily declining numbers of Japanese air attacks.

naval gunfire into these and other Japanese air strips. The strikes prevented the enemy from using the facilities against the approaching amphibious armada of Adm. Wilkinson.

At 7:26 A.M., elements of the US 3d Marine Division, the van of Maj. Gen. Alexander A. Vandegrift's I Marine Amphibious Corps debouched from amphibious craft and stormed across the beach at Torokina just north of Empress Augusta Bay on Bougainville's west

coast. The site had many advantages; fighters based at Munda in New Georgia were in range, the area's soil was suitable for airfield construction, and surrounding mountains would help delay the arrival of Japanese reinforcements. Perhaps of greatest importance, the bay area was not strongly defended.

This proved fortunate, because the 270 defending Japanese soldiers, who fought almost to the last man, took a heavy toll of marines: 78 killed and 104 wounded. Direct air and naval gunfire support of the troops ashore was not particularly effective that day. In addition, rough seas caused a large number of landing craft to broach in the surf, and this delayed the landing of supplies and equipment, as did several enemy air attacks. Despite these difficulties, by nightfall the marines of Maj. Gen. Allen H. Turnage's division had secured the beachhead.

In the early morning hours of November 2, the Japanese mounted another threat — this time from the sea. Vice Adm. Sentaro Omori brought his force of two heavy cruisers, two light cruisers, and six destroyers south against the American beachhead at Empress Augusta Bay. In the battle of the same name, Adm. Merrill's surface warships sank the light cruiser *Sendai* and the destroyer *Hatsukaze*.

Below: Marines move through a typical Bougainville swamp. This is a mortar crew, with the man second from left carrying the tube and others toting bags filled with mortar shells. As in New Guinea, the mortar proved very important on Bougainville.

The fleet also added to the pounding of Rabaul. On November 5, Adm. Sherman's Task Force 38 sortied into the waters of the northern Solomon Sea to launch 97 aircraft against the air and naval forces concentrated at the Japanese redoubt. Dive bombers, torpedo bombers, and fighters pounced on warships in the harbor and aircraft parked wingtip to wingtip on surrounding airfields. The carrier planes put out of action three heavy and two light cruisers and two destroyers. Of greater significance, the Japanese fleet was compelled to retire from Rabaul for the relative safety of the base at Truk further to the north. Only six days later, Task Force 38, reinforced with three more carriers, struck again. Once again the naval aviators strafed and bombed enemy aircraft on the strips around Rabaul.

The month-long Allied aerial campaign devastated Japanese air strength. Of 173 planes deployed forward to Rabaul by the enemy, 121 were destroyed. The Japanese navy lost another 70 aircraft. When the enemy withdrew his carrier aircraft to Truk on November 12, it was tacit admission that Operation *RO* had failed miserably.

Meanwhile, the fight for Bougainville continued. On November 13, Adm. Wilkinson, as prescribed in the current amphibious warfare doctrine, turned over operational control of the forces ashore to Marine Maj. Gen. Roy S. Geiger, who had earlier replaced Vandegrift. By mid-month, the Army's 37th Infantry Division, now blooded veterans of New Georgia, arrived to increase the odds against the enemy.

The Japanese did not have an easy time reinforcing Bougainville. On the night of November 24, the war-weary destroyers of Arleigh Burke's "Little Beavers" squadron intercepted five enemy destroyers off the northern coast. The American warships forced their foe to withdraw to the north and then pursued them to Cape Saint George off New Ireland, in the process sinking three of the enemy vessels. This last naval engagement of the Solomons campaign amply demonstrated the US Navy's increasing dominance at sea.

For the remainder of 1943, the two divisions ashore at Torokina expanded the beachhead against moderate opposition from the Japanese, who still blindly expected the Allied main effort to hit southern Bougainville. On December 15, Gen. Griswold and his XIV Corps relieved Geiger and the I Marine Amphibious Corps. New units entering the beachhead included the Army's Americal Division and a battalion of the Fiji Infantry Regiment. Behind them in the perimeter, eight American engineer battalions and a New Zealand engineer brigade worked feverishly to improve the old Japanese air strip near the bay and to construct two more. Their efforts paid off on December 17, when aircraft based at Torokina launched their first air strike against Japanese bases on Rabaul.

Above: During early 1944, the Truk group of islands received heavy attention from American carrier-borne air power. Here, at the end of April, Douglas SBD Dauntless dive-bombers prepare to destroy the radio direction-finder unit on Ulalu islet.

Below: In a two-day raid on Truk during February, American warplanes sank more than 200,000 tons of shipping and destroyed 275 aircraft. This is the destruction of Dublon island's seaplane base by a combination of fragmentation and incendiary bombs.

Operations on the other side of the Solomon Sea were also going well. MacArthur's forces cleared Japanese defenders from the area around Finschhafen on New Guinea and in mid-December crossed over to the island of New Britain. The Army's 112th Cavalry seized Arawe on the south coast on the 15th and was soon reinforced by the Guadalcanal veterans of the 1st Marine Division. By the end of the month American forces had seized all of Cape Gloucester on New Britain's north shore.

Leaders in Washington now considered further measures to encircle Rabaul and reduce the offensive capability of Japanese air and naval forces based there. On December 20,

MacArthur approved Halsey's plan to seize Green Island, almost due east of Rabaul. Possession of Green Island would enable Halsey's fighter aircraft to cover the planned Allied seizure of Kavieng, northwest of Rabaul. Between February 15 and 20, 1944, a force of Americans and New Zealanders landed on Green Island and killed the 100 men of the defense force. Allied fighters and PT boats soon operated from there.

Throughout the early months of 1944, Allied air and naval forces poured a deluge of fire into the Rabaul bastion. The 600 land-based bombers, fighters, and other aircraft of Gen. Kenney and Marine Maj. Gen. Ralph J. Mitchell, who replaced Twining as Commander, Air Forces, Solomons, repeatedly hit the Japanese. By February, enemy warships rarely put in at Rabaul and after the 19th of that month, Japanese fighters did not rise to contest the skies with Allied planes. After March, American naval vessels confidently approached the coast off Rabaul to bombard targets ashore.

The 21,000 tons of bombs and shells dropped on Rabaul throughout the war cost the enemy dearly. The Japanese lost 30 naval vessels, 154 large cargo vessels, and 517 barges. Hundreds of precious airplanes and their crews were killed in defense of this Japanese Gibraltar of the Pacific.

At this juncture, American actions in the neighbouring Central Pacific theater had an even greater influence on Japanese plans for the defense of Rabaul

Below: The George Medal was created by Maj. Donald Dickson, 1st Marine Division. It was cast when the division returned to Melbourne, after Guadalcanal. This highly-prized, but unofficial decoration was awarded to members of the Marine Corps who fought there. *US Marine Corps Air-Ground Museum.*

than the ever-approaching forces of Halsey and MacArthur. For, on the last day of January 1944, Adm. Nimitz' Navy-Marine Corps team opened the campaign for the Marshall Islands with landings on Kwajalein Atoll.

Then on two successive days in mid-February, the fast carrier task force of Adm. Raymond A. Spruance unleashed crushing air strikes against Japanese forces at Truk. Between 250 and 275 enemy aircraft were destroyed or damaged, as were numerous naval vessels caught in the harbor. With the American seizure of Eniwetok Atoll in the Marshall Islands on February 17, 1944, it was clear that the Allied trans-Pacific advance would flank Rabaul far to the north.

The circle closed from the west as well. On February 29, MacArthur's Southwest Pacific forces landed on Los Negros in the Admiralty Islands, northwest of Rabaul. Although enemy resistance continued there well into the spring, by mid-March 1944 American forces were in control of these strategically placed islands.

Almost as a reflex action, on March 20, South Pacific forces carried out the last planned operation of the Solomons campaign, the capture of Emirau Island (which had replaced Kavieng as an objective), far to the northwest of Rabaul. The enemy was nowhere to be found.

There was little the Japanese could do during March 1944 to fend off the Allies' crushing embrace of Rabaul. It was not uncommon in the Pacific war, however, for the Japanese command to adopt desperation measures and they now did so on Bougainville. Belatedly, Lt. Gen. Harukichi Hyakutake concentrated the 15,000 men of his 17th Army in front of the beachhead at Torokina and prepared to push the Americans into the sea.

This would be no easy task. Holding the Torokina perimeter in early March 1944 was Gen. Griswold's XIV Corps of two Army infantry divisions, the 37th and the newly arrived Americal, and additional special units. Allied forces totaled 62,000 men. Further, since the landing the previous November, the Americans had developed fighting positions protected by thousands of mines, miles of barbed wire, hundreds of interlocking machine guns, and multiple mortar and artillery tubes sighted on all likely avenues of approach.

On March 8, 1944, General Hyakutake opened his attack with a heavy artillery bombardment of targets within the American perimeter. The following day, Japanese infantry assaulted fortified positions on Hill 700 held by units of the 37th Infantry Division. The enemy infiltrated the American lines but failed to break through to the rear. For the next three days, in vicious, hand-to-hand combat, the federalized Ohio National Guardsmen worked to push the enemy off the hill.

The initial Japanese attack was followed on the 10th by a thrust from the east against redoubts defended by men of the Americal Division (known during the Vietnam War as the 23d Infantry Division). The enemy seized one prominent terrain feature, South Knob of Hill 260, and then attempted, but failed, to storm nearby North Knob. The American soldiers were no more successful in counterattacking. Repeated assaults on South Knob could not budge the dogged Japanese troops. The American artillery batteries within the Torokina perimeter then concentrated their fire on the enemy salient, pouring 10,000 rounds onto South Knob. By the 15th, the decimated Japanese attack force was compelled to retreat to the east.

The last of Hyakutake's planned attacks kicked off on March 11, when the men of Colonel Isaoshi Magata's crack 45th Infantry Regiment moved against the 37th Infantry Division line at the base of Mt. Nampei. Enemy penetrations were minimal, and subsequent counterattacks by the division's 129th Infantry and elements of the 754th Tank Battalion forced the Japanese, by March 17th, to cease their fruitless effort. A desperate, final attack on the Torokina perimeter on the 23rd was repulsed with heavy loss.

In their offensive, the enemy killed 263 men of the XIV Corps. But the ill-fated operation resulted in the death and wounding of 8,000 Japanese soldiers, over half of the army committed to battle. On March 27, Gen. Hyakutake conceded the obvious and withdrew his spent forces from the unbroken American perimeter.

This bloody finale in the fight for Bougainville was an appropriate end to the bitter, 18-month Allied-Japanese struggle for the Solomon Islands; islands which pointed like an arrow at the heart of the Japanese Far Eastern Empire.

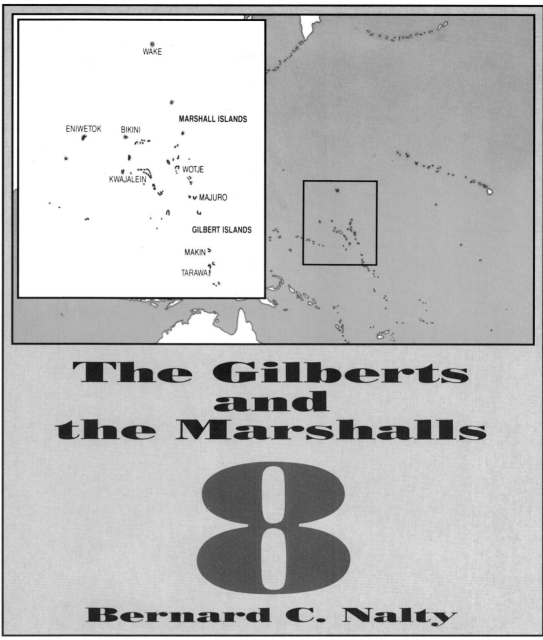

The Gilberts and the Marshalls

8

Bernard C. Nalty

By the end of 1942, the war against Japan entered a new phase, shifting from the defensive to the offensive. The Battle of Midway in June ended the threat to the Hawaiian Islands, while breaking the back of the Japanese carrier force. A succession of naval battles from the Coral Sea in May to the Tassafaronga Strait on the last night of November, some of them tactical victories for the Japanese, together with the grueling advances in New Guinea and the Solomon Islands, ensured the security of Australia and the supply line from Hawaii and the United States. In these circumstances, even though victory remained far from won, Adm. Ernest J. King, the Chief of Naval Operations, addressed the possibility of knifing westward through the central Pacific, while the forces of Gen. Douglas MacArthur and Adm. William F. Halsey converged on the Japanese redoubt at Rabaul, New Britain. At the Casablanca Conference in January 1943, Adm. King and Gen. George C. Marshall, the Army Chief of Staff, persuaded the Anglo-American Combined Chiefs of Staff to agree to operations against the Gilbert Islands, a

prewar British possession, and two island groups in the Japanese Mandates, the Marshalls and Carolines. While preparing for this offensive, the Americans would continue the advance on Rabaul, which Allied strategists expected to capture sometime in 1943, and drive the Japanese from their outposts in the Aleutians, Attu and Kiska, occupied at the time of the Battle of Midway.

King hoped to execute, insofar as resources permitted, the strategy outlined in the prewar Orange Plans, which called for a naval expedition westward from Hawaii. After World War I, with Japan in control of the central Pacific islands that a defeated Germany had acquired from Spain, American naval strategists realized that the US Fleet would have to seize operating bases, like Truk in the Carolines, to sustain the advance through the Japanese Mandates. In the early 1920s, Maj. Earl H. Ellis of the Marine Corps claimed for his service the mission of storming ashore to capture the required bases, drawing up tactics and estimates of the manpower needed for the seizure of such exotic

US Marine Corps Headgear, Small Arms and Rifle Grenades

1 Container for .30 caliber ammunition in eight round clips (left). Container for 600 rounds of .30 caliber ammunition for M1 carbine (right)
2 World War I style campaign hat
3 Model 1917 A1 steel helmet
4 Lightweight tropical helmet
5 Collapsible field hat
6 US rifle M1 Garand with M7 grenade launcher attachment on muzzle. The rifle grenade attached is spigot-launched. .30 caliber blank cartridges for launching grenade can be seen nearby
7 US carbine M1, .30 caliber, with grenade launcher attachment on muzzle. Open pack of grenade-launching blank cartridges can be seen nearby.
8 USMC personal flotation bladder. Inflatable, for amphibious landings.
9 Amber parachute flare
10 Spigot-launched rifle grenade Type M9A1. This type of grenade was used mainly for the delivery of smoke or burning phosphorous
11 Spigot-launched rifle grenade
12 Spigot-launched rifle grenade

Scott A. Duff, Richard Kos, William Thomas, William Ricca Collections

atolls as Eniwetok, Wotje, and Maleolap in the Marshalls. Possessing a brilliant imagination, though erratic in his behavior, "Pete" Ellis died before the techniques and equipment of amphibious warfare were perfected. In 1923, he perished on Koror in the Palaus, possibly from acute alcoholism, during a freelance reconnaissance of the Japanese Mandates. The circumstances of his death — he was traveling as a civilian in an area where Japan discouraged visitors — gave rise to the legend of Ellis the master spy, but at the time the islands had no defenses worth spying on.

The really important contributions to the development of amphibious warfare were being made by Ellis the planner, rather than Ellis the spy, and by the largely anonymous innovators who experimented with naval gunfire in support of a landing force and devised such prosaic things as combat loading, whereby the supplies an assault force needed first would be stowed nearest the hatches of the transports. The key equipment for seizing defended beaches came from engineers like Andrew Jackson Higgins, inventor of a landing craft that could beach itself and afterward withdraw to deep water, and Donald Roebling, grandson of the builder of the

Brooklyn Bridge (and greatgrandson of its architect), who invented a tractor for rescue work in the Florida Everglades that proved equally adept at clawing through surf and scrambling across coral reefs or sandy beaches. By the time that King set about reviving the centerpiece of the Orange Plan, the basic items of equipment for amphibious operations stood ready, the necessary manuals had been written, and the problems of supply and fire support had been addressed. In theory, marines could storm and seize a defended beach, but the theory remained untested in combat.

In May 1943, five months after the

The US grenade launching attachments could be used by the M1 Garand, M1 carbine and Model 1903 rifle — since all these weapons had the same .30 caliber. The rifle grenade is a concept that goes back almost as far as the rifle itself, and indeed a cup discharger device was developed by the British in the 1740s. The trench warfare of World War I brought the idea back into vogue: crudely put, a grenade could be sent further than a man could throw, if it were blown off the end of a rifle by means of a blank cartridge.

talks at Casablanca, the Anglo-American political and military leaders met at Washington to review the strategy for that year. At this conference, called Trident, the American Joint Chiefs of Staff urged an intensification of the war against Japan and the adoption of a target date for the invasion of France. Their British counterparts sought to follow up the conquest of North Africa with further operations in the Mediterranean area. The available resources in manpower and *materiel* (with the exception, as yet, of landing craft) enabled the Allies to establish a date of May 1, 1944, for the cross-channel invasion, to carry the war to Sicily and Italy, and to attack the Marshall Islands (en route to the Carolines), while at the same time continuing the two-pronged offensive against Rabaul.

The Marshalls group presented a challenging objective, consisting of 32 atolls and separate islands, arranged in two parallel chains that ran generally southeast to northwest over a distance of almost 300 nautical miles (555km). Facing an operation of this magnitude, the staff of Adm. Chester W. Nimitz, Commander in Chief, Pacific Ocean Areas, soon realized the wisdom of first attacking the Gilberts, a group of 16 islands and atolls southeast of the Marshalls. Since Japan had occupied the Gilberts in December 1941, these islands might not prove as formidable as the Marshalls, administered since World War I by the Japanese, who in 1940 had embarked on a program of fortification. However logical this reasoning, Tarawa Atoll in the Gilberts turned out to have some of the more powerful defenses encountered during the war in the Pacific. The availability of troops also influenced the choice of the Gilberts over the large atolls of the widely scattered Marshalls. A thrust into the Marshalls would require two battle-tested divisions, the planners believed, but only one was available: the 2d Marine Division, which had fought at Guadalcanal. Another possible choice, the 7th Infantry Division, faced its combat debut in the Aleutians and afterward might require rest and refurbishment before joining in the fighting in the Central Pacific Area. The 27th Infantry Division was readily available, but the unit had helped garrison the Hawaiian Islands and lacked the training or experience to undertake a bitterly contested amphibious landing.

The projected attack on the Gilberts would be the second American foray into those islands. In August 1942, a band of Marine raiders under Col. Evans F. Carlson had attacked Makin Atoll, landing from the submarines *Nautilus* and *Argonaut*. In a confused operation, Carlson's executive officer, Maj. James

Right: Photographed from the light carrier *Cowpens*, this is the *Astoria* class heavy cruiser *Minneapolis* refueling at sea during the operations around the Gilbert islands. Such far-flung operations emphasized the skill and reliability of the fleet train.

Roosevelt, a son of the president, almost drowned in a raging surf, 21 marines died in overcoming Japanese resistance, and nine were left behind when the raiders withdrew. The Japanese captured and executed the Americans who remained on the atoll.

Operation Galvanic, the expedition against the Gilberts scheduled for late 1943, would team inexperienced soldiers with combat-hardened marines, the green 27th Infantry Division with the tested 2d Marine Division, and the composition of the force caused Adm. Nimitz to reorganize his theater headquarters to include a number of Army officers in key staff assignments. He insisted, however, upon retaining command of operations in the Central Pacific Area, while continuing to serve as Commander in Chief, Pacific Ocean Areas,

Below: Marines parade on the hull of the submarine *Argonaut* on return to Pearl Harbor in August 1942. The marines had just completed a raid on Makin Island in the Gilberts group, securing valuable intelligence about Japanese strength.

which also embraced the North Pacific and South Pacific. Nimitz, moreover, commanded the Pacific Fleet, and he established a new component, the Fifth Fleet under Adm. Raymond A. Spruance, to invade the Gilberts and undertake subsequent operations in the mid-Pacific region. During the Gilberts campaign, Rear Adm. Charles A. Pownall assumed command of the carrier forces, and Rear Adm. John E. Hoover controlled the land-based aviation, which included squadrons of the Army Air Forces. As at Guadalcanal and New Georgia, Adm. Richmond Kelly Turner bore the responsibility for landing the assault troops, in this instance Marine Maj. Gen. Holland M. Smith's V Amphibious Corps. Holland Smith relied upon Maj. Gen. Julian C. Smith's 2d Marine Division, which would seize Tarawa Atoll, and Maj. Gen. Ralph Smith's 27th Infantry Division, the assault force for Makin Atoll. Turner himself led the task force bound for Makin, while Rear Adm. Harry W. Hill commanded the amphibious force destined for Tarawa.

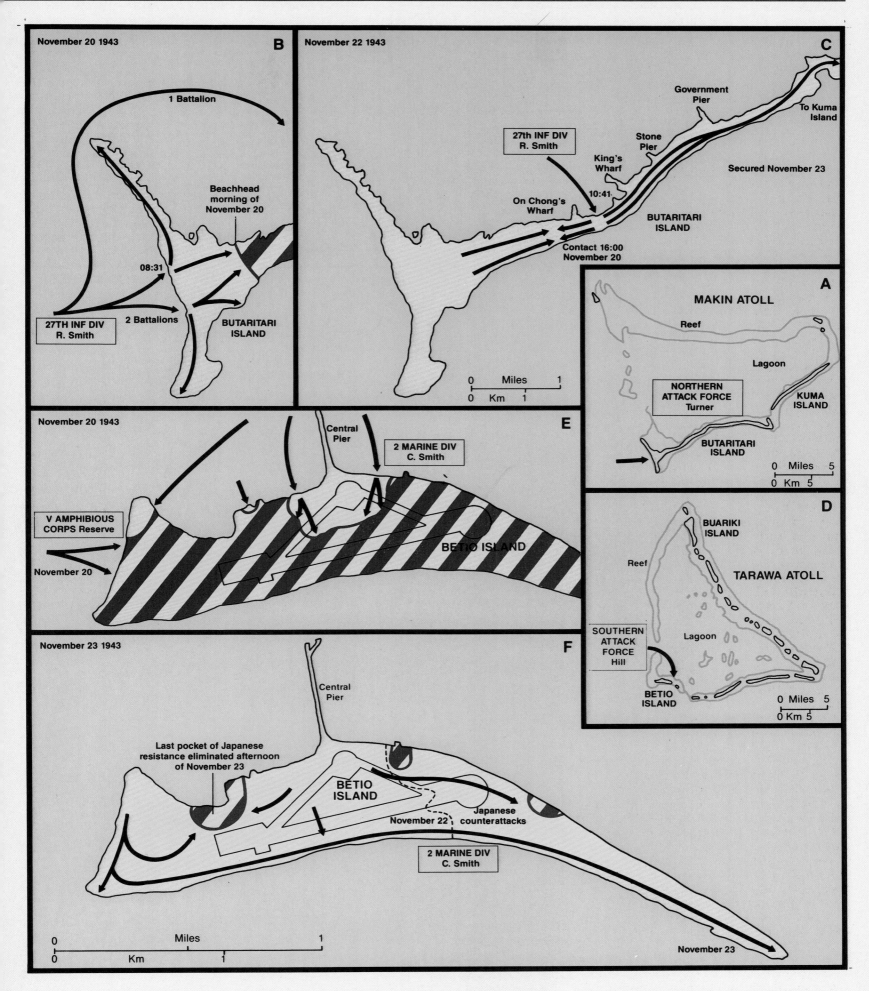

B — November 20 1943

1 Battalion

Beachhead morning of November 20

08:31

27TH INF DIV R. Smith

2 Battalions

BUTARITARI ISLAND

C — November 22 1943

Government Pier

To Kuma Island

Stone Pier

27th INF DIV R. Smith

King's Wharf

Secured November 23

10:41

On Chong's Wharf

BUTARITARI ISLAND

Contact 16:00 November 20

Miles 0 1
Km 0 1

A

MAKIN ATOLL

Reef

Lagoon

NORTHERN ATTACK FORCE Turner

KUMA ISLAND

BUTARITARI ISLAND

Miles 0 5
Km 0 5

E — November 20 1943

Central Pier

2 MARINE DIV C. Smith

V AMPHIBIOUS CORPS Reserve

November 20

BETIO ISLAND

D

BUARIKI ISLAND

Reef

TARAWA ATOLL

Lagoon

SOUTHERN ATTACK FORCE Hill

BETIO ISLAND

Miles 0 5
Km 0 5

F — November 23 1943

Central Pier

Last pocket of Japanese resistance eliminated afternoon of November 23

BETIO ISLAND

November 22

Japanese counterattacks

2 MARINE DIV C. Smith

November 23

Miles 0 1
Km 0 1

THE INVASIONS OF MAKIN AND TARAWA

Maps A, B and C
Butaritari Island was the main objective of the infantry division invading Makin Atoll. The initial naval bombardment left the defenders comparatively unharmed, and they emerged to man a defensive line across the island as the American forces moved ashore. It took three days to secure the island.

Maps D, E and F
Betio Island was the main objective of the marines at Tarawa Atoll. The landing force launched its attack from inside the lagoon. The majority became stuck on a reef at low tide and those who had reached the island had to fight hard to hold the beachhead against the defenders who were well dug-in. On the second day artillery and tanks were landed in numbers and began to reduce the Japanese strongpoints. The defenders were pushed back. A final *banzai* charge ended organised resistance.

US Edged Weapons

1 Model 1942 machete with 18-inch (45-cm) blade and canvas scabbard
2 US Marine Corps medical corpsman's knife, with brown leather scabbard
3 US Navy utility knife Mk 1, with issue leather scabbard
4 M3 trench knife with M8 olive drab plastic scabbard
5 US Navy and Marine Corps utility knife, Mk 2, with issue leather scabbard. Note the reduction in size from the Mk 1
6 M1941 Johnson spike bayonet and scabbard

7 M1905 E1 bayonet with M7 plastic scabbard. This bayonet is a shortened M1905, fitted with a World War II scabbard
8 M1905, but has a spear point rather than a knife point as 7. Items 7 and 8 are alterations to obsolete patterns
9 M1 bayonet as manufactured for use with the M1 Garand rifle
10 M1905 bayonet with M1910 scabbard, used with Model 1903 rifle
11 Model 1942 bayonet with issue scabbard, used with Model 1903 A3 rifle and M1 Garand rifle

Scott A. Duff

In the jungle wilderness in which so much of the Pacific War was fought, edged weapons took on an important role. The use of machetes to clear undergrowth became essential, and fighting knives were found to have important advantages as weapons. They were silent, needed little maintenance, and in the hands of a trained man could be used without a moment's hesitation. They could also be used as tools. The widespread use of edged weapons of this type can be discovered in the number of obsolete bayonets of World War I vintage that were adapted to World War II uses.

Such was the "wiring diagram," or organizational chart, which Turner and Hill short-circuited as soon as the fighting began. Rather than work through Holland Smith as corps commander, Hill dealt directly with Julian Smith and Turner with Ralph Smith. Turner did, however, make use of Col. William D. Eareckson of the Army Air Forces, whom he had selected as Support Aircraft Commander. Instead of relegating Eareckson to a purely advisory role, as he did Holland Smith, Turner put him in control of all aircraft, regardless of service, supporting operations at Makin and Tarawa.

In the plan for Operation Galvanic, the untested 27th Infantry Division received the easier assignment, the capture of Makin Atoll, defended by some 800 Japanese naval infantry, aviation personnel, and Korean laborers under Lt. (j. g.) Seizo Ishikawa. On November 20, 1943, amphibian tractors based on Roebling's invention landed the first wave of some 6,500 soldiers on Butaritari Island. The preliminary naval bombardment pinned down the defenders, but when the fires lifted, Ishikawa's garrison emerged from cover, manned a defensive line across the narrow island, and waited for the Americans to approach.

The advance proceeded slowly, for the terrain canalized movement and light tanks sank turret-deep in shell holes torn in the road. Sluggish after sedentary months of garrison duty, the troops of the 27th Infantry Division performed hesitantly at times, imposing severe demands on small-unit leaders like Sgt. Michael Thompson, who crawled close to a Japanese position, killed a machine gunner and four riflemen, and enabled his platoon to move forward. This kind of individual heroism proved necessary to restore momentum after sniper fire, for instance, had driven the Americans to cover. Despite the disparity in numbers — eight to one in favor of the assault force — not until the evening of November 23 could Gen. Ralph Smith announce: "Makin taken."

During the fight for Makin Atoll, the attacking soldiers suffered 218 casualties, 64 of them killed in action or dead of wounds, while only one of the Japanese naval infantry and 105 laborers survived to become prisoners. The US Navy lost 43 killed and 19 wounded when a turret exploded in the battleship *Mississippi*. Another 644 Navy men perished when the Japanese submarine *I-175* torpedoed and sank the escort carrier *Liscome Bay*, as it provided air support for Ralph Smith's troops.

At roughly the same time that elements of the 27th Infantry Division landed at Butaritari Island, the 2d Marine Division stormed the far more formidable beaches of Betio Island in Tarawa Atoll. The legend that heavy guns captured at Singapore defended Betio is untrue, but the Japanese had 51 artillery pieces of their own, varying from 37-mm field guns to 8-inch coast defense weapons, plus 35 heavy machine guns mounted singly or in pairs. Many of the larger weapons fired from protected emplacements that hugged the surface of the low-lying island. Rear Adm. Keiji Shibasaki's garrison of at least 3,000 naval infantry and 600 laborers had in a comparatively brief time turned Betio into a maze of strongly built bunkers dug into the coral and protected by log barriers and barbed wire. Although built primarily as shelters rather than firing positions, the bunkers provided both protection against all but the heaviest weapons and limited fields of fire.

A fringing reef enhanced the effectiveness of Shibasaki's defenses. This obstacle lay in the path of Julian Smith's marines as they approached the beaches of the narrow island, just 800 yards (731m) wide but 13,500 yards (12,344m) long. In late December, at high tide, the water over the reef would be deep enough to permit the passage of landing craft as well as amphibian tractors or amtracs (also called landing vehicles, tracked, or LVTs), but no one could be sure what the depth would be on November 20. To delay, however, would invite further discussion among the Combined Chiefs of Staff, a possible conflict with amphibious operations elsewhere, and perhaps cancellation. The assault on Betio had to go ahead as planned, even though F. L. G. Holland, an Australian familiar with Tarawa, predicted no more than three feet (0.9m) of water over the reef on November 20, a foot less than the boats needed. As a result, Julian Smith warned his subordinate commanders that those marines not in amphibian tractors could expect to wade hundreds of yards from the irregularly shaped reef to the assault beaches.

Adm. Hill's warships pounded Betio with 3,000 tons of shells in just two and one-half hours on the morning of D-Day,

Above: Launching the attack on Tarawa Atoll, Adm. Harry W. Hill and members of his staff watch the bombardment of Betio from the bridge of *Maryland*, while the battleship's own 16-inch guns pound the Japanese defenses just prior to the marines' assault.

but much of the bombardment consisted of flat trajectory fire delivered at close range, which tended to glance off the bunkers that hugged the island's surface. The shells, moreover, had instantaneous rather than delayed-action fuzes and exploded on contact before penetrating the log emplacements that protected the defenders. As a result, the shelling stunned the Japanese and killed some of them, but all too many survived and took advantage of the premature lifting of naval gunfire to open fire on the marines.

The amphibian tractors churning toward shore were scheduled to touch down at 9:00 A.M.; to avoid accidentally firing into the assault waves, Hill ceased firing at 8:55. The tractors, however, moved slower than planned and were 15 to 27 minutes from their assigned beaches when the ships' guns fell silent. Since concussion from the 16-inch guns of the battleship *Maryland,* which Hill had chosen as his flagship, knocked out his radios, he could not fine-tune the bombardment. Worse yet, the aircraft that were to conduct a last-minute strafing of the beaches arrived a few minutes later than planned, but too early entirely to bridge the gap that had opened between the cessation of naval gunfire and the arrival of the tractors on their assigned beaches.

The first marines to land that morning were members of the 2d Marines's scout-sniper platoon, commanded by 1st Lt. William D. Hawkins. They scrambled from a landing craft, rather than an amphibian tractor, at the end of a pier that extended from the shoreline,

beyond the reef, to deep water. Hawkins and his men used flamethrower to incinerate Japanese machine-gunners emplaced on the pier and thus eliminated a source of enfilade fire against the waves of tractors wallowing past en route toward the island.

Thanks to the scout-snipers and the lingering effect of the preparatory bombardment, three rifle battalions of the 2d Marines, commanded by Col. David M. Shoup, got ashore but moved only 100 yards (90m) inland before a log embankment stopped the amphibian tractors that were carrying them. Shoup's men worked their way inland, rolling over the logs and crawling forward, or running at a crouch when possible. As they located the dust of the muzzle blasts from concealed Japanese weapons, they pinpointed the strongpoints and destroyed them.

Behind the tractors came the landing craft, which fetched up on the reef, forcing the marines to climb out and wade, burdened by their equipment, through chest-deep water churned by Japanese bullets. A battalion of the 8th Marines plunged into the water some 700 yards (635m) from shore; an estimated 70 percent of the men in the first wave were killed or wounded, and in subsequent waves the casualties proved worse. Nevertheless, Julian Smith's marines kept coming, and by dusk perhaps 3,500 had dug in ashore, although they clung to a beachhead only 300 yards (270m) deep. On that bloody first day, 1,500 members of the assault force had been killed or wounded.

Events of the second day foretold the doom of the Japanese garrison. The 10th Marines — the division's artillery regiment — manhandled a battery of 75-mm pack howitzers into position behind an embankment thrown up by bulldozers and fired pointblank into Japanese bunkers. A few tanks also went into action; two of them, in conjunction with 5-inch gunfire from two destroyers in the lagoon, enabled Maj. Michael P. Ryan's 3d Battalion, 2d Marines, to clear the western end of Betio, providing a comparatively broad and secure beach for landing reinforcements and supplies. By mid-morning of November 21, Shoup could report, correctly, that ''. . . we are winning.'' After dark, Shibasaki acknowledged defeat, radioing: ''Our weapons have been destroyed and from now on everyone is attempting a final charge.''

Elements of the 6th and 8th Marines took over from Shroup's 2d Marines and advanced yard by yard, pushing the remaining Japanese into the narrowest part of the island, from which the survivors launched a suicide attack on the night of November 22 and the early morning of the 23d. After this *banzai* assault, the marines returned to the offensive, reaching the eastern tip of Betio after killing perhaps 4,500 defenders who resisted as long as they lived. Fewer than 150 surrendered, most of them Korean laborers. The 2d Marine Division lost almost 1,000 killed and more than 2,000 wounded in the conquest of Betio.

Besides seizing Makin and Tarawa, the Americans captured several lesser atolls in the Gilberts. Components of the 2d Marine Division landed at Abaiang, Maiana, and Marakei, but the Japanese occupied only Abaiang, which served as the outpost for a handful of coastwatchers. The reconnaissance company of V Amphibious Corps seized Apamama Atoll; the 23 Japanese stationed there were killed or committed suicide in this action, which completed Operation Galvanic.

Since the Gilberts would provide a stepping stone to the Marshalls, planning for the conquest of the Marshalls proceeded even as the marines prepared to wrest Tarawa from a determined enemy and the soldiers sought to capture Makin from its defenders. By the end of October, Nimitz realized that he could not attack the Marshalls by the tentative D-Day of January 1, 1944. The assault troops — the new organized 4th Marine Division and 22d Marines and the veteran 7th Infantry Division, which had fought in the Aleutians — would not

Below: A vital link in the command of an amphibious operation, of the type undertaken at Tarawa, was the ship-to-shore communication link. This is Pfc Merle Newberg USMC, who acted in this capacity on the *Maryland* until concussion from the ship's guns knocked out the antennas.

be ready until the end of that month, and the extra time could be used to repair ships and landing craft damaged in the Gilberts. Operation Flintlock, the campaign against the Marshalls, was rescheduled for January 31.

At first, American planners intended to hit three objectives simultaneously — Wotje and Maleolap Atolls on the eastern fringe of the group and Kwajalein Atoll at the center. The battle for Tarawa and the ongoing buildup of Japanese defenses in the Marshalls raised doubts about the wisdom of dividing the effort among three objectives. Of the three, Kwajalein seemed the most dangerous, for its capture required the penetration of waters dominated by Japanese aircraft based at Wotje, Maleolap, Jaluit, and Mille. Rear Adm. Forrest P. Sherman, a former aircraft carrier commander now serving on the staff of Adm. Nimitz, believed, however, that the new *Essex*-class fast carriers could neutralize enemy air power throughout the island group. Each of these warships, which displaced 27,100 tons, carried 80 or more aircraft, including the new Grumman F6F fighter, and mounted 40-mm antiaircraft guns in quadruple mounts, plus 12 5-inch dual-purpose weapons that could employ the new radar proximity fuze, which exploded when it came within killing range of an airplane. For the Marshalls fighting, Nimitz would have four of these new carriers, the prewar *Saratoga* and *Enterprise*, and four new 11,000-ton light carriers, built on cruisers' hulls, each of which carried 45 aircraft.

Spruance, Turner, and Holland Smith, the bloodshed at Betio freshly in mind, argued against an attack on Kwajalein. They conceded that amphibious forces could seize the atoll, but they worried that Japanese aircraft would prey upon the ships of the task force and the supply vessels, thus isolating the objective once it had been taken. Nimitz became convinced, however, that the fast carriers could do all that Sherman claimed. Kwajalein Atoll at the heart of the Marshalls would be the objective, and anyone who opposed the move should step aside and be replaced. Faced with this choice, the dissenters accepted the decision. Yet, as a concession to their concern about plunging so deeply into the Marshalls, Nimitz agreed to seize lightly-held Majuro Atoll in the eastern part of the group to obtain an anchorage that would bring the fleet a little closer to Kwajalein.

Although he agreed to participate, Spruance may still have had his doubts about Flintlock. In any event, he insisted that the fast carriers of Task Force 58, commanded by Vice Adm. Marc A. Mitscher, hammer the airfields in the Marshalls. In addition, Army bombers were attacking them from bases in the recently captured Gilberts.

Kwajalein Atoll, an irregular grouping of reef-girdled islands more than 500 nautical miles (926km) northwest of

Japanese Light Machine Guns

1 Type 99 (1939) light machine gun, caliber 7.7mm, with 30 round magazine in position
2 Type 96 (1936) light machine gun, caliber 6.5mm with 30 round magazine in position
3 Type 91 (1931) tank/vehicle machine gun. This weapon has a caliber of 6.5mm and features a unique hopper feed mechanism on its side. This enables the gun to utilize the standard five round rifle clip of ammunition. This type also featured a telescopic sight, which is missing
4 Type 91 (1931) tank/vehicle machine gun. This is a modified Type 11 featuring an ammunition feed hopper and a large 1.5x telescopic sight affixed to the top — an unusual feature which was quite common to Japanese light machine guns. This weapon includes an optional bipod, and is without its wooden stock
5 Light machine gun used for training purposes. The weapon is of 6.5mm caliber. In this example the top-loading magazine is not in place

US Army Ordnance Museum

Japanese light machine guns feature a number of interesting characteristics. These include the hopper feed system for ammunition and the use of a fixed telescopic sight. Weapons *1, 2,* and *5* also have lugs beneath the barrel for a bayonet attachment; an unusual Japanese approach to these weapons.

Tarawa, presented the next objective. Once again, Spruance commanded the Fifth Fleet, Turner the Joint Expeditionary Force, and Holland Smith the Expeditionary Troops, which consisted of Maj. Gen. Charles H. ''Cowboy Pete'' Corlett's 7th Infantry Division, the 4th Marine Division (Reinforced) under Maj. Gen. Harry Schmidt, and the Majuro Landing Force, built around Lt. Col. Frederick B. Sheldon's 2d Battalion, 106th Infantry, 27th Infantry Division. Turner commanded the attack force that would send Corlett's soldiers against Kwajalein Island at the southeastern corner of the atoll. Forty-four nautical miles

(81km) to the northwest, Rear Adm. Richard L. Conolly would land Schmidt's marines on Roi-Namur, twin islands connected by a causeway. Adm. Hill, who had landed the 2d Marine Division at Tarawa, commanded the expedition bound for Majuro.

On paper at least, Holland Smith now functioned as a corps commander, assuming responsibility for operations ashore from the time the assault troops established a beachhead until they secured the objective. During Flintlock, however, the expected duration of the fighting, perhaps four or five days at the most heavily defended objective, and

the distance involved left Corlett, Schmidt, and also Sheldon largely on their own. Nevertheless, the Kwajalein operation defined the role of the amphibious corps commander for future campaigns.

Of the three objectives included in Operation Flintlock, Majuro seemed the easiest. Chewing fiercely on his cigar, Holland Smith flatly declared that no more than a couple of rifle squads defended the atoll, an estimate that proved overly conservative. Actually, the Japanese withdrew from Majuro before Hill's ships arrived.

In contrast, perhaps 2,000 troops of

US MARINES, ASSAULT ON TARAWA ATOLL

The marine on the left wears the two piece combat fatigues of camouflage herringbone twill which was introduced in 1943, the man on the left wears a mixture of camouflage jacket and olive green trousers. Marines on Tarawa were armed mostly with M1 Garands (shown here on the right), and .30 caliber carbines; though the Browning Automatic Rifle (carried by the man on the left) and portable flamethrowers were also used.

various kinds, some 600 of them trained as infantry, and 1,000 laborers defended Roi-Namur, the site of the headquarters of Vice Adm. Michiyuki Yamada's 24th Air Flotilla, which controlled the naval air forces throughout the Marshalls. The Kwajalein Island garrison included 1,750 trained infantry, most of them soldiers rather than sailors; some 5,000 laborers were also available there or on nearby islets. Bunkers, heavy guns, and automatic weapons guarded the main objectives, but the defenses lacked depth and mobile reserves. The Japanese could be expected to fight to the last man.

Operation Flintlock served as the testing ground for new tactics and equipment devised as a result of the fighting in the Gilberts. On D-Day at Kwajalein and Roi-Namur, the soldiers and marines seized nearby islets, mere coral outcroppings, and set up field artillery to support the main landings and the subsequent fighting on the next day. Armored amphibian tractors, called LVT(A)s, took their places in the assault waves, firing 37-mm cannon as they thrashed toward shore, while landing craft, infantry, fitted out as gunboats, dubbed LCI(G)s, launched rockets in support of the landings. An amphibious truck, the Army-developed DUKW, helped haul supplies and ammunition for the 7th Infantry Division, a task that LVTs performed for the marines. These innovations reflected the hard lessons learned at Tarawa. The artillery, the LCI gunboats, and the cannon-carrying tractors could cover any last-minute gap in the preparatory bombardments, and reinforce the naval gunfire. The use of amphibious trucks and amphibian tractors to carry supplies would ensure a steady flow of cargo to the forces advancing inland and, when unloaded, provide a means of rapidly evacuating the wounded.

Despite confusion among the inexperienced amphibian tractor crews, whose navigational errors sometimes put artillerymen on the wrong islets, the guns were in position to cover both landings on D-Day plus 1 — February 1, 1944. At Kwajalein Island, the operation unfolded largely as planned. Two battleships steamed within 2,000 yards (1,800m) of shore to blast gaps in a wall that barred egress from the assault beaches, and the first waves started ashore on schedule. The 32d and 124th Infantry landed on the western beaches, at the bend of the hook-shaped objective, and began a systematic and successful four-day campaign. The soldiers killed all but a handful of the Japanese on the island at the cost of 173 killed and 793 wounded. In the meantime, the 4th Marine Division was overrunning the

Japanese defenders of Roi-Namur.

Unforeseen difficulties and accidents marred the Roi-Namur operation from the outset. Scarcely had Adm. Conolly's warships destroyed the known defensive batteries when word came that the landing ships tank (LSTs) were having difficulty lowering the amphibian tractors to the tank deck, from which they would drive through the open bow doors to the troop transports, the assembly areas, the line of departure, and finally the assigned beach. On one LST, the elevator jammed, and on the others, fitting the newer-model LVTs onto the elevator proved harder than expected. As a result of delays on board the LSTs, the assault waves formed behind schedule, and the landing had to be postponed from 10:00 A.M. to 11:00 and the climactic naval bombardment adjusted accordingly. Adm. Conolly issued the necessary

Above: The small area of Kwajalein did not permit sophisticated maneuvers, so the destruction of the Japanese garrison's complex of defensive bunkers was undertaken by artillery firing at pointblank range or, as here, by flamethrowers.

order and then received a report that the Japanese were counterattacking one of the offshore artillery positions. Even though aerial observers could not verify the report, Conolly had no choice but to divert aircraft, naval gunfire, and artillery fire to deal with the possible threat, which never materialized.

The last-minute false alarm caused no further delay, however. The landings on Roi and Namur took place one hour later than originally planned. The 23d Marines stormed ashore at Roi, encountered almost complete devastation, and, aided by tanks, advanced across the island by dusk, overcoming brave but

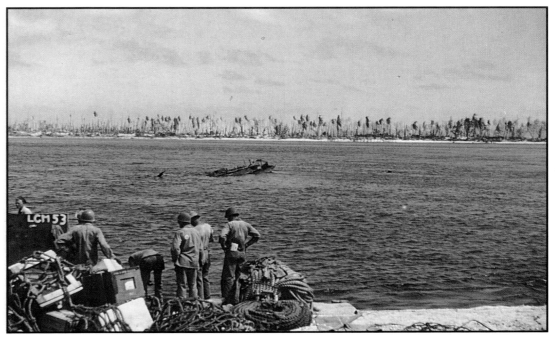

Right: This view from a causeway or large pier on Kwajalein in the Marshalls group in February 1944 reveals the devastation caused by the 7th Infantry Division's operation to capture the island. American losses had been small in proportion to the numbers employed.

disorganized resistance. The defenses of Namur proved stronger, but by early afternoon the advance of the 24th Marines was on schedule. Infantrymen of the regiment's 2d Battalion were attacking a massive concrete bunker when the Japanese defending the area scrambled from cover and fled. After a shaped charge had punched a hole in the wall of the structure, a marine hurled a satchel charge inside, and the entire building vanished in a cloud of flame and smoke. An officer standing on the beach saw "trunks of palm trees and chunks of concrete as large as packing crates . . . flying through the air." The bunker had contained warheads for aerial torpedoes; all that remained was a hole "as large as a fair-sized swimming pool." Despite the explosion, which killed 20 marines and wounded 100 others, the 24th Marines conquered Namur by mid-afternoon of February 2. The victory at Roi-Namur exacted a toll of 313 killed and 502 wounded from the assault forces. Of the defenders, fewer than 100 survived to become prisoners of war.

Having seized the Gilberts and Majuro and Kwajalein Atolls in the Marshalls, Nimitz and his principal commanders looked ahead to the next objective, the huge natural anchorage of Eniwetok Atoll in the western-most Marshall Islands. The logic of such a move seemed inescapable, even to the Japanese. "Will the enemy attack Eniwetok?" asked Norio Miyada, a non-commissioned officer stationed at the atoll. In his diary, he answered his own question: "He will attack this island after attacking Roi."

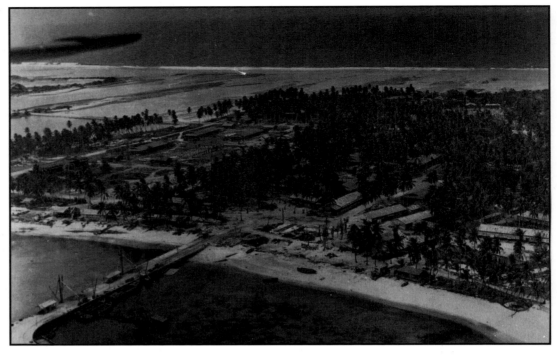

Below: As warships and supply vessels maneuver in the lagoon of Eniwetok atoll on February 18, 1944, American tanks move across the airstrip on Engebi toward the islet's northern tip, where the last Japanese defenders were positioned.

The Americans would come, but exactly when? Miyada expected a slow advance by what he called the "hackneyed method of island hopping."

For a time, Nimitz did plan to move slowly, attacking Eniwetok on May 1, but he soon realized that the Japanese were reinforcing the atoll. The longer the delay, the more savage the fighting. Mopping up continued at Kwajalein Atoll when Turner recommended an immediate attack on Eniwetok. Spruance agreed, and Nimitz approved the accelerated timetable. On February 15, the 106th Infantry of the 27th Infantry Division and the 22d Marines, assigned to V Amphibious Corps, would assault the atoll's three main islands — Eniwetok, Parry, and Engebi. Adm. Hill, the veteran of Tarawa and Majuro, commanded the expedition, and Marine Brig. Gen.

Above: Careful aerial reconnaissance of islands such as Namur generally revealed the damage inflicted by the pre-invasion bombardment, but often failed to spot the main Japanese defensive positions, which were well sited and cleverly camouflaged.

Thomas E. Watson served as troop commander.

The mimeograph machines had just finished turning out the plan for Operation Catchpole, the conquest of Eniwetok, when a major change had to be made. Nimitz postponed D-Day until February 17 so that the fast carriers could neutralize the major Japanese base at Truk, 670 nautical miles (1,241km) to the southwest of Eniwetok. In two days, February 17 and 18, Mitscher's carriers battered Truk, shooting down two-thirds of the defending fighters and putting the airfields out of action, at least temporarily. The American airmen found no major units of the Japanese navy in the harbor but sank some lesser warships and an estimated 200,000 tons of merchant shipping. Never again would the Imperial Japanese Navy attempt to use Truk as a major base.

On February 17, the first day of the strikes against Truk, Hill's expedition steamed through the broad entrance to Eniwetok lagoon to seize the lesser islands needed as artillery positions to support the next day's assault on Engebi, the first major objective. Two battalions of the 22d Marines landed behind a naval bombardment supplemented by the fire of LCI(G)s and began fighting their way through a tangle of spider holes — foxholes covered by woven mats or pieces of driftwood — connected by tunnels to central bunkers. To locate the troublesome spider holes, marines threw smoke grenades into the bunkers and watched for fumes to rise from the camouflaged positions.

Parry and Eniwetok Islands promised even harder going. Documents captured at Engebi revealed that 300 troops

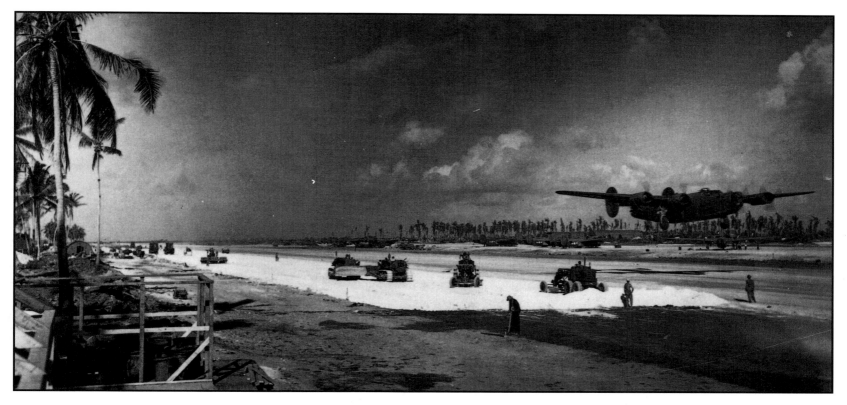

defended Parry and twice that number Eniwetok, more than American intelligence had predicted. Consequently, Hill decided to mass his forces against Eniwetok before seizing Parry. Two battalions of the 106th Infantry landed at Eniwetok on February 19 but soon became bogged down amid the same sort of defenses the marines had encountered on Engebi. Col. Russell A. Ayers, commander of the 106th Infantry, committed his reserve, the 3d Battalion,

Below: Though the fighting for Eniwetok lasted only a short time, it was still a typically hard-fought battle. Downing cups of coffee after returning to their assault transport, these marines had been involved in two days and nights of intense combat.

22d Marines, at mid-day, sending one Army battalion toward the narrow end of the island, while the other advanced in the opposite direction alongside the marines. What should have been a comparatively straightforward operation became complicated when Ayers ordered a night attack with the Marine and Army battalions advancing abreast. Since they would be without the support of tanks, the marines stood fast, but the soldiers pushed ahead, inadvertently bypassing many Japanese whose emplacements could not be seen by the uncertain light of flares. On the following morning, the enemy emerged from concealment, crossed the line between the battalions, and attacked the Marine

Above: As soon as Eniwetok was in American hands, the engineers of the "Seabees" moved in to create a crushed coral airstrip that allowed long-range aircraft such as this Consolidated B-24 Liberator to move straight into residence.

command post. This proved to be the last concerted action in the fight.

On February 22, the 22d Marines attacked Parry. Resistance proved savage, but Marine medium tanks came ashore just in time to destroy three Japanese light tanks leading a counterattack against the beachhead. At the height of this fight, a misdirected salvo from one of the supporting warships exploded amid the combatants, knocking out two Marine tanks but inflicting severe casualties among the Japanese infantry. Within two days, the fighting ended. During Catchpole, Marine units suffered 254 killed and 555 wounded; the 106th Infantry lost 94 killed and 311 wounded. Only 66 of the Japanese defenders of Eniwetok Atoll remained alive.

The campaigns in the Gilberts and Marshalls demonstrated that trained Army or Marine Corps divisions, supported by naval gunfire and air strikes, could seize a defended island. American amphibious forces tested their tactics and equipment in the Gilberts, corrected the most glaring deficiencies, and in less than a month, January 31 to February 24, vaulted the Marshall Islands to within 1,000 nautical miles (1,800km) of the Marianas. Majuro, though overshadowed by the vast lagoon at Ulithi, which was occupied later in the year, provided a valuable advanced anchorage for the Pacific Fleet. Moreover, the fast carriers and their Grumman F6F Hellcat fighters proved superior to land-based Japanese air power. In neutralizing Truk, Mitscher's Task Force 58 removed a major threat to the advance to the Marianas.

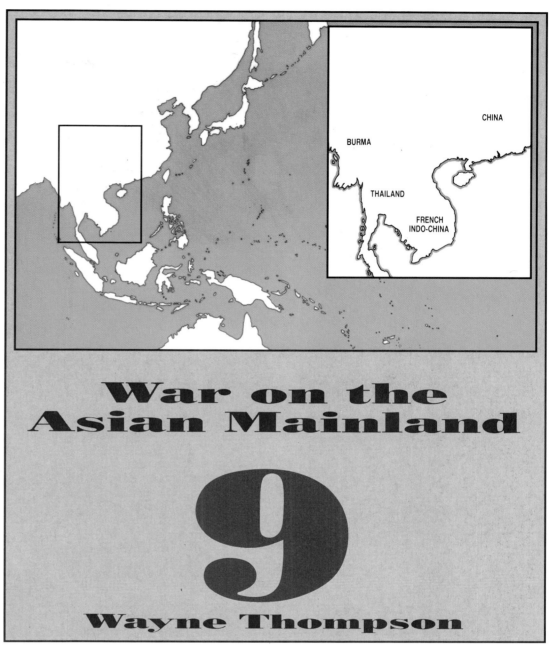

War on the Asian Mainland

9

Wayne Thompson

At the end of 1943 Chiang Kai-shek at last gave his American military adviser, Lt. Gen. "Vinegar Joe" Stilwell, unfettered command of a pair of Chinese divisions. "Put down December 18, 1943 as the day," Stilwell crowed, "when for the first time in history, a foreigner was given command of Chinese troops with full control over all officers and no strings attached." He was eager to clear the Japanese out of northern Burma and put through a new road from Ledo, India, southeast to intersect with the Burma Road from China. He hoped that the success of his Chinese troops might encourage Chiang to send a dozen divisions from China southwest down the Burma Road to join the force pushing southeast from India and open a ground route for American supplies.

To break through Chiang's unwillingness to commit forces to battle, Stilwell had created a Chinese force in India where it could be of no other use to Chiang. A remnant of the Chinese army which had been driven out of Burma into India with Stilwell in 1942 formed the nucleus of the two divisions Stilwell had equipped and trained at Ramgarh in

central India. The rest were brought to Ramgarh in transport planes which otherwise would have returned empty from China. Since these planes were China's only link to the outside world, they were filled on the India-China flight with supplies deemed more precious than the Ramgarh force. Chiang would only retrieve those troops if they fought their way across Burma.

Stilwell's personal Christmas carol of 1943 was "jungle bells, jungle bells, jungle all the way." He was glad to have any excuse to get out of the Chinese capital at Chungking (Chongqing), were he was offended daily by the obvious corruption and reluctance to fight the Japanese. Chiang presided over rather than controlled the warlords who ruled the regions of southern and western China not yet conquered by the Japanese. American aid more often enriched the Chinese hierarchy than supplied Chinese troops. There were some well-equipped divisions directly under Chiang's control, but these he hoarded for the inevitable civil war with the communist forces of Mao Tse-tung (Mao Zedong). Although this practice

Commonwealth Personal Equipment

1 Map case, large
2 Map case, small, two types
3 Pattern 1937 large pack
4 Mess tin
5 Wire cutters
6 Communications bag or valise
7 Ankle boots
8 Large wire cutters
9 Battle lantern/flashlight
10 Pattern 1937 web gaiters
11 Issue combat socks
12 Shell dressing/first aid bandage
13 Pattern 1937 webbing harness, consisting of belt, braces and two universal pouches for ammunition
14 Pattern 1942 canvas battle jerkin, for additional equipment carriage
15 Pattern 1943 light respirator satchel
16 Small personal haversack
17 Mk 1 steel helmet
18 Pattern 1937 webbing harness, with universal pouch (left) and pistol ammunition pouches (right)
19 Pattern 1942 entrenching tool
20 Personal sewing kit
21 Gas mask with case
22 Cloth covered canteen

Allan Cors: 1, 6-8, 13, 14; Pritchard Collection: 2-5, 9-12, 15-22

Most of this personal web equipment is the British standard pattern introduced in 1937. Among the more unusual items here is the canvas battle jerkin *14*. This was introduced in 1942 primarily for use in amphibious landings by commandos. The light-weight canvas was meant to be easily jettisonable in water. The gas respirator in case *21* was an item rarely seen towards the end of the war. It consisted of a tin canister holding the air filter, a rubber hose long enough to allow some movement, and a rubber face mask.

infuriated Stilwell, Chiang was right to think that he could count on the Americans to defeat the Japanese and that his more deadly enemy was Mao.

Mao made much better use of the war with Japan, for though he too was hoarding his forces, he was doing more than just that. After the disastrous Hundred Regiments Campaign of 1940, communist forces avoided pitched battle and reverted to harassing the Japanese. In this way the communists could play the leading role in fighting the Japanese without suffering severe losses. The techniques of peasant insurgency (which Mao had developed before the war) enabled the communists to organize guerrilla forces behind Japanese lines. Peasant hostility to the Japanese was transformed into allegiance to communist guerrilla leaders. While Chiang was conserving his forces for civil war, Mao was already quietly waging it.

Even had Chiang's bureaucracy been more honest and more competent, it is doubtful that it could have withstood the combined assault of Japanese invasion and communist insurgency. Having lost China's trade and industry to the Japanese, there was no real economic base for a military establishment exceeding 5,000,000 troops. Chungking could only print more currency, with the consequence that inflation ran wild. Yet despite inflation and corruption, China made a major contribution to the defeat of Japan. The great land mass of China simply proved too big for the relatively small islands of Japan to swallow while fighting off American offensives in the Pacific.

Throughout the war with the United States, Japan had to keep more than 1,000,000 soldiers in China. Many who got their initial combat experience there were pulled out to fight in the Pacific, but greener troops from Japan were sent to take their place. In Japan's fantasy of empire, the Chinese and other conquered peoples were expected to embrace their conquerors as allies against the white race; puppet governments and puppet armies would administer the Greater East Asia Co-Prosperity Sphere cheaply — or rather, profitably — just as the British had long ruled India with an army of Indians.

Even in China it did prove fairly easy for the Japanese to find collaborators who would form a puppet government. In Burma (Myanmar) the nationalist movement readily embraced the Japanese as a way to throw out the British. The Burmese nationalist student leader Aung San had been arrested by the Japanese in China, where he had gone seeking the help of Chinese communists. But in exchange for his release he agreed to collaborate with the Japanese. They sent him to Hainan Island, where he and his Thirty Comrades were trained in guerrilla warfare. The Thirty Comrades included Ne Win, who would rise to power after the war and Aung San's assassination. Their collaboration led to the establishment of an "independent" Burma in the summer of 1943 with the older, more pliable Ba Maw as president and Aung San as minister of defense.

At the same time the Japanese established an Indian National Army composed of some 40,000 Indian prisoners held in Burma. An Indian nationalist leader, Subhas Chandra Bose, took command of this force which was expected to inspire the independence movement in India to join forces with the Japanese to overthrow the British. This development might have frightened the British a year earlier, when an Indian civil disobedience campaign had led to imprisonment of Mohandas Gandhi and rioting in Calcutta. By the summer of 1943, however, the British were more confident that they could combat a Japanese invasion of India without worrying about their empire immediately disintegrating behind them.

At the beginning of 1944, when Stilwell was leading his two Chinese divisions from India into northern Burma, he hoped that at long last not only the Chinese but also the British might be ready to take the offensive in Burma. It was a notable feature of the situation that the senior general most eager to fight was the one whose government had failed to provide him with substantial ground forces. As Stilwell described his predicament, he and "Peanut" (his nickname for Chiang) were "on a raft with one sandwich between us, and the rescue ship heading away from the scene." Stilwell could only attack when Chiang provided troops. This fact combined with Stilwell's obvious contempt for most Chinese and British leaders considerably reduced his influence on them.

In Burma, Stilwell was supposed to be subordinate to the Supreme Allied Commander of South East Asia Command

Above: Seen with Generalissimo and Madame Chiang Kai-shek in April 1942, Lt. Gen. Joseph "Vinegar Joe" Stilwell was the Chinese leader's chief of staff and the most important figure in improving the combat efficiency of the Chinese army. The relationship between Stilwell and the Nationalist Chinese leader was never an easy one, however, and a split finally came during the Japanese offensive of 1944, when Chiang ordered Stilwell and his New Chinese Army to abandon their Burma campaign and come to his aid.

(SEAC), Adm. Lord Louis Mountbatten, whom Stilwell called "The Glamour Boy." This handsome, great-grandson of Queen Victoria had parted ways with Stilwell over the importance of retaking Burma sooner rather than later. Mountbatten shared Churchill's view that Singapore was more important and that an amphibious operation against Sumatra would lead to an early return to Singapore. Since sufficient resources were not yet available for a Sumatra campaign, Mountbatten tried to persuade Churchill, Roosevelt, and Chiang at the Cairo Conference in November 1943 to go along with an amphibious operation against the Andaman Islands off the Burma coast. Although Chiang wanted the British to undertake an amphibious operation against Burma itself, the Chinese leader could not see much point in the Andaman operation. Nor could Roosevelt, but the American president talked Chiang into accepting it as part of a bargain by which the British would seize the island, so that Chiang could send his Yunnan divisions across the Salween River and down the Burma Road.

This bargain promptly collapsed when landing craft had to be withdrawn for the invasion of France. Indeed the associated Cairo and Teheran conferences did much to wean Roosevelt from his enthusiasm for Chiang. Roosevelt had hoped to establish Chiang as leader of one of the four great powers which would dominate the postwar world. But Stalin and Churchill were having none of it. Stalin insisted on the parallel conference at Teheran to exclude Chiang,

Right: A bomb train moves toward a B-24 bomber of the British Strategic Air Force within the Allied Eastern Air Command. This force undertook much of the strategic bombing effort in southeast Asia against targets mainly in Burma and Malaya.

who had been present at Cairo, and Chiang's status was further undercut by Stalin's promise to enter the war against Japan after the defeat of Germany. Under these circumstances no one should have been surprised that Chiang seemed uncooperative, for the ground was being cut from under his feet.

After Cairo, Stilwell could not be sure what the Chinese and British were going to do with their ground forces. The prognosis for air forces was more certain, at least with respect to the strength employed. Against a shrinking Japanese air force of fewer than 200 aircraft in Burma, nearly 600 British and American fighters were already engaged in operations there together with 150 bombers under an American commander, Maj. Gen. George E. Stratemeyer. This force would double by the end of 1944, while the Japanese in Burma continued to lose

THE WAR IN BURMA,
OCTOBER 1943 — FEBRUARY 1945

Map A
In 1943, the Japanese had control of northern and central Burma, cutting off Nationalist Chinese forces and Maj. Gen. Chennault's aircraft from their source of supplies which came from ports in India. To circumvent this, an airlift was begun in late 1942 from Ledo in Assam, 500 miles (800km) across the Himalayas. This became known as the "Hump" route.

Map B and C
The first Allied offensive actions in Burma met with mixed success. The Arakan campaign of December 1942 was turned back, but the first Chindit expedition of February-March 1943 was reckoned a success: infiltrating themselves behind enemy lines and cutting the Mandalay-Myitkyina railway (Map C). The next Allied offensive in January 1944 (Map B) came in northern and western Burma. In the north, Merrill's Marauders led an attack with the Chinese towards Myitkyina, while the Chindits operated in strength behind the Japanese lines. To the west, the XV Corps attacked towards Akyab. In March, however, the Japanese launched counteroffensives in Arakan and towards Imphal and Kohima. In Arakan they were held by XV Corps and thrown back, while Imphal and Kohima were reached but not taken. Facing stiffening resistance, heavy casualties and the monsoon, the Japanese began to withdraw in July 1944.

Map D
The Allies now went on to the offensive across Burma. Fighting through the monsoon, the Fourteenth Army pushed on towards Mandalay, supplied through Akyab. The capture of Mandalay was planned by Slim as a vast pincer movement. The IV Corps would cross the Irrawaddy downstream and in an armored thrust capture Meiktila, thus cutting off the Japanese line of retreat, while the XXXIII Corps attacked Mandalay itself. The plan worked brilliantly and Mandalay fell on March 29, 1945.

Commonwealth Sniper Equipment

1 Camouflaged Denison smock with hood
2 Camouflage face veil
3 Ordnance storage and carrying chest for rifle No.4, Mk 1 (T) sniper rifle and accoutrements
4 Rifle No.4, Mk 1 (T) sniper rifle, with No.32 telescopic sight, leather carrying sling and five round clip of .303 caliber ammunition
5 Mk 1 steel helmet with netting for camouflage
6 Scout telescope, leather-covered with a brass body. This type of telescope was issued to snipers and observer teams
7 Leather carrying case with shoulder strap for scout telescope
8 Black leather, hob-nailed ankle combat boots; black pebble finish
9 Camouflage trousers worn with Denison smock
10 Metal case and leather lens caps for No.32 telescopic sight. The case is carried in the rifle's storage chest
11 Pattern 1937 binocular case
12 Pattern 1937 web gaiters
13 Issue combat socks with reinforced heel and toe and padded sole

*Allan Cors: 1, 3, 4, 6-10;
R.A. Pritchard: 2, 5, 11-13*

The No.4 Mk 1 (T) rifle (4), was specially designed for the sniping role. The No.32 telescopic sight was specifically designed for use with this rifle. Among the rifle's special features is a cheek piece on the top of the stock and a leather carrying strap instead of the standard web sling. Care and maintenance instructions concerning this specialist equipment can be seen pasted to the lid of the carrying case (3). The Denison smock (1), and camouflage veil (2), are pieces of uniform usually associated with airborne troops, for whom they were developed after 1941. The camouflaged and showerproof Denison was a large pullover over-jacket worn over the battledress and under the web equipment. It fastened with a zip running from throat to chest. The jacket was usually also lined for warmth.

aircraft not only to Allied attack but also to meet the needs of Japanese units in the Pacific. Stratemeyer's Eastern Air Command protected its own bases in India, escorted cargo aircraft flying between India and China, and pounded Japanese lines of communication in burma and Thailand. Heavy bombers struck Rangoon's docks and rail yards repeatedly; as in raids against Germany, Royal Air Force heavy bombers operated at night while the Army Air Forces operated during the day.

Less satisfactory had been medium bomber raids against bridges, several of which proved remarkably durable. Bom-

bing accuracy against bridges did begin to improve by chance on January 1, 1944, when an American B-25 dropped its bombs while pulling up to avoid a tree and lofted them so that they were falling almost perpendicular when they hit. That bridge went down, and the new technique was used later to good effect against other bridges. But the Japanese were able to keep their rail lines open much of the time and with forced labor even build a new line connecting Bangkok and Rangoon. Tens of thousands of brutally treated Malayans, Chinese, Burmese, Indians, Australians, British, and others died building the Thailand-

Above: A mule train of the 5307th Composite Unit, generally known as "Merrill's Marauders" after its first commander. This unit operated in northern Burma alongside Chinese formations as part of Stilwell's Northern Combat Area Command.

Burma railroad. As the postwar novel and motion picture *Bridge on the River Kwai* would emphasize, erecting bridges absorbed much of this deadly effort. Yet on a single day in 1945, American B-24s (heavy bombers with more range than medium B-25s) would claim destruction of 30 bridges built over many months at the cost of so many lives.

Although the American contribution to the Burma campaign was principally air power, Stilwell's Chinese divisions were accompanied in early 1944 by 3,000 American troops — the first American ground combat unit in the China-Burma-India theater. The Americans were volunteers from other units, many with experience fighting the Japanese in the Pacific. Their commander was Brig. Gen. Frank D. Merrill, and they became famous as Merrill's Marauders. Their job was to provide Stilwell with a long range penetration group comparable to Maj. Gen. Orde Wingate's 77th Indian Infantry Brigade, the "Chindits," composed of Gurkha, Burmese, Indian, and British troops.

The Chindits caught Roosevelt's attention in 1943 when they operated for six weeks behind Japanese lines in Burma. While Stilwell was pleased to get American soldiers, he was dismayed to learn that they would be commanded by Wingate, whose unusual fervor to fight seemed to entail not a little arrogance and fanaticism. Stilwell did manage to wrest Merrill's Marauders from Wingate, and in any case Wingate's effort in 1944 supported Stilwell's offensive.

Wingate had learned from losing a third of his force in 1943 that he would need a lot of air transport, and he had persuaded Gen. Arnold of the US Army Air Forces to provide him with an air commando group of transports, gliders, fighters, and light bombers. Here was the model of the American air commandos who were to return to Southeast Asia during the Vietnam War. They were romanticized from the beginning by the cartoonist Milton Caniff in his strip "Terry and the Pirates," whose hero Flip

Corkin was drawn from the actual commander, Col. Phil Cochran.

Cochran's air commandos were the most famous part of a much larger airlift effort which made possible the success of all the allied campaigns in Burma's jungles during 1944 and 1945. Never had ground campaigns depended so completely on air transport. In Stilwell's case, Wingate and Cochran placed a force of 14,000 men 250 miles (400km) behind Japanese lines (athwart the rail link to Rangoon), while Merrill's Marauders made short penetrations around the Japanese flanks and the Chinese pushed southeast toward the Burma Road. It was an effective combination even after Wingate was killed in a plane crash in late March, and Merrill had to be evacuated following a heart attack. The rapidity of Stilwell's advance was facilitated by the decision of the Japanese to gather 100,000 of their

250,000 troops in Burma for an offensive into India southwest of Stilwell's operation.

In March 1944, the three divisions of Lt. Gen. Renya Mutaguchi's Fifteenth Army together with Burmese and Indian troops (including a full division of the Indian National Army) moved across the Chindwin River toward the plain of Imphal, a ten-mile-wide breach eroded by the Manipur River in the mountains separating India and Burma. It was to prove a fatal error; Mutaguchi would lose at least half his force in the decisive battles of the war for Burma. The British commander at Imphal, Lt. Gen. William J. Slim, had been hoping for a Japanese offensive there and planned to defeat it with three Indian divisions in place and two others which could be brought north from coastal Arakan where they had just helped defeat a Japanese offensive intended to pin them down. Before long he would also require a British division and an East African one.

One of the principal advantages of Slim's Fourteenth Army was the commander himself. Slim had a rare ability to assess his mistakes coolly in time to take corrective action. In this ability he judged himself superior to the Japanese generals he encountered. Like Stilwell, Slim had tasted the bitterness of defeat in 1942 and was eager to transform his British and Indian divisions into a victorious army. His own account of converting *Defeat into Victory* remains the best book on the Burma campaign, for his balanced judgments stride forth clothed in fine prose.

So competent and likable was "Uncle Bill" Slim that even Stilwell approved of him and agreed to serve under him in Burma. This arrangement was all the more extrordinary because Stilwell outranked Slim in the hierarchy of South East Asia Command. They saw in each other someone who knew much about Asia and much about war. Both had memories of World War I — Stilwell of St Mihiel and Slim of Gallipoli. Although Slim had spent more years in India than

Left: An A-2 flying jacket worn by Tech. Sgt. R. C. Vandurberry, 5th Air Force. Below: A-2 jacket with the image of "Dragon Lady" from the comic strip "Terry and the Pirates." *War Memorial Museum of Virginia.*

Above: Lt. Gen. Sir William Slim was one of the ablest British commanders of World War II, and despite his command's low priority in men, equipment and supplies, he turned the Fourteenth Army into a capable, indeed formidable, fighting machine.

Stilwell had in China, Slim always felt a little uncomfortable in the jungle. He preferred the deserts of the Middle East where he had fought in both world wars. "The desert suits the British," he wrote, "and so does fighting in it. You can see your man." On one occasion during World War I, he so well marked the position of a Turk he had shot in Iraq that after the battle he could return to help his victim.

But calm, flexibility and compassion do not guarantee victory, and Slim was thankful to the Japanese in Burma for making errors more consequential than his own. While he was still gathering his reinforcements, the Japanese could have taken the railhead at Dimapur and cut the ground supply route not only for Slim's force but for Stilwell's too. Indeed the airlift to China also depended on the railroad running north from Calcutta through Dimapur to Ledo. Slim would later admit that Dimapur would have fallen easily to the Japanese division which instead laid siege to the Indian Army post at Kohima on a ridge over which passed the road connecting the railhead and the plain of Imphal.

Japanese preoccupation with Kohima's 3,000 British, Indian, and Gurkha defenders permitted a British division to reinforce Dimapur and reach Kohima before the end of April. But Japanese forces continued to hold the Kohima-Imphal road and surround the plain through May, when the summer monsoon turned their ground supply routes to mud and Mutaguchi was losing even more men to hunger and malaria than to Slim's firepower. Meanwhile, aircraft had steadily reinforced and continually supplied the defenders of Imphal. Occasional Japanese air strikes on the Imphal airfields could not stem the flow, and the Japanese lacked a comparably large fleet of cargo aircraft. In any case the Japanese had already lost the battle for control of the air over Burma, and Japanese cargo aircraft could no longer survive there.

Mutaguchi had hoped for a quick victory at Imphal which would leave him in possession of captured British supplies. His Indian troops were also expected to confuse and subvert the defending Indian troops. Instead the leader of Japan's Indian force, Subhas Chandra Bose, quarreled with Japanese generals about proper conduct of the campaign, and his Indian division made only a token contribution. Mutaguchi fired all of his Japanese division commanders, but he and his boss in Rangoon, Lt. Gen. Masakazu Kawabe, were also quickly removed.

After the Japanese withdrew into Burma in June 1944, Slim waited for drier weather to pursue them. Early in 1945 he would show them how to cut an enemy's line of communication. While the Japanese sought to stop his frontal attack across the wide Irrawaddy River at Mandalay, Slim sent an armored force a hundred miles (160km) down the river to Pagan, where the tanks were ferried across and then raced east to cut the railroad from Rangoon at Meiktila. By then the Japanese had already been cleared from northern Burma and a road was open from Ledo, India, to China.

Stilwell's north Burma offensive had bogged down around Myitkyina in the summer of 1944, and although Chiang had finally permitted 70,000 of his troops in Yunnan to attack the Japanese on the Burma Road, not until January 1945 did the two Chinese forces converge. Nevertheless, taking the Myitkyina airfield in May 1944 proved more important than the subsequent effort to open a road to China. Since the Japanese could no longer fly from Myitkyina, American cargo aircraft could take a more southern route avoiding the higher mountains to the north and consequently lifting a heavier load at lower altitude on a more direct route to China. This change, together with the introduction of larger C-54 transports, permitted the Army Air Forces to create an air transportation system which would carry more than twice the monthly tonnage carried by the Ledo-Burma road and oil pipeline. If the weight of trucks is subtracted from the road's contribution, the airlift was moving supplies at a rate five times greater. In July 1945 alone, more than 500 cargo planes of the Air Transport Command's India-China Division took more than 70,000 tons of supplies to China.

By 1945 the China airlift had come a long way from its fragile beginning. When the Japanese closed the Burma Road in the spring of 1942, the American

Above: A Browning .50 caliber water-cooled antiaircraft machine gun, with sight and ammunition hopper. Right: the same type of weapon being used behind Japanese lines in Burma by men of Orde Wingate's Chindits. *War Memorial Museum of Virginia.*

effort to replace the road with airlift had taken more than half a year to reach the ridiculously inadequate rate of 1,000 tons per month. The requirements for an effective airlift included not only sufficient aircraft, spare parts, and aircrews, but also airfields in India (as well as China) and an improved rail link between the Indian airfields and Calcutta's docks. So long as the cargo planes had to fly above 18,000 feet (5,400m) to clear the "Hump" of the eastern Himalayas, four-engine C-54s could not be used, and should a two-engine C-46 lose an engine enroute, its crew was rarely seen again.

In early 1943, with the airlift still providing less than 3,000 tons a month, Chiang Kai-shek insisted that it reach 10,000 tons a month before he would authorize Stilwell to take any action in Burma. Not that Stilwell would be permitted to allocate much of the airlifted supplies to Chinese ground forces — Chiang wanted most of those supplies for his American air force under the command of Maj. Gen. Claire Chennault,

BRISTOL BEAUFIGHTER

For many people, the de Havilland Mosquito was the twin-engined fighter of World War II; but the Japanese had a greater fear of another British "twin," namely the Bristol Beaufighter. Robust, fast and, most important of all, heavily armed, it made its presence felt early on with a daring attack on a ceremony to celebrate the emperor's birthday. As more and more low-level attacks were carried out with devastating results, the Japanese signalled their awe — and fear — of the big fighter by dubbing it "Whispering Death." As the war dragged on, more and more successes were achieved as the Beaufighter continued its valuable contribution to the eventual Allied victory.

who promised to win the war with air power.

Chennault's relationship with Chiang was everything Stilwell's was not. By focusing on air power, Chiang could keep his ground forces intact for the coming struggle with the communists. Impatient with this policy, Stilwell had made little effort to conceal his contempt for Chiang. Chennault, on the other hand, was grateful to Chiang not only for supporting air power, but also for rescuing him from a dead-end career in the Army Air Corps.

When he retired from the Army in 1937 to become Chiang's air adviser, Chennault was a 43-year-old captain whose strong advocacy of the ability of fighter aircraft to stop bombers had made him unpopular with Air Corps leaders. Nevertheless he was himself also an advocate of bombers, and it was his hope to attack Japan from China with American B-17s. Before the Marco Polo Bridge incident of July 1937, Chennault had toured Japan looking for potential targets. But when he went to Washington

Commonwealth Crew Served Weapons, and Sub-Machine Guns

1 British Bren Mk 1 light machine gun .303 caliber; magazine-fed and gas operated
2 Pattern 1937 Bren ammunition pack
3 British PIAT (Projector, Infantry, Anti-Tank), with its 2.5lb bomb in position
4 PIAT training projectiles
5 Boys antitank rifle Mk 1, .55 caliber with box magazine detached
6 Pattern 1937 web equipment with ammunition pouches
7 British Sten Mk III, 9mm sub-machine gun with 32 round magazine in place
8 British muzzle-loading 2-inch mortar with shell

9 Pattern 1937 Sten gun magazine pouch with loading tool
10 Australian Austen Mk 1 9mm sub-machine gun with silencer, canvas hand-guard and breech cover
11 British Sten Mk IIS sub-machine gun with silencer, canvas hand-guard and breech cover
12 British Lanchester sub-machine gun Mk1
13 50-round magazine for 12
14 British Sten Mk V with No.4 bayonet fixed
15 Scabbard and frog for No. 4 bayonet
16 Waterproof sleeve for 14
17 British Sten Mk VI

US Army Ordnance Museum:
1, 5, 7, 8, 10-12, 17; Allan Cors
Collection: 2-4, 6, 9, 13-16

The Bren gun (*1*), was the basic infantry support weapon for Commonwealth forces, and was introduced into the British Army in 1938 to replace the Lewis gun. It derived its name from its place of development — Brno in Czechoslovakia — and its place of manufacture — Enfield in Britain. The PIAT (*3*) was a crude, but effective antitank weapon. Its hollow-charged projectile was fired by means of a strong spring mechanism which detonated a charge in the projectile's tail. This gave it a range of about 350 yards (315m). The weapon also proved successful in destroying buildings in house-to-house fighting. The Boys antitank rifle (*5*) on the other hand never proved successful. The development of thicker tank armor made this product of early-1930s thinking obsolete before World War II broke out.

in 1940 seeking B-17s, all he could get were 100 P-40 fighters and the volunteers to fly them.

Those P-40s with painted shark's teeth and contract pilots who were nicknamed "Flying Tigers" gave Americans something to brag about during the dark early days after Pearl Harbor. Their exploits in Burma and China made an impression on Americans, Chinese and Japanese far greater than was warranted by so small a force. Before the American Volunteer Group (as the Flying Tigers were officially designated), Chiang's capital at Chungking had experienced harsher bombing than any other city up

to that time. With the aid of a network of Chinese ground observers, Chennault was able to provide a surprisingly effective air defense. This demonstration of the effectiveness of fighters against bombers, however, dissuaded neither Chennault nor Chiang from the belief that given enough bombers and the right tactics they could wreak havoc not only on Japanese positions in China, but on Japan itself.

Stilwell together with the Commanding General of the Army Air Forces, "Hap" Arnold, tried to rein in Chennault and subordinate him to their purposes, but (except in the case of Chiang)

Chennault had never been a good subordinate. Enjoying relationships with Chiang and Roosevelt far stronger than Stilwell's, Chennault made the most of them. He wriggled out from under the control of Brig. Gen. Clayton Bissell's Tenth Air Force in India and in early 1943 was given command of his own Fourteenth Air Force. In presidential aide Thomas G. "Tommy the Cork" Corcoran, Chennault had a friend close to Roosevelt, and Chennault himself came to Washington with Stilwell in April 1943 to debate allocation of airlifted supplies to China. Chennault won handily — of the 7,000 tons per month prescribed by

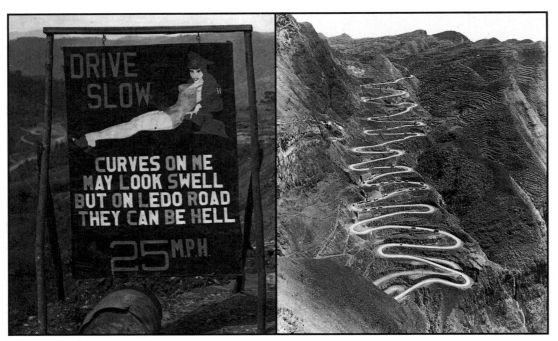

Above: The strategically vital supply route to southwestern China through northern Burma was a major engineering triumph, but was a nightmare of a driving experience that demanded great concentration on the part of truck crews.

Roosevelt, Chennault was to get the first 4,500 tons (which was more than the total then being delivered). Stilwell, who thought the president "frothy," grumbled and growled and did not persuade.

Chennault promised more for a smaller investment, which was the primary consideration in the theater with the lowest priority. But Stilwell did have a good argument against emphasizing air power in China, even if he was not always able to present his case convincingly. In Stilwell's view, an air attack strong enough to hurt the Japanese would provoke them to invade southern China and take the offending airfields. The addition of a group of B-24s to Chennault's air force in the spring of 1943 did add weight to his attacks on Hankow (Hangzhou), Canton (Quangzhou), Hanoi, and Haiphong, and for the first time Formosa could be bombed. Fourteenth Air Force's attacks on the Yangtze River and coastal shipping were particularly damaging.

In the spring of 1944 Stilwell's prediction seemed to come true. The Japanese sent a force of some 250,000 soldiers from north China into the south and another 50,000 west from Canton. This First Offensive (*Ichi-Go*) was launched by Gen. Shunroku Hata while Mutaguchi's offensive against Imphal was still underway. In both cases the Japanese were looking for a victory to counterbalance their defeats in the Pacific. The conquest of southern China would connect them with Southeast Asia via a land route invulnerable to submarines and sea mines, and also less vulnerable to air attack, since Chennault's airfields would be swept up simultaneously.

Although Stilwell had made an accurate forecast that Chiang's divisions would be unable to protect Chennault's

Right: B-4 bag of Sgt. James Abbott, 322 Troop Carrier Squadron, 14th Air Force. The bag carries the 14th's famous 'Flying Tiger' emblem. Far right: A-2 flying jacket bearing the badge of the 5th Air Force.
War Memorial Museum of Virginia.

bases, it is doubtful that shifting airlifted supplies from Fourteenth Air Force to those divisions would have made much difference, either in their ability to defend or the Japanese decision to attack. As Stilwell knew all too well, there was no way to assure that infantry supplies reaching China also reached the soldiers who needed them. The five Chinese divisions by then under his direct control in India and Burma were well equipped and relatively immune from the corruption which plagued the bulk of Chiang's army. Stilwell had also insured that 12 divisions in Yunnan Province on the Burma border were among the best equipped in China. Now over Stilwell's objections, most of the Yunnan force was pulled from the Burma campaign to face the Japanese onslaught in China. Chiang, of course, was also eager to find some way to retrieve Stilwell's own Chinese divisions from Burma.

Whereas Stilwell was upset that Chiang would want to end the Burma

campaign so near to its successful conclusion, Chiang complained bitterly that his American adviser was consumed by a relatively inconsequential effort in Burma while the Japanese were launching their major offensive of the war in China itself. There the forces engaged dwarfed those in any other action of the Pacific conflict. About 1,000,000 Chinese and Japanese troops were ultimately involved, and Chinese resistance was tougher than the Japanese or the Americans had expected.

At first the Japanese offensive proceeded according to schedule. After capturing Changsha in mid-June, the Japanese moved south down the railroad toward Hengyang. The Chinese had ripped up the track before them. Japanese repair efforts were foiled by heavy rain, frequent flooding, and Chennault's Fourteenth Air Force with its composite wing of Chinese and American pilots. Japanese trucks were forced to drive through the mud at night and even then they were harassed from the air, as were Japanese supply boats on the Hsiang River (Xiang Jiang).

At Hengyang, Maj. Gen. Fong Hsien-chueh's Tenth Army made a determined stand, holding the Japanese at bay for more than a month. Then Chiang cut off supplies to Fong for fear that he and his boss Gen. Hsueh Yueh were involved in a plot to overthrow the government. Chennault even begged Stilwell to divert airlifted supplies from Fourteenth Air Force to Fong, but Stilwell, bogged down in Burma, also reversed himself and turned aside Chennault's request both as a waste of resources in a lost cause and as interference in Chinese politics. Chennault did not have sufficient fuel to sustain his support of Fong, whose forces gave way at the beginning of August. Chennault's air bases at Kweilin (Guilin) and Liuchou (Liuzhou) were also overrun by the end of the year.

Stilwell's success in Burma together with Chiang's worsening predicament in China prompted President Roosevelt to promote for a time Gen. Marshall's suggestion that Stilwell be given command of all Chiang's forces in China as well as in Burma. To facilitate this transition,

Above: The Curtiss P-40 was the celebrated fighter of the "Flying Tigers" or American Volunteer Group, which in 1942 became the core of the China Air Task Force, which was in turn expanded into the 14th Air Force. All were commanded by Claire L. Chennault.

Stilwell became the fifth American four-star general of the war. But Chiang was not about to surrender so much authority to Stilwell. Their long feud now caught fire. Roosevelt sent Maj. Gen. Patrick J. Hurley, who had been Secretary of War in the Hoover administration, to negotiate a workable arrangement. Chiang held his ground and in October 1944 Roosevelt replaced Stilwell with Lt. Gen. Albert C. Wedemeyer, who had been Deputy Chief of Staff of South East Asia Command under Mountbatten.

As for Chennault, his pleasure in Stilwell's departure was dampened by the loss of his airfields in southeastern China. His bases in the southwest (including his headquarters base at Kunming) were not seriously threatened, but his importance to the war effort declined as did China's as a whole. No longer did it seem necessary to establish an American base on the Chinese coast before invading Japan. The invasion of Japan might even prove unnecessary if

Left: A selection of safe-passage documents or 'Blood chits'. These were carried or sewn into jackets by aviators flying over Asia. If forced down, messages in local languages told locals which side the aviator was on.
John T. Frawner Collection.

the new long-range B-29 bombers could hit the Japanese Home Islands hard enough. This use of air power was not out of line with Chennault's thinking, but his ambition to command such an effort was not to be fulfilled. During the last six months of 1944, B-29s did launch from Chinese bases, but not under Chennault's control and not to much effect.

Gen. Arnold of the US Army Air Forces sent the B-29s to China as a way of keeping them out of the hands of Gen. Douglas MacArthur and Adm. Chester W. Nimitz, the principal commanders in the Pacific, until the Mariana Islands had been captured from the Japanese and made ready to support B-29 operations against Japan. Consequently, Arnold chose to press ahead despite the obvious impracticality of airlifting large amounts of aviation gasoline to China for extensive B-29 operations. The prospect of early bombing raids against Japan easily won the president's support, especially since Arnold promised that 150 B-29s in China would be nearly self-sustaining — they would carry their own fuel and bombs and other supplies from India to China with the assistance of only 20 cargo aircraft.

In a highly unusual move, Arnold made himself commander of the new Twentieth Air Force, through which he would control all B-29 operations from his headquarters in Washington. He put Brig. Gen. Kenneth B. Wolfe in charge of the B-29s that would stage through China, designating him to command the subordinate XX Bomber Command. Wolfe, who had supervised B-29 production, now found himself squabbling with Chennault and Stilwell over the allocation of airlift tonnage. The problem of sustaining so many bombers in China was exacerbated by their great size (about twice that of the B-17 or the B-24) as well as the haste with which they had been developed and produced. Not only did they consume enormous quantities of gasoline (seven B-29 sorties over the Hump to provide enough gasoline for one sortie against Japan), but their engines frequently failed and had to be returned to the United States.

Wolfe's tenure at XX Bomber Command was brief. His first raid from bases near Calcutta against a railroad repair shop in Bangkok did little damage; nor did his first raid from Chinese bases in Szechuan (Sichuan) against Japan on June 15, 1944 — only one bomb did any real harm, to the great Yawata steel works on the southern island of Kyushu. Arnold brought Wolfe back to the United States and sent out Maj. Gen. Curtis E. LeMay, who had been possibly the most innovative American bomber commander in Europe.

Not even LeMay could do much with

Above: After serving as Adm. Lord Mountbatten's deputy in South East Asia Command, Lt. Gen. Albert C. Wedemeyer (center) succeeded Stilwell as commander of American Forces in the China-Burma-India Theater and as Chiang's chief of staff.

the logistical situation he found in China. Japan suffered hardly at all from B-29 strikes so long as they had to be launched from China, since LeMay could only launch three or four strikes a month from there and only those against relatively close targets in China and Formosa could carry much weight. LeMay did not always see the merit in these closer targets, and he agreed to Chennault's request to bomb Hankow (Hangzhou) on the Yangtze River only after Washington insisted. But the Hankow raid turned out to be perhaps the most successful strike LeMay launched from Chinese bases. It was his first major incendiary raid in the Far East, and the Chinese industrial city burned satisfactorily.

By then American forces had taken the Marianas and Twentieth Air Force's XXI Bomber Command was already using them to attack Japan with B-29s readily supplied by ship. In another month LeMay would begin to move his B-29s to the Marianas.

Gen. Chennault in Kunming also dealt with a communist (Vietnamese in this case) who was assisting downed American pilots and providing target intelligence. Although Chennault gave an autographed photograph of himself to Ho Chi Minh, their slight acquaintance would not develop, and official American friendships with Asian communists would end with the world war. Chennault's genuine and enduring friendship with Chiang Kai-shek would last long after Mao forced Chiang to seek refuge on Formosa in 1949. But Mao's victory so embittered American politics that for decades few Americans could appreciate the loss of 10,000,000 Chinese lives in China's war against Japan.

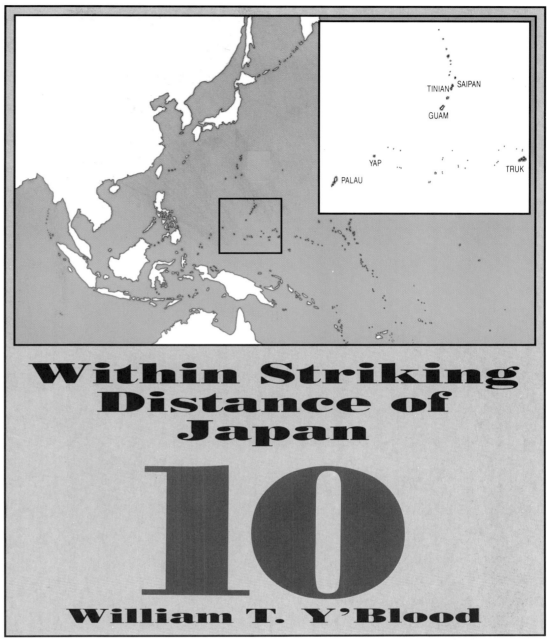

Within Striking Distance of Japan

10

William T. Y'Blood

On June 15, 1944, just nine days after the Normandy landings, the largest invasion force up to that time in the Pacific (some 127,500 troops and 535 vessels of all types) invaded the Marianas. That the Marianas would even be invaded had not been an easy decision. Although the islands had figured in prewar naval planning, when in 1943 the question of which route to follow to Japan — Southwest Pacific, Central Pacific, or both — was discussed, only Adm. Ernest J. King fully realized the importance of the Marianas and pushed hard for their inclusion in the strategic planning of the Combined Chiefs of Staff (made up of the American Joint Chiefs of Staff and their British counterparts).

King, who was Chief of Naval Operations and Commander-in-Chief, United States Fleet, began pushing for a Marianas operation at the January 1943 Casablanca Conference. He made little headway at that time, although the conferees did endorse planning for a Central Pacific drive. At the Trident Conference, held at Washington in May, the concept of a two-pronged advance was approved, with the Central Pacific route being the main one. But the Marianas did not appear on the list of objectives. In August, at the Quadrant Conference in Quebec, King was able to get the Marianas placed in the strategic timetable as at least an alternative operation. Perhaps more important, however, was the ally King gained at the conference: the commander of the Army Air Forces, Gen. Henry H. Arnold.

Arnold had a new weapon, the B-29, which he was eager to use. At the Quadrant Conference, he estimated that by October 1944 he would have enough of the big planes to bomb Japan. But at this time it appeared that the only place the B-29s could be based for that purpose was China, which was not an especially appealing choice to the planners of the Army Air Forces. However, B-29s using bases in the Marianas would be well within range of Japan, plus logistics and construction problems would be more easily solved in the islands than in China. Both Arnold and King applied pressure on the Combined Chiefs of Staff planners to consider the Marianas as a target. Finally, during the Sextant Confer-

Japanese Handguns and Accoutrements

1. Type 96 (1894) double action revolver, of 9mm caliber, with holster, shoulder belt, neck lanyard and boxes of cartridges
2. Type 94 (1934) semi-automatic pistol, of 8mm caliber, with early style leather holster and cartridge pouch
3. Sugiura semi-automatic pistol, of 7.65mm caliber. Made in a Japanese arsenal in China, this is a very rare handgun
4. Nambu semi-automatic pistol Type B, of 7mm caliber, with holster and ammunition
5. Modified Nambu semi-automatic, Type A, of 8mm

caliber, with holster, magazine and pistol cartridges
6. Model 1903 Colt semi-automatic pistol, of 7.65mm caliber, with Japanese-made holster and box of ammunition
7. Type 14 (1925) Nambu semi-automatic pistol, of 8mm, with early leather holster, magazine, lanyard, cleaning rod and cartridges
8. Mid-period holster. The body is of rubberized fabric but the flap is of leather
9. Type 14 (1925) Nambu semi-automatic pistol, of 8mm caliber, with rubberized fabric holster, lanyard and cartridges

Eugene C. Gibson Collection

The Nambu semi-automatic pistol (numbers *4, 5, 7* and *9*) was the standard Japanese handgun of the war. First introduced in 1909, it resembled on outside appearance an Italian design. This first model was modified in 1925 and reissued. It was a reasonably well-designed and well-made weapon, which worked on the closed breech principle by short recoil, the breechblock being locked during firing by a special locking piece below it. This piece was carried down after firing, allowing the block to make its rearward journey, compressing the return spring which provided the energy for the forward action. The magazine was of standard type with a guide stud working in a slot on the right hand side to help compress the spring for the last few rounds. The trigger guard was sometimes made sufficiently large to allow the pistol to be used in a gloved hand. It was reliable but lacked stopping power.

ence at Cairo in December 1943, the Combined Chiefs directed that a two-pronged "mutually supporting" advance, Southwest Pacific and Central Pacific, was to be used in the Pacific. Both routes would converge on the Luzon-Formosa-China area in the spring of 1945. To the dismay of Gen. Douglas MacArthur, in case of conflicts the Central Pacific route would take precedence.

After the Combined Chiefs directive reached him, Adm. Chester W. Nimitz, the Commander-in-Chief Pacific Ocean Areas (CinCPOA) and Commander-in-Chief Pacific Fleet (CinCPac), issued a tentative campaign plan, Granite, which was modified just two weeks later. In the initial Granite plans, the Marianas were not to be assaulted until November 1944, three months *after* both Truk and the Palaus were to be taken. This sequence began to unravel during meetings in late January 1944 to coordinate these operations. At this time Nimitz proposed either taking Truk on June 15, 1944, followed by the Marianas on September 1 or bypassing Truk altogether and moving the Marianas operation up to June 15. Most of the planners (from the Southwest, South, and Central Pacific commands) present at these meetings were not enthusiastic about a Central Pacific offensive. Even Nimitz was now lukewarm to the idea and considered recommending that MacArthur's advance be the primary route.

MacArthur was elated by his apparent victory at these meetings, but his elation was short-lived. An angry Adm. King quickly informed Nimitz that making the main advance along the New Guinea coast was "not in accordance with the decisions of the Joint Chiefs of Staff . . ." It was not until March 12, 1944, however, that the Joint Chiefs of Staff issued a directive ordering MacArthur to isolate Rabaul, undertake further operations up the New Guinea coast, and prepare to assault Mindanao on November 15, 1944, while Nimitz was to bypass Truk, seize the Marianas on June 15, 1944, followed by the Palaus on September 15. Formosa or Luzon was targeted for February 15, 1945.

The campaign in the Marianas, which went under the name Operation Forager, was a joint one involving troops from both the Marine Corps and the Army. Saipan was the first island to be taken, with a target date of June 15. The invasion of Guam was to follow quickly, landings on June 18 being tentatively approved. An assault on Tinian, last of the islands to be taken, was to occur after Saipan had fallen.

Overall commander for Forager was Vice Adm. Raymond A. Spruance, who also commanded the Fifth Fleet. Under him were two attack forces: the Northern Attack Force (Task Force 52) and the Southern Attack Force (Task Force 53). Task Force 52 was commanded by Vice Adm. Richmond Kelly Turner, who was also in charge of the Joint Expeditionary Force (Task Force 51), which had the job of taking all three islands. Commanding Task Force 53, the Guam assault force, was Rear Adm. Richard L. Conolly, nicknamed "Close-in" Conolly because of his willingness to pound coastal defenses from close range. Finally, tactical command of the troops ashore was the responsibility of Lt. Gen. Holland M. Smith, USMC.

The 2d and 4th Marine Divisions were scheduled to make the Saipan landings, while the Army's 27th Infantry Division was to be held in reserve. The two Marine divisions were also to be used on Tinian. For the Guam landings, the 3d Marine Division and the 1st Provisional Marine Brigade were to make the assault, with the 77th Infantry Division in general reserve.

In May, it had been estimated by the Americans that no more than 10,000 Japanese were on Saipan. Just before the invasion this figure was revised to between 15,000-17,600, but even this estimate was way off the mark. Actually, there were close to 30,000 Japanese troops. The Japanese command organization was typically complicated. Saipan was jointly commanded by Lt. Gen. Yoshitsugu Saito and Vice Adm. Chuichi Nagumo. Saito commanded the bulk of the forces; Nagumo, who had led the attack on Pearl Harbor and commanded the carrier force at Midway, had fallen from grace and was now, for all intents, just in charge of a small administrative organization of less than 7,000 men. Fortunately for the Americans, US submarines had disrupted the passage of construction supplies to Saipan, so that the enemy could not build their planned defenses. Still, there were enough natural defensive positions available and enough troops to man them to ensure that the attackers would receive a nasty welcome.

Several days before the landings, Task Force 58 struck the Marianas, and the

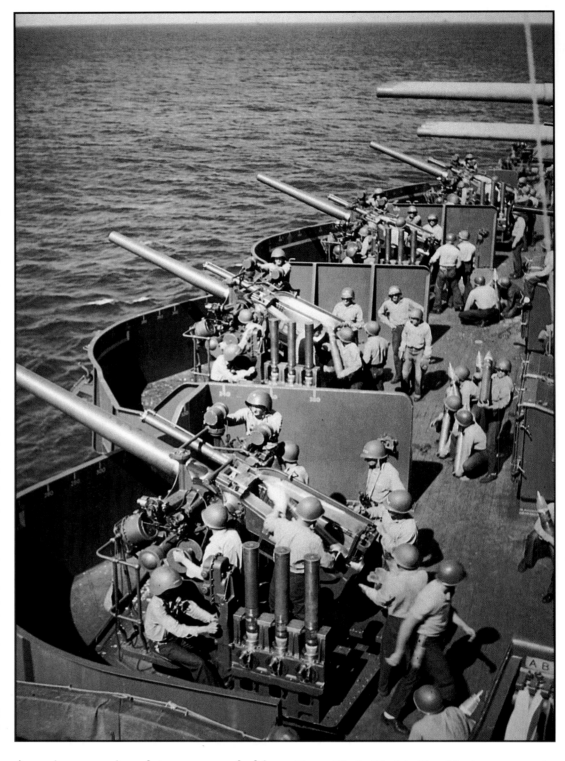

American carrier planes succeeded in preventing the Japanese from launching any serious attacks from the island's fields. These raids also put a serious crimp in the Japanese plans to use these airstrips during the big naval battle that was to come. The use of the fast battleships of Task Force 58 to provide pre-invasion bombardment was less successful. These warships were not used for shore bombardment and many of their shells were wasted on obvious (but, really, unimportant) targets, such as a sugar mill at Charan Kanoa, while more important targets were overlooked. Only when the old battleships took over on June 14 did this situation improve, but there was little time left to do an adequate job. When the marines stormed ashore the next day, they found the Japanese waiting amid many undamaged positions.

Above: The battleship *New Mexico* prepares to open fire against Japanese positions on Saipan. To this task she could bring the considerable firepower of twelve 14-inch guns in four triple turrets and fourteen 5-inch guns in single mountings.

At 5:42 on the morning of the 15th, the traditional command was given to begin the assault: "Land the landing force." The landings took place on a two-division front of about four miles (6km). Assigned to the left-hand, or northern, beaches was the 2d Marine Division. The 4th Marine Division was to land on the right-hand beaches. It was not quiet as the waves of troop-carrying amtracs, escorted by armored amphibian tractors, called LVT(A)'s and carrying 75-mm guns, left the line of departure for the beaches. There was a continuous drum roll of ships' guns firing, the whine and shriek of planes from escort carriers as they strafed the beaches, the throaty growl of the motors of the LVTs. But soon more sounds, unwelcome sounds, joined in the din. These were the sounds of enemy guns firing and shells landing in the midst of the assault waves. Most of the amtracs made it to the beach, but there were greasy smoke columns staining the air that showed where some had not been as fortunate.

At 8:44 A.M., the first wave touched down and within 20 minutes some 8,000 troops were put ashore. But the landings were not going smoothly. On the left, a northerly current had pushed the landing craft off to one side and, thus, many of the 2d Marine Division troops landed too far to the north and on the wrong beaches. This created a dangerous gap between the two divisions which required heavy fighting to close. The roughest time on D-Day was had by a battalion of the 25th Marines of the 4th Marine Division. At least four large artillery pieces situated directly in front of the marines caused heavy casualties and kept them pinned down on a beachhead just 12 yards (11m) deep.

As night fell, the marines were on Saipan to stay, although they had gained only half of the planned beachhead and the bothersome gap between the two divisions remained. Some 20,000 troops had been put ashore, but a tenth of these became casualties. During the night, the Japanese attempted three massed counterattacks but were repulsed with cruel losses. When dawn broke on June 16, the marines renewed their advance, albeit against strong resistance. It was apparent that Saipan was not going to be an easy battle.

Meanwhile, Adm. Spruance had received disturbing news — the Japanese fleet was on the move and obviously heading for the Marianas. He promptly called a meeting with Turner and Holland Smith. During this meeting, the American commanders decided that: the 27th Infantry Division would go ashore immediately (because of the fierce opposition, the Marine divisions could use some help anyway); the Guam landings would be postponed; Task Force 58's screen would be augmented by ships (cruisers and destroyers) from the bombardment group; troops and supplies would be unloaded until dark on the 17th, whereupon the ships would retire 200-300 miles (320-480km) to the east; and in case the Japanese did get around Task Force 58, the old battleships and the remaining vessels in their screens would take up position 25 miles (40km) west of Saipan.

Indeed, the Japanese were coming and in force. Operation *A-GO*, like so many of the Imperial Navy's previous plans, envisaged as "decisive" fleet action, this time in the Palaus and Western Carolines. If the Americans invaded the Marianas, land-based aircraft there would lead the counterattack, and then the US forces would be "lured" to the areas where they would be defeated. In

actuality, the only ones lured were the Japanese, who fell for MacArthur's attack on Biak on May 27 and began to concentrate against that invasion. (The concept of a two-headed attack in the Pacific was showing dividends.) But when it became obvious that the main attacks were taking place in the Marianas, the Japanese changed direction and sailed east to seek their enemy in the Philippine Sea.

The force the Japanese had assembled — the 1st Mobile Fleet — was indeed powerful. Its commander, the able Vice Adm. Jisaburo Ozawa, had the fine new 29,300-ton carrier *Taiho*, the veteran carriers *Shokaku* and *Zuikaku*, plus five smaller carriers. Among the screening vessels were the superbattleships *Yamato* and *Musashi*, three other battleships, 13 cruisers, and 27 destroyers. Other vessels formed a supply force. But this imposing force had a weakness which proved to be a major factor in its defeat: there were only 450 planes available at the start of *A-GO* and the crews flying them were ill-trained, some with only a couple of months of training. And what kind of force would be opposing the Mobile Fleet?

Vice Adm. Marc A. Mitscher's Task Force 58 was an awesome armada. When it sortied from Majuro for the Marianas, it took almost five hours to clear the lagoon! Under Mitscher's command were 15 carriers, 7 fast battleships, 10 cruisers, and 60 destroyers. Aboard the flattops were 902 planes flown by well-trained airmen. Beginning June 11, Mitscher's force hit the Marianas for

Below: Japanese dead litter the western shore of Saipan after the landings by the 2d and 4th Marine Divisions on June 15, 1944. As this photograph suggests, the Japanese tried unsuccessfully to halt the Americans on their eight landing beaches.

several days in preparation for the invasion. Following these initial raids, two task groups were sent north to neutralize the airfields in the Bonins, particularly those on Iwo Jima. Although two days of strikes were originally intended, when Spruance learned of the movement of the Mobile Fleet, he told the task group commanders to restrict their attacks to the 16th and to rendezvous with the rest of Task Force 58 on June 18. Despite poor weather, the attacks on Iwo Jima and other fields in the Bonins group were successful and it was several days before the Japanese were able to mount an aerial assault against the American ships off Saipan.

By the time the units of Task Force 58 had rejoined, Adm. Spruance had no doubt that the Japanese were heading his way. Filipino coastwatcher and submarine sightings had confirmed the movement of the fleet eastward. Despite his preparations and his well-founded belief in the superiority of his forces, Spruance was worried. He was concerned that the Japanese might make an end run around him and strike at the forces on and just offshore of Saipan. On the 17th, Spruance issued what appeared to be an aggressive battle plan, but in spite of a message from Nimitz counting "on [Spruance] to make the victory decisive," Spruance was already considering holding his forces back and accepting a first attack by the Japanese.

The Japanese launched numerous air searches on the 18th, the Americans not as many. With a decided range advantage for their aircraft, the Japanese spotted the Americans first. During the afternoon, Task Force 58 was seen about 200 miles (320km) west of Saipan, and Ozawa began preparations for a launch against the Americans the next morning. Unaware that both the land-based planes

Japanese Army Uniforms and Equipment

1 Field cap. This pattern was introduced into service in 1938. Indicative of Japanese resource problems, this cap is made of woven grasslike material
2 Field cap
3 Cotton full-length field trousers with securing tapes
4 Cotton tropical half breeches
5 Cotton tropical shorts
6 Tropical lightweight helmet made of cloth-covered bamboo and cork. Note the yellow army star on the front
7 Model 1932 steel helmet with canvas cover
8 Light cotton bag for storage of effects
9 Khaki painted three-piece aluminium mess tin, shown open here
10 Personal patriotic flag with inscriptions
11 Japanese copy of German Model 1924 hand grenade. Note that the cap has been removed, revealing the cord which ignited the time-fuze when pulled
12 Issue spectacles
13 Metal cigarette case with image inside
14 Packs of cigarettes
15 Utility knife
16 Brass bugle
17 Iron climbing spikes
18 Pair of *Tabi*

Eugene C. Gibson: 5-7, 13, 14, 18; US Marine Raider Museum: 1-4, 8-12, 15-17

and their bases in the Marianas had been decimated, Ozawa continued with the *A-GO* plan to use the bases for refueling and rearming and the planes to beef up the attacks.

At 1:15 A.M. on the 19th, a prowling PBM finally found the Mobile Fleet. But in one of those "fog of war" situations, the message never reached Spruance. He would remain unaware of the enemy's actual position until next day. Ozawa, meanwhile, knew exactly where Task Force 58 was, and beginning at 8:25 A.M., sent his first attack group heading east — to its destruction. Before the day was over, Adm. Ozawa would launch 374

(including floatplanes) of his 473 operational aircraft against Task Force 58. Only 130 would return to their ships.

The 19th of June would go down in naval history as the "Great Marianas Turkey Shoot." Saddled with inexperienced fliers, picked up by radar long before they were in range, and — unknown to them — with a Japanese language officer on Mitscher's flagship listening in on their radio chatter, the Japanese attackers were no match for the well-trained Americans with (at this time in the war) their superior aircraft. When the slaughter was over, 294 enemy planes (including 50 land-based

aircraft) had been shot down. The vast majority had fallen to the guns of the F6F Hellcats; only 19 were shot down by antiaircraft fire. In comparison, the Americans lost just 31 planes, some of these in operational accidents. On this day the Japanese carrier force was shattered forever.

While his fliers were undergoing their ordeal, Ozawa was having problems of his own. A pair of American submarines found the Mobile Fleet and sank two of its carriers! The *Albacore* hit Ozawa's flagship, the brand-new *Taiho*, at 9:11 A.M. with one torpedo, but this one "fish", coupled with extremely poor

Among these items are the three most common types of cotton field trouser: the long trousers, shorts and half breeches (4). The breeches were worn gathered below the knee with wool or cotton puttees, which extended down to the ankle. They could also be worn without these. The canvas and rubber *Tabi* boot (18) was a piece of essentially jungle gear. It is characterized by the split toe and fastening at the heel. The iron climbing spikes (17) were worn tied to footwear to allow for easy climbing of trees. They were often used by snipers.

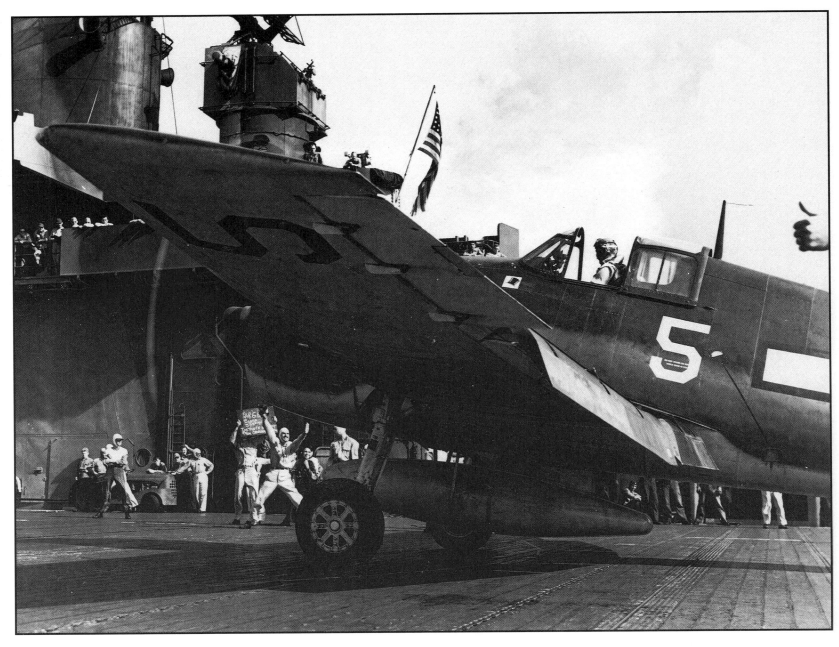

damage control by the carrier's crew, caused the ship to blow up and finally sink with heavy loss of life almost ten hours later. Meanwhile, the *Shokaku* ran afoul of the *Cavalla* and was speared by four torpedoes. The resulting explosions ripped the Pearl Harbor veteran apart, again with heavy casualties. Along with the loss of life and the two vessels, 22 more planes went down with the carriers.

June 19 had been a disastrous day for the Japanese, but Ozawa was no quitter and, misled by inaccurate if not dishonest reports of glowing successes, planned another attack. But first, he had to replenish his ships. This he proposed to do on the 21st. During the afternoon of June 20, however, the Mobile Fleet was at last sighted by the Americans; an event of which Adm. Ozawa was quickly aware.

Two search planes from Task Force 58 spotted the Japanese ships at about 4:00 in the afternoon. When Mitscher received the first plane's report, he immediately began launching an attack force of 240 aircraft. (Because of malfunctions, only 226 planes made the strike.) He realized that because Spruance had held the ships close to the Marianas the previous day, it was going to be a strike at extreme range with his planes having to make night landings afterwards or perhaps running out of fuel on the way back, but the target was worth it. As his planes were being launched, Mitscher received some disquieting news: the second search plane had found an error in the earlier sighting report and the Japanese were 60 miles (96km) farther west; some 275 miles (440km) from Task Force 58! Mitscher held back a second strike, but the planes in the air were committed.

When the Americans reached the Mobile Fleet around 6:30 P.M., there were only about 30 minutes of daylight left, and in the gathering dusk the attack that took place turned into a wild, incoherent brawl. The setting sun coloring the clouds vivid hues, the enemy throwing up a dazzling display of antiaircraft fire, both combined to create a spectacular but deadly scene. In the ensuing attack, the carrier *Hiyo* suffered fatal hits and two oilers were sunk, four other carriers were damaged, as well as the battleship *Haruna*, the cruiser *Maya*, the destroyer *Shigure*, and another oiler.

Above: Deck crew of the carrier *Yorktown* prepare for the launch of a Grumman F6F-3 Hellcat fighter during the Battle of the Philippine Sea. These powerful and well-flown fighters exacted a devastating toll on Japan's poorly flown and obsolete aircraft.

Eighty Japanese planes were lost during the battle over the Mobile Fleet; six American planes fell to the flak, while another 11 were shot down by the defending fighters. Adm. Ozawa started out what became known as the Battle of the Philippine Sea with 473 aircraft. At the end of it he had only 47 left.

The Americans now had to return to their carriers and make night landings, something which many fliers had never done. On the flight back planes began to go down — some damaged, others out of fuel. Those planes that did make it back to Task Force 58 found it lit up like Broadway, for Adm. Mitscher had ordered the lights turned on to guide his planes back. What now ensued, however, was utter chaos. Running low on fuel, some with damaged planes and desperate for a place to set down, pilots tried to land on any carrier (and, occasionally, other ships) that would take them. Before this wild scene quietened, 82 planes were

US NAVY PILOT

This figure of a naval fighter pilot wears a one-piece flying suit and life preserver, together with a lightweight flying helmet. His personal armament consists of a knife and .45 caliber semi-automatic pistol. This is held in the M3 shoulder holster on his left side. He also carries spare pistol ammunition in the pouch on his belt. The knife and pistol were survival aids should he be unfortunate enough to be shot down.

to take their own lives when faced with defeat.

Tinian was the last island to be taken in the Marianas. The invasion was unusual in that it was preceded by a land bombardment from nearby Saipan. The marines landed where they were not expected, and a Japanese counterattack was broken on the beachhead. The defenders were then forced back into the southern tip of the island. There they were surrounded and their force destroyed.

THE INVASION OF GUAM

Maps E and F
The attack on Guam followed the Saipan operation. After a lengthy bombardment, elements of the III Amphibious Corps landed ashore. The Japanese then launched a series of heavy counterattacks against the beachheads, which were beaten off. The battle now swung in the Americans' favor. Moving out of the beachheads, the south of the island was taken and Army and Marine units began a push towards the final Japanese defensive positions in the northeast of the island. It was here that organized resistance ended.

THE BATTLE OF THE PHILIPPINE SEA

Map A
The Japanese saw in the American invasion of the Marianas an ideal opportunity for the decisive fleet action for which they had planned so long. Towards Task Force 58, the covering force for the Mariana landings, the Japanese sent the combined carrier and battleship force of their 1st Mobile Fleet. Despite the impressive size of this force, the Japanese had far fewer carrier-borne aircraft than the Americans, and their pilots were largely inexperienced. Other factors also weighed against them: the land-borne aircraft and facilities on the Marianas, on which they were relying for support, had already been largely destroyed, and the American task force knew they were coming.

Nevertheless, on the first day of the battle, it was the Japanese who found the Americans first. A first strike was ordered, and the Japanese commander Adm. Ozawa sent up nearly every aircraft he had. The American planes found this force and in the air battle later known as the "Great Marianas Turkey Shoot", decimated it before it could reach its target.

While the Japanese were losing their aircraft, a submarine attack on the Mobile Fleet sank two of their carriers.

Map B
Unaware perhaps of how serious his position was, the Japanese commander decided to keep his force in the area of operations and continue the engagement. On the second day of the battle, the position of his fleet was found by the Americans, and an air strike was launched. Despite being at the very limit of their range and the fact that it was nearly dark, the American aircraft severely damaged the Japanese fleet and destroyed all but 47 of their carrier aircraft.

THE INVASION OF SAIPAN AND TINIAN

Maps C and D
The landings on Saipan began the American invasion of the Marianas. Two divisions of marines and a reserve infantry division were to make the assault. Unfortunately the Japanese strength on the island was seriously underestimated and the landings proved very difficult. To make matters worse, the appearance of the Japanese fleet forced the withdrawal of the supporting naval force, Task Force 58. The reserve division was therefore brought ashore. The struggle for the island then became characterized by the appalling terrain and the suicidal will of the defenders; a particularly unpleasant element since a large number of Japanese civilians also chose

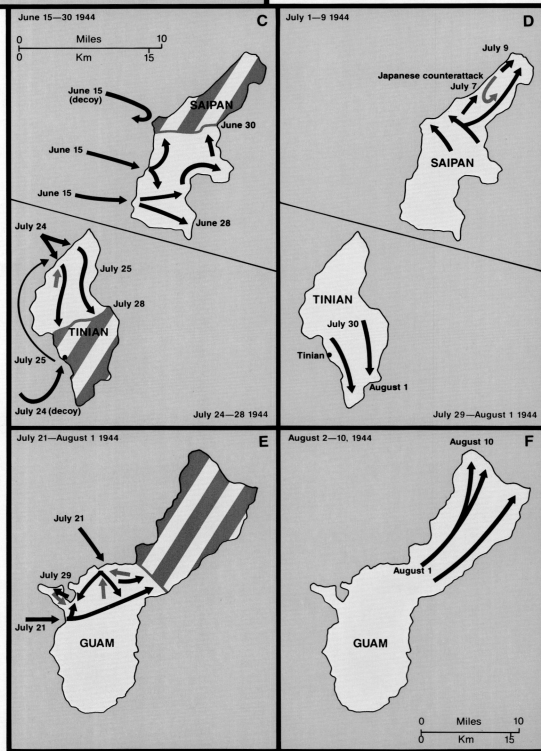

lost, most after running out of fuel. Fortunately, because of superb rescue efforts, only 16 pilots and 33 crewmen were lost.

Task Force 58 attempted to chase the Mobile Fleet the next day, but Adm. Ozawa had decided to head back to safety and the biggest carrier battle of the war was over. Although it had been an American victory, the battle left a bitter taste in the mouths of many of the victors. The passive and somewhat defensive maneuvers of Adm. Spruance had not set well with the carrier aviators. Despite Adm. Nimitz' desire for a "decisive victory", Spruance had held back and, in the view of the fliers, the victory was less decisive than it could have been. Unknown to the Americans, Japanese carrier aviation had been destroyed, but all that they could see was that the all-important carriers had been allowed to escape. The desire to get those carriers would lead another admiral into making a serious mistake several months later.

In the meantime, the situation on Saipan, which seemed in doubt when Adm. Spruance went to fight the Mobile Fleet, had turned in the American's favor. To beef up the attack, two regiments of the 27th Infantry Division landed on the 16th and 17th, the third regiment coming ashore on the 20th. A Japanese counterattack led by over 40 tanks against two companies of the 2d Marine Division on the night of the 17th was smashed so completely that enemy tanks never again played a major role. By the 18th, Saipan was cut in two as elements of the 4th Marine Division reached Magicienne Bay on the east coast.

On June 20, the main American offensive began to take shape as the 2d Marine Division on the left, the 27th Infantry Division in the middle, and the 4th Marine Division on the right took up positions to push toward Saipan's northern tip, Marpi Point. In the meantime, units of the Army division began clearing enemy positions in the southern part of the island. This latter action ended disastrously when the remaining enemy troops there broke through thinly held lines to launch an unsuccessful *banzai* attack on the newly-captured Aslito Airfield. Then, when the offensive to the north resumed on the 23d, the attack of the 27th Infantry Division bogged down amid treacherous terrain (soon to be known as Death Valley) and tenacious Japanese resistance. The marine divisions surged ahead of the Army unit, leaving open flanks in the middle. An irate Holland M. Smith lived up to his nickname of "Howling Mad", and relieved the 27th's commander, Maj. Gen. Ralph Smith. The resulting uproar was felt all the way back to Washington and the controversy created bitter feelings between the two services and their supporters that exist even today.

Although the 27th Infantry Division had a new commander, it was still fighting in appalling terrain and its for-

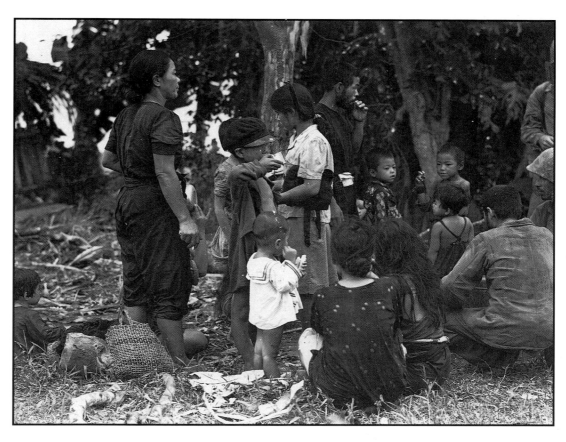

Above: Many Japanese civilians leapt to their deaths from Saipan's cliffs, and others hid in the island's many caves. These people are among the groups that emerged from hiding on July 12 after pleas delivered to them over a loudspeaker system.

Below: A Marine command post extemporized from a shell or bomb crater in the Guam beachhead on July 21, 1944. Control of fluid beachhead situations was often difficult, so it was very important for commanders to be well up with their men.

ward progress remained slow. Still, by the end of June the division had moved forward and, as the island narrowed, replaced the 2d Marine Division on the left side of the line, so that the marine unit could pull back into reserve. But early on the morning of July 7, a screaming swarm of what was estimated as 3,000 enemy troops, some armed only with rocks or spears, launched probably the largest *banzai* attack of the war against the 105th Infantry Regiment. Two Army battalions were almost wiped out by the charge which carried through to artillery batteries further back. Finally, the onslaught was stopped but losses to the Americans had been heavy. Nevertheless, this attack, born of desperation,

was the last gasp for the defenders. Adm. Nagumo and Gen. Saito committed suicide, as did many other of their troops. Soldiers were not the only ones choosing suicide; as the Americans reached Marpi Point on July 9, they were horrified to see thousands of Japanese civilians throwing themselves off the cliffs into the sea, drowning themselves and their children in the surf, or blowing themselves up. Accustomed to seeing enemy soldiers deliberately seek death, the Americans were sickened by the needless sacrifice by women and children.

Although Saipan was declared secure on the 9th, Japanese stragglers continued to make trouble for some time.

Allied Handguns

1 US pistol belt, Model 1938 with magazine pouch, Model 1918; M3 trench knife; Model 1916 holster and Model 1911 A1 semi-automatic pistol
2 Model 1911 semi-automatic pistol — with open slide
3 M3 shoulder holster for 2
4 Liberator pistol, .45 caliber single shot
5 French Model 1935 S semi-automatic pistol
6 French Model 1935 A 7.65mm semi-automatic pistol
7 Commonwealth holster for Canadian No. 1 Mk 1 semi-automatic pistol
8 Canadian No. 1 Mk 1 Inglis-Browning 9mm semi-automatic pistol

9 Leather holster, Model 1911 Mills pistol belt for use with 11
10 British Mk VI Webley revolver, .445 caliber
11 Model 1917 Smith and Wesson revolver
12 British Mk IV Webley revolver
13 Model 1917 Colt revolver
14 British Mk V Webley revolver
15 Victory Model .38 caliber Smith and Wesson revolver
16 British Webley .38 revolver No. 2, Mk 1
17 British Enfield revolver No. 2, Mk 1

US Army Ordnance Museum: 4, 12-14; Allan Cors Col: 5-8, 16, 17; Pritchard Col: 1-3; Laurence Beyer Col: 9-11; William LePard Col: 15

The Liberator pistol (*4*) was a smoothbore weapon made from sheet steel by General Electric. It was designed for mass airborne delivery to partisan units. The Canadian No. 1 Mk 1 pistol (*8*) features an attached wooden stock/holster, while the British Webley No. 2 Mk 1 (*16*) is shown with the Pattern 1937 web holster and cartridge pouch. The open top holster and belt with *17* were designed for the use of tank crew, being worn on the thigh.

Saipan was not cheap. Of over 14,000 casualties, 3,674 were soldiers and 10,437 were marines; the Japanese lost about 30,000 troops dead, and civilian casualties, mostly by suicide, were near 8,000. Saipan was only the first step, however. Guam and Tinian were to follow.

The assault on Guam by the III Amphibious Corps finally took place on July 21. Because the 27th Infantry Division had been used on Saipan, the 77th Infantry Division bolstered the attack. The delay in the Guam landings resulted in that islands receiving a continuous 13-day naval and air bombardment.

When the 3d Marine Division and the 1st Provisional Marine Brigade stormed ashore on the 21st, they were able to carve out substantial beachheads. It was evident that the bombardment had played havoc with the Japanese defenses but it was also evident that of the estimated 27,000 Japanese on Guam (in actuality only about 18,500), there were more than enough defenders still left to offer fierce resistance. On the evening of the 21st, the 77th Infantry Division's 305th Infantry came ashore to help the 1st Marine Brigade secure the beachhead.

Over the next few days the rest of the

Army division came ashore and relieved the 1st Marine Brigade in the southern portion of the island. The new task for the brigade was the capture of Orote Peninsula which separated the two beachheads. Before this assault took place, however, a full-scale coordinated counterattack fell upon the American lines. On the evening of July 25-26, as many as seven separate attacks were sent against the positions of the 3d Marine Division in the north, and each time the enemy was sent reeling backwards. Bottled up on Orote Peninsula, another contingent of defenders attempted to smash through the brigade's lines with as little success as their comrades to the north. When the fighting was over, approximately 3,500 Japanese, including up to 95 per cent of the officers in the attacks, had been killed. Although Lt. Gen. Hideyoshi Obata was on Guam and was responsible for the defense of the Marianas, he had left the immediate defense of Guam to Lt. Gen. Takeshi Takashina, who realized that Guam was lost; all he could do now was inflict as many casualties on the Americans as possible.

On July 29, the 1st Marine Brigade reached the tip of Orote Peninsula, securing the vital airfield located there. While the brigade had been fighting for the peninsula, the 3d Marine Division and the 77th Infantry Division had secured the Force Beachhead Line and patrols from the Army Division had scouted the southern portion of the island. Few Japanese were found by these patrols. It was obvious that the main defenses were in the north. The 3d Marine Division turned north, while the 77th Infantry Division cut east, then wheeled to the left to join the marines in as continuous a line as the jungle and hilly terrain permitted.

Initially, the invaders encountered feeble resistance as they moved forward, but this changed as the Americans neared the enemy's main areas of resistance. Over the next few days

several vicious actions took place in both the army and marine sectors. Agana, the largest city in the Marianas, fell to the marines on the 31st. During another action, Gen. Takashina was killed by US tank fire. Near the tiny village of Barrigada, a lone enemy tank, flushed out of hiding, sped through the 77th Infantry Division's lines, causing few casualties but creating a great deal of chaos before finally disappearing back into the jungle.

On August 3, the 3d Marine Division captured the village of Finegayan and the next day Mount Barrigada fell to the soldiers. The Japanese began to fall back toward a final defensive position centered on Mt. Santa Rosa, near the

Above: American soldiers blast a Japanese strongpoint on Guam's Orote peninsula. The weapon on the right is a 37-mm antitank gun M3, which was by then obsolete in its original role and therefore used in the Pacific theater for tasks such as this.

northeast tip of Guam. The Americans tried to close with the defenders as quickly as possible, but heavy jungle growth slowed the advance as did numerous diehards and occasional tanks, and the 1st Provisional Marine Brigade had to come forward to help with the advance. By the 8th, however, the 77th Infantry Division had cleared Mt. Santa Rosa and the marines had reached Ritidian Point, the island's northernmost point. Two days later the entire island

Right: Another method of dealing with Japanese bunkers was the satchel charge, which contained a large quantity of high explosive and produced a result such as that seen here as American soldiers destroy a Japanese position on Guam's Orote peninsula.

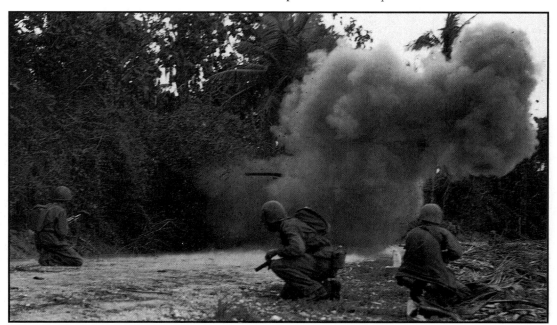

was overrun by the Americans. Although the island was declared secured on the 10th, a sizable number of Japanese stragglers remained at large, a few even surviving for several years after the war ended. Nevertheless, the entire Japanese garrison of about 18,500 was eventually either killed or captured. The cost to the Americans was 7,800 including 2,124 killed or died of wounds. By far the greatest number of casualties were incurred by the marines.

There was one final island taken in the Marianas. This was Tinian; the last to be assaulted but the quickest taken. Just three miles from Saipan, Tinian was the least mountainous of the Marianas and was well-suited for use by the B-29s. The Japanese already had exploited the terrain and had built two excellent airfields plus two more of somewhat lesser quality. Because of its closeness to Saipan, Tinian would be a unique operation: pre-landing bombardment with artillery on Saipan taking part was one of the most extensive in the Pacific during the war; unit commanders down to even platoon level were able to make almost daily flights over their objectives, thus offering the invaders an unparalleled chance to scout the terrain and enemy positions; and this would be a shore-to-shore operation, one of the few carried out in the war.

The Japanese, totalling about 8,000 army and navy troops, expected the landings to be either on the southwestern shore near Tinian Town or on the east coast at Asiga Bay, the two sites with the best beaches. The narrow, cliff-lined beaches on the northwest coast near the Ushi Point airfield seemed an unlikely alternative. However, it was near Ushi Point that the marines came ashore. On July 24, as a diversionary force feinted toward the Tinian Town beaches,

Below: Vice Adm. Richmond K. Turner studies the island of Tinian from Saipan, using captured Japanese observation glasses. Awaiting his turn is Lt. Gen. Holland M. Smith (right), the commanding general of Fleet Marine Forces Pacific.

Above: Marines shelter from a tropical downpour under the eaves of a Japanese farmhouse on Tinian, which had a large population of ethnic Japanese. Sustained operations were extremely difficult in the monsoon type of weather.

marines of the 4th Marine Division stormed over these tiny beaches, meeting relatively light resistance. By nightfall, a beachhead almost a mile deep was established and the marines awaited the expected counterattack. It was not long in coming, but the three separate and seemingly uncoordinated drives that comprised the counterthrust were soon beaten back. When the fighting ended, over 1,200 enemy dead littered the area and the Japanese defense of Tinian had been irrevocably broken.

The next day, as the 4th Marine Division expanded its beachhead, the 2d Marine Division joined the operation, and the two divisions made rapid progress toward the southern tip of the island. As the marines advanced, they were supported by Army P-47 fighters that had recently arrived at Saipan. For the first time in the Pacific these planes used a fearsome weapon that would be employed with great success throughout the rest of the war — napalm. By the 31st, the Japanese were compressed into about a five-square-mile (8km²) pocket backed up to the ocean. It was here that the Japanese made their last stand. A counterattack on the evening of the 31st was a failure, and the next afternoon when the marines reached the south coast, Tinian was declared secured. Almost 2,000 Americans were killed and wounded in what some considered a "perfect" amphibious operation; in return the Japanese lost their entire force. Like Saipan and Guam, however, a number of defenders had escaped detection and were still being hunted down months later.

Following the fall of Saipan, one anguished Japanese official remarked, "Hell is on us." A few months later, "hell" in the form of the B-29 was, indeed, upon Japan. Construction of the Marianas fields began almost immediately after the fields had been captured. On Saipan, Isely Field (formerly Aslito airdrome) was in full operation by mid-December 1944 and the first Tokyo mission (on November 24) was flown from it; two B-29 airfields on Guam were put into operation by July 1945, with the first Japan mission being flown in February; a third Guam airfield became the XXI Bomber Command headquarters; two more ex-Japanese fields on Tinian were reconstructed for the B-29s and were available for use in February and March. It was from the old Ushi Point field, now renamed North Field, that a B-29 named *Enola Gay* took off on August 6, 1945, bound for its moment in history.

Securing MacArthur's Flank

11

William T. Y'Blood

American strategy in the Pacific did not visualize attacking every island stronghold of Japan. And as the war progressed, the idea of bypassing, of "leapfrogging", certain enemy possessions to attack other, more vulnerable, targets became an even more attractive prospect. So it was when the eastern Marshall Islands were bypassed and Kwajalein and Eniwetok invaded instead. Those islands (Wotje, Maloelap, Mille, Jaluit) now to the rear of the US advance were left to "wither on the vine", their defenders reduced to fighting for survival, scrabbling for a few vegetables and subsisting mainly on fish.

But being left to "wither" did not mean being left alone. The islands in the Marshalls and other enemy positions, such as Nauru (west of the Gilberts) and Rabaul and Kavieng in the South Pacific, were visited often, sometimes daily, by US and Allied airmen. These raids had the purpose of keeping the Japanese occupied, at the same time killing some, and also giving green newcomers to the battlefield some first-hand experience in a combat situation. While most of these missions were little more than boring "milk runs", the Japanese were not defenseless. More than one flier found this out to his regret.

Truk, too, wound up being one of those bypassed strongholds. Up until 1944, Truk was a mysterious fortress which Westerners had been unable to approach. It was known to be a major base for the Japanese Combined Fleet and was believed to be so studded with weapons that it received the sobriquet "Gibraltar of the Pacific". Actually, that group was relatively weakly defended, with only about 11,000 army and navy troops present in mid-February 1944, and only some 40 antiaircraft guns scattered around the islands.

But this the Americans did not know — not yet. The thought of attacking this "fortress" caused some concern with the planners, who in late 1943-early 1944 already were thinking that bypassing Truk might be a good idea. Nevertheless, during meetings at Pearl Harbor in late January 1944, Truk was still considered an objective, with an invasion date set for August. Before committing his full resources against Truk, however, Adm. Nimitz wanted to see just what

Japanese Arisaka 7.7mm Longarms

1 Type 99 (1939) Arisaka long rifle. Almost identical to the Type 38, but of larger caliber (7.7mm)
2 Type 99 (1939) 7.7mm Arisaka rifle, early manufacture, with folding monopod and antiaircraft sights, both extended
3 Type 99 (1939) 7.7mm rifle
4 Type 99 (1939) 7.7 rifle, late manufacture, so-called 'last ditch' rifle, with non-adjustable rear sight. Late production bayonet affixed. Bayonet scabbard is of wood with string mounts and metal toe
5 Type 99 (1939) 'Naval Special' 7.7mm, with heavy receiver. Note muzzle cover at the end of the barrel
6 Type 2 (1942) 7.7mm paratroop take-down rifle, disassembled
7 A child's ⁷/₈ scale Type 38 training rifle. Military training played an important part in the raising of Japanese boys. This type of training aid was an integral part of that indoctrination
8 Type 30 (1897) bayonet with tropical rubberized canvas frog
9 Ammunition pouches for 30 rounds

Eugene C. Gibson Collection

Contrary to the belief of some individuals, Japanese arms and equipment were quite serviceable and deadly effective. Although Japan never placed emphasis on semi-automatic rifle and sub-machine gun development, the use of light and heavy machine guns was well developed, particularly adapted to Japanese jungle fighting tactics. While their equipment did not meet Western standards, it was nevertheless well-made, functional and efficient.

Japanese ordnance opted for a small caliber round in 1897 with the adoption of the Arisaka system. By the beginning of World War II, it was obvious that the 6.6mm round was underpowered, and so a 7.7mm round was adopted. Unfortunately, or fortunately, depending on your point of view, the transition could not be made due to wartime needs, and both calibers were used concurrently.

As the war went on and Allied bombing took its toll of Japanese industry, emergency measures, manufacturing short cuts and non-critical substitutions were utilized. Early Arisakas with nicely finished wood and well finished, blued metal were replaced by arms with rough, unfinished stocks, barrels with obvious lathe marks and areas where spot welds were still needed. Handgun and machine gun production also deteriorated. These 'last ditch' weapons have become quite collectable in recent years.

kind of reaction would be provoked if his carriers attacked Truk. An attack was planned for March.

The surprising ease with which Kwajalein fell enabled Nimitz to move his carrier attack up to mid-February. On February 4, Americans got their first look at mysterious Truk when a Marine PB4Y (the Navy version of the B-24) pierced the veil of secrecy shrouding the atoll. What the fliers saw was impressive — the superbattleship *Musashi,* a couple of carriers, ten or so cruisers, 20 destroyers, and numerous merchant vessels. Truk was going to offer some good pickings for the planes of Task

Force 58. But the Japanese realized what the appearance of the reconnaissance plane meant and almost immediately began pulling the Combined Fleet units back to the safer waters of the Carolines and the Home Islands. It was the last time the sailors of Combined Fleet saw Truk.

When the Task Force 58 aircraft pounced on Truk on February 17 and 18, most of the major naval units were gone. Nevertheless, some 50 merchant ships, a smattering of warships, and 365 planes (many laying over before proceeding on to Rabaul) were found. Before the Task Force 58 fliers were finished, the Japanese lost about 200,000 tons of

ships, including 2 cruisers, 4 destroyers, 24 marus (transport ships), and 75 percent (275) of their planes.

The American airmen were not the only ones to score during this two-day strike. On the 17th Task Force 58's gunnery ships, led by the battleships *New Jersey* and *Iowa,* circled the atoll, catching some fleeing Japanese vessels in the process. In a running gun battle, the US ships sank a light cruiser, a destroyer, and a trawler. United States' submarines were not left out of the action either. The day before the Task Force 58 planes struck, the submarine *Skate* hit the light cruiser *Agano* with three torpedoes

JAPANESE INFANTRY, HEAVY MACHINE GUN CREW

These two infantrymen are using the Type 92 air-cooled heavy machine gun. Their uniform comprises khaki jacket and breeches with cross-taped puttees. They wear hobnailed leather boots rather than the lighter split-toed canvas and rubber *Tabi* shoe. The standard Japanese helmet is worn, secured by tapes tied under the chin. Both carry their kit in a canvas hold-all secured round the body.

while she was attempting to escape Truk, and sent her to the bottom.

American losses in this very successful strike were light — 25 planes lost and about 40 men killed among the aviators and aboard the carrier *Intrepid*, when that flattop was damaged during the one counterattack the enemy was able to mount. When Task Force 58 retired from the arena on the evening of February 18, Truk was revealed as a hollow shell. A second carrier raid in April reinforced this revelation. There was no doubt that with its thousands of soldiers Truk would be dangerous if landings were attempted. It was equally obvious that now with no naval or air support, it would pose no problems if bypassed.

Gen. MacArthur began the process of bypassing Truk when he invaded the Admiralties on February 23, thus outflanking Truk to the south. The isolation of Truk became official on March 12, when the Joint Chiefs of Staff presented a new timetable and list of targets to the Pacific commanders, Nimitz and Gen. MacArthur. MacArthur was directed to continue his advance up the back of New Guinea and to the islands off the Vogelkop Peninsula, then invade Mindanao in November. While MacArthur was gaining control of New Guinea (either by isolating the Japanese, as at Wewak, or assaulting their positions directly, as at Hollandia and Biak), Nimitz was to keep Truk neutralized, invade the Marianas, then strike at the Palaus in mid-September. To accomplish these tasks, most of the Army troops from Adm. Halsey's South Pacific Area command (now a secondary theater) went to MacArthur, while Marine and most of the naval units were assigned to Nimitz.

Following the Marianas operation, Adm. Nimitz' next task was the assault on the Palau Islands. Part of the Caroline Islands, the Palaus lay about 530 miles (240km) east of Mindanao and about the same distance north of New Guinea, and were the main Japanese position in the Carolines. By taking these islands, Nimitz would secure MacArthur's right flank as he drove for the Philippines. Initially, the entire group of over 100 islands in the Palaus was to be taken or neutralized, but when information was received that the Japanese were reinforcing the islands — primarily their main positions on the largest island in the group, Babelthuap — Nimitz decided to limit his attack to three islands — Angaur, Peleliu, and Ngesebus — in the southern Palaus.

Peleliu was the site of a pair of enemy runways, and the flat southern portion of the island was capable of being developed into an even larger airfield complex. The terrain to the north of the runways, known as Umurbrogol Mountain, which should have been obvious to the US planners, apparently did not unduly alarm them. Hidden under a carpet of trees and scrub brush, it was only after

Above: Dublon Island in the Truk group comes in for another attack from American carrier-borne air power. By this time the value of Truk to the Combined Fleet had disappeared, but substantial forces were still located in the islands.

the landings that this area (with its nightmarish aspect of caves, ridges, gorges, and pinnacles at last revealed) created concern and some apprehension. Just a few hundred yards off Peleliu's north shore was Ngesebus, a small flat island which appeared to be capable also of airfield construction.

The other island to be captured was Angaur, ten miles (16km) south of Peleliu. Smaller than its northern neighbor, Angaur was densely wooded but, except for the northwest portion of the island, relatively flat and suitable for airfield development. Adm. Nimitz chose two other objectives for capture. One was Yap, about 300 miles (480km) northeast of the Palaus, and the site of a major airfield and a large garrison. The other was Ulithi Atoll, a necklace of small islands surrounding a magnificent lagoon, and another hundred miles (160km) northeast of Yap. Few Japanese were stationed at Ulithi.

The forces Nimitz gathered for Stalemate II (the capture of the southern Palaus, Yap, and Ulithi) were formidable. In fact, before it was over, some 250,000 Marine, Navy, and Army personnel would take part in Stalemate II. In overall command of the operation was Adm. Halsey. In August, Halsey replaced Spruance in command of the Fifth Fleet, bringing with him a new designation for the force — Third Fleet. Actually, there was little change in the structure of the fleet. For the most part, the ships remained the same, only the leaders switched. Thus, while Halsey took the ships to sea, Spruance and his staff were ashore planning the next operation and vice versa.

For Stalemate II, Halsey split his force into two major parts. One, in which he retained direct command, was the Covering Forces and Special Groups (Task Force 30). This force was built basically around the fast carriers of Task Force 38. The other major organization was Rear

Adm. Theodore S. Wilkinson's Joint Expeditionary Force. The Expeditionary Force was actually a headquarters section of the Third Fleet's III Amphibious Force (Task Force 31), which Wilkinson also commanded. Wilkinson wore one more hat for his operation, that of the Eastern Task Force commander.

Under the Joint Expeditionary Force were two more units — Rear Adm. George H. Fort's Western Attack Force (Task Force 32), which was assigned Peleliu and Angaur, and Wilkinson's Eastern Task Force (Task Force 32), which was to be used at Yap and Ulithi. Leading the ground forces was Maj. Gen. Julian S. Smith (USMC), Commander, Expeditionary Troops. Maj. Gen. Roy S. Geiger (USMC) commanded the Western Landing Force and Troops, also known as the III Amphibious Corps. Two divisions made up the principal ground units used at Peleliu and Angaur. One, the veteran 1st Marine Division, would assault Peleliu. The other, the 81st Infantry Division (minus one regimental combat team), was going into combat for the first time and was assigned Angaur. The force scheduled to take Yap was the XXIV Corps, with the 7th, 77th, and 96th Infantry Divisions. The regimental combat team of the 81st Infantry division not scheduled for Angaur was given the task of subduing Ulithi.

The 1st Marine Division was coming from its so-called "rest area" on Pavuvu in the Russell Islands. Pavuvu was probably one of the worst sites imaginable for a rest camp — sodden, disease-ridden, too small for proper training, and lacking in adequate facilities for almost any task or activity. Just leaving Pavuvu

US Marine Raider Fighting Knives and Machetes

1 Marine Raider machete and leather sheath. The design of the handle can also be seen in knife 4
2 Marine Raider Ka Bar knife
3 Australian fighting knife with steel blade and all aluminum handle and knucklebow combination
4 Marine Raider Gung Ho knife. This weapon was designed specifically for Carlson's 2d Raider Battalion, and is a development from the Marine machete 1. Its blade is 9 inches (22 cm) long the same type as 4.
5 Marine Raider knife. The same type as 4. In exactly the same condition as it was issued. The knife is still in its protective oiled paper complete with acceptance certificate
6 US Marine Raider stiletto, with sheath. This knife was developed from the British Fairbourne-Sykes (F-S) fighting knife by Lt. Col. Clifford H. Shuey USMC, specifically for the Raiders
7 Variant of 6, with sheath
8 Variant of 6
9 Theater manufactured Marine Raider fighting knife
10 Theater manufactured Marine Raider fighting knife
11 Theater manufactured Marine Raider fighting knife
12 Marine Raider patch

US Marine Raider Museum

The Marine Raider Gung Ho knife (*4* and *5*), was manufactured specifically for Carlson's 2d Raider Battalion. They were made by Collins & Co. of Hartford, Conn, and were distributed to the men during July-August 1942. The Raider stiletto (*6*, *7*, and *8*), was based on a British designed commando knife. The Raider knife differs from the British type in that it has a one piece, die-cast aluminum alloy grip. It is the poor quality of this alloy that is making these knives increasingly difficult to find undamaged by time. The Marine raider patch insignia (*12*), is believed to have first been designed after the unit returned from Guadalcanal in 1943. The Raider skull (a popular Raider emblem) is superimposed on the Southern Cross badge of the 1st Marine Division - an insignia also designed after Guadalcanal.

was a relief to the marines, who undoubtedly preferred to take out their frustrations on the Japanese.

Until April 1944, the Palaus remained pretty much a sleepy rear-echelon base, a staging area for Japanese units moving elsewhere. This changed dramatically, however, with the fall of the Marshalls, the air attacks on Truk, and, then, a spectacularly successful raid on the Palaus by Task Force 58 in March. Faced with the possibility of an attack there, the Japanese sent the 14th Division (a veteran division from the Kwantung Army of Manchukuo) to the Palaus in late April to take over the defense.

By September, following a period of realignments of the division's units to various islands, the Japanese defense of the Palaus stabilized. The bulk of Lt. Gen. Sadae Inoue's 14th Division was stationed on Babelthuap and Koror, the latter being the site of the division's headquarters. On Peleliu, Col. Kunio Nakagawa, commander of the 2d Infantry and the island's garrison, had almost 10,500 men (of which two-thirds were combat troops) from his regiment, plus battalions from the 15th Infantry and the 53d Independent Mixed Brigade. Maj. Gen. Kenjiro Murai was also on Peleliu, but Nakagawa was actually in charge of

the defense. Apparently, Murai was there solely to counterbalance the senior naval officer, a rear admiral.

Nakagawa would be the first Japanese commander officially to use new tactics against the invaders. *Banzai* attacks were out. Instead, a defense in depth was established, with well-prepared fall-back positions. A solid reserve was to be used in reasoned and massive counterattacks. All of the probable landing beaches were mined, defensive positions were superbly camouflaged, contained heavy firepower, and were physically very strong. And there was always the Umurbrogol, with its warren of caves, that

The first two United States Marine Corps Raider Battalions were activated in February 1942, specifically to undertake amphibious, commando-style raids in the Pacific. The 1st Battalion took part in the Guadalcanal landings, while companies of the 2nd Battalion took part in the defense of Midway and the raid on Makin Island. The 3rd battalion was organized in Samoa in September 1942, and the 4th on the West Coast that October. The 3rd took part with the 2nd in operations in the northern Solomons and Bougainville, while the 4th would join the 1st for the campaign on New Georgia. The need for specialized assault battalions receded after 1943, and in response, the four Raider battalions were brought together on Guadalcanal in February 1944, and there reconstituted into the 4th Marine regiment.

Japanese Army Equipment

1 Medical corpsman's first aid case, open, with contents displayed
2 Hospital banner
3 Metal medicinal container
4 Mirror in pouch from kit *1*
5 Small scissors from kit *1*
6 Packet of tablets
7 Wound description tag to be affixed to an injured soldier
8 Pocket surgical kit with forceps and scalpel
9 Packet of bandages from first aid case *12*
10 Medicinal container from first aid case *12*
11 Drugs and suture needles from first aid case *12*
12 First aid case
13 Medical personnel brassard
14 Roll of medicinal tape

15 Packets of medicinal powder
16 Engineer's drafting instruments and case from map case *25*
17 Infantry issue binoculars 6x magnification, with case
18-20 Personnel items carried in *25*
21 Camera from item *25*
22 Artillery officer's measuring tape
23 Pair of ear plugs in wooden box, carried by artillery officer
24 Late 1944 pattern officer's sword
25 Map case carried by officers and NCOs
26 Issue wrist watch

US Marine Museum: 2-7, 14-22, 24-26; Eugene C. Gibson: 1, 8-13, 23

This collection of Japanese Army equipment includes a Japanese Red Cross banner (2) from the home front. In translation it reads: 'Japan Red Cross, Hiroshima branch.' The banner is a souvenir of the ground-breaking ceremony of a new hospital there. (Ground-breaking is Shinto ceremony.) The Army medical equipment carried in first aid cases 1 and 12, seems quite simple by comparison with Allied medical kits. Through lack of resources and conscious design, Japanese medical services were of much poorer quality than those of its opponents. The spirit of the Japanese soldier was to fight and die, if need be at the place where he stood. The necessity then for an organization to save him for another day was not recognized by Japanese commanders, and medical services in Army units were often simply neglected.

could be used for a last-ditch effort. Nakagawa made sure that any attempt to take Peleliu would be bloody.

Angaur was another story. Maj. Ushio Goto had only one battalion of the 59th Infantry, plus supporting troops, to defend the island. His total force numbered only about 1,400 men and he did not have many artillery pieces. Nevertheless, he had prepared strong defensive positions and, like Nakagawa, Maj. Goto was ready to make the invaders pay dearly.

To provide cover for the Palau landings, on September 9-10, Halsey sent the planes of Task Force 38 against enemy airfields on Mindanao. Opposition was very weak and many Japanese planes were destroyed. Buoyed by the results of these attacks, Halsey canceled further strikes on Mindanao to concentrate instead on Japanese fields in the central Philippines. In a three-day attack, September 12-14, the Americans once again had a field day, destroying some 200 Japanese planes, sinking or damaging many ships, and wreaking considerable devastation to ground installations. Halsey was sure the Philippines were an empty shell (which was completely false as would be found out) and on September 13, made a startling

THE DEFENSE OF PELELIU

Maps A and B
The Japanese had learnt valuable lessons from previous assaults on their islands, and on Peleliu new defensive tactics were used. Heavily fortified and well-armed strongpoints were used in conjunction with a reserve kept ready for counterattacks; there were to be no *banzai* charges. The Japanese also made full use of the terrain, especially the hill mass of the Umurbrogol which they turned into a warren of defensive positions.

and far-reaching recommendation.

In a message to Nimitz, he proposed that the Palaus, Yap, and Mindanao landings be canceled and, instead, these troops be used to strike at the center of the Philippines, at Leyte. Nimitz approved the cancellation of the Yap landings but decided that the Palau operation was too far along to stop. Meanwhile, Nimitz sent signals to MacArthur and the Joint Chiefs of Staff, in mid-September 1944, the latter meeting at that time with their British counterparts in Quebec at the Octagon Conference.

MacArthur was en route to Morotai to observe those landings and was maintaining radio silence, but his chief of staff, Lt. Gen. Richard K. Sutherland, knew this was the opening MacArthur sought to strike at the heart of the Philippines. Sutherland quickly radioed back that Halsey's recommendations were agreed with, and that an assault on Leyte be mounted on October 20. The Joint Chiefs of Staff also acted with breath-taking speed. Within 90 minutes of the receipt of Halsey's recommendations and Nimitz and MacArthur's agreements, the Joint Chiefs ordered Leyte invaded and the Yap, Talauds, and Mindanao operations canceled.

Additionally, the Joint Chiefs of Staff directed that the XXIV Army Corps, scheduled for the Yap landings, be assigned to the Leyte assault; that all shipping used in the Palaus be sent to the Southwest Pacific after unloading to help provide extra lift for the Sixth Army's movement to Leyte; that all fire support ships and escort carriers used in Stalemate II be assigned temporarily to the Seventh Fleet for use at Leyte; and that Ulithi be taken immediately. Thus, in mid-September, the plans so carefully crafted in the spring suddenly became so much waste paper — except for Angaur and Peleliu.

The pre-invasion bombardment of Peleliu began early on the morning of September 12, as Rear Adm. Jesse B. Oldendorf's fire support group of 5 battleships, 8 cruisers, and 14 destroyers began its slow, methodical bombardment of the island. Assisting in this task were planes from 11 escort carriers, the largest grouping yet of these vessels in the Pacific. Soon this bombardment began to strip away the vegetation to reveal the convoluted terrain of the island. None of the Americans gave much thought to this terrain — not yet.

Pleased with the progress of the bombardment and unaware of the cave structure of the island and the toughness of some of the prepared positions,

Oldendorf made an unfortunate remark on the evening of the 14th. "We have run out of targets", he radioed the commander of Task Force 32. If any Japanese was listening, he must have smiled.

But Oldendorf was not the only invader exuding confidence. Maj. Gen. William H. Rupertus, the 1st Marine Division commander, was equally sanguine about the operation. In a letter issued to his troop the day before the landings, he predicted a tough operation, but a "quickie" that would be over in three or four days. Many marine officers felt later that this belief that Peleliu would be a speedy task had an effect on tactical operations throughout the battle.

September 15, 1944, was D-Day for Peleliu. Initially, the sky over the island that morning was bright and almost cloud-free, but this soon changed as coral dust churned up by the naval gunfire and smoke from burning vehicles and structures smudged the sky. Offshore, amphibian tractors, LVTs and LVT(A)s, carved the water in circles as they awaited to begin the charge toward land. Because of the reef protecting Peleliu's western beaches, the marines in the assault waves were carried by amtracs. Later waves were shuttled to the reef by LCVPs (ramped landing craft) and transferred to LVTs and DUKWs (amphibian trucks) returning from the beach.

Marine ranks, but the defenses were somewhat weaker here, probably because the airfield covered most of this area. Nonetheless, there were enough prepared positions still operating to add to the casualties. By mid-afternoon, however, elements of the 5th Marines were just short of the eastern shore.

To the south, on the right flank of the beachhead, the 7th Marines met scattered resistance at first, but this stiffened as the marines pushed inland against a series of well-organized positions. A mangrove swamp, which had not shown up on the marines' maps, helped to slow the 7th Marines' progress.

So far the Japanese, adhering to Nakagawa's defensive plans, had been content to launch just small counterattacks. But at 4:50 in the afternoon, they mounted a combined infantry-tank attack across the airfield. This was no *banzai* attack; the infantrymen moved with the skittery bounds followed by the quick drops to the earth that marked the veteran soldier. Fortunately, the attack was not coordinated. The light tanks (lighter than their American counterparts and more properly described as tankettes) raced full bore across the airfield toward the marine lines, leaving their infantry far to the rear.

The resulting action was a slaughter. Marine M4 medium tanks, 37mm antitank guns, bazookas, grenades, even a 500-lb bomb dropped by a plane from an escort carrier, ripped the attack to pieces. Exactly how many Japanese tanks were actually involved is still open to question: the confusion of the battle created all sorts of claims, but it is known that eleven of the enemy vehicles did not

At 8:00 A.M., the first wave crossed the line of departure and headed for the island. Thirty-two minutes later, the first amtracs ground ashore. The landing beaches were under heavy fire and soon the carcasses of LVTs and DUKWs littered the area, along with the bodies of many marines. The 1st Marines landed on the left-hand beaches and found themselves in difficulty almost immediately. The regiment landed under the shadow of a 30-foot (9-m)-high coral ridge which had gone unnoticed earlier and which was swarming with angry Japanese. Also, many of the enemy strongpoints were left completely untouched by the naval and air bombardment and were now swiftly reoccupied by the defenders.

The most important piece of real estate at this end of the beachhead was a piece of land extending into the water and which received the name, The Point. From The Point, the defenders could fire into the division's flank. After a two-hour battle, The Point was silenced, but the company which accomplished this task found itself cut off from the

remainder of the regiment and spent the next 30 hours defending its gains.

It was in the center of the beachhead, in the 5th Marines zone, where the greatest advances were made. This area was flat, with many palm trees. Enemy shelling caused many casualties in the return to their own lines. Casualties to the enemy infantrymen are unknown but they must have suffered heavily also. Several other attempts to breach the marine lines during the day likewise met with failure.

By nightfall, the marines carved out a perimeter about 2,800 yards (2,500m) long but, except where the 5th Marines had crossed the island, one only some 400-700 yards (360-630m) deep. This beachhead cost the 1st Marine Division 210 dead and 901 wounded, plus many others felled by the searing heat, which climbed at times to over 100 degrees. These results were not what the marines expected; still, Gen. Rupertus and many of his men remained optimistic that the defenders would soon break and the battle would end.

Over the next few days, the 1st Marine Division pushed forward, completing the capture of the vital airfield and moving into the shadow of the Umurbrogol hill mass. The fighting was intense and the marines suffered numerous casualties. It was now evident that Peleliu was not going to be a "quickie" operation. However, on the 16th when Rupertus still felt that the battle was going well and no reinforcements were

needed, the 81st Infantry Division had been released from its reserve role so that it could attack Angaur. Thus, reinforcements were not going to available right away. (Rupertus may have had another reason for sending the Army troops to Angaur. He intensely disliked the Army and did not want to share with the other service any "glory" that might arise from the Peleliu battle.)

The 321st and 322d Regiments of the 81st Infantry Division landed on Angaur on the morning of September 17. There was little opposition and within 30 minutes all the assault waves were ashore. Most of Goto's defenders were caught out of position and it was some time before they were able to react. Resistance eventually developed but the Japanese were unable to prevent the Army troops from expanding their beachhead. Almost as much of a problem as the Japanese was the dense jungle. At some points it proved to be impassable.

Over the next four days, the 81st Infantry Division pushed the Japanese into the northwest corner of Angaur. Feeling that the main resistance was over, the 81st's commander, Maj. Gen. Paul J. Mueller, declared the island secured on

the 20th and released his 321st Infantry for use on Peleliu. However, despite being declared secured, the toughest fighting for the island lay ahead. Major Goto established a smaller version of the Umurbrogol on Angaur's northwest corner. Here he fought until killed on October 19. After that, the soldiers cleaned out most of the remaining Japanese. By the 23d, the action on Angaur was over except for the tracking down of stragglers. Already, Army Air Forces B-24s were operating from the field that was built following the landings.

On Angaur, only 59 Japanese were captured. The rest, around 1,400, were killed or chose to die by their own hand. For the Americans, Angaur cost 264 men killed and 1,355 wounded or injured. It wasn't a Peleliu type of casualty list but it was bloody enough.

In the meantime, the 81st Infantry Division's third regiment, the 323d, occupied Ulithi on September 23. The only Japanese found — two — were already

Below: A marine involved in the fighting for the Palaus looks carefully for Japanese snipers. Ignoring their own safety and waiting for just the right moment, such snipers could hide for days and then cut down several Americans before being killed.

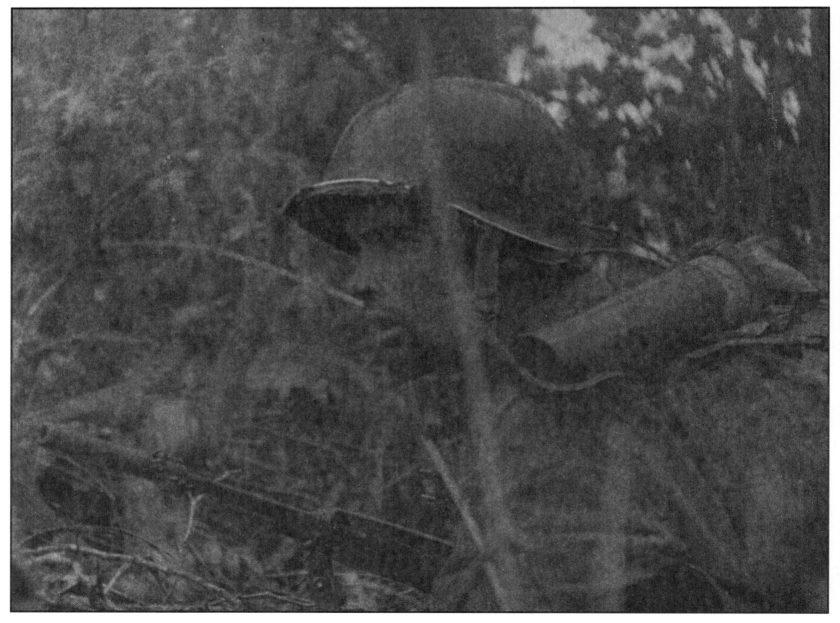

dead, and the process of turning the atoll into a major base began apace. By early October, the lagoon was being used by the fast carriers. Before the war ended, the Ulithi anchorage was to prove its value many times over.

While the Angaur and Ulithi operations were coming to a successful close, the fighting on Peleliu became more savage. The initial objectives of the invasion force, particularly the airfield, had been attained within a week of the landing. Marine aircraft began close air support operations from the field on the last days of September. The missions were among the shortest of the war, the pilots often not even raising their landing gear after takeoff before having to drop their bombs or napalm. Even with air support, close-range artillery and tank fire (if any of these weapons could be brought to bear in the mazes of gorges and peaks), the only way the Japanese were going to be defeated was by the foot-by-foot progress of the infantrymen. And although Gen. Rupertus refused to acknowledge the fact, his division was being bled white.

By the 21st, the 1st Marines were virtually finished and had to be relieved. The regiment suffered an almost 60 percent loss of its authorized strength (one battalion losing almost three-quarters of its strength). This was the highest casualty rate *any* Marine unit would take in the war. At last, Rupertus recognized the severity of his division's losses and realized that the Army troops would have to be called in. On September 23, the 321st Regimental Combat Team landed on Peleliu to relieve the 1st Marines and was in action the next day.

The Umurbrogol was isolated on September 27 and Ngesebus was captured on the 29th after a two-day fight. This small island was found to be useless for airfield construction. By October 1 almost all of Peleliu was captured — only the Umurbrogol remained.

Above: Photographed on October 13, 1944 and flying with its landing gear lowered, probably to keep its speed down, a Vought F4U Corsair fighter bomber of the 2d Marine Air Wing napalms the Japanese in a gorge behind Five Sisters Peaks on Peleliu.

Bloody Nose Ridge; Death Valley; Pope's Ridge; Wildcat Bowl; China Wall. These were just a few of the names the Marine and Army troops gave to the topographical features in the Umurbrogol. Yet, even a name like Death Valley fails to convey the horror of the fighting that took place there.

The fighting in this jumble of pock-marked rotting coral was slow, grinding, punishing on all who took part. The front lines, if they can even be called lines, sometimes moved forward only a few feet. Slowly, the Umurborgol Pocket was reduced, but the 1st Marine Division was wearing out. Finally, relief of the division by units of the 81st Infantry Division began on October 15. On the 20th, responsibility for the battle passed to Gen. Mueller, the 81st's commander.

For the next month, the army troops methodically smashed the pocket.

Below: Seen at the burial of American dead on Peleliu are two of the assault force's senior commanders, namely Maj. Gen. William H.Rupertus (right) of the 1st Marine Division and (left) Colonel Lewis Puller of the 1st Marines.

There was no great urgency to finish the job; the airfield was already in operation; the Japanese were contained; and the task was not worth risking the soldiers' lives unnecessarily. Not in four days, as Gen. Rupertus predicted rashly, but 74 days later, on November 27, the battle was declared over. This does not mean that all the Japanese defenders were dead. In 1947, a group of 27 Japanese surrendered. Amazingly, one last survivor, a Korean, remained hidden on Peleliu until 1954 when he finally gave himself up.

Peleliu was a brutal battle — one of the bloodiest of the war. It cost the 1st Marine Division 1,252 dead and 5,274 wounded. The 81st Infantry Division suffered 277 killed and 1,000 wounded on Peleliu, plus another 26 dead and 1,354 wounded on Angaur. And these figures do not include the hundreds of men temporarily incapacitated by heat, fatigue, disease. For the Japanese it was even worse. Of the almost 12,000 men on both islands, only 361 were captured.

Was Peleliu worth it? In hindsight, probably not. Although Adm. Nimitz, who did not have a clear intelligence picture of Japanese strength in the Palaus, still believed the assault on Peleliu and Angaur was necessary, the capture of the Marianas and MacArthur's advance up New Guinea effectively flanked the Palaus. The Japanese Navy's carrier power was destroyed in the Battle of the Philippine Sea and Peleliu was to play no part in subsequent Japanese plans for a final decisive fleet action. Even after Peleliu and Angaur were captured, the airfields on these islands were little more than way stations for planes traveling elsewhere. Only Ulithi became a valuable base for the US Navy in the last months of the war. Nevertheless, the valor shown by the marines and soldiers on Peleliu and Angaur should not be forgotten.

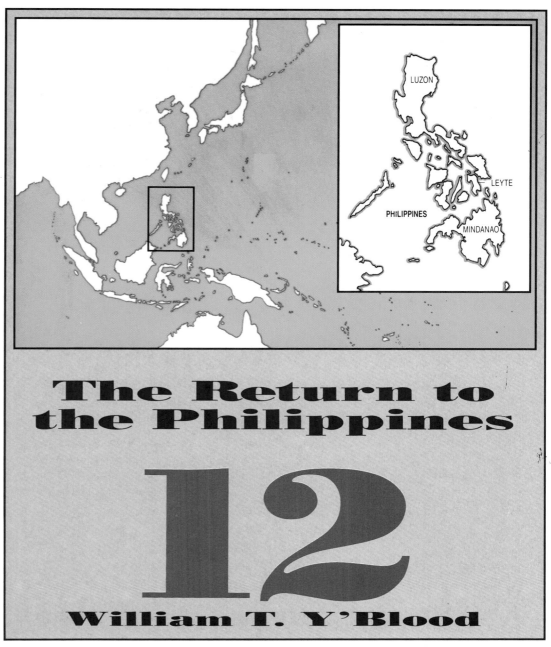

The Return to the Philippines

12

William T. Y'Blood

For months the Joint Chiefs of Staff debated whether the American attack across the Pacific should be aimed at the Philippines, specifically Luzon, or at Formosa and the China coast, or if the advance should be split between the two arenas. Pressing hardest for the Philippines was Gen. Douglas MacArthur. Any operations in the Philippines would be under his command and he felt he had made a pledge, not just to the Filipinos but also to the world, that he would return to those islands. Arguing just as forcefully for Formosa was Adm. Ernest J. King, who believed that attacking that island was the best way to cut Japan's lifeline to the Netherlands East Indies and Southeast Asia, while providing a strategically stronger location than Luzon for a final assault on Japan.

On March 2, 1944, the Joint Chiefs of Staff had tentatively selected Formosa as the "first major objective" of the Pacific advance, with Luzon a possibility if that operation proved necessary. But this was only a tentative decision and many months of wrangling lay ahead as, first, MacArthur and his partisans argued for the Philippines, then King and his

followers presented their point of view.

Prior to the invasion of the Marianas, it was apparent to the Joint Chiefs that operations were going well and further operations in the Pacific could be accelerated. In fact, in June they even considered the possibility of bypassing both Formosa and the Philippines. MacArthur refused to accept this, and in July, presented the Joint Chiefs with his latest strategic plan — Reno V. In this plan, Sarangani Bay on Mindanao was to be assaulted on October 25, 1944, followed by landings on Leyte about November 15, southeastern Luzon in mid-January 1945, and Lingayen Gulf, Luzon, on April 1, 1945.

Reno V, if accepted, meant that a Formosa operation would have to be postponed until October of 1945. This was unacceptable to the Joint Chiefs of Staff, particularly Adm. King. But as the Joint Chiefs thrashed out this conflict, MacArthur met in late July with Adm. Chester W. Nimitz, Commander-in-Chief, Pacific Ocean Areas, and President Roosevelt at Pearl Harbor. When MacArthur left that meeting, he believed he had converted the president to his

Japanese Naval Insignia and Accoutrements

1 Paper parade flag bearing the emblem of the Imperial Japanese Navy. In translation the flag reads: 'Patriotic Ladies Society, Kyoto Branch'
2 Dark blue wool junior officer's cap.
3 White cotton enlisted man's cap
4 Private purchase silk pillow case with motifs of anchor, battleship, and the Imperial Japanese Navy ensign
5 Naval parade saber and scabbard. This pattern sword was developed around the 1900s and was in use until the end of the war. It was adopted by all commissioned officers.
6 Model 1883 modified, commissioned officer's dirk and scabbard
7 Naval officer's cap insignia
8 Two-piece, interlocking brass navy belt plate and black leather belt with hangers. This belt and plate was adopted by all officers
9 Private purchase naval belt buckle
10 Enlisted ranks insignia: the cherry blossom
11 Sleeve insignia of an Ordinary Seaman
12 Sleeve insignia of a Leading Seaman
13 Sleeve insignia of a Petty Officer First Class
14 Sleeve insignia of a Chief Petty Officer

US Marine Raider Museum

The Japanese Navy field cap (*2* and *3*) was of the same pattern as that used by the Japanese Army, and was introduced during the war. Naval ratings also wore the Western-style dark blue square rig and flat round cap. The white cap (*3*) is part of a white working rig of cap, loose pullover jacket, and trousers. The ratings badges (*11, 12, 13,* and *14*) were worn on the sleeves of all ratings; these four are of a late pattern insignia. The Navy emblem of the cherry blossom (also in evidence on silk pillow case *4*) was given different colors to distinguish the different branches of naval service. These colors included yellow for sea service, blue for aviation, and red for medical; other branches included construction and pay. Navy personnel serving on land, of which the Japanese Marines are an example, wore a special uniform of olive drab drill.

views. Roosevelt had told MacArthur that the Philippines would be taken; he *had not*, however, canceled the Formosa operation nor had he said which of the two options would come first.

And there the strategy for forthcoming operations in the Pacific remained stuck. Both MacArthur and King continued to forcefully present their differing ideas on the proper strategy. The joint planning staff continued to churn out variations of the two strategies. Finally, on September 1, the Joint Chiefs of Staff approved MacArthur's plan for an invasion of Mindanao followed by an attack on Leyte around December 20.

Afterward the American forces might advance on Formosa or Luzon as the planners decided.

At this juncture, Adm. William F. Halsey made a startling recommendation to bypass Yap and the Palaus and strike directly at Leyte. Although MacArthur, through his intelligence organizations, knew the Philippines were stronger than Halsey realized, he seized this unexpected opportunity to launch an attack into the center of the Philippines and thus commit the United States to retaking the islands. He radioed the Joint Chiefs that Leyte could be assaulted on October 20.

Approval for this operation came quickly — after only 90 minutes — and MacArthur's cherished dream of returning to the Philippines was on its way to becoming reality. MacArthur also believed that an attack on Leyte would enable him to advance the Luzon landings to December 20. The possibility of invading Luzon so soon made an assault on Formosa a much less attractive option, particularly since it appeared that Nimitz would require many more service troops for that operation than were then available. Also, Japanese advances in China had diminished the strategic importance of the area. Reluctantly, Adm. King agreed to the postponement of any operations against Formosa and that proposal receded into the background, never to emerge again as a serious topic.

For his return to the Philippines, MacArthur had an immense amount of resources under his command. Lt. Gen. Walter Krueger's Sixth Army, about 200,000 strong, would make the assault on Leyte. Assigned the southern beaches near Dulag were the 96th and 7th Infantry Divisions of Maj. Gen. John R. Hodge's XXIV Corps. Originally scheduled to attack the island of Yap, the XXIV Corps still had its transports combat-loaded for that operation, which created some problems because of the vastly different terrain that would be encountered initially on Leyte. Also, the two divisions would still use during the landings the amphibian tractors (amtracs) that were to have been employed over the coral reefs at Yap.

Landing on the northern beaches near Tacloban were the 1st Cavalry and 24th Infantry Divisons of Maj. Gen. Frank C. Sibert's X Corps. Unlike the XXIV Corps divisions, these units would utilize ramped landing craft rather than amtracs for their landings. Held in reserve by Krueger were the 32d and 77th Infantry Divisions and the 6th Ranger Battalion.

Also under MacArthur's command was the Seventh Fleet, led by Vice Adm. Thomas C. Kinkaid. Kinkaid's force was split into three units: Task Force 77 (which Kinkaid commanded directly) would cover the landings and included the close support vessels and escort carriers; Task Force 78, under Rear Adm. Daniel E. Barbey, was the Northern Attack Force assigned the Tacloban beaches; Vice Adm. Theodore S. Wilkinson's Task Force 79, the Southern Attack Force, would land the XXIV Corps over the Dulag beaches. The Seventh Fleet was a tremendous aggregation of ships, over 700 vessels, of which many were borrowed from Nimitz. The job of the Seventh Fleet was to get the troops ashore and support them. The job of protecting the troops and of covering the entire operation was that of Halsey's Third Fleet.

But MacArthur did not control the Third Fleet; Halsey reported directly to Nimitz. Thus the American command at Leyte was not unified but divided — a

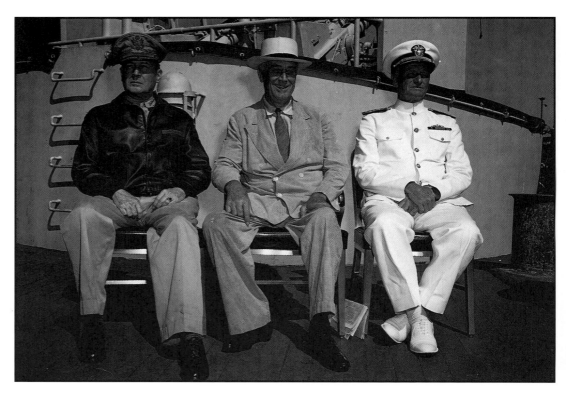

Above: Seen on board the heavy cruiser *Baltimore* at Honolulu on July 26, 1944, President Roosevelt is flanked by the men who were the driving force behind the American effort against the Japanese, namely MacArthur and Nimitz.

Below: Later in the war, the Japanese placed much faith in the capabilities of the superbattleship *Yamato*, which with her sister ship *Musashi* was designed with the protection and firepower to fight a group of smaller American battleships.

setup ripe for confusion. What, for example, would Halsey do if the Imperial Japanese Navy intervened? He was supposed to cover the Leyte operation for MacArthur but he was also to destroy the enemy fleet for Nimitz; this latter task would become his primary mission if enemy warships approached. And Halsey was passionate when it came to destroying the enemy fleet, especially its carriers. Like a number of other officers, notably many aviators, he felt that Adm. Raymond Spruance had "failed" to destroy the enemy during the Battle of the Philippine Sea and he was not about to let that happen again.

Yet, if the US command was unwieldy and potentially risky, that of the Japanese was in a far worse position. Throughout the war, Japanese army and navy operations were seldom truly coordinated; one of the services would initiate a plan without consulting the other, then call upon the other for assistance when difficulties arose.

Although Japanese operations in the Philippines were planned jointly by both services, in conducting them, the army and navy (especially the latter) each went its own way.

Following the fall of the Marianas, the Japanese devised a new set of plans for a "decisive" battle. Named *SHO-GO* (Victory Operation), the plan was actually a set of four plans covering various parts of the shrinking Japanese empire. The likeliest point of attack was considered to be the Philippines and *SHO-1* covered this possibility; *SHO-2* concerned Formosa and the Ryukyus; *SHO-3* was southern and central Japan; and *SHO-4* involved the Kuriles and northern Japan.

SHO-GO required a careful husbanding of resources to meet the American threats. Only after MacArthur and Nimitz showed their hand could the defenders throw their full strength against the invaders. For the Japanese navy, this involved yet another

THE BATTLE OF LEYTE GULF

Map A
Under the Japanese *SHO-1* plan, four separate naval forces would converge on the American Philippines invasion fleet: three would force their way north and south of Leyte, catching the invader's transports between them in Leyte Gulf and destroying them. At the same time a carrier force approaching from the north would decoy the covering American fleet. Things did not go as planned. Two American submarines found the Japanese 1st Striking Force near the island of Palawan; they attacked and sank two heavy cruisers. The Americans, now alerted to the presence of the Japanese, then attacked the 1st Striking Force with carrier aircraft as it passed through the Sibuyan Sea. Damage was sustained but the Force carried on. This battle of the Sibuyan Sea was the first of the Leyte Gulf engagements.

Map B
The following day, October 25, the Japanese Southern Force attempted to force a way through the Surigao Strait. Here it was met by a Group of battleships, cruisers, destroyers and PT Boats which inflicted severe damage on the Southern Force. This action became known as the Battle of Surigao Strait.

Map C
The next action, the Battle off Samar, took place as the 1st Striking Force cleared the San Bernadino Strait on the morning of the 25th and ran up against a far lighter American force of escort carriers and destroyers. The American ships forced a Japanese withdrawal, though with heavy losses to themselves.

Map D
The final action, the Battle of Cape Engano, took place to the north, where the Japanese carrier force was caught by American carrier planes. Heavily damaged by these, the Japanese were saved from total annihilation when the battleships of Task Force 34 were ordered back to support the 7th Fleet.

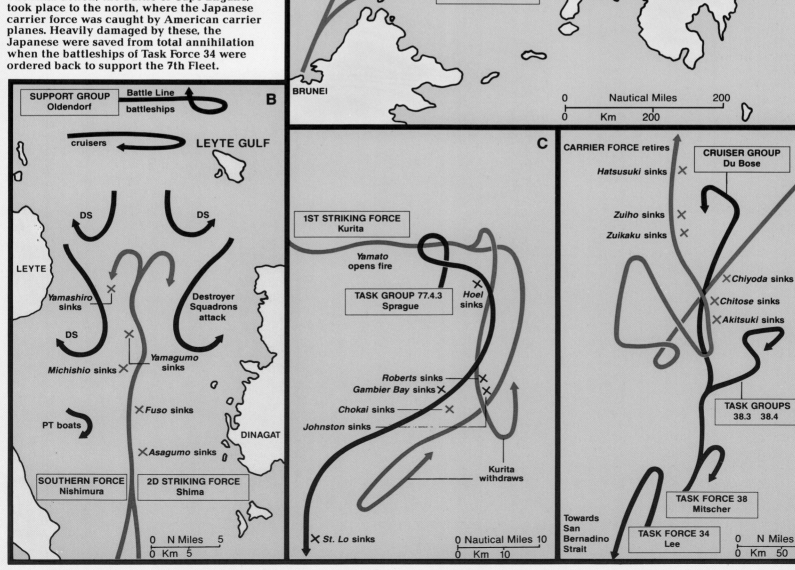

A — October 23—26 1944

PHILIPPINE ISLANDS

CARRIER FORCE Ozawa · October 25

3D FLEET Halsey

LUZON

2D STRIKING FORCE Shima

Manila

Princeton sinks ✕

Battle of the Sibuyan Sea October 24 — Air attacks *Musashi* sinks

SAMAR

LEYTE

7TH FLEET Kinkaid

1ST STRIKING FORCE Kurita

Atago sinks ✕

Maya sinks ✕

PALAWAN

MINDANAO

SOUTHERN FORCE Nishimura

0 — Nautical Miles — 200
0 — Km — 200

BRUNEI

B

SUPPORT GROUP Oldendorf · Battle Line battleships

cruisers · LEYTE GULF

DS · DS

LEYTE

Yamashiro sinks ✕

Destroyer Squadrons attack

DS

Michishio sinks ✕ · *Yamagumo* sinks

✕ *Fuso* sinks

PT boats · DINAGAT

✕ *Asagumo* sinks

SOUTHERN FORCE Nishimura · 2D STRIKING FORCE Shima

0 N Miles 5
0 Km 5

C

1ST STRIKING FORCE Kurita

Yamato opens fire

TASK GROUP 77.4.3 Sprague · *Hoel* sinks ✕

Roberts sinks ✕
Gambier Bay sinks ✕
Chokai sinks ✕
Johnston sinks

Kurita withdraws

✕ *St. Lo* sinks

0 Nautical Miles 10
0 Km 10

D

CARRIER FORCE retires · CRUISER GROUP Du Bose

Hatsusuki sinks ✕

Zuiho sinks ✕
Zuikaku sinks ✕

✕ *Chiyoda* sinks
✕ *Chitose* sinks
✕ *Akitsuki* sinks

TASK GROUPS 38.3 38.4

TASK FORCE 38 Mitscher

Towards San Bernardino Strait

TASK FORCE 34 Lee

0 N Miles 50
0 Km 50

US Army Uniforms and Equipment

1 Herring bone twill one piece overalls worn by tank crews and vehicle maintenance personnel
2 Leather combat boots of the double buckle type
3 Issue olive drab flashlight
4 Model 1936 pistol belt with water canteen in Model 1910 cover, and Model 1942 first aid pouch
5 Model 1911 semi-automatic pistol with leather holster and Model 1918 pistol magazine pouch
6 Model 1936 musette bag/all purpose pack
7 Armor crewman's helmet
8 Field cap of herring bone twill
9 Aviator's survival vest
10 Aviator's leather helmet
11 Summer weight army aviator's one piece suit
12 Inflatable life preserver vest, known as a "Mae West"
13 A2 leather flying jacket with the insignia of the "Jolly Rogers," 90th Bomb Group, Pacific theater
14 Leather toilet kit with the insignia of the 20th Air Force
15 Field shoes
16 Silk escape and evasion maps carried by aviators

Dale E. Biever: 1, 3, 8-16
Pritchard Collection: 2, 4-7

The armor crewman's helmet (*7*) was made of lightweight materials and was pierced with holes for ventilation. The helmet was heavily padded and was designed to be worn over a second close-fitting fabric helmet or knitted "jeep cap". The flexible leather earpieces on the helmet also featured holes; these were to allow the wearer to use headphones for communications inside the vehicle. Over the crown of the helmet can just be seen a snap-fastened leather strap. This was used to hold a pair of tank goggles in place.

The leather A2 flying jacket (*13*) features the insignia of the 90th Bombardment Group, nicknamed the "Jolly Rogers". The 90th Bombardment Group served in the Solomon Islands and Guadalcanal between 1942 and 1943, then transfered to mainland China, from where it operated until the war's end.

complicated plan that required exquisite timing. For *SHO-1*, the plan eventually used, the Japanese assembled a strong force, but one that, at the time of the landings, was weakened by having to operate in widely separated components.

From Singapore came Vice Adm. Takeo Kurita's 1st Striking Force, a powerful unit consisting of 5 battleships (including the *Musashi* and *Yamato*), 10 heavy and 2 light cruisers, and 15 destroyers. The 2d Striking Force, under Vice Adm. Kiyohide Shima and consisting of two heavy cruisers, a light cruiser, and seven destroyers, had left its base in the Ryukyus by the start of

SHO-1 and was in the Pescadores off Formosa preparing to escort a convoy. Shima's force was brought into the plan on the 21st, too late to coordinate an attack with Vice Adm. Shoji Nishimura who was to advance through Surigao Strait. The woefully misnamed Main Force was commanded by Vice Adm. Jisaburo Ozawa and came from Japan. His force was made up of four carriers (carrying only 116 planes — not many more than those carried by a single *Essex*-class carrier), two "hermaphrodite" carriers (battleships fitted with bobtailed flight decks), three light cruisers, and eight destroyers. A fourth contingent, until October 22 a part of the 1st Striking Force, was Nishimura's group of two battleships, a heavy cruiser, and four destroyers. Nishimura's ships split from the 1st Striking Force on October 20 to join with Shima's vessels and force their way through Surigao Strait.

The *SHO-1* plans looked good on paper but required that everything work to perfection. While Ozawa and, in the initial plans, Shima decoyed Halsey to the north, Kurita would streak through San Bernardino Strait north of Leyte, and Nishimura would bull his way through Surigao Strait to the south. The Japanese forces would meet in Leyte Gulf, crushing the American transports between them, then fall upon Halsey who by this time would be caught out of position. Both land-based air and the pitifully few planes Ozawa had left would make all-out attacks against the Americans in support of these movements. In a nutshell, this was how the plan was supposed to work. But, like many nutshells, it cracked easily.

Meanwhile, the Japanese Army was attempting to ready its units for the upcoming battle. Overall command of the Japanese Army forces in the Southwest Pacific was vested in Field Marshal Hisaichi Terauchi. The primary commander in the Philippines was Gen. Tomoyuki Yamashita, ''The Tiger of Malaya'', who commanded the Fourteenth Area Army. However, he had only reached the islands on October 6, in relief of the previous commander, and had hardly familiarized himself with the tactical situation when the Americans struck. Yamashita did not command the Fourth Air Army, which was led by Lt. Gen. Kyoji Tominaga, who reported directly to Terauchi. Subordinate to the Fourteenth Area Army was Lt. Gen. Sosaku Suzuki's Thirty-Fifth Army, which was responsible for the defense of the central and southern Philippines, including Leyte. On Leyte itself was Lt. Gen. Shiro Makino's 16th Division — about 20,000 troops. Initially in the Japanese view, Leyte was not to be the site of the ''decisive'' battle in the Philippines; that ''honor'' was to befall Luzon.

Above: Fulfilling a promise he had made to himself, the Philippines and the world, MacArthur strides toward the Philippine shore from a landing craft, escorted by American and Filipino officers of his Southwest Pacific Area staff.

Thus, on the date of the US landings, Leyte was relatively weakly defended.

The *SHO* plans began to fall apart when the Third Fleet (during its covering operations for the Leyte landings) struck Luzon, Formosa, and the Ryukyus between October 10-13. Believing that these raids portended an invasion of Formosa, the Japanese prematurely activated *SHO-2*. In the process, they lost close to 600 planes, aircraft that would have been used against the Americans on Leyte if they had been available, and almost lost Shima's force, which squandered precious fuel in trying to execute the *SHO-2* plans. The waste of fuel, rather than American action, prevented Shima from cooperating with Nishimura, though both forces entered

Surigao Strait independently of one another.

The battle for Leyte opened on October 17, when US Army Rangers landed on several small islands protecting Leyte Gulf. At last the Japanese knew for sure the target and alerted the fleet for *SHO-1*. A bit slower in reacting to these landings, however, was the Japanese army which did not set in motion their part of *SHO-1* until the next day. Also that afternoon, the Imperial General Headquarters activated *SHO-1* in separate orders to the army and navy.

Up until this time, the Japanese had anticipated fighting the decisive battle for the Philippines on Luzon. For some time, though, Field Marshal Terauchi had pressed for fighting this battle wherever the Americans landed. In Tokyo, the Japanese finally agreed to Terauchi's plan, especially since it seemed (wrongly as it turned out) that Halsey's carriers had been damaged severely in the Formosa attacks. The decision to switch the decisive arena to Leyte was made on the 18th, but Terauchi and Yamashita were not informed of this until late on the 20th, after the Americans landed on Leyte. Yamashita was not happy with this decision, believing that Luzon was still the prime target and that throwing everything into a defense of Leyte would result in the loss of Luzon. Nevertheless, he followed orders.

The Seventh Fleet ships began pounding Leyte on the 19th. Aircraft from the escort carriers swarmed all over the target area, disrupting traffic and,

Left: Apparently untroubled by current events, a water buffalo continues to graze as a supply-laden amphibious tractor rumbles past. Such vehicles were essential in supplying the 1st Cavalry Division as it fought in the mountains west of Carigara.

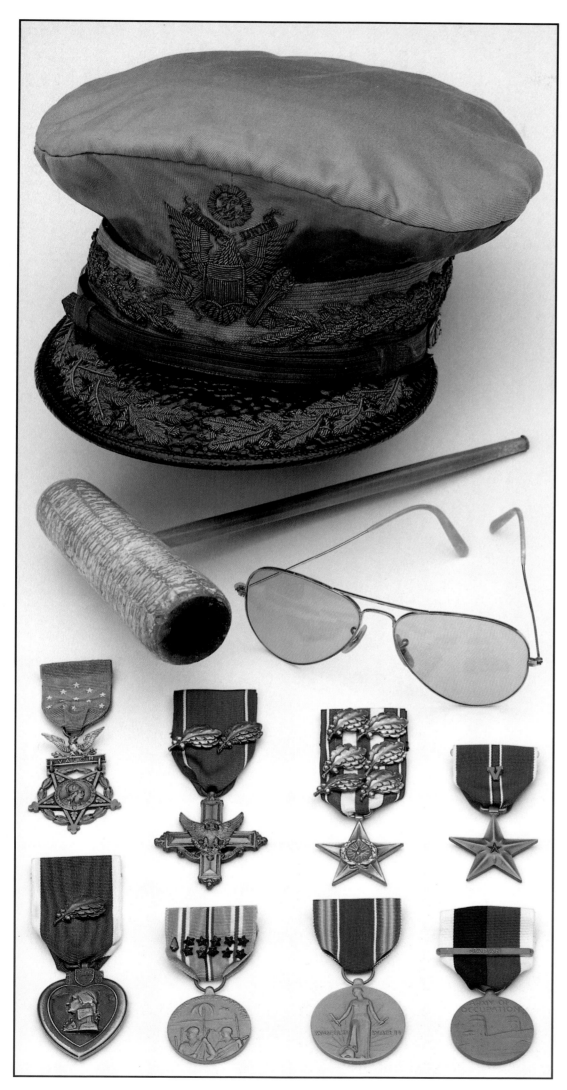

Left: General officer's service cap, corn cob pipe, sunglasses and decorations of General MacArthur. The decorations are (from left to right), the Medal of Honor; Distinguished Service Cross with two Oak Leaf Clusters; Silver Star with six Oak Leaf Clusters; Bronze Star; Purple Heart with Oak Leaf Cluster; Asiatic-Pacific Campaign Medal with battle stars; World War II Victory Medal and Army Occupation Service Medal with Japan clasp. *MacArthur Memorial Collection.*

incidentally, causing the Japanese on Leyte to fire off almost all of their antiaircraft ammunition. Air opposition was light, most of the Japanese planes having been destroyed or put out of action during the Formosa and Luzon carrier attacks. Although the Americans did not realize it, this meant that the air element of *SHO-1* was already out of kilter.

On the morning of the 20th the four US divisions stormed ashore near Dulag and Tacloban. The attack caught Gen. Makino in the midst of moving his command post from near Tacloban to a point about nine miles (14km) inland. For close to 48 hours, he was out of touch with Yamashita and Suzuki.

Resistance on the northern beaches proved relatively light, though the defenders put up a strong fight at Hill 522 before that position was taken. By nightfall, the 1st Cavalry and 24th Infantry Divisions held a five-mile (8km) long line from Tacloban to Hill 522. Besides the opposition offered by the Japanese, the attackers had to battle through an extensive area of swamps and jungle.

The Dulag area was where Makino had been expecting a landing and the defenses were stronger there. Particularly nettlesome to the attackers was Catmon Hill, which overlooked the entire beachhead and where the Japanese had emplaced a number of artillery pieces. It took until the 24th before the troops of the 96th Infantry Division were able to drive the defenders off the hill. Like the soldiers to the north, the XXIV Corps infantrymen also had to contend with large areas of swamp.

Some of the heaviest fighting during the first few days took place in the 7th Infantry Division's sector. Here the Army troops ran into a series of well-organized defensive positions, along with a number of enemy tanks. About four hours after the initial landings, shortly after 2:00 P.M., MacArthur, accompanied by members of his staff and Philippine president Sergio Osmena, splashed ashore. As astonished GIs watched, MacArthur strode to a hastily set up microphone and, in an emotion-choked voice, declared, ''People of the Philippines, I have returned!''

Over the next few days, the beachhead was enlarged and secured. As the Americans pushed inland, the fighting grew more intense. Particularly sharp and bloody actions were fought at Palo, Tabontabon, Catmon Hill, and at the Buri airstrip. By the 26th, Gen. Makino's division had suffered over 75 percent losses and now was reduced to less than 5,000 men. Although some Japanese

US Marine Corps Uniforms and Equipment

1 USMC Model 1941 field transport pack assembly, including camouflage poncho, M1942 bayonet, knapsack above haversack, with M1910 entrenching tool (with cover) attached
2 USMC M1944 reversible camouflage poncho
3 USMC camouflage mosquito head net
4 USMC all metal utility folding pocket knife
5 Standard US K (field) rations — this box is breakfast
6 US two piece metal mess tin, with lid in place
7 P-38 can opener
8 Standard US canned (or C) ration
9 Standard three piece mess kit, including knife, fork and spoon, all items carried inside item 6
10 USMC 1941 marching pack assembly
11 US M1941 aluminum canteen with cup
12 Hand-held radio receiver/transmitter, the BC-611-c, better known as the ''walkie-talkie''
13 USMC undershirt
14 USMC undershorts
15 USMC field socks
16 Personal medical kit
17 US M1923 cartridge belt
18 US M1 carbine
19 M1 cleaning rod

William H. Thompson Jr.: 18, 20; Scott A. Duff: 2-4, 6-7, 10, 11, 16, 19; Richard A. Kos: 1, 9, 12, 17; Dale E. Biever: 5, 8; Elliot R. Laine Jr.: 13-15

The USMC M1941 marching pack assembly, (10), consists of the M1942 bayonet and scabbard fastened to the side of the knapsack. The M1910 entrenching tool in its cover can be seen fastened on the back of the knapsack.

The personal medical kit (16), designed for jungle use, consists of, amongst other things, insect repellent and a tube of antiseptic ointment.

The M1923 cartridge belt (17), features, together with the nine ammunition pouches, the US M1910 canteen with United States Marine Corps cover, and two variations of the personal first aid pack. The outer casings of each of these can be seen next to the pouches. The M1 carbine (18) carries two spare magazines in its stock pouch. A cleaning rod for all types of .30 caliber weapons is stored within case 19.

reinforcements (primarily from the 30th and 102d Divisions) began landing at Ormoc, on Leyte's west coast, on the 23d, they were not strong enough to have any impact on the battle until early in November.

The only Japanese units that could have any effect on the battle in these early days of the invasion were the ships of the Imperial Japanese Navy which had been gathered for just such a purpose. Ozawa's carrier force left the Inland Sea on the 20th; Kurita's 1st Striking Force departed Brunei Bay, Borneo, two days later, followed a few hours later by the ships of Nishimura's unit; Shima's 2d

Striking Force sailed south a bit later. Their target — Leyte Gulf and the US transports and covering vessels.

Kurita was to steam through the Palawan Passage and thence through San Bernardino Strait. The route through the Palawan Passage lay outside the search sectors of American patrol planes, but it was hazardous nonetheless. Somewhat narrow, it was bordered on one side by an area of shallow water and reefs aptly known as the Dangerous Ground. And Palawan Passage was made even more dangerous by the presence, unknown to Kurita, of a pair of American submarines, the *Dace* and *Darter*.

Left: The *Cleveland* class cruiser *Birmingham* comes in close to lend fire-fighting assistance to the stricken carrier *Princeton*. An enormous explosion in *Princeton*'s stern soon afterwards severely damaged the cruiser. The carrier later sank.

At 1:16 on the morning of the 23d, the two submarines were lying close to each other on the surface, exchanging information, when their radars picked up a surface contact in the passage. Swiftly they took up the chase and soon saw a large group of ships. A contact report was sent, the first indication to the Americans where the Japanese were and where they were heading. Splitting up, the *Dace* and *Darter* were able to get on both sides of the enemy formation. Shortly after 6:00 A.M., the *Darter* fired a spread of six torpedoes at the first ship in the line of enemy vessels. The chosen target was the cruiser *Atago*, Adm. Kurita's flagship, and four of the torpedoes pierced her steel sides. It took only 18 minutes for her to sink.

The *Darter* was already firing at the second ship in line, the heavy cruiser *Takao*, before the first "fish" had struck the *Atago*. The *Takao* was luckier than her sister ship; although hit by two torpedoes which ripped off her rudder and two propellers, she survived but had to return to Brunei Bay in the company of some destroyers.

The *Darter* did not monopolize the action. On the other side of the formation, the *Dace* fired six torpedoes at the cruiser *Maya*. Four hit and sent the unfortunate vessel to the bottom in just four minutes. While escaping the inevitable, though in this case a very desultory, depthcharging, the *Darter* ran aground on Bombay Shoal. Her crew was taken off by the *Dace* but the submarine had to be scuttled by explosive charges and gunfire. All in all, however, the loss of a submarine was more than made up by the sinking of two heavy cruisers, and the disabling of a third.

By shortly after dawn of the 23d, the Americans were well aware that the Japanese navy was on the prowl and heading toward Leyte. Halsey brought his Third Fleet closer to the island and began to prepare a hot reception for the Japanese. One of his task groups was stationed east of Luzon, another about 50 miles (80km) east of San Bernardino Strait, a third was off Samar. Halsey's fourth task group had been sent to Ulithi for replenishment, but was hastily recalled. This last group did not see any action during the first stages of the battle. Kinkaid, also, began to prepare for what was shaping up to be a major naval battle.

On the morning of October 24, Halsey was informed by one of his search planes that Kurita's ships were rounding the island of Mindoro and apparently heading for San Bernardino Strait. Halsey quickly issued orders for his task groups to concentrate and prepare to attack. Hardly had he given these orders than Task Group 38.3 was hit by attacks by Luzon-based aircraft. Most of these planes were shot down, but one escaped to plant a bomb on the light carrier *Princeton*'s flight deck. At first it was believed the damage was minor but a raging fire soon developed. Although the cruiser *Birmingham* and a destroyer came alongside to help fight the blaze, they were soon drawn away from his task by more air attacks, these coming from Ozawa's carriers. These raids drew Halsey's attention to the north, which was what the Japanese wanted.

When the *Birmingham* returned to her firefighting tasks, it appeared that the carrier's crew had everything under control. Suddenly a tremendous blast ripped apart the *Princeton*'s stern and ravaged the cruiser drawn up alongside. The carrier could not be saved and was eventually sent to the bottom with US torpedoes. Casualties on the cruiser actually were much more severe than those on the carrier, and she, too, was knocked out of action.

Revenge was swift, however. At about the time the *Princeton* and *Birmingham* were undergoing their ordeal, Kurita's force was being treated even more roughly by Halsey's planes. Over 250 aircraft, in five air attacks, pounced on the Japanese as they steamed through the Sibuyan Sea. The mighty *Musashi* was sent under, but only after taking 19 torpedoes and 17 bombs. A heavy cruiser was damaged severely enough to be sent back to Brunei but most of the other ships escaped relatively unscathed in what became known as the Battle of the Sibuyan Sea. (The Battle of Leyte Gulf was made up of four widely separated actions, of which this was the first.) The American fliers over-optimistically reported heavy damage to the enemy and that the ships were

Right: PT boats played an important role in the Battle of Surigao Strait. As part of Rear Adm. Oldendorf's Bombardment and Fire Support Group, they kept the Japanese under attack for over three hours, and later in the battle undertook rescue duties.

retreating to the east. Kurita, indeed, did head eastward for a time but by late afternoon he was again heading for San Bernardino Strait.

Buoyed by his pilots reports, Halsey was ready to write off this portion of the Japanese fleet, even after his night search planes reported the enemy was drawing closer to the strait. But Halsey was after supposedly "bigger" game, the Japanese carriers which had finally been spotted to the north. Having taken the bait, he sped north to join battle with Ozawa. San Bernardino Strait was left wide open.

Earlier in the day, Halsey had issued a proposed battle plan to his task force commanders. In it he announced that Task Force 34, consisting of four battleships, five cruisers, and fourteen destroyers, was to be formed *when he directed,* to take on the big ships of the Japanese fleet. This message was intended only for his commanders, but copies were sent to Nimitz and King solely for their information. Kinkaid, although not an addressee of this message, intercepted it and believed that Task Force 34 had been formed and was stationed off San Bernardino Strait. This misconception also prevailed in Hawaii and Washington. But Halsey had not directed its implementation and when he turned north, all of his ships went with him.

Meanwhile, Nishimura's force had also been spotted and attacked. It was obvious that this enemy unit was heading for Surigao Strait. Adm. Kinkaid prepared a very unfriendly welcome for these intruders. At the northern entrance of the strait was Rear Adm. Jesse B. Oldendorf's Bombardment and Fire Support Group of 6 old battleships, 4 heavy and 4 light cruisers, 28 destroyers, and 39 patrol torpedo (PT) boats. The heavy ships were drawn up across the neck of the strait, while most of the "tin cans" lined each side and the PTs were stationed even further into the strait.

The PTs first sighted the Japanese ships at 10:50 P.M. and for the next three hours they kept Nishimura's force under observation or attack. A little before 3:00 A.M. on the 25th, the destroyers joined the fray. In a series of charges over a period of less than an hour, the destroyers sank two enemy "tin cans", and damaged Nishimura's two battleships, the *Fuso* and *Yamashiro.* Shortly before 4:00 A.M., Oldendorf's battleships and cruisers added their fire as they "capped the enemy's T". The *Fuso* blew up at 3:38 A.M. and the *Yamashiro* went under about 40 minutes later. Of Nishimura's force, only two vessels survived temporarily.

Following behind Nishimura was Adm. Shima's group of ships. (Although Shima and Nishimura were to have coordinated their efforts, this never took place. One theory for this failure was that Shima was senior to Nishimura and refused to obey a junior officer.) When Shima took a look at the burning vessels in Surigao Strait, he did not like what he

saw. After seeing one of his cruisers damaged by PT torpedoes, he liked it even less and decided to retire. For all intents, the Battle of Surigao Strait (the second of the Leyte Gulf actions) was over. It had been a smashing victory for the Americans. Over the next few days, US aircraft hunted down the survivors of this battle. Of Nishimura's seven vessels, only one (a destroyer) would survive. Shima's vessels were luckier, although not much. Two of his cruisers and four destroyers were able to sail away from this debacle.

But while the Japanese attempt to push into Leyte Gulf from the south was thwarted, the effort by Kurita came close to succeeding. Without interference from any patrolling US aircraft, his ships passed through San Bernardino Strait with no problem and by 12:35 A.M. on the 25th, Kurita had entered the open waters of the Philippine Sea. He headed east for about two and one-half hours before turning southeast toward Leyte Gulf. The air attacks on his ships in the Sibuyan Sea had rattled Kurita and, although pleasantly surprised that he had not been spotted, he still viewed the coming hours with some trepidation.

In his path to the south lay three groups of "jeep" carriers and their escorts. Two of these groups would only be involved in the action known as the Battle off Samar through the actions of their aircraft. The third, however, would meet the enemy face to face. Rear Adm. Clifton A.F. Sprague's Task Unit 77.4.3 (codenamed "Taffy 3") consisted of six slow, thin-skinned escort carriers, three destroyers, and four destroyer escorts. The largest gun any of these ships had was a five-incher. Yet these "popguns"

Below: The escort carriers and destroyers of Taffy 3 come under heavy attack from the 14-and 18-inch guns of Japanese battleships during the Battle off Samar. Water spouts from Japanese shells can be seen to the left, while a carrier burns.

would be firing defiantly at ships carrying 18-inch, 14-inch, and lesser caliber guns in just a few hours. Of this, though, the American sailors were as yet blissfully unaware.

Shortly after 6:30 A.M. the sailors of Taffy 3 were surprised to see black bursts of flak sprout over the northern horizon. This antiaircraft fire was aimed at one of the escort carriers' search planes. It wasn't much longer before lookouts on the US ships could see the distinctive "pagoda" masts of some of the Japanese vessels. The Americans were no more surprised at running into the enemy than were the Japanese, who thought (and continued to believe throughout most of the battle) they had encountered Halsey's carriers.

Shaken by the sudden appearance of enemy ships, Kurita gave a disastrous order, "General attack!" Instead of a carefully orchestrated attack, his ships now joined in an undisciplined charge toward the enemy. Sprague immediately brought his ships around to the east, into the wind, and began launching planes. The *Yamato* opened fire at 6:58 A.M., the other ships joining in soon after. Towering geysers of colored water (dye marker was used by the Japanese to spot the fall of their shells) began to creep up on the wildly maneuvering carriers. "They're shooting at us in Technicolor!" an excited sailor on a carrier yelled. To throw off the aim of the Japanese, Sprague ordered his ships to make smoke, which they did with alacrity.

Frantic messages for help to Halsey from both Sprague and Kinkaid (who now knew where Kurita's force was) filled the air. They also wanted to know where was Task Force 34. But Halsey was too far away and was already attacking Ozawa's ships. The only help Taffy 3 would get was from its own planes, plus more from the other two carrier units, and its screening vessels. Like angry hornets, the planes swarmed over the Japanese force. Many of the planes carried no armament at all; they had been launched too fast for that. Others carried just a few bombs, primarily suitable for the ground support missions they were to have flown that day. Few had torpedoes.

The Taffy 3 destroyers and destroyer escorts charged the oncoming enemy vessels. It was an unequal fight but, surprisingly, the "little boys" were able to keep the Japanese off balance. Their magnificent fight entailed a high price, though. The *Hoel, Johnston,* and *Samuel B. Roberts* were sunk and virtually all the other escorts damaged. Several of the "jeeps" were also damaged and one, the *Gambier Bay*, was sunk after absorbing at least 26 hits ranging in size from 14-inch to 4-inch.

The attacks by Taffy 3's screen and the constant air attacks rattled Kurita and shortly after 9:00 A.M., and on the verge of victory, he recalled his ships and turned north for San Bernardino Strait. For almost two and a half hours Taffy 3 had been under nearly constant shelling, but except for the three escorts and the *Gambier Bay*, it had come through battered but intact. The little boys had defeated the giants.

In the meantime, Halsey had found what he had been seeking, the Japanese carriers, and the fourth action of the Battle of Leyte Gulf, the Battle of Cape Engano was being fought. This was an aptly named battle, for Engano is Spanish for "deceit" or "lure", and Ozawa had lured Halsey perfectly. With few aircraft to protect their ships, the Japanese were sitting ducks. The Pearl Harbor veteran carrier *Zuikaku* was blasted to the bottom, as were the three other light carriers. Several other ships were heavily damaged and succumbed later to submarines or the surface vessels Halsey sent after them.

While Ozawa's ships were being pounded, Halsey had been receiving a string of increasingly urgent pleas for help from Kinkaid. Halsey was annoyed because he thought that Kinkaid had plenty of firepower to handle any incursion by the Japanese into Leyte Gulf. It was only after Kinkaid radioed that the battleships were low on ammunition that he realized there was a serious problem to the south. Also, Halsey noticed that most of the messages had taken over an hour to reach him, but by now he was too far away to have any effect on the battle.

About this time Halsey received a message from Nimitz that sent him into a rage. The message read, "Where is, repeat, where is, Task Force 34. The world wonders!" Halsey believed the message to be an insult but, actually, the last sentence was irrelevant "padding" that one of Halsey's radiomen had inadvertently left in. Halsey fretted over this message for almost an hour more before forming Task Force 34 at 10:55, long after Kurita had turned back for the strait. With all of his battleships, along

Above: Two destroyer escorts lay down smoke to protect their carriers during the Battle off Samar. Totally outgunned by the Japanese battleships, the destroyers' only hope in attack was to rely on their speed to get in close enough to launch their torpedoes.

with one of his carrier groups, he headed back for San Bernardino Strait. At this time, he was just 42 miles from Ozawa's battered force.

In what became known as the "Battle of Bull's Run", Halsey's battleships accomplished almost nothing. He just missed Ozawa's force and he missed Kurita's by a long way, although a straggling destroyer was sunk just after midnight on the 26th. Kurita was not out of the woods yet. One final air attack by Halsey's planes on the morning of October 26 resulted in the sinking of a cruiser and a destroyer and further damage to Kurita's battered force.

With this attack and some attacks by Army planes that sank another cruiser, the Battle of Leyte Gulf was over. The greatest battle in naval history had been a smashing victory for the Americans. Some 26 ships, of 305,710 tons, were lost by the Japanese in the main battles, plus several others in peripheral actions. Only six ships, totalling about 36,000 tons, were lost by the Americans. All except one of these losses had been in Taffy 3.

As the sounds of naval gunfire faded away over the ocean, another terrifying weapon made an appearance — the *kamikaze*. Pilots from many nations had deliberately crashed their aircraft into the enemy, but usually as a last resort. The Japanese, however, made this method an official tactic. The first *kamikaze* units were organized in the Philippines and made their first attacks on October 21, with a landing craft, infantry (LCI) and a tug the first of a long string of victims to be sunk. It was not until the 25th, however, that a *kamikaze* sank a major target. During the morning two escort carriers of the southern group of escort carriers were damaged at about the same time Taffy 3 was undergoing its ordeal. Then, shortly after Kurita's vessels turned back and allowed Taffy 3 to escape, another group of *kamikazes* arrived. Aboard the *St Lo*, her men were beginning to unwind from the tension of the past hours when a *kamikaze* hurtled down through the "jeep's" flight deck and onto the hangar deck. Uncontrollable explosions and fires were kindled and the carrier sank about half an hour later. Several other

Below: Crew members of the stricken Japanese carrier *Zuikaku*, last survivor of the Pearl Harbor Strike Force, salute as the ensign is lowered after the ship had taken fatal bomb and torpedo hits in the Battle of Cape Engano on October 25.

Taffy 3 carriers were also damaged by *kamikazes*. It was an eye-opening introduction to the menace of the *kamikaze*.

Ashore, the American GIs pressed steadily forward against mounting resistance. As Stanley Falk, the author of a history of the Leyte fighting, has written, it was a race for reinforcements between both sides as to who would win. The invaders actually held about a five-to-one edge in ground troops; air power was more even. The Leyte airfields were to have supported large numbers of planes from the Army Air Force, but the topography of the island was not conducive to airfield building on a grand scale. Not only this, but rain was very heavy throughout the battle, causing many of the fields to be rendered unusable temporarily or even to the state of having to be abandoned. Because the Army planes were not available yet in force, Halsey's carriers had to remain until late November to provide support, long past the date when they were due to retire.

Most of the Japanese reinforcements

Below: In the Battle off Samar, the escort carrier *St Lo* was one of six such ships in 'Taffy 3' (Task Unit 77.4.3). After being hit by a Mitsubishi A6M Zero in this *kamikaze* attack, the ship was torn by terrible internal explosions and sank.

Above: Surrounded by a miasma of smoke from her antiaircraft guns, a Japanese hybrid battleship/carrier (either *Hyuga* or *Ise*, neither carrying aircraft) comes under attack in the Battle of Cape Engano. Both ships survived the battle and the war.

came ashore at Ormoc, and the Americans attempted to stop this activity through numerous air attacks on the convoys. These were often spectacularly successful, but almost as often the reinforcements were able to get through. In fact, by early December, the Japanese had over 60,000 men on Leyte. The Americans continued to move slowly through the morass of wet jungle and mud, repeatedly being slowed by the terrain and the weather. But Gen. Krueger's advance was also measured, enabling the Japanese to erect strong defenses. At the key crossroads town of Carigara, on Leyte's north coast, these defenses proved to be especially difficult to reduce.

Krueger sent some of his troops across the southern tier of mountains to begin attacking toward Ormoc from the south; others went straight across the mountains toward the town. But all these maneuvers proved time-consuming and debilitating to the soldiers; there had to be a better way to end this battle. An "end-around" landing at Ormoc turned out to be the way to do it. The newly-arrived and fresh 77th Infantry Division

was selected for this task. Loaded out at Dulag, the division landed three miles (5km) south of Ormoc on December 7. Ormoc fell three days later, where upon the division commander radioed the 7th Infantry Division and the 11th Airborne Division (which had entered combat in late November), "Have rolled two sevens in Ormoc. Come seven. Come eleven."

In an ironic twist of fate, December 7 saw the destroyer-transport *Ward* fatally damaged by enemy planes during the landings. Three years earlier, the *Ward* had fired the first shots at Pearl Harbor when she sank a midget submarine. And the man now commanding the destroyer which fired the torpedoes that finally sank the *Ward*, William W. Outerbridge, had been her commander on that momentous day in 1941.

While the Ormoc landings had been going on, the Japanese made their own, albeit ill-fated, attack, Operation WA, which was intended to recapture American airstrips near Burauen by means of a coordinated ground and airborne attack. As it turned out, communications prevented such coordination, and the attack (which took place between December 6 and 11) failed dismally. Also a failure in this operation was Japanese intelligence, because the Americans had abandoned as unusable the very airfields that were being attacked, and few US planes were still operating from them.

On December 25, the town of Palompon was captured, ending the major fighting on Leyte. Control of mopping-up operations was turned over to the Eighth Army, and the Sixth Army staff departed to take part in the Luzon landings. "Mopping-up" is really a misnomer as the Eighth Army fought many sharp battles with the surviving Japanese, killing many but losing many also. This phase of the battle lasted over four months, until May 5. Leyte cost the Americans 3,500 dead and another 12,000 wounded or incapacitated. For the Japanese it was much worse. Some 60,000 men did not come back from Leyte and fewer than 400 prisoners were captured.

Because of the weather and the terrain, Leyte did not become the site of major airfields. However, the island did prove very useful as a supply base and staging area for further operations in the Philippines. Additionally, Leyte was used extensively during the waning months of the war by naval units for replenishment and repair as well as a facility for rest and recreation.

Yamashita had not wanted to make Leyte the site of the decisive battle in the Philippines, but he had been overruled by his superiors. When Leyte fell, it was only a matter of time before the rest of the Philippines would follow. Having lost some of his best troops on Leyte, now he was forced to change his tactics regarding the defense of Luzon. Despite the loss of these men, his new tactics forced the invaders to pay a heavy price for the conquest of Luzon.

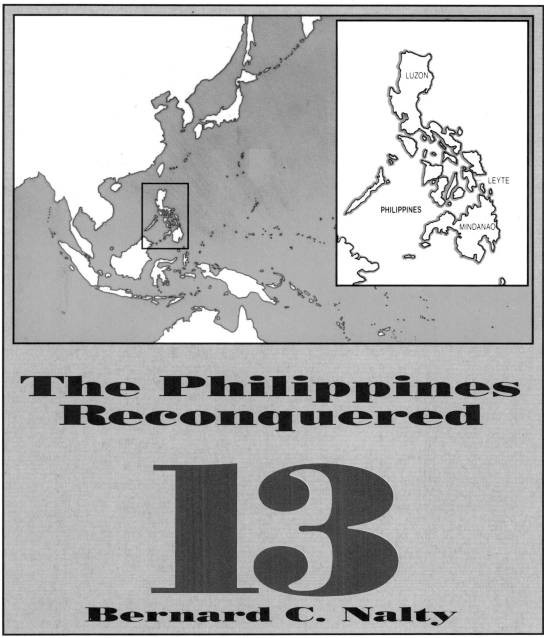

The Philippines Reconquered

13

Bernard C. Nalty

''Where do we go from here, Douglas?'' President Roosevelt was supposed to have asked Gen. Douglas MacArthur in July 1944, during their only wartime meeting.

MacArthur, who had just described a landing at Mindanao in the southern Philippines, replied: ''Leyte, Mr. President, and then Luzon.''

Whether embellished or not, the story illustrates MacArthur's commitment to the Filipinos, whom he had abandoned in 1942 and was determined to liberate. Luzon, the largest and most populous of the Philippines, some 40,000 square miles (64,000km²) with 12 million inhabitants, represented an important step on a road that began in the mud and jungle of New Guinea and would end in Tokyo Bay. For MacArthur, the recapture of Luzon was an obligation.

Whereas MacArthur was determined to redeem his pledge to return to the Philippines, Adms. Ernest J. King, the Chief of Naval Operations, and Chester W. Nimitz, the Commander-in-Chief, Pacific Ocean Areas, sought the best means to accelerate the war against Japan. The thrust from the Gilberts through the Marianas had seized secure airfields within B-29 range of Japan and wiped out the corps of naval aviators that the Japanese had reconstituted after the American victory at Midway. King and Nimitz intended to take advantage of this momentum, bypass Luzon, seize Formosa, and gain a lodgment on the Asian mainland. Gen. George C. Marshall, the Army Chief of Staff, at first sided with the Navy, and Gen. Henry H. Arnold, Commanding General of the Army Air Forces, believed that B-29s based on Formosa could join those based in China and the Marianas in battering Japan. As the summer of 1944 ended, Nimitz turned his attention to Okinawa, half as far from Japan as Formosa and, with an area of 467 square miles (1,167km²), only one thirtieth as large. Adm. William F. Halsey, commander of the Third Fleet, also favored eliminating Formosa from the list of objectives and seizing Luzon and Okinawa as stepping stones to Japan. Repelled by the vision of bombs falling on the largest city of the Philippines, King asked Halsey's chief of staff, Vice Adm. Robert B. Carney ''Do you want to make a London out of Manila?'' ''No sir,''

US Personal Effects

1. Soldiers' stationery set
2. V mail paper
3. Plastic match safe
4. Pack of Lucky Strike
5. Packs of matches
6. Songbook
7. Metal-cased pocket Bible
8. Armed services edition paper-backed books
9. First aid pouch
10. Issue technical manuals
11. Flashlights
12. First aid manual
13. Carlisle-pattern bandage
14. Booklet of medical tags
15. Carlisle battle dressing
16. Private purchase, Red Cross donation sewing kits
17. Red Cross playing cards
18. Private purchase pornographic playing cards
19-20. Wrist compasses
21. Government issue metal case compasses
22. Identification tags (dog tags), two variants
23. M1 helmet
24. Personal collapsible canvas wash basin
25. Issue undershirt
26. Issue undershorts
27. Issue socks
28. Toilet kit
29. Shaving mirror and cover
30. Canister of foot powder
31. Two piece mess kit
32. Mess kit utensils
33. Jungle food storage bag
34. Packet of toilet paper
35. Doughboy prophylactic kit
36. Variant prophylactic kit
37. Issue plastic whistle

Dale E. Biever: 1, 2, 3, 4, 5, 7, 8, 10-25, 28, 30-37; Howard Hendricks: 6, 9, 26-27, 29

Most of these artifacts were issue items, or available to the troops through private purchase or institutional donation. They are designed primarily to keep up the troops' morale, maintain his spiritual well-being and keep him occupied during periods of inactivity. If they all failed to keep him engaged in wholesome pursuits, there were always the prophylactic kits to protect him during the unwholesome ones. Personal hygiene was always an important item, and the M1 helmet is shown in one of the uses it was put to in the field, namely that of wash basin.

Carney replied, "I want to make an England out of Luzon," for he and Halsey envisaged the island as a base for further air and amphibious operations.

The Joint Chiefs of Staff finally decided the question of Formosa or Luzon strictly on the basis of the more efficient use of military and naval resources. King, a diehard supporter of Formosa, argued that an assault on Luzon would require six weeks of support by the fast carriers of the Pacific Fleet. MacArthur responded that escort carriers could take over as soon as the amphibious forces were ashore and provide air cover until landing fields were ready for shore-

based Army aircraft. Moreover, the Formosa operation, followed as planned by a landing in China, would tie up the fast carriers even longer and place the fleet in danger from Japanese forces on bypassed Luzon. This reasoning persuaded even King, and on October 3, 1944, the Joint Chiefs of Staff directed MacArthur to seize Luzon, while Nimitz took Iwo Jima and Okinawa. The invasion of Formosa was postponed indefinitely.

Once again, MacArthur insisted upon advancing under an umbrella of land-based aircraft, and he chose the island of Mindoro, just south of Luzon, to

provide the airfields he needed. As the invasion force steamed toward Mindoro, a *kamikaze* hit the cruiser *Nashville*, killing three senior officers and wounding the commander of the assault troops, Brig. Gen. W. C. Dunckel, but the landings went ahead as planned. On December 15, Rear Adm. R. S. Berkey's task force opened fire on the beaches near San Jose in southwest Mindoro, and Dunckel's soldiers splashed ashore. Both the American commanders knew Mindoro well; Berkey had surveyed the waters around the island in 1935, and Dunckel had driven its roads as a tourist during prewar duty in the Philippines.

US Marine Airborne Uniforms and Equipment

1 Marine parachutist's blue denim helmet, worn in the early days of Marine airborne operations
2 Marine herring bone twill jump smock with padded elbows and pockets
3 Marine camouflage jump smock — reversible, with padded elbows
4 Ammunition bag for Johnson light machine gun clips. The bag takes 12 clips, each of 20 rounds
5 Johnson Model 1941 light machine gun, .30 caliber, with web carrying sling. Bipod has been removed

6 Johnson Model 1941 semi-automatic rifle
7 Unique spike bayonet and frog for 6
8 Marine parachute rigger's kit, including sewing needles, wood-handled stitching awl, packing hook, temporary locking pins, line separator, and large and small fids
9 Canvas and rubber jungle boots
10 First pattern smooth leather jump boots
11 Non-issue parachutist's fleece lined vest
12 Parachutist's utility knife and scabbard

United States Marine Corps Air-Ground Museum

During the war in the Pacific, American and allied airborne operations were rare events, though those which were carried out were notable for their success. The theater of operations, though vast, for the most part made airborne operations hazardous, due to the invariably dense jungle conditions on the ground. Nevertheless it was these very conditions which made delivery of troops from the air such an attractive proposition. If it could be achieved, a drop could flank the enemy and avoid a slow slogging march in the process. It was this thinking that led to the highly successful coastal 'hops' by airborne troops in New Guinea. A more traditional massed parachute assault, such as those witnessed in Europe, was undertaken on the fortress island of Corregidor in the Philippines.

Japanese attacked Berkey's warships off the beaches, sinking two LSTs. The escort carrier *Marcus Bay* sustained minor damage, though one sailor was decapitated by the wing of an enemy fighter skimming the flight deck. Ashore, resistance proved scattered, as Dunckel's force — principally the 19th Regimental Combat Team of the 24th Infantry Division and the 503d Parachute Regimental Combat Team — quickly overran four airfields, three active and one abandoned, and set up a perimeter embracing San Jose.

Once Dunckel's men had seized a beachhead, Japanese aviators attacked the ships supplying the force. One *kamikaze* tried to dive through the open doors of an LST but miscalculated and exploded on the sands. More successful were the suicide pilots who damaged a liberty ship, a destroyer, and two more LSTs. Of the 750 soldiers on board the two landing ships, 107 perished. One of the survivors, Sgt. William A. Schnor, had both feet cut off; other soldiers bandaged his wounds, wrapped him in a life-jacket, and enabled him to swim to a nearby destroyer.

How should Japan react to the American invasion of Mindoro? Field Marshal Hisaichi Terauchi, who from

Saigon commanded Japanese forces in the Philippines, wanted to fight, as he had fought for Leyte. Gen. Tomoyuki Yamashita, the conqueror of Malaya now in command on Luzon, recommended writing off Leyte and Mindoro. Yamashita wanted to concentrate every man, bullet, and grain of rice on Luzon, and hold out there as long as possible. Terauchi prevailed, reinforcing Leyte, but he could find no more than a few hundred men for Mindoro, and their counterlanding failed.

Meanwhile, the Imperial Japanese Navy tried to intervene. On Christmas Eve, Rear Adm. Masanori Kimura sailed from Cam Ranh Bay, Indochina, with two cruisers and six destroyers to shell the American forces at San Jose. A Navy patrol bomber sighted Kimura's task force, misidentifying a 10,000-ton cruiser as the battleship *Yamoto*, displacing 70,000 tons and mounting 18-inch guns. Since no major warships were near at hand, Army aircraft and wooden-hulled torpedo boats had to intercept the Japanese, driving off Kimura's marauders, but not before they had damaged a torpedo boat and a freighter and lobbed a few shells into the beachhead. As the enemy withdrew, a torpedo boat finished off a destroyer damaged by aerial attack. The Army lost 26 aircraft to enemy fire or in crash landings.

While the Americans were securing airfields on Mindoro to cover the invasion of Luzon, Task Force 38, the carrier strike force of Halsey's Third Fleet, launched fighter sweeps of the airfields on Luzon that destroyed 270 Japanese aircraft, 208 of them on the ground, and then steamed toward a refueling rendezvous east of the Philippines. On December 17, the seas grew too rough for refueling. Two hoses parted as the battleship *New Jersey*, Halsey's flagship tried to take on oil, and the destroyer *Maddox* almost collided with the tanker *Manatee*. By mid-day, the decks of the escort carriers were pitching so violently that they could neither launch nor recover aircraft. Two returning pilots were ordered to abandon their fighters and parachute into the raging sea; they did, and a destroyer rescued them.

Early in the afternoon, in response to orders from Halsey, Vice Adm. John S. McCain, the commander of Task Force 38, broke off refueling, except for three destroyers with almost empty bunkers. Despite the plummeting barometer, winds that skimmed spindrift from the wave tops, and seas that caused plates to groan and ripple in the hulls of smaller ships, the realization dawned all too slowly that a typhoon was bearing down on the Third Fleet. As late as the morning of the 18th Halsey hoped to resume refueling, for weather forecasts did not yet reflect reality. Not until 1:45 in the afternoon, when the storm was at its worst, did Halsey issue a typhoon warning, and by this time three destroyers had perished in the storm. A court of inquiry

blamed the captains for not breaking formation to save their ships, but the entire fleet, from Halsey to the newest ensign, had been slow to realize the danger. Besides the three ships that capsized, killing all but 72 of the 800 officers and men on board, another half dozen ships sustained severe damage. Often survival resulted as much from luck as from seamanship.

Since the Eighth Army fought at Leyte and provided the assault force for Mindoro, MacArthur dispatched the Sixth Army, under Lt. Gen. Walter Krueger, to conquer Luzon. Krueger's army consisted of I Corps, under Maj. Gen. Innis P. Swift (the 6th and 43d Infantry Divisions), and XIV Corps, commanded by Lt. Gen. Oscar W. Griswold (the 37th and 40th Infantry Divisions), and the Army Service Command, under Maj. Gen. Hugh J. Casey, with the 25th Infantry Division, 13th Armored Group, 158th Regimental Combat Team, and 6th Ranger Infantry Battalion in army reserve. Atop the pyramid of command was MacArthur (a five-star General of the Army since December 1944), the commanding general of the Southwest Pacific Area and the Army Forces in the Far East. His principal commanders, besides Krueger, were: Lt. Gen. Robert L. Eichelberger of the Eighth Army; Lt. Gen. George C. Kenney of the Allied Air Forces; Gen. Sir Thomas A. Blamey of the Allied Land Forces, mainly Australians with a few troops from the Netherlands East Indies; and Vice Adm. Thomas C. Kinkaid of the Allied Naval Forces. Kinkaid took command of the naval expedition that would land Krueger's forces on Luzon. Except for Blamey, an Australian, all the senior officers were Americans.

The basic plan for the reconquest of Luzon called for Krueger's forces to seize a beachhead at the Lingayen Gulf, drive

the length of the island's central plain, capture Manila, and gain control of Manila Bay. The invasion force sailed in two elements — the fire support ships, escort carriers, mine-sweepers, and underwater demolition teams, under Vice Adm. Jesse B. Oldendorf, whose flag flew from the battleship *California*; and the amphibious shipping with Adm. Kinkaid. Both set out on January 2, 1945, from a rendezvous off Leyte, but Kinkaid's ships moved more slowly. Oldendorf, in the lead, ran a gauntlet of suicide attacks as he steamed past Leyte and Negros, then swung northward past Panay, through the Mindoro Strait, to Luzon and the Lingayen Gulf.

As Oldendorf's ships approached Mindoro Strait, a *kamikaze* dived into the escort carrier *Ommaney Bay*, starting fires that doomed the vessel. On January 5, the *kamikazes* returned, penetrating a screen of 68 Navy and Army fighters to damage the cruisers USS *Louisville* and HMAS *Australia*, the escort carrier *Manila Bay*, and the destroyer escort *Stafford*. On the morning of January 6, Oldendorf's fire support ships began their bombardment and stirred up yet another nest of *kamikazes*, which in two days of savage action sank three American destroyers — *Long*, *Hovey*, and *Palmer* — and damaged several other ships, including the previously hit cruisers *Louisville* and *Australia* and the battleship *New Mexico*. Meanwhile, Kinkaid followed in Oldendorf's wake, and once again the *kamikazes* made repeated attacks, damaging an American LST, an Australian landing ship, and a transport,

Below: Seen while fighting a typhoon off the Philippines in December 1944, the fleet carrier *Hancock* and battleship *New Jersey* were typical of the highly effective major warships built and placed in service by the US Navy during World War II.

Above: Prisoner of war memorabilia. (From the top.) Arm brassard worn by HQ surgeon. Red Cross brassard. Arm brassard of officer of the day (medical). (Right.) Wooden POW sick tag. Cigarette holder. Hand-carved clothes peg. Photograph of the medical staff, Fort Sternberg General Hospital, Manila, taken spring 1941. Obverse and reverse of notification card of capture by Japanese. *MacArthur Memorial Collection.*

and forcing two escort carriers to retire temporarily from action.

On the morning of January 9, 1945, Vice Adm. Daniel E. Barbey's San Fabian Attack Force landed General Swift's I Corps near that town, while the Lingayen Attack Force, under Vice Adm. Theodore S. Wilkinson, put Griswold's XIV Corps ashore near the towns of Lingayen and Dagupan. Opposition proved scattered despite potentially strong defensive positions in caves beyond the San Fabian beaches. Lt. Col. Russell Volckmann, the American leader of a Filipino guerrilla force, told MacArthur's headquarters that the Japanese would not defend the beaches, and events proved him right.

Volckmann had based his prediction on a copy of Yamashita's battle plan found during December in the wreckage of a Japanese airplane. The document called for the defenders to fall back from the coastline to form three major redoubts. The 80,000-man Shimbu Group, under Lt. Gen. Shizuo Yokoyama, assumed responsibility for Manila and the Bicol Peninsula southeast of the city. Northwest of the city, Maj. Gen. Rikichi Tsukada commanded the Kembu Group, with some 30,000 men, half of them sailors reporting to Rear Adm. Ushie Sugimoto, which defended an area including Clark Field and Bataan Peninsula. Yamashita himself retained

command of the Shobu Group, numbering 152,000, which controlled Baguio, the summer capital, the hills north of Manila, and the food-producing Cagayan Valley. As MacArthur had retreated to Bataan, Yamashita planned to fall back into the mountains of northern Luzon, carrying off the harvest of the Cagayan Valley, and resisting as long as he could. The only alternative to this kind of delaying action was a suicidal attack on the beachhead, in effect handing Luzon to MacArthur.

Despite the assurances from Volckmann, MacArthur and Krueger expected a counterattack. As a result, I and XIV Corps advanced cautiously onto the central plain. While I Corps protected Krueger's left flank and rear, XIV Corps, with the 37th and 40th Infantry Divisions, gradually gathered momentum in the drive toward Manila. On the boundary line between XIV and I Corps, elements of the 40th Infantry Division overran Camp O'Donnell, the northern terminus of the Bataan Death March. The prisoners had been evacuated long before, and the Japanese fled, leaving warm rice in the mess hall; only the American graves remained. The two divisions encountered determined resistance from the Kembu force, dug in among the hills overlooking the rail line and main road leading to Clark Field and beyond it to Manila. The Japanese made

intelligent use of difficult terrain; when American infantry silenced one cave, enemy gunners opened fire from another. Tanks, tank destroyers, and self-propelled howitzers crashed through bamboo thickets and crawled up rocky inclines to fire directly into the defensive positions. By the end of January, XIV Corps had overrun Clark Field and seized the hills beyond.

Meanwhile, MacArthur went ahead with plans to land XI Corps of Eichelberger's Eighth Army on the west coast of the island near the Bataan Peninsula. After coming ashore on January 29, XI Corps overran the prewar naval base of Olongapo and collided with elements of the Kembu Group at Zig Zag Pass. For two weeks, the 38th Infantry Division, at a cost of 250 killed and 1,150 wounded, fought its way through a web of interlocking defensive positions, concealed by dense jungle, in a vicious action that kept the Japanese from retreating onto Bataan Peninsula.

Overestimating the Japanese on Bataan, who numbered about one-fifth of the anticipated 6,000, Krueger dispatched the 151st Infantry of the 38th Infantry Division by boat to Mariveles at the peninsula's southern tip, where the troops disembarked and advanced along roads on either side of Mount Mariveles. Meanwhile, the 149th Infantry of the same division and the 1st Regimental

US PARATROOPER, CORREGIDOR, FEBRUARY 1945

This figure wears a two-piece olive drab combat suit. As was common practice in combat zones, no insignia is worn. Olive drab material also covers his M1 helmet. His combat boots are of the leather double buckle type. His braces are of the standard type, and he carries binoculars around his neck. On the stock of his M1 .30 caliber carbine he carries a pouch with two spare clips of ammunition.

Combat Team of the 6th Infantry Division moved southward along the western shore of Manila Bay to Pilar, where the highway forked. There the force divided, part advancing across the peninsula and the other continuing southward. MacArthur, who had gone to Bataan just once during the desperate times of 1942, chose to visit the front. A P-38 pilot saw the general's motorcade, assumed it was Japanese, but fortunately requested permission before he attacked. Maj. Gen. William C. Chase, who commanded the operation, overheard the transmission, realized that MacArthur was the target, and prevented the strike. By February 21, after scattered skirmishing, Krueger controlled Bataan.

The island fortress of Corregidor, nicknamed The Rock, which had surrendered to the Japanese in May 1942, did not figure in Yamashita's scheme of defense, but as long as it remained in enemy hands, it impeded American use of Manila Bay. Consequently, MacArthur directed Krueger to seize the fortress. Sixth Army headquarters decided to drop 2,000 paratroops of the 503d Regimental Combat Team from low-flying C-47s onto the island's parade ground and golf course, while 1,000 soldiers of the 34th Infantry stormed ashore from landing craft. The attackers faced more than 5,000 Japanese, most of them sailors ill-trained for infantry combat, and the enemy commander, navy Capt. Akira Itagaki, lacked the communications to control the defense. On the morning of February 16, after a naval bombardment and air strikes, the first of the parachutists landed, secured the drop zone, and opened fire in support of the amphibious landing on the shoreline below.

The Americans enjoyed an incredible stroke of luck at the outset, when a squad of paratroops, blown wide of the drop zone, landed around an observation post where Itagaki happened to be. The captain died in the ensuing firefight. Deprived of his leadership, the defenders fought courageously, at times suicidally, but without tactical cohesion. Not only did they cling to defensible positions, counterattacking those that were captured, they fought to the death for caves and foxholes that had no real importance. Suicidal gestures proved common; sometimes they took the form of *banzai* attacks, but on three occasions groups of Japanese gathered in ammunition dumps and blew themselves up, killing or wounding any Americans who happened to be nearby. On February 26, the battle for Corregidor ended when some 200 of the enemy gathered in an underground magazine and detonated the contents; besides killing the last of the defenders, the blast hurled an American tank 50 yards, showered shards of rock on warships 2,000 yards away, and killed or wounded 200 American soldiers.

Although Corregidor held the key to Manila Bay, a few islands remained

Above: Parachutes litter the battlefield of Corregidor. American paratroopers and infantry defeated 5,000 fanatical but ill-trained Japanese. Some of the defenders touched off massive explosions, sacrificing themselves to kill the attackers.

Below: American troops land on Fort Drum (inset) on April 13, 1945. Lying on the southern side of the entrance to Manila Bay, Fort Drum was pitted and blackened by an aerial bombardment and by shellfire from the nearby island of Corregidor.

under Japanese control as late as mid-April. The most formidable was El Fraile, a reef which a prewar engineering project had converted into Fort Drum, concrete with a skin 20 to 36 feet (6-11m) thick. Fortunately, the four 14-inch and four six-inch guns had been silenced during the 1942 fighting and never repaired. Indeed, the place seemed deserted until Japanese machine gunners killed one member of the crew of a patrol torpedo boat that tied up there. The 38th Infantry Division received the assignment of capturing Fort Drum and did so on April 13 at the cost of one man wounded. A landing ship came alongside the fort, taking advantage of a blind spot, and a rifle company scrambled across a ladder rigged from the conning tower to the concrete deck. The assault force strung hoses, pumped oil into the ventilating system, and put 600 pounds of explosives in place. After a false start when a hose broke, the troops relit the fuze, reembarked, and watched for the blast. The initial explosion scarcely dented the fort, but burning oil reached the magazine, filled with ammunition stored since before the war, and the entire island erupted in a thunderclap.

Personal Clothing and Effects of Prisoners of War Held in the Philippines

1 Reissued khaki short-sleeved cotton shirt
2 Reissued British pattern tropical shorts. The conditions in the prison camps reflected perhaps in the very heavy patching of this garment
3 Japanese bugle with tassels. This instrument was used by the captors to sound the various formations throughout the day
4 Reissued British blue wool pajama trousers
5-6 Reissued British Army pajama shirt and trousers

7 US mess tin used throughout the years of imprisonment; the lid was signed by fellow prisoners at liberation
8 Camp English dictionary kept by a POW
9 Scavenged tin disk cover
10-12 Various scavenged food containers
13 Knife made in prison
14 Shoes cut down from old riding boots
15 Ledger of POW records kept by the Japanese camp authorities

Milwaukee Public Museum: 1, 2, 4-6, 8-14; US Army Quartermaster Museum: 3, 15; Gary Pagel, Milwaukee, Wisconsin: 7

Items 3, 7, and 15 are non-related. All the other objects were brought back to the United States from prison camp by Col. William H. Braddock, a camp medical officer. Col. Braddock was sent to the Philippines in 1941. At the capture of the islands by the Japanese he was imprisoned and held for four years until the islands were liberated.

During the battles for Bataan and Corregidor, the fears of Adm. King (promoted to Fleet Admiral in December 1944) were realized: in a month-long battle the Americans and Japanese inflicted worse destruction on Manila than the German *Luftwaffe* had visited upon London. On January 27, the 37th Infantry Division attacked from Clark Field toward Manila, but after just three days MacArthur lost patience and berated the troops for a "noticeable lack of drive and aggressive initiative." Whether because of MacArthur's prodding or the failure of Japanese resistance to crystalize, the drive accelerated, with the 1st Cavalry

Division, temporarily attached to XIV Corps, advancing on the left of the infantrymen. Maj. Gen. Verne D. Mudge, commander of the cavalry division, organized two motorized "flying columns", complete with tanks and artillery, that crossed the Pampagne River and lunged toward Manila. A race developed between the two divisions in which the infantry unit was slowed by blown bridges and unfordable streams. On February 3, elements of the 8th Cavalry of Mudge's division reached the Tuliahan River, just north of Manila, and found that the defenders had rigged the stone-piered bridge for demolition. A

bomb disposal expert on loan from the Navy, Lt. (j. g.) James P. Sutton braved hostile fire, ran onto the structure, and cut the sputtering fuze. Thanks to Sutton, who earned the Army Distinguished Service Cross for his exploits ashore, the cavalrymen reached the outskirts of Manila that same evening, roughly 12 hours before the infantrymen.

While the 37th Infantry and 1st Cavalry Divisions advanced on Manila from the north, the 11th Airborne Division, under Maj. Gen. Joseph M. Swing, closed in from the south. Gen. Eichelberger had considered and, for various reasons, rejected several plans

THE RECONQUEST OF THE PHILIPPINES

Map A
During the summer of 1944, a decisive strategic debate took place among the commanders of the United States' Pacific forces. The subject of that debate was the choice of objectives in the next step towards Japan's Home Islands. The choice lay between Formosa, Okinawa, and Luzon in the Philippines. For Gen. MacArthur, forced to leave the Philippines in 1942, Luzon had to be the target. After much discussion, the Joint Chiefs of Staff agreed to both an invasion of Luzon and a central Pacific drive towards Okinawa.

The need to provide land-based air cover for the Luzon invasion, meant that preparatory operations needed to take place to secure airfields. Leyte was already in American hands, having been invaded on October 20, 1944, but the island was unsuitable for aircraft, and so part of the island of Mindoro was taken.

In the meantime, the Japanese were organizing their defense of Luzon. This was to be based around three group areas set back inland from the coastline. By far the largest of these would be situated in the north of the island, where food supplies were plentiful and a fighting withdrawal could take place into the mountains to the north.

The American invasion plan was to seize an area around Lingayen Gulf and advance south towards Manila and Manila Bay.

Map B
Two army corps landed at Lingayen Gulf on January 9, 1945. While I Corps pushed towards the north and east, The XIV Corps began the drive south towards Manila. While these moves were taking place, the XI Corps was landed on the west coast of the island to the south of the advance. Their task was to block any Japanese retreat into Bataan.

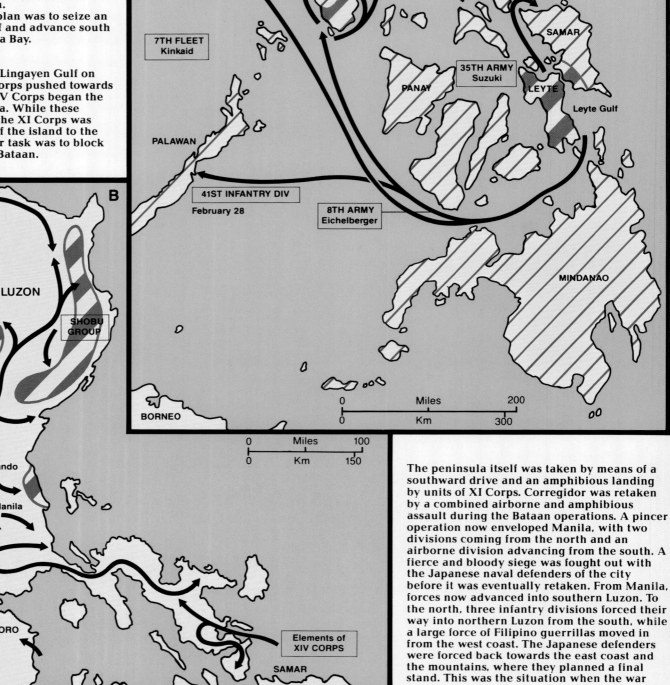

The peninsula itself was taken by means of a southward drive and an amphibious landing by units of XI Corps. Corregidor was retaken by a combined airborne and amphibious assault during the Bataan operations. A pincer operation now enveloped Manila, with two divisions coming from the north and an airborne division advancing from the south. A fierce and bloody siege was fought out with the Japanese naval defenders of the city before it was eventually retaken. From Manila, forces now advanced into southern Luzon. To the north, three infantry divisions forced their way into northern Luzon from the south, while a large force of Filipino guerrillas moved in from the west coast. The Japanese defenders were forced back towards the east coast and the mountains, where they planned a final stand. This was the situation when the war came to an end.

for using Swing's paratroopers before finally deciding upon an amphibious landing at Nasugbu Bay south of the entrance to Manila Bay. The division's two glider regiments, the 187th and 188th Infantry, waded ashore and began advancing along Route 17 which crossed a range of mountains and swung northward toward the city. The 188th Infantry, spearheading the attack, encountered strong resistance that delayed Eichelberger's plan to reinforce the column by dropping the division's other regiment, the 511th Parachute Infantry. On February 2, however, the 188th Infantry secured the proposed drop zone on Tagaytay Ridge, where the 511th Infantry parachuted the following day. Although only a fourth of the troops landed within the zone, some of the others coming down among banana trees as far as five miles (8km) away, injuries were few, and the division pushed rapidly toward Manila. Since the paratroops had not jumped since New Guinea and the C-47s had never conducted an airborne operation, the drop was bound to be flawed.

By February 4, American troops had raced to the outskirts of Manila, as engineers replaced the bridges the Japanese had destroyed north and south of the city so that truck convoys could deliver food, fuel, and ammunition. Truck maintenance proved spotty at best, and the gravel roads rapidly wore the tread from tires. Aircraft helped ease the logistical strain; C-47s flew drums of gasoline and other cargo to Nasugbu Bay and later to Tagaytay Ridge, eliminating a bad stretch of gravel highway. While C-47s assisted the advance from the south, dive bombers of Marine Corps Aircraft Groups 24 and 32, flying from an airstrip at the Lingayen beaches, guarded the exposed flank of the 1st Cavalry Division and scouted ahead of the flying columns. The marines attempted only one close support mission, but the cavalrymen and the defenders were too close. A series of dry runs demoralized the enemy, who fled even though the aircraft had not fired a shot. Army fighters and attack aircraft, whose pilots had scant experience in close air support, bombed and strafed in front of both pincers closing on Manila. Accidental attacks on friendly troops happened all too frequently, causing Krueger to warn Kenney that "these repeated occurrences are causing ground troops to lose confidence in air support and are adversely affecting morale". Kenney heeded the warning, and cooperation between air and ground improved.

Yamashita had not intended to defend Manila. He knew he could not feed the million or more residents and doubted that he could defend so large an area with vast tracts of inflammable wooden buildings. In contrast, Rear Adm. Sanji Iwabuchi, commander of the largely independent Manila Naval Defense Force, proposed to defend the city to the last man. Gen. Yokoyama, Yamashita's

principal subordinate in the Manila area, concentrated his forces north of the city, but he did not forbid Iwabuchi to fight using navy troops.

Iwabuchi discovered few good defensive positions except in the Intramuros, the old walled city, and among nearby public buildings, schools, and other earthquake-resistant structures. After blowing up every outlying facility having even marginal military value, he ordered his poorly trained men into the defensive zone. Minefields, barbed wire, trenches, and the hulks of trucks and trolleys canalized the American advance toward the sandbagged buildings. The Manila Naval Defense Force manned a formidable position, but one that lacked either depth or fully integrated fields of fire.

To limit the destruction, MacArthur imposed restrictions on air strikes and area bombardment by artillery. Despite the limitations, progress was initially encouraging, for the 8th Cavalry battered down the gates of Santo Tomas University and freed some 3,500 civilians interned there. The prison commandant, Lt. Col. Toshio Hayashi, made hostages of 275 of his charges until a senior American officer, Gen. Chase, guaranteed a safe passage for him and his guards. Troops of the 37th Infantry Division freed the captives at Old Bilibid prison, and the 7th Cavalry captured part of the city's water system. After these victories, however, the attack became a prolonged and bloody struggle for each successive block and fortified building within the city.

On February 12, the American divisions completed the encirclement of Iwabuchi's sailors. Yokoyama's army forces to the north tried unsuccessfully to launch a diversionary attack so that the defenders of Manila could escape, but a retreat did not figure in the naval

Above: This 2,000lb bomb was released by a Curtiss SB2C Helldiver carrier-borne dive-bomber over the Pasig River in Manila, but its trajectory took the bomb across the city to hit a target in Manila harbor, a location well to the west of the drop point.

officer's plans. His forces resisted as American riflemen — supported by flame throwers, grenades, and direct fire from tanks, tank destroyers, and artillery — attacked one building after another and killed the Japanese inside. Potentially the strongest of the fortified structures was the post office, a warren of tiny cubicles, but the enemy unaccountably failed to reinforce the stronghold, although tunnels connected it with the Intramuros.

The final battle for the Intramuros began on February 17, when artillery fire punched holes in the 16-foot(5m)-high walls, 40 feet(12m) thick at the base and tapering to 20 feet(6m) at the top. MacArthur refused to allow a massive aerial bombardment, so the attackers relied on artillery fire that rained down throughout the night of February 22-23. When the shelling ended at 8:30 A.M. on the 23d, troops advanced through the breaches in the walls or crossed the Pasig River in assault boats and attacked from the more exposed northern side. Fighting continued within the walled city until February 26; outside the walls,

Below: Much of Manila, including the national assembly's building, (the last Japanese-held position in the city) was devastated in the fighting that followed the senseless decision of Japanese naval forces to hold the city in direct disregard of Yamashita's orders to pull out.

Above: Filipino guerrillas parade before boarding an American landing craft for delivery to a point behind the Japanese lines. The guerrillas had been a thorn in the side of the Japanese since 1942, and now played a more overt offensive role.

pockets of Japanese resisted until March 3. Subjected to an unceasing pounding, out of contact with their senior commanders, and facing certain death, the sailors took out their anger and frustration on defenseless civilians, committing acts of senseless brutality. The battle claimed the lives of 1,010 American soldiers, and 5,565 suffered wounds. An estimated 100,000 Filipinos perished in the fighting, which all but leveled the core of the city. The Japanese dead numbered perhaps 16,000, three-fourths of them sailors of the Manila Naval Defense Force.

Once Manila had been captured, MacArthur planned to advance in two directions from the city. Krueger's Sixth Army was to overrun southern Luzon, including the Bicol Peninsula, and at the same time attack to the northeast destroying Yokoyama's forces and securing Manila's water supply. For the drive to the south, which lasted some 70 days, Krueger teamed the 11th Airborne Division, from Eichelberger's Eighth Army, with the 158th Regimental Combat Team and Filipino guerrillas. The clearing of southern Luzon began with an attack from the vicinity of Tagaytay Ridge and ended when this force made contact with the troops that had landed on April 1 near Legaspi at the tip of the Bicol Peninsula.

In the meantime, the 6th and 43d Infantry Divisions advanced on the dams northeast of Manila, seizing a succession of fortified ridges and mountain passes to capture Ipo Dam on May 17 and Wawa Dam on the 28th. At Ipo Dam, patrols from the 43d Infantry Division had reached the structure, but had withdrawn, when a band of guerrillas arrived and raised the American flag. Resentment flared, for the infantrymen believed that the Filipinos had stolen the glory of raising the flag, but this quickly subsided as the fighting continued.

Krueger's Sixth Army next closed in on Yamashita's final redoubt, even though only the 32d, 33d and 25th Infantry Divisions and Volckmann's Filipino

guerrillas were immediately available. Advancing abreast, the three American divisions attacked on February 21 in an attempt to crash through to the Cagayan Valley. Krueger wanted the products of this fertile area to help feed the liberated populace of Luzon; Yamashita needed the harvest to sustain the soldiers of the Shobu Group.

Initially chosen to fight a holding action southwest of Baguio, the summer capital, the 33d Infantry Division forced the Japanese to retreat, though grudgingly. Gen. Swift, the commander of I Corps, realized, however, that he would be hard pressed to send reinforcements if Yamashita were to counterattack the overextended American division, and instead kept a tight rein on the advance. Not until early April, when Krueger shifted the 37th Infantry Division northward from Manila, could Swift team the two units in an attack that captured the high ground dominating the bridge across the Irisan River gorge. When the defenders beat back a frontal attack spearheaded by self-propelled howitzers and tank destroyers, riflemen of the 148th Infantry, 37th Infantry Division, outflanked the Japanese strongpoint. Repeated frontal attacks followed by flanking movements and aided by air strikes broke through, killing an estimated 500 Japanese at the cost of 40 killed and 160 wounded, and enabling the 33d Infantry Division to overrun Baguio.

Meanwhile, the 25th and 32d Infantry Divisions tried to break through to the north before the Japanese had dug in, but the defenders were ready. The 32d Infantry Division ran into powerful defenses at the Salacsac Passes, where the enemy emplaced machine guns in caves to cover the trails, and plotted mortar or artillery concentrations on the

gullies that might provide cover for flanking movements. The Americans nevertheless succeeded in working their way around Salacsac Pass No. 2 and attack the strongpoint from the flanks and rear; Salacsac Pass No. 1 also had to be reduced in similar fashion. While some of the troops wiped out the isolated pockets of Japanese, others pushed forward, seizing the village of Imugan at the end of May. The advance to Imugan cost the division some 3,000 killed or wounded and twice that number evacuated because of illness or exhaustion.

To the right of the 32d Infantry Division, the 25th Infantry Division encountered similar difficulties. In the sector of the 27th Infantry, a hill mass that included Mount Myoko threatened to block the advance, until the regimental commander, Col. Philip F. Lindeman, was flown over the area and discovered a bypass. One of Lindeman's battalions maintained pressure on Mount Myoko, while another outflanked it. The successful flanking movement neutralized the Mount Myoko strongpoint but created a tortuous supply route upon which Lindeman's advance elements depended. Air drops eased the supply situation until troops of the 37th Infantry Division relieved Lindeman's battalion at Mount Myoko, and the 35th and 161st Infantry of the 25th Infantry Division came abreast of the 32d Infantry Division on the left and prepared for the final drive.

While the American infantry divisions advanced from the south, the US Army Force in the Philippines (Northern Luzon), as Volckmann's guerrillas were now known, attacked from the west coast toward the Cagayan Valley, threatening the rear of Yamashita's force. The guerrillas then joined the 6th and 32d Infantry Divisions in maintaining pressure on the surviving Japanese, who withdrew into the mountains for the final battle.

While the fighting raged for northern Luzon, MacArthur sent Eichelberger on a succession of amphibious landings that recaptured the southern Philippines, where guerrillas had been harrying the enemy. On February 28, elements of the 41st Infantry Division landed at the narrow waist of Palawan Island and rapidly seized Puerto Princesa and its airfield. Desultory fighting lasted until April.

Airfields on Palawan were to have provided air cover for an assault on the Zamboanga Peninsula of Mindanao Island early in March, but construction moved too slowly. A postponement would have been necessary, save that Filipino guerrillas held the airstrip at Dipolog on Zamboanga. Troops landed in C-47s at the beachfront airstrip on March 8, and 16 Marine Corps fighter-bombers arrived to fly cover for the amphibious landing two days later. Once ashore, two regiments of the 41st Infantry Division drove the Japanese from the peninsula; more than 6,000 of the enemy were killed or died of starvation during the

Below: Japanese army officer's sword, of the *Shin-gunto* type, first introduced in 1933-4. It is the most common of all Japanese military sword furniture, and was carried as a weapon throughout World War II. This one belonged to Gen. Tomoyuki Yamashita, commander of the defending forces on Luzon. The sword blade itself is signed 'Fujiwara' and dates from between 1640-80. There is a general's tassel tied to the hilt, and on the scabbard is a leather combat cover. This sword was surrendered by Gen. Yamashita on September 2, 1945 when the Japanese forces on Luzon capitulated. The document to the left is Gen. MacArthur's personal copy of the instrument of surrender of Japanese forces on the Philippines. It was signed at Baguio, Luzon, is dated September 3, 1945, and carries Yamashita's signature.
West Point Museum.

retreat, at a cost of 220 Americans killed and 665 wounded.

From Zamboanga, MacArthur moved toward Borneo, landing first at Basilan, then in the Tawi Tawi group, and on Jolo. The theater commander had hoped to use Adm. Sir Bruce Fraser's British Pacific Fleet in attacking Borneo during March, but Fraser's aircraft carriers became committed to the Okinawa campaign. As a result, Borneo was not invaded until May 1, when Australian troops, under Lt. Gen. Sir Leslie Morshead, supported by American and Australian warships, seized a beachhead at Tarakan. Other Australians landed at Brunei Bay in June and in July at the oil refining center of Balikpapan. The vast land mass of Borneo, almost 270,000 square miles (432,000km²), defied conquest, and

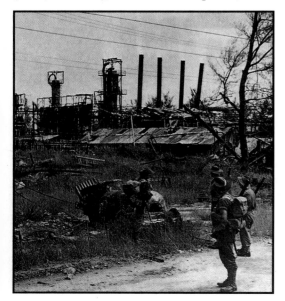

Left: Men of the 13th Australian Infantry Battalion inspect the ruins of the oil refinery at Lutong on the northeastern side of Borneo. The Japanese wrecked the installation before pulling back when the Australians landed and advanced in June 1945.

while the Australians carved out the three beachheads, some 2,000 of their fellow soldiers, held prisoner in the interior, perished almost to a man as they slaved to build an airfield for their captors.

MacArthur's westward drive from the Zamboanga Peninsula coincided with the liberation of the central Visayan Islands and eastern Mindanao. While the 41st Infantry Division was freeing Zamboanga, the 40th Infantry Division landed at Panay, the westernmost of the central Visayans on March 18 and quickly overcame the Japanese garrison. This division invaded Negros on April 2 and spent almost the entire month eliminating the defenders of the mountainous north. Meanwhile, the Americal Division invaded Cebu and Bohol in the eastern part of the group and linked up with the 40th Infantry Division on Negros at the end of April.

The invasion of eastern Mindanao got underway on April 17 and 18, when elements of the 24th Infantry Division seized some offshore islets and a sector of the coast near the base of the Zamboanga Peninsula. A formidable band of guerrillas under Col. Wendell W. Fertig, another of the Americans who had refused to surrender in May 1942, controlled parts of the island, but Mindanao was a large and rugged place, totaling 36,500 square miles (57,600km²),

defended by 43,000 Japanese troops. Its reconquest required the use of two infantry divisions, the 24th and 31st, and elements of three others, the 40th, 41st, and Americal. On June 30, Eichelberger reported that organized resistance had ended, but isolated skirmishes flared until Emperor Hirohito on August 15 ordered his troops to surrender.

Yamashita still held out on Luzon when Japan surrendered. He came down from the mountains knowing full well that he would be held responsible for the atrocities committed by Japanese troops in the Philippines. "There is only one person who can be responsible", he said, "and that is me". Gen. MacArthur insisted upon a trial, and a military commission found Yamashita guilty of war crimes, even though the evidence showed that he had prevented local commanders from murdering Americans held prisoner on Luzon and had no direct connection with the crimes that were committed. MacArthur intended to hang Yamashita at Manila on the anniversary of Pearl Harbor, December 8, 1945, but the attorneys representing the Japanese officer appealed the decision to the Supreme Court of the United States. Two of the justices considered the trial a travesty of justice, but a majority held that only the convening authority could reverse the decision of a military commission. Since MacArthur declined to intervene, Yamashita went to the gallows on February 23, 1946; across the international date line, it was February 22, Washington's birthday. Yamashita died as a symbol of the violence that Japan had unleashed upon the world.

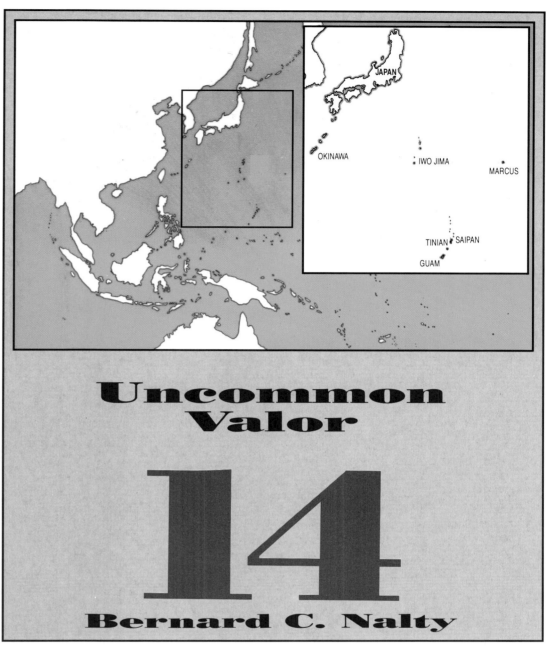

Uncommon Valor

14

Bernard C. Nalty

Iwo Jima, the Sulphur Island, takes its name from the mineral springs that bubble there. Covering just eight square miles (20km²), it is one of the Volcano chain, and an extinct volcano, 546-foot (166m) Mt. Suribachi, looms at the narrow end of the island, which has been compared in shape to everything from a pork chop to an ice cream cone. During early 1944, a few Japanese trapped rainwater in cisterns, for there were no fresh streams or springs on the island, as they tended gardens, grew and refined sugar cane, and distilled sulphur in huge pots. Despite the island's trifling economic value, when the war entered its final phase, Iwo Jima suddenly became strategically important, for it lay 760 miles (1,222km) from Tokyo, near the midpoint of the route flown by B-29s from the Marianas to bomb Japan.

The defense of Iwo Jima rested in the hands of Lt. Gen. Tadamichi Kuribayashi and a garrison that ultimately numbered 20,000. In May 1944, before the Americans had seized the Marianas and developed airfields there, Gen. Hideki Tojo, Japan's prime minister, chose Kuribayashi to take command at Iwo

Jima, assuring the 53-year-old cavalryman that he was the best qualified officer for the assignment. Tojo may have been impressed by Kuribayashi's first-hand knowledge of Americans, for the new garrison commander had been an assistant military attaché at Washington and a student of cavalry tactics at Fort Bliss, Texas. Kuribayashi had traveled widely in the United States, living for a time in a rooming house in Buffalo, New York. What Tojo prized may not have been Kuribayashi's familiarity with the ways of Americans but rather his resourcefulness and determination. A letter written to his brother to announce his departure for Iwo Jima provided an insight into Kuribayashi's character. "I may not return from this assignment," he wrote, "but let me assure you that I shall fight to the best of my ability, so that no disgrace will be brought upon our family."

On June 24, 1944, two days after he arrived at Iwo Jima, Kuribayashi experienced his first air raid. American carrier aircraft shot down 66 of the hundred airplanes on hand to defend the island. In the future, Japanese aircraft would

United States Firearms

1 US rifle Model 1917, of .30 caliber, together with bayonet, scabbard and box of ammunition
2 US rifle Model 1903 A1, the 'Springfield', of .30 caliber together with bayonet, scabbard and ammunition
3 US rifle Model 1903 A3, of .30 caliber with grenade-launcher attachment
4 US carbine M1, of .30 caliber, with three individual rounds, a spare magazine and a magazine pouch
5 US rifle Model 1903 A4, of .03 caliber, in sniper configuration
6 US rifle M1, Garand, of .03 caliber complete with bayonet and scabbard

7 Bandolier of ammunition, as issued, for the M1 Garand
8 US pistol Model 1911 A1, of .45 caliber
9 US pistol Model 1911, of .45 caliber
10 US revolver, Smith & Wesson, Model 10, of .38 caliber, the Victory Model
11 US Colt revolver Model 1917
12 US Smith & Wesson revolver Model 1917, of .45 caliber
13 Holster and web belt. The .45 cartridge clips are for use in 11 and 12

Pritchard Collection, 1-5, 7-9; Howard O. Hendricks Collection, 6; William LePard Collection, 10; Laurence J. Beyer Collection, 12, 13; Dale E. Biever Collection, 11

not operate from Iwo Jima but rather stage through the two airfields and one auxiliary airstrip to attack the new American bases in the Marianas. In preparation for the invasion that he considered inevitable, the general ordered the civilian residents sent home and had his men begin burrowing into the rock, hewing out additional cisterns to capture rainwater for the increasing number of soldiers, along with concealed gun positions and blast-resistant shelters.

As early as mid-July, with Saipan securely in American hands, attention shifted to Iwo Jima, where Gen. Henry H. Arnold, the Commanding General,

US Army Air Forces, wanted to operate three airfields, one as a staging area for B-29s based in the Marianas and the others for escorting fighters. As if to dramatize the importance of Iwo Jima, the Japanese over the weeks staged bombers through the island to attack the airfield on Saipan, destroying 15 B-29s and severely damaging more than 40 others. American firepower failed to neutralize Iwo Jima, which continued to serve as a site for early-warning radar and a refueling base for nuisance air raids. As Kuribayashi expected, an amphibious assault would be necessary.

Adm. Raymond A. Spruance assumed

overall command of the Iwo Jima operation. Adm. Richmond Kelly Turner served as the Joint Expeditionary Force Commander, and Marine Lt. Gen. Holland M. Smith was Commanding General, Expeditionary Troops. In command of the fighting ashore was Maj. Gen. Harry Schmidt, whose V Amphibious Corps consisted of the 4th Marine Division (Maj. Gen. Clifton B. Cates), the 5th Marine Division (Maj. Gen. Keller E. Rockey), and the 3d Marine Division (Maj. Gen. Graves B. Erskine). The basic plan called for the 4th and 5th Marine Divisions, each with one of its three regiments in reserve, to

Over two million US Model 1917 rifles (*1*) were fabricated for use in World War I, but very few saw service. They were reissued to US and Allied forces at the start of World War II. The US Model 1903 A1 rifle (*2*) was a modification of the standard shoulder arm of World War I. This rifle saw extended use into 1943 by all branches of the service. The light, semi-automatic US M1 carbine (*4*) was an extremely popular weapon, despite being underpowered; over six million were fabricated by contractors during the war. Manufacture of the US rifle M1 Garand began in 1936, but insufficient numbers were in service by the beginning of the war, necessitating continued use of the Model 1903 rifle.

The US pistol M1911 A1, (*8*) is one of the best known handguns in the world. Fabricated by Colt, Remington, Springfield Armory and several other contractors, production ran into millions. US pistol M1911 (*9*), was the immediate predecessor of the M1911 A1; the differences were minor, such as real wood instead of plastic grips. US revolver, Smith & Wesson, Model 10 Victory Model (*10*), was carried by pilots in branches of service and various service personnel. Large numbers were supplied to allies. US Model 1917 Colt revolver (*11*); a total of 151,700 of this arm were manufactured during the war. US Model 1917 Smith & Wesson revolver (*12*); some 153,311 of this arm were produced during the war.

land abreast on the southeastern beaches, from the vicinity of Mt. Suribachi to a rock quarry where the shoreline flared seaward. The 3d Marine Division, in corps reserve, could land over the same beaches to reinforce the assault divisions. Once ashore, elements of the 28th Marines, 5th Marine Division, would swing to the left and capture Mt. Suribachi, which dominated the narrower portion of the island, while the rest of the landing force overran Airfield No. 1, inland of the assault beaches, advanced to the opposite shore, and pivoted to the right, seizing the rugged plateau at the wider end of the island, where the Japanese had built Airfields No. 2 and No. 3, the latter a partially completed auxiliary airstrip.

In preparation for the invasion, B-24s from the Marianas, joined at times by B-29s, hammered the island, but the critical element in softening the defenses would be naval gunfire. Generals Smith and Schmidt wanted the Navy to pound Iwo Jima for ten days, but Adm. Turner replied that his warships had time and ammunition for only three days of concentrated shelling. When the Marine Corps generals objected, Turner agreed to a fourth day, only to be overruled by Spruance, who intended to launch a carrier strike against targets in Japan on the same day that the cruisers and old battleships opened fire on the objective.

Spruance believed that his attack would prevent the Japanese navy from challenging the Iwo Jima landings, but he could not launch the strikes until three days before the invasion. The problem of timing persuaded Spruance to limit Turner to a three-day bombardment prior to the assault, scheduled for February 19, 1945. Actually, Spruance scrimped on the shelling to no purpose, since the Japanese by this time no longer had the warships, aircraft, or fuel to intervene decisively in the waters off Iwo Jima.

Determined to do his best, whatever the odds against him, Kuribayashi adopted a scheme of defense that was easy to coordinate and required a minimum of maneuver. Weeks of aerial bombing had shaken the defenders who were short of food and water, but morale improved when the troops celebrated the 2,605th anniversary of the legendary founding of Japan, February 11, with rice cakes and what remained of the wine and beer. The general issued instructions for his batteries to hold their fire during the preliminary bombardment, allow the American assault waves to advance perhaps 500 yards (455m) inland, and then hit the marines with every weapon that could be brought to bear. Afterward, he proposed to fall back grudgingly, fighting from prepared positions, avoiding being caught in the open,

Above: Consolidated B-24 Liberator bombers pound the Japanese defenders on the volcanic island of Iwo Jima in December 1944. The Americans wanted the island as a forward air base, for it contained two airfields with a third under construction.

and conserving Japanese lives while killing as many Americans as possible. Kuribayashi forbade suicide charges, for he intended to win the battle, wearing down the attackers as he gave ground until the Japanese were superior in

Victory in Europe

On May 7, 1945, as B-29s based in the Marianas were bombing Japanese airfields that might be used by *kamikazes* for further attacks on Allied warships, the fighting in Europe ended. A German delegation entered a small room in the Supreme Headquarters, Allied Expeditionary Forces, at Reims, France, sat at a makeshift table, and signed the instruments of surrender. Hitler was already dead. On April 30, while Soviet troops fought their way through the streets of Berlin, he had killed himself in his underground bunker. The first objective of the basic Anglo-American war plan — the defeat of Germany — was thus accomplished. All the destructive might the allies could muster would now be turned against Japan. Indeed, the transfer of men and machines from Europe to the Far East was already under way.

On March 15, 1945, elements of the Royal Navy — four aircraft carriers, two battleships, and lesser warships, supported by a hastily improvised fleet train — reported to Fleet Adm. Nimitz, the American Commander-in-Chief, Pacific Ocean Areas. The British Pacific Fleet saw combat at Okinawa, where *kamikazes* scored hits on the carriers *Formidable*, *Indefatigable* and *Indomitable*, but failed to penetrate the armored decks. Later, the British force bombed and shelled targets in Japan, as

the time for the projected invasion of the Home Islands drew nearer.

Preliminary plans for the conquest of Japan called for seizing a lodgment in November 1945 on the island of Kyushu, (Operation Olympic), followed early next year by Operation Coronet, the invasion of Honshu and the capture of Tokyo. Army and Marine Corps divisions that had been fighting the Japanese in the Pacific would storm ashore on Kyushu, and troops would redeploy from Europe in time for Coronet and any subsequent operations against other of Japan's Home Islands. The first major units to arrive from the European Theater of Operations was the

Above: The Soviet flag flies above the Reichstag in Berlin. Taking the city cost the forces of Gens. Zhukov and Konev over 300,000 casualties. The city fell on May 2; Germany surrendered five days later.

Eighth Air Force, which established itself on Okinawa in mid-August, but the airfields there proved so crowded that the newly arrived squadrons could not immediately go into action. The airmen, sailors and troops earmarked for the invasion looked forward with dread to the battle for Japan, but the atomic bomb intervened. The Eighth Air Force was not needed, nor were the divisions and the massed fleets; there would be no fight to the death for the Home Islands.

numbers and firepower, and only then launching a counterattack.

On February 17, the second day of bombardment before the scheduled assault, cruisers and old battleships pounded the invasion beaches and the high ground beyond, while mine-sweepers checked for mines. Landing craft armed with rockets opened fire and dropped off underwater demolition teams, frogmen, who searched for obstacles, which the defenders had not been able to install because of deep water and swift currents. Since landing craft lunged shoreward behind a curtain of rockets and naval gunfire, Kuribayashi's troops assumed that this was the invasion, and in their fear and excitement, they forgot his instructions to hold their fire. Mortars and carefully concealed coastal defense batteries suddenly cut loose. Six Japanese shells hit the heavy cruiser *Pensacola* wounding more than a hundred of the crew and killing 17; a direct hit on a destroyer killed seven and wounded 33. The crews of the rocket-firing landing craft suffered grievously. The dead and wounded lay in pools of blood on the decks, and fires burned onboard, as a half dozen of them wallowed without power on a hostile sea. Only one of the landing craft sank, however, and all but one of the frogmen returned safely after reconnoitering Iwo Jima's beaches. Since the Americans withdrew behind a smokescreen, the Japanese concluded that they had beaten off an attempted landing.

The day's events proved as sobering to the Americans as they were encouraging to the Japanese. The violent and accurate fire from the island demonstrated that the defenses had thus far survived. As a result, Turner revised his plans for the third day of shelling, and on the 18th the fire support ships, including five old battleships, closed within a mile and a half (2.5km) of shore and methodically blasted the suspected strongpoints dominating the assault beaches. Despite showers that hampered the airborne observers adjusting the fire of the warships, more than half the targets fired upon were destroyed or heavily damaged, but far too many pillboxes and artillery positions escaped detection or survived the naval gunfire to oppose the next day's landings.

On the morning of February 19, the marines started for the island, amphibian tractors leading the way, after more than 8,000 shells, from 5-inch to 16-inch, exploded on the beaches and beyond in a savage 30-minute barrage. From the air, the amphibian tractors seemed like bugs skittering across a pond, but the heavy machines actually were flailing half-submerged through the water, the spray thoroughly soaking the marines packed inside. The first of the vehicles crunched ashore one minute before 9:00 A.M., 29 minutes after Admiral Turner signaled the assault waves to start for shore. Within 15 minutes four waves landed, the marines rolling over the sides of the

Above: Sailors of the attack transport Hansford hoist an LVT(A)4 from the hold into the water before the assault on Iwo Jima. Armed with a turreted 75-m howitzer, the LVT(A)4 was an armored assault vehicle based on the standard amphibious tractor.

Below: Men of the 4th Marine Division storm ashore on February 19, 1945, as the Iwo Jima operation begins. Right from the landing, the marines faced fanatical resistance in what was to become one of the bloodiest battles of the entire Pacific campaign.

tractors to begin scrambling up the embankment beyond the beach — a struggle since each man carried 80 to 120 pounds (32-48kg) of equipment.

For roughly half an hour, scattered small-arms fire crackled above the black volcanic sand and an occasional mortar shell exploded as the marines attacked the pillboxes defending the beaches. The lull resulted in part from the fire discipline that Kuribayashi had drummed into his troops and in part from the numbing effect of the naval bombardment. Indeed, one Japanese soldier, one of only ten men in his unit who survived the D-Day bombardment, confessed that he was so dazed and demoralized that he fled into the broken ground beyond the invasion beaches and hid in a cave until he could surrender. Taking advantage of the effect of the shelling, 1st Lt. Frank B. Wright and a handful of men from his platoon crossed the island, flushing the defenders from one strongpoint after

another and killing them. When the marines came within sight of the ocean, the island came alive with fire from rifles, mortars, and machine guns hidden among the rocky outcroppings. The nature of the battle swiftly changed; Wright and the men with him were cut off until the rest of the platoon could fight its way forward and join them. Other platoons had the same experience, initially advancing rapidly against disorganized enemy resistance and then finding themselves pinned down by deadly fire.

Meanwhile, the buildup continued. Troops, artillery, armor, and supplies kept coming ashore despite heavy losses. The driver of a bulldozer, whose assigment was to cut a path inland for the tanks, started forward when the bow ramp of his landing craft dropped; before him, the incline was littered with dead and wounded marines, but he had no choice save to lower the blade and carve

Allied Machine Guns

1 Vickers Mark 1 medium machine gun, of .303 caliber, water-cooled. Fabricated by various Royal Ordnance factories, this weapon saw continuous service with British forces from its introduction in 1912 right up until 1968, and proved itself an incredibly reliable weapon

2 Browning M2 heavy machine gun, of .50 caliber, air-cooled. Developed in the years immediately before World War II, the M2 saw service in an infantry support role, as well as being mounted on tanks and other vehicles. It proved itself effective in ground-to-ground, air-to-ground and antiaircraft roles

3 Browning Model 1919 A4 air-cooled light machine gun, of .30 caliber. Introduced just after World War I, this weapon was used extensively during World War II as a company support weapon, and was also used in a variety of vehicle mounts. Towards the end of World War II it was modified with a rifle-type butt, a pistol grip and a bipod

US Army Ordnance Museum

out the roadway. The men fighting inland had to have the fire of tanks.

Amphibian trucks driven by soldiers of the Army's Quartermaster Corps brought ammunition ashore for the two artillery regiments, the 13th Marines and the 14th Marines, that landed with the assault force. On the return trip to pick up more shells, the drivers carried away the wounded. Two of the truck companies consisted of black soldiers, and the Marine Corps, which like the Army reflected the racially segregated nature of American society, used black units to keep ammunition and supplies moving from the beach to the advancing riflemen and other forward units.

The marines saw few Japanese that first day, except for the dead. Occasionally, one of the enemy might pop up as he tried to escape from a doomed pillbox or to move from one position to another, but most of the defenders remained invisible. All too obvious was the fact of sudden death. A marine might lay on the sand lifeless, his wristwatch still ticking. An officer, shot in the throat, was thought to be dead, but he kicked violently when someone tried to bury him; carried away on a stretcher, he died in surgery on board one of the ships. Almost 30,000 marines landed during the first day, and more than 2,500 were killed or wounded.

The second day of fighting saw incredible acts of courage by both Japanese and Americans. Pointblank fire from the battleship *Washington* ripped into the steep slopes of Mt. Suribachi, causing landslides that exposed some artillery positions and buried others. Despite the hail of explosives, the defenders tried to carry out Kuribayashi's order of the day to "defend Iwo Jima to the bitter end . . ." Individual Japanese soldiers sprinted from cover to place mines in the path of approaching Marine tanks in a suicidal attempt to disable the vehicles. Among

The Vickers Mark 1 machine gun (1) was a development of the Maxim gun, and was first seen in 1912, though it did not reach the British Army until after the outbreak of World War I. In 1913 the United States ordered several thousand of these weapons, built around a .30 caliber, but delivery was slow and very few saw service with the US Army in France during 1917-18. The Vickers was replaced soon after the war by the American-produced 1917 Browning machine gun.

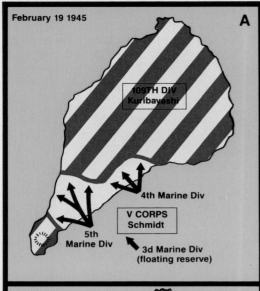

February 19 1945 **A**

109TH DIV
Kuribayashi

4th Marine Div

V CORPS
Schmidt

5th
Marine Div

3d Marine Div
(floating reserve)

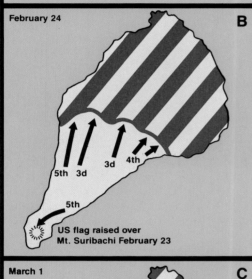

February 24 **B**

5th 3d 3d 4th

5th

US flag raised over
Mt. Suribachi February 23

March 1 **C**

5th 3d 3d 3d
4th
4th

March 9 **D**

5th 3d 3d
3d
4th
4th

THE INVASION OF IWO JIMA

Map A
It was to further the aims of the air campaign against the Japanese Home Islands that one of the bloodiest land battles of the Pacific War was fought. Iwo Jima was needed by the Americans as a support base for its B-29s on the Mariana Islands, while for the Japanese the island held a vital early-warning radar station and three airfields that could be used to launch raids on American bases.

The invasion force comprised of three Marine divisions. The plan was to land two divisions on the beaches on the southeast of the island. Forces would then advance towards the opposite shore, while also attacking Mt. Suribachi and Airfield No. 1 to the south and north.

The Japanese strategy of defense was to make the high ground on the island (Mt. Suribachi and the plateau to the northeast), centers of resistance. The Americans would be allowed to land and then be attacked from fixed positions. A battle of attrition would result, with the Japanese launching counterattacks only when numbers were in their favor.

After an aerial and naval bombardment that had lasted for months, the marines landed on the beaches to very little defending fire. It seems that the bombardment had done its work. As the marines pushed inland, however, Japanese fire became more and more intense and accurate. By the end of the first day some marines had reached the farther shore, but the majority were pinned down on the beachhead and were taking heavy casualties.

Map B
On the second day, the attack on the base of Mt. Suribachi began in earnest, and marine units began to secure the farther shore. The main drive to the northeast, however, remained bogged down under the sheer virulence of the Japanese defense. At the end of the second day it was decided to begin committing the reserve division. The third day of the battle saw Suribachi surrounded by marines; the attack up its slopes began the day after. The crater rim was reached on that day, but it was to be another six days before all the pockets of resistance were destroyed and the mount secured.

Map C
The reserve division was committed in its entirety in a bid to secure Airfield No. 2 and the high ground above it. The airfield was taken, but the marines then ran up against a heavily defended area of hills, ridges and depressions that would become known as the Meat Grinder.

Maps D and E
The destruction of the chain of Japanese strongpoints including the Meat Grinder ended organized resistance on March 9, but there would be another two weeks of fighting before Iwo Jima could be called secure.

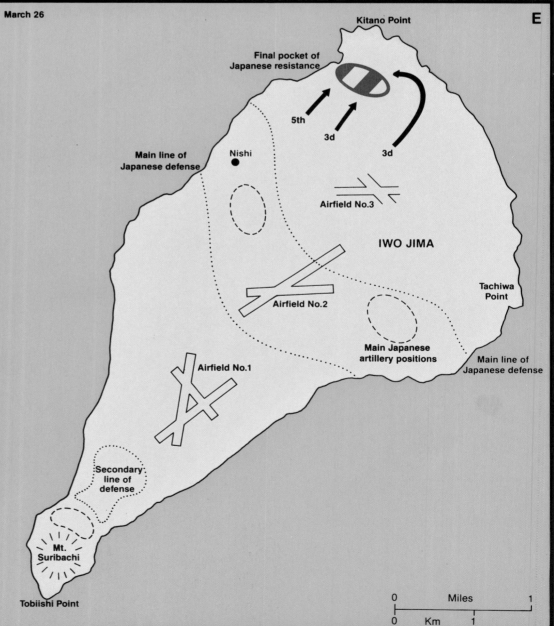

March 26 **E**

Kitano Point

Final pocket of
Japanese resistance

5th
3d
3d

Main line of
Japanese defense

Nishi

Airfield No.3

IWO JIMA

Tachiwa
Point

Airfield No.2

Main Japanese
artillery positions

Main line of
Japanese defense

Airfield No.1

Secondary
line of
defense

Mt.
Suribachi

Tobiishi Point

0   Miles   1

0   Km   1

Left: A naval chaplain comforts a marine artilleryman. The wounded man's battery was only 50 yards (45m) away on the south side of Airfield No.1, where V Amphibious Corps committed its reserve, the 3d Marine Division, on February 20.

found a piece of pipe for a flagstaff and unfurled the colors. A Marine Corps combat photographer, Sgt. Lou Lowery, took a picture, while Robeson stood out of the scene and made fun of Lowery and his ''Hollywood marines.'' From the beach, Secretary of the Navy James V. Forrestal, who had witnessed the landings, saw the flash of red, white, and blue high above him. He turned to Gen. Smith and said: ''Holland, the raising of that flag on Suribachi means a Marine Corps for the next 500 years.''

Schrier's battalion commander, Lt. Col. Chandler Johnson also saw the flag unfurled and sent his runner to get a larger one that would be visible from a greater distance. About three hours later, a group of five marines and a sailor — Pfc. Ira Hayes, a Pima Indian; Pfc. Franklin Sousley; Sgt. Michael Strank; Pfc. Rene Gagnon; Cpl. Harlan Block; and Pharmacist's Mate 3d cl. John H. Bradley — took down the first flag and replaced it with one from LST 779. Joe Rosenthal, an Associated Press photographer, took a picture of this second flag-raising, a masterpiece of dramatic composition that served to inspire the heroic sculpture by Felix de Weldon at the Marine Corps War Memorial in Arlington, Virginia.

The fate of the flag-raisers testifies to the savagery of the fight for Iwo Jima. Only six of the 12 men in the two groups survived the battle — Schrier, Michels, and Lindberg from Lowery's picture, plus Hayes, Gagnon, and Bradley from the Rosenthal photograph. Also killed in action was Lt. Col. Johnson, who sent for the larger flag.

During the struggle for Suribachi, the Japanese defenders sold their lives dearly and avoided the kind of *banzai* charge

the marines, Pvt. Jacklyn H. Lucas, a 17-year-old who had lied about his age when he enlisted three years earlier, threw himself onto a grenade, absorbed the blast with his body to save the lives of others, and survived to receive the Medal of Honor. Lucas had a reputation as a troublemaker, but on this day he was a hero.

On the bloody second day, the marines cut the island in half. While the 23d and 25th Marines of the 4th Marine Division and the 27th Marines of the 5th Marine Division fought their way to the northeast, onto the central plateau, and toward Airfields No. 2 and No. 3, the 28th Marines of the 5th Marine Division advanced toward Mt. Suribachi. Under the command of Col. Harry B. Liversedge, nicknamed ''Harry the Horse'' when he played football in college, the regiment clawed its way forward, taking advantage of air strikes and fire from warships and marine artillery. Tanks were to have supported the advance but fuel and ammunition arrived late, and the armored vehicles had trouble finding a route forward that did not come under mortar or artillery fire adjusted by observers on the slopes of the volcano. At last, tanks mounting 37-mm guns or flamethrowers began attacking the pillboxes barring the approaches to Mt. Suribachi, but rain and the abruptly steepening slopes immobilized the armor. The battle for the mountain became a seemingly endless succession of attacks with flamethrowers and explosive charges against caves and concrete bunkers, but unremitting pressure shattered organized

Japanese resistance on Mt. Suribachi. Perhaps 300 of the enemy still survived on the morning of February 23, but they clung to isolated strongpoints, out of contact with each other and with Kuribayashi's headquarters at the opposite end of the island.

On that same morning, the fourth day of the battle, marine patrols advanced to the very top of the mountain, passing flame-blackened caves and bunkers uprooted by naval gunfire. One of the patrols, led by 1st Lt. Harold G. Schrier, carried a small American flag that his battalion adjutant had brought ashore from the transport *Missoula*. At the rim of Suribachi's crater, Schrier's marines — Sgt. Ernest I. Thomas, Jr.,; Sgt. Henry O. Hansen; Cpl. Charles W. Lindberg; Pfc. James R. Michels; Pfc. James Robeson; and Pvt. Louis Charlo, a Crow Indian —

Right: In one of the most celebrated images of World War II, men of the 28th Marine Regiment raise the ''Stars and Stripes'' above Mt. Suribachi on February 23. It was to be more than another month before the last Japanese resistance ended on Iwo Jima.

Japanese Machine Guns

1 Lewis machine gun of a 1932 type. This weapon has a caliber of 7.7mm and is seen here in its antiaircraft configuration. This example features its 47 round drum magazine in position, together with an extra drum

2 Type 92 (1932) heavy machine gun. This air-cooled weapon has a caliber of 7.7m and features a telescopic sight on the receiver, and a flash suppressor over the end of the barrel. Its stripper clip of ammunition can be seen in position. Note the adjustable 'spade' type wooden grip. Mobility was an important part of Japanese machine gun tactics, and the tripods of these weapons, including the one here, have lugs at the feet to allow carrying poles to be inserted

3 Air-cooled Type (1941) machine gun. This weapon is of 7.7mm caliber. It features a 'spade' grip and flash suppressor

4 Stripper ammunition clips of 7.7mm caliber, complete in their original cardboard packing boxes

US Army Ordnance Museum, 1-3; Eugene C. Gibson Collection, 4

that, in the long run, would have made the job of the marines easier. Similarly, Japanese aviators sought to trade one life for hundreds of American lives. About 50 *kamikazes* took off from an airfield near Tokyo on February 21, refueled in the Bonin Islands, and attacked the fleet off Iwo Jima. Five suicide pilots jumped the aircraft carrier *Saratoga*, two of them crashing into the hull and exploding deep within the ship. Almost two hours later, another *kamikaze* nosed over, dived on the damaged carrier, and released a bomb that penetrated the flight deck and prevented the launching of aircraft. As *Saratoga* withdrew from

the fight with more than 300 crewmen killed or wounded, another group of *kamikazes* attacked the escort carriers provided air support for the marines ashore. One of the aircraft hit *Lunga Point*, drenching the flight deck with blazing gasoline but causing only minor damage. Another escort carrier, *Bismarck Sea*, suffered hits by two *kamikazes* and erupted in a ball of fire, probably when torpedoes stored on the hangar deck exploded; the stricken ship remained afloat for an hour, giving 625 of the more than 900 officers and men on board an opportunity to escape. The *kamikazes* also sank an LST, together

with the auxiliary vessel *Keokuk*.

Although the sight of the American flag over Suribachi inspired the marines and profoundly discouraged the Japanese, who had expected the mountain redoubt to hold out for weeks rather than days, the capture of the volcano marked the end of just one phase of a long and deadly campaign. On February 20, the second day of the battle, when the 28th Marines wheeled to advance on Suribachi, the rest of the 5th Marine Division and the 4th Marine Division began fighting their way northward. The same rainstorm that slowed the attack up the slopes of the volcano interfered with

The Japanese took an early interest in the machine gun, and during their war with Tsarist Russia in 1904-5, were one of the first nations to use them in an offensive capacity. Their choice of design was based around the air-cooled French Hotchkiss gun, which fired the characteristic stripper clip of ammunition.

a plan to move the 21st Marines of the 3d Marine Division into line in place of the 25th Marines, which had suffered severe casualties advancing through broken terrain on the far right of the assault beaches. The 21st Marines moved forward on the morning of February 22, but the fresh regiment relieved the 23d Marines on the boundary between divisions, instead of the 25th Marines as originally planned. The Japanese realized what was happening and laid down fire which delayed but could not prevent the change of regiments. Next to the 21st Marines, but on the opposite side of the division boundary, Gen. Rockey replaced the bloodied 27th Marines with the 26th Marines, so that V Amphibious Corps was able to maintain pressure all along the line, advancing between 200 and 1,000 yards (182 and 910m).

The next readily defined objective was Airfield No. 2, and on the morning of February 24 the marines attacked behind a naval bombardment lasting 75 minutes, an artillery barrage, and an airstrike. Tanks crossed the division boundary and reinforced the armored elements of the 4th Marine Division in storming the airfield. Mines and antitank guns stopped the advance, but not until the attack had gained 500 yards (455m) and reached the near edge of the objective.

In order to sustain the momentum thus generated, Gen. Schmidt committed the remainder of Gen. Erskine's 3d Marine Division to join the regiment, the 21st Marines, already in action in the center of the corps zone. On the morning of February 25, the 9th Marines attacked through the positions of the 21st Marines on the first of three days of bloody fighting that ended with the capture of Airfield No. 2 and the hills just to the north. The 21st Marines then took up the cudgel and battered its way through Motoyama Village to the high ground just south of Airfield No. 3. Throughout the fighting in this sector, the Japanese resisted from caves all but impervious to artillery fire; only the flamethrower could kill the defenders or drive them deeper underground, so that marines with charges could seal the openings.

While 3d Marine Division fought for the territory between Airfields No. 2 and No. 3, the 5th Marine Division attacked toward Hill 382 and the 4th Marine Division toward Hill 362A. Neither objective could be bypassed, and the marines took them both, though at a terrible cost. On March 1, the 28th Marines, the conquerors of Suribachi, stormed Hill 362A in the face of mortar and artillery concentrations that killed or wounded 224 of the assault troops. Despite the casualties, the regiment overran the hill in two days of fighting and advanced along the ridge line beyond.

Unlike the comparatively isolated stronghold of Hill 362A, Hill 382 formed but one element in a defensive maze: dug-in tanks and sturdy bunkers mounting artillery and antitank guns guarded

Above: Sitting amongst a huge pile of used cartridge cases, this crew of a Browning machine gun fight it out with defenders at the base of Mt. Suribachi, three days after the invasion began. Empty ammunition boxes and a water can are also in evidence.

Below: Two configurations of the Browning Model 1917 A1 water-cooled machine gun — ground mount (left) and antiaircraft mount (right). Developed originally for World War I, this model was introduced in 1936. *US Army Ordnance Museum.*

the approaches to the hill; next to the hill itself was a moonscape of ridges and draws called Turkey Nob; and farthest to the right and dominated by Turkey Nob was a huge depression nicknamed the Amphitheater. This entire complex — Hill 382, Turkey Nob, the Amphitheater, and the broken ground that linked them — came to be called the Meat Grinder, and with good reason. The battle for the Meat Grinder lasted two weeks, as the Japanese clung stubbornly to every yard until killed by bazookas (which fired a rocket designed to penetrate the armor of tanks), flamethrowers, grenades, or explosive charges.

MARINE WITH FLAMETHROWER, IWO JIMA

This marine wears the olive drab combat fatigues of herringbone twill, common at this period of the war. His web gaiters are worn outside the trousers and his helmet is covered in a cloth camouflage cover. His personal armament includes a large fighting knife and .45 automatic pistol. The M2-2 portable flamethrower he carries was a company support weapon first used in New Guinea. By the end of the war over 24,000 had been made.

During the savage battle for the Meat Grinder, the 5th Marine Division captured Hill 362B and the 3d Marine Division attacked Hill 362C. The assault on Hill 362C was one of the few night attacks by American forces in the entire Pacific war. Gen. Erskine realized that Marine units had fallen into the habit of attacking in the morning light, and he obtained permission to move out before daybreak. The troops eased forward under cover of darkness on the morning of March 7 and, as Erskine expected, caught the Japanese by surprise. Not until daylight did the defenders realize that the marines were at their throats; a firefight erupted, but by mid-afternoon the objective had been captured.

The interlocking defenses laid out by Kuribayashi — a semicircle from Hills 362A, B, and C to the Meat Grinder — had been broken. The Japanese general had no communication with his soldiers, who were hungry and thirsty, groggy from lack of sleep, resigned to death, but nonetheless determined to keep on killing as long as they could. In these desperate circumstances, the Japanese in the zone of the 4th Marine Division attempted a counterattack on the night of March 8. A few of Kuribayashi's men launched a *banzai* charge with shouts and wild firing, but most of them took advantage of the jagged ground and tried to infiltrate along the regimental boundary between the 23d and 24th Marines. The results proved disastrous for the Japanese, as their general had feared when he directed his men to fight from prepared positions — 650 killed by mid-morning of March 9. This Marine victory and the capture of the Meat Grinder on the following day signaled the end of organized resistance, although some savage fighting lay ahead as the marines subdued the last of the Japanese.

Three isolated strongpoints still held out, one in front of each of the Marine divisions. The Japanese facing the 3d

Above: Men of the 5th Marine Division on the ruins of Hill 165 during March 17, 1945. The division had advanced along the western side of Iwo Jima, and was now only a little short of Kitano Point where all Japanese resistance ended on March 25.

Marine Division were concentrated in Cushman's Pocket, southwest of Hill 362C, named for Lt. Col. Robert E. Cushman, Jr., the commander of the 2d Battalion, 9th Marines, one of the three battalions that helped eliminate it. As Kuribayashi had ordered, the defenders of Cushman's Pocket fought from concealment, forcing the marines to attack each position in succession with flame-throwers, the 75-mm guns of medium tanks, and finally explosive charges. Of the 450 or more men trapped in the pocket, perhaps 40 surrendered, some of them Korean laborers rather than Japanese soldiers. Finally, on March 15, the 60 or so survivors threw away their lives in a final charge.

The 4th Marine Division encountered a comparable force of Japanese fighting from caves and pillboxes among the ravines that run from the plateau to the surf, just north of the invasion beaches. The members of a psychological warfare team tried to broadcast a surrender

appeal before the final assault but could not. Their gasoline-powered generator, and its backup, refused to start, and the loudspeakers remained mute. On March 12, without prior warning, the Americans attacked. Judging from the ferocity of their resistance, the Japanese could not have been persuaded to give up, for the marines had to fight yard by yard until they reached the ocean after a four-day struggle.

Meanwhile, on March 11, the 5th Marine Division attacked the third enemy stronghold, Bloody Gorge, near Kitano Point at the northern tip of the island. As in the other division sectors, the assault troops, aided by fire from tanks, worked their way through a jumble of draws and ridges honeycombed with caves. The defenders might open fire from any direction, sometimes hiding underground until the marines passed and then cutting loose with machine guns or rifles. Fighter-bombers dropped 500-pound (200kg) bombs as the infantry advanced, aiming for blockhouses and the mouths of large caves. The extent to which the Japanese had tunneled into the volcanic rock became obvious when a bomb plummeted into a cave, exploded, and sent smoke billowing from fissures in the broken ground 200 to 300 yards (182 to 273m) away. Kuribayashi, who had moved his headquarters to this part of the island, radioed Tokyo on the night of March 17 that he intended to launch a final attack. In a poem he intended as his last testament, he wrote:

> Shells and bullets are gone, and we perish
> Remorseful of failure to fulfill our assignments.

The promised attack, if it did take place, passed unnoticed amid the general

Below: Only 216 of Iwo Jima's defenders survived to become prisoners of war. Here one of these men shows men of the US Marine Corps a cave used as a Japanese supply dump. The island was honeycombed with caves and man-made excavations.

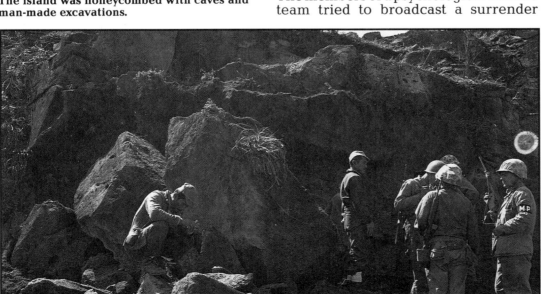

Left: Iwo Jima was an ideal emergency landing point for Boeing B-29 Superfortress bombers on their way back to the Marianas from raids on Japan. The first such aircraft arrived on the island during March 4, as the fighting still raged around it.

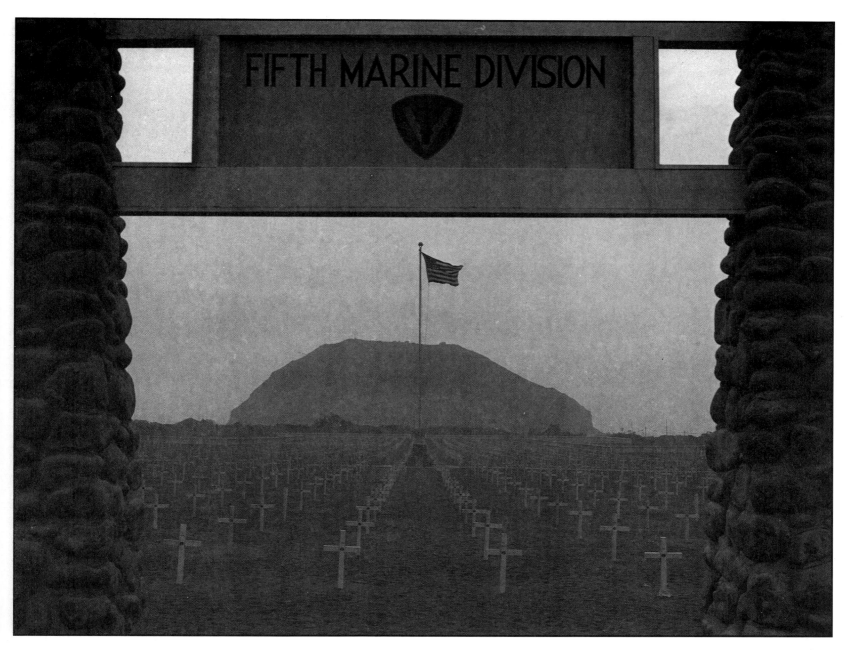

violence. On March 23, he again broke radio silence in a final farewell to his superiors at Tokyo.

The battle for Iwo Jima ended on March 25 in an American victory but, at the cost of almost 6,000 men killed and more than 17,000 wounded. Said Fleet Adm. Chester W. Nimitz, the Commander in Chief, Pacific Ocean Areas, in formally announcing the end of the

Above: It is more than fitting that the cemetery of the 5th Marine Division should lie under Mt. Suribachi. This is the dominating feature at the southern end of Iwo Jima, and its capture cost the division very heavy casualties.

fighting: ''Among the Americans who served on Iwo Jima, uncommon valor was a common virtue.'' Of the 20,000 defenders, only 216 survived to become prisoners of war; all the others died, many of them sealed forever in the caves from which they had resisted.

In American hands, Iwo Jima provided airfields from which P-51s could escort B-29s against Japan and where damaged bombers could land rather than risk flying an additional 600 miles to the Marianas. On March 4, while the battle still raged, a B-29, short on fuel because of the added drag created by a jammed bomb-bay door, landed safely on the island. This was the first of 2,251 bombers, with more than 22,000 crewmen on board, to make emergency landings there. Clearly, Iwo Jima, which had cost so many lives, also saved them, even though many of the B-29s that landed there might well have reached the Marianas or ditched safely at sea.

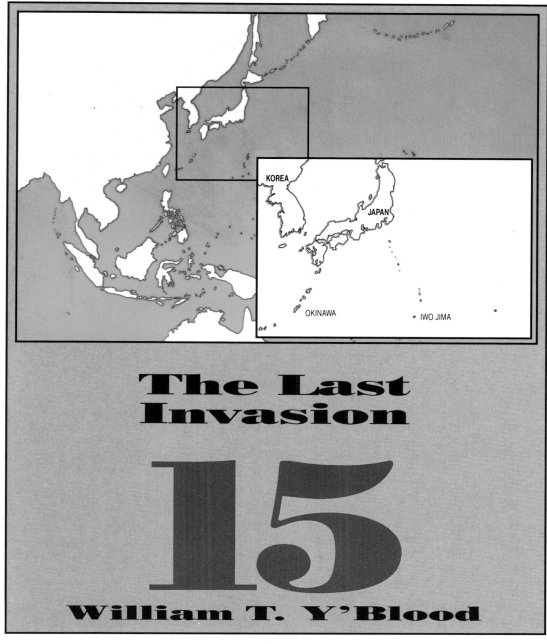

The Last Invasion

15

William T. Y'Blood

By the spring of 1945, the Japanese must have felt that the wolf was at their front door. Instead of sheep's clothing, however, this wolf was clad in the green drab of a marine, the olive drab of a soldier, the blue of a sailor, and the khaki of a flier. Army Air Force B-29s had begun bombing Japan on a regular basis in November 1944, and Navy carrier planes joined in with heavy attacks on the Home Islands in February and March 1945. Iwo Jima (only 660 nautical miles (1,222km) south of Tokyo) was assaulted on February 19, 1945, and after a bloody battle, fell a month later. It was obvious to the Japanese that the Americans would need to take one more objective before launching a final assault on Japan, and that objective was Okinawa.

It was equally obvious to the American planners that an invasion of Okinawa was required in order to secure air bases and the real estate necessary to handle the huge amount of supplies that would have to be gathered for the final assault on Japan. The possibility of invading Okinawa had surfaced in July 1944 but it was not until October, when the debate over Luzon or Formosa was resolved in

favor of Luzon, that an attack on Okinawa became possible.

On October 3, 1944, the Joint Chiefs of Staff directed Adm. Chester W. Nimitz to seize one or more positions in the Ryukyu Islands by March 1, 1945, later postponed to April 1. The Ryukyus stretch about 790 nautical miles (1,463km) in an arc from Kyushu to Formosa. Okinawa, 60 miles (96km) long and the largest of the some 140 islands in the chain, lies almost in the center of the Ryukyus and is about 350 nautical miles (648km) from Kyushu.

Planning for the invasion, codenamed Operation Iceberg, began immediately after receipt of the directive. In overall command of Iceberg was Adm. Spruance, who wore many hats. At Okinawa he was Commander, Central Pacific Task Forces (the overall command organization), Commander, Fifth Fleet, and Commander, Covering Forces and Special Groups (Task Force 50). As commander of Task Force 50, Spruance had at his disposal the fast carriers of Adm. Mitscher's Task Force 58 and an organization making its first appearance in the Pacific: the British Carrier Task

US Army Uniforms and Equipment

1. Model 1928 field pack with Model 1910 entrenching tool attached on the back
2. Enlisted man's raincoat
3. Army service gas mask and carrier. The filter is inside the carrier
4. Shelter half with securing pegs, and supporting pole
5. Field shoes
6. M1 steel helmet
7. Herring bone twill shirt
8. Herring bone twill field trousers
9. Herring bone twill field jacket
10. M1938 canvas leggings
11. M1910 pick/mattock, disassembled
12. M1937 Browning Automatic Rifle (BAR) magazine belt
13. M1918 A2 BAR
14. M1943 field jacket
15. Buckle boots
16. M1 helmet with net band
17. Field trousers with braces
18. Service machete
19. M1 Garand rifle
20. Olive drab field trousers
21. M1943 entrenching tool
22. M1945 field pack
23. M1923 cartridge belt and combat straps
24. Grenade carrier
25. M1910 hand axe and carrier
26. First aid pouch with Carlisle first aid pouch
27. M1910 canteen, cup, and cover

Dale E. Biever: 1-3, 5-6, 11-14, 24, 25; Pritchard Collection: 4, 10, 15, 17-19, 21, 26; Howard E. Hendricks: 7-9, 16, 20, 22, 23, 27

The herring bone twill olive green fatigues replaced the khaki drill 'chino' service dress in 1942 (elements of uniform on the left). The infantry then was issued with a one piece combat overall that was found to be far too impractical for jungle use. At the time of its introduction, the overall was to be found in both olive green and camouflage material. A two-piece combat suit of herring bone twill was introduced from 1943 onwards, also in camouflage colors. The overalls were phased out in spring 1944. The camouflage colors were also dropped from the two-piece herring bone twill suit and from spring 1944 it was found only in olive drab. The final infantry combat uniform of the war was the two-piece olive drab poplin uniform introduced in spring 1945, which served until the war's end (elements of uniform on the right).

Force (Task Force 57). The carriers of Task Force 57 were to neutralize the southern Ryukyus, or the Sakishima Gunto.

Vice Adm. Richmond K. Turner, commanded the Joint Expeditionary Force (Task Force 51). His job, as in so many landings before, was to land the troops that would capture the island. Under his command were the Amphibious Support Force (Task Force 52), consisting of escort carriers, gunboats, minesweepers, and the like; the Gunfire and Covering Force (Task Force 54), of old battleships, cruisers, and destroyers; the Northern Attack Force (Task Force 53),

which would land marines over the northern beaches; the Southern Attack Force (Task Force 55), which would carry the Army troops; and the Expeditionary Troops (Task Force 56), charged with seizing Okinawa.

Lt. Gen. Simon Bolivar Buckner, Jr., commanded the Expeditionary Troops. Following the assault phase, Buckner, as Commander Tenth Army, would handle the ground phase of the operation. Tenth Army, a joint organization, was a powerful force and, although the army itself was not combat-tested, its component units were veteran outfits.

The XXIV Corps (Southern Landing

Force), under Maj. Gen. John R. Hodges, consisted of the 7th and 96th Infantry Divisions. The Northern landing Force was composed of the 1st and 6th Marine Divisions of Maj. Gen. Roy S. Geiger's III Amphibious Corps. Additionally, the 77th Infantry Division was to open the battle by capturing the islands of the Kerama Retto, about 15 nautical miles (27km) west of Okinawa, prior to the main landings; the 2d Marine Division would conduct a feint toward southeast Okinawa, also in anticipation of the main landings; the 27th Infantry Division was in floating reserve; and the 81st Infantry Division was in area reserve. Except for the 81st Infantry Division, all of the divisions would eventually fight on Okinawa.

Over 180,000 soldiers, marines, and attached naval personnel made up the assault force. Supporting these troops were close to 1,500 ships of all types and sizes. In magnitude, Operation Iceberg rivaled D-Day at Normandy as the largest amphibious operation of the war. The very size of the objective, 467 square miles (1,210km²), its proximity to the Home Islands, and its defenses dictated the size of the invasion force.

Although the Japanese defenders had nowhere near the number of troops as the attackers, other factors helped to even the odds somewhat. Given the task of defending the Ryukyus, in particular Okinawa, was Lt. Gen. Mitsuru Ushijima's 32d Army, built around the 24th and 62d Infantry Divisions. (Fortunately for the invaders, a third division, the 9th was transferred to Formosa in December in response to the invasion of the Philippines. The division, incidentally, never did get to the Philippines.) Still, when the invasion of Okinawa took place, Ushijima had about 77,000 Japanese troops, another 20,000 men of the *Boeitai* (the Okinawa Home Guard), and approximately 10,000-15,000 other Okinawan natives available for his army.

Ushijima's troops knew the ground very well and carefully prepared it for a defense in depth centered upon three defense lines in the southern part of the island near Shuri. The terrain in the south is relatively flat and highly cultivated, but is broken by numerous ravines, ridges and escarpments. In the north, a couple of battalions defended the Motobu Peninsula and Ie Shima, a small island just three and one-half nautical miles (6.5km) off the peninsula. The northern part of the island is very rugged and heavily forested. Behind the Hagushi beaches on the west coast, where the Japanese expected correctly that the landings would be made, only a small delaying force dug in.

The 32d Army intended to deny the Americans the use of Okinawa until the *kamikazes* and other air and naval units could destroy the invasion fleet. For a delaying action of this sort, the Japanese were well equipped. They had more artillery available than had yet been seen in the Pacific, and they used it with deadly efficiency. Moreover, the 32d Army had more antitank guns, mortars, automatic weapons, and ammunition than normal for such a force. This oversupply was caused, generally, from the inability of the Japanese to ship this material on to the Philippines as had been intended. Ushijima's men made grim use of this windfall.

Finally, there was the *kamikaze*. Although its use in the Philippines resulted in heavy damage to Allied shipping, the Okinawa campaign would be unique in the ferocity of the *kamikaze* attacks. Unlike the earlier battles where the suicide planes were used in small groups, Okinawa would see them employed in great masses.

Admiral Mitscher's Task Force 58 made the opening moves in Operation Iceberg. In an attempt to prevent enemy aircraft from interfering with the landings, planes from Mitscher's carriers

Above: Lieutenant colonel's uniform of the 637th Tank Destroyer Battalion. This unit served in the capture of Luzon. Includes winter combat helmet, jacket, trousers, gloves, and boots peculiar to the armored service. *War Memorial Museum of Virginia.*

attacked airfields and installations on Kyushu on March 18-19. These attacks were productive, the Americans claiming some 528 enemy aircraft destroyed. The Japanese countered that only 163 planes were lost in the air but conceded that an undetermined number were destroyed on the ground. Whatever the totals were, these losses effectively prevented the Japanese from launching a major aerial attack until almost a week after the landings.

Task Force 58 achieved this success at great cost, however. The carriers *Enterprise, Yorktown, Intrepid,* and *Wasp* were hit, most by regular bombers, and incurred severe casualties. But it was the *Franklin* that endured the greatest agony. Struck by two bombs while she was launching a strike, the carrier was turned into a raging inferno. For a time, the ship seemed doomed, but heroic efforts by her crew and ships standing alongside eventually quelled the fires. The *Franklin* took grievous losses — 724 dead and another 260 wounded out of a crew of about 2,600 — yet she was able to steam back to the United States for repairs. Her damage was so extensive, and the war ended so soon afterwards, that she never returned to action.

Making the initial assault in the Ryukyus was the 77th Infantry Division,

Left: An American battleship pounds Okinawa. Between March 23 and 31, the aircraft and guns of Adm. W.H.P. Blandy's force of escort carriers and heavy warships delivered a vast weight of bombs and shells onto the island's defenses.

THE INVASION OF OKINAWA

Map A

The initial landings on Okinawa would be undertaken by two complete corps. Beaches to the north of the landing zone would be attacked by two Marine divisions of the III Amphibious Corps, while to the south two infantry divisions of XXIV Corps would land.

The Japanese decided to use the island's terrain to maximum effect, and organized their defense on three lines in the south, manned by two infantry divisions. Here the country was flat, but broken with ravines and escarpments. The north of the island, being forested and hilly, was left lightly defended. The overall strategy was for the land battle to delay the Americans for as long as possible while naval assaults and mass attacks by *kamikaze* units destroyed the invasion fleet.

The initial landings went well for the Americans, and by the fifth day of the invasion, two important airfields had been secured and the island had been cut in two.

Map B

Marines now moved into the north of the island through difficult terrain to pin down and destroy its defenders. This was achieved in reasonable time. To the south, however, American forces had hit the first of the Japanese defense lines. Progress was slowing and casualties began to mount. At the same time, *kamikaze* attacks had begun to take their toll of the invasion fleet.

Map C

The Japanese defenders were now concentrated in and around the heavily fortified Shuri area. For five days American infantry battered away at it, but little progress was made in breaking through the defensive line. American divisions were now reinforced. Attacks again went in; these failed at first but finally the first line broke. A major Japanese counterattack now occurred, but was thrown back. The Americans again went on the offensive; there was progress but it was slow and bloody. The breakthrough finally came around the flanks which isolated and destroyed the last pockets of organized Japanese resistance.

US Combat Rations

1-3 K rations. Developed by Dr. Ancel Keys of the University of Minnesota, and the Subsistence Research Laboratory. They consisted of three boxes, one for each meal of the day, containing a reputedly balanced and edible meal; all self-contained and ready to eat

4 Major meat component of K rations and tin of cheese spread. Each meal contained a tin of meat product together with a key to open it

5 Wood spoons

6 Pack of issue toilet paper

7 Pack of chewing gum

8 Pack of chewing gum

9 Packets of cigarettes

10 Sachets of brand-named instant coffee

11 Sachet of instant coffee

12 Soluble soup cubes

13 Box of granulated sugar

14 Pack of matches, with a malaria warning printed on the back

15 Hard crackers

16 Bar of sweet chocolate

17 Full unopened ration pack of sugar, confection and biscuits. The open pack has individual servings of dry, ready-to-eat cereal inside

US Army Quartermaster Museum

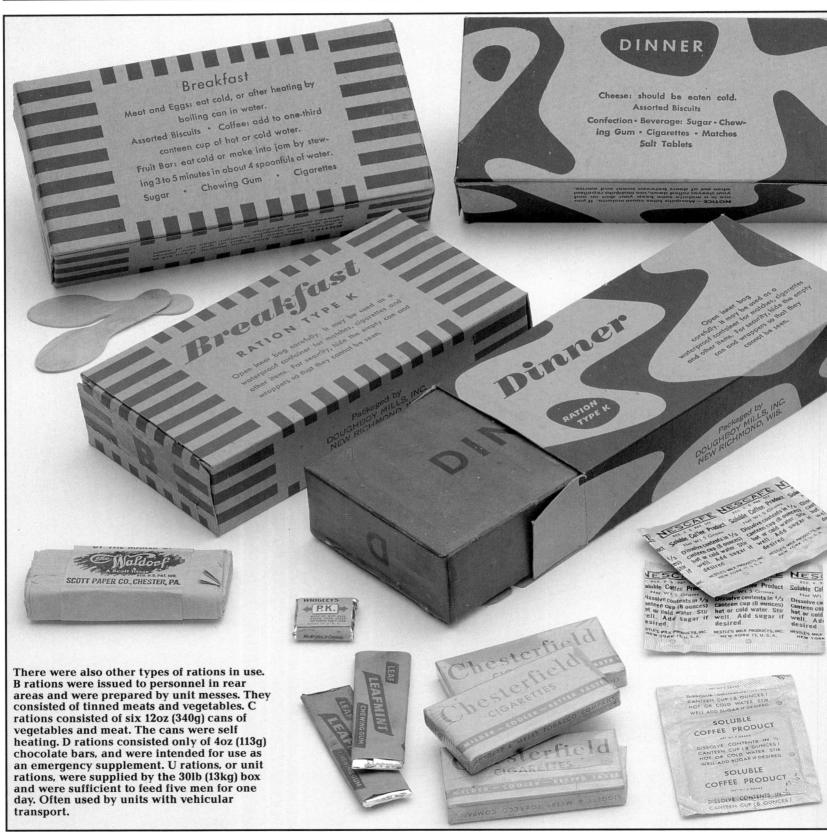

There were also other types of rations in use. B rations were issued to personnel in rear areas and were prepared by unit messes. They consisted of tinned meats and vegetables. C rations consisted of six 12oz (340g) cans of vegetables and meat. The cans were self heating. D rations consisted only of 4oz (113g) chocolate bars, and were intended for use as an emergency supplement. U rations, or unit rations, were supplied by the 30lb (13kg) box and were sufficient to feed five men for one day. Often used by units with vehicular transport.

which began landings on islands in the Kerama Retto on the morning of March 26. The capture of these islands was intended to provide a protected anchorage, a base for supply and repair vessels, and a seaplane base. By March 29, after some 15 separate landings, the 77th Infantry Division controlled the Keramas. Two days later, elements of that division made an unopposed landing on Keise Shima, a group of four tiny islets eight miles (12.8km) west of the city of Naha. From these islands 155-mm guns could cover most of southern Okinawa. Two battalions of these guns quickly went into place and played a major role through-

out the remainder of the campaign.

Casualties in this entire operation were relatively light and the Americans reaped an unexpected benefit when they discovered and captured a nest of suicide boats in the Keramas. Hundreds of these small boats, each carrying two 250-lb (112-kg) depth charges, were to have been used in suicide attacks on the invasion fleet, but the capture of the islands nullified these plans.

The importance of these islands became evident even before the shooting came to an end there. Vessels scourged by *kamikazes* gathered in the anchorage to seek succor from the

repair ships. But even the Kerama Retto would not be immune to the *kamikazes* and the sobriquets "Bogey Gulch" and "Suicide Gulch" for the anchorage were well earned. Nevertheless, throughout the entire campaign, the Kerama Retto remained a vital acquisition for the Americans.

April 1 was Easter Sunday. It was also L-Day (the only time the letter was used to designate an assault landing). But it was also April Fools' Day and the Japanese had a trick to play on the Americans. At 5:30 A.M., the pre-landing bombardment began. Between then and 8:30 A.M., when the first

US Special Weapons

1 Model 1919 A6 Browning light machine gun .30 caliber. This arm was produced in an effort to provide a more effective weapon than the Browning Automatic Rifle. It was no more than a Model 1919 with a shoulder stock and bipod added

2 M1 metal ammunition boxes. Painted olive drab (OD), these boxes carried loaded 250 round belts of machine gun ammunition for the Model 1919 A6 and Model 1919 weapons

3 M2-2 flame thrower

4 M1 A1 rocket launcher, 2.36-inch. This electrically-fired smooth-bore weapon had a maximum range of 400 yards (360m). At America's entry into the war, it went into service extremely fast: 5,000 were completed within one month in 1942. They proved highly portable and effective infantry weapons and were used with most effect against light and medium armor.

5 M6 A1 hollow charge rocket, 2.36-inch for use in 4

6 M6 A1 practice rocket, 2.36-inch for use in 4

War Memorial Museum of Virginia: 1-5; Dale E. Biever Collection: 6

The 2.36 rocket launcher was also known popularly as the bazooka, after a comic wind instrument in an American radio show. There was nothing humorous about this particular bazooka though. The finned rocket was loaded into the back by the second man of the firing team. The rocket was connected by an electric firing wire to batteries in the launcher. The firer simply took aim through the open sight on the side of the launcher and ignited the rocket's motor by pressing the trigger. Because the rocket blast went straight through the tube, there was no recoil, though those around had to take care not to stand behind the firer when a rocket was being launched.

The M2-2 portable flame thrower was a version of a simple but particularly nasty weapon that had first been developed in Germany in the early 1900s. The flamethrower worked by firing a stream of inflammable liquid by means of compressed gas, then igniting it.

landing craft touched down, over 100,000 rounds of shells and rockets plastered the landing beaches and surrounding areas. It was the heaviest concentration of naval gunfire ever in a landing operation.

The initial objectives of the Tenth Army were the two airfields, Yontan and Kadena, located a mile inland. It had been estimated that the fields could be secured by L plus 5. By L plus 10 the invaders were to advance on a line facing south near the village of Futema, splitting the island. In the north, a line was to be formed near Ishikawa, and most of the Katchin Peninsula taken by L plus 15.

Because of the severity of the fighting in the earlier Pacific battles, particularly Peleliu and Iwo Jima, together with the nearness of the Home Islands, most of the invasion troops expected the landings to be bloody and fiercely contested. Thus it came as quite a surprise to the Americans that they met little resistance when they stormed ashore on Okinawa.

Ushijima had not planned on making a stand on the beaches and had positioned just light forces in the area to fight a delaying action. These Japanese troops did even less of a job in delaying the US forces than Ushijima had ordered, which

infuriated him, but there was little he could do now. By nightfall, the two important airfields were in American hands at a remarkably light cost in dead and wounded. Ironically, some of the heaviest casualties had been suffered by the force making the diversionary feint at southeast Okinawa when it had been attacked by *kamikazes*.

Over the next few days the Tenth Army consolidated and expanded its beachhead, reaching the east coast of the island on April 3 and successfully cutting the island in two. The following day the XXIV Corps wheeled south while the marines of the III Amphibious Corps

Left: The Japanese deployed to Okinawa a large number of suicide craft such as these two boats captured on the Mobotu peninsula. The *Shinyo* class craft carried a 4,400lb explosive charge or two depth charges, and could reach a speed of 25 knots.

turned to face toward the north.

In the south, the 7th Infantry Division was on the left (east) flank and the 96th Infantry Division was on the right (west) flank. As these two divisions drove south, resistance stiffened and casualties began to increase. The army troops had run into the outposts of Ushijima's main defense lines. An especially troublesome position confronting the soldiers of the 7th Infantry Division was known as the Pinnacle. Frontal assaults proved to be fruitless against this well-protected position and the Pinnacle fell only after a surprise flank attack. The toughness of the fighting around the Pinnacle brought the Americans back to reality following the euphoria of the first days after the landings.

Meanwhile, the marines in the north fought the terrain as much as the enemy. Most of the Japanese defenders retreated slowly into the Motobu Peninsula, where a 1,200-foot (360-m)-high

Left: A Kawasaki Ki-61 "Tony" fighter dives toward the escort carrier *Sangamon* in a suicide attack on May 4, 1945. The attack missed the carrier by less than 25 feet (7m), but the explosion beside the waterline still caused considerable damage.

mount, Yae Take, had been turned into a well-organized defensive position. Other defenders melted into the jungle to wage guerrilla warfare, but marine patrols combed the jungle and neutralized them. One regiment of the 6th Marine Division secured the entire northern portion of the island by April 19, encountering little opposition.

Motobu Peninsula and Yae Take were another story. The peninsula was mountainous and heavily forested which restricted movement. The Japanese were well dug in. Nevertheless, by April 14, the 6th Marine Division was in position on three sides of Yae Take and was patrolling the fourth side. Over the next few days, in savage fighting (sometimes hand to hand), the marines took the crest of Yae Take but were unable to drive the enemy off the rest of the mountain. Finally, a surprise attack up an almost sheer cliff routed the Japanese. The fighting in northern Okinawa (primarily on Motobu Peninsula) cost the marines over 1,200 casualties, including 236 dead, but the Japanese losses were much worse. Only 46 became prisoners; over 2,500 others were killed.

While the marines mopped up Motobu Peninsula, the 77th Infantry Division assaulted Ie Shima. Although small, the island boasted a large airfield complex. It also had some extremely rugged terrain and a lot of fanatical defenders. Approximately 2,000 Japanese were expecting the attack, as were some 5,000 civilians still on the island. One of the most striking things about this battle was how many civilians, including many

women, took an active part in the fight.

The 77th Infantry Division surged ashore on the morning of April 16 and by evening the airfields were taken. Resistance, though, was strong and would remain so throughout the battle, particularly as the attackers moved into the broken terrain. Especially tough nuts to crack were the 600-foot (180m)-high Pinnacle (not to be confused with the other Pinnacle on Okinawa) and Bloody Ridge. Eventually, the division had to commit all three of its regiments in order to clear out the defenders.

Although Ie Shima was declared secure on the 21st, for almost five days afterward the soldiers were killing defenders who refused to give up. Like so many of the actions during the Okinawa campaign, Ie Shima was a bloody, vicious brawl. Over 4,700 of the defenders, both soldiers and civilians, were killed. American losses totaled 218 killed or missing and 902 wounded, and many of the wounds suffered in the battle were unusually severe. One of the casualties of Ie Shima was famed war correspondent Ernie Pyle, celebrated for his stories about ordinary servicemen doing a dangerous and unheralded job, who was killed by machine-gun fire when he raised his head to see where the fire originated.

Despite the cost in lives, Ie Shima was an excellent acquisition for the Americans. By mid-May a fighter group was operating from the island and the radars that had been quickly installed proved their value over and over as they spotted the *kamikazes* that continued to roar down from Japan.

As the fighting on Okinawa rose in intensity, offshore the ships of the Navy were undergoing an assault of unprecedented ferocity. An integral part of the defense of Okinawa was an operation named *Ten-Go*. This presaged the use of *kamikazes* in massed attacks. The Japanese hoped to gather over 4,500 aircraft to use in these attacks, but the fast carrier and B-29 raids on Japan reduced the planes immediately available when the battle opened to only 735.

Individual *kamikazes* attacked the invasion fleet from the beginning, and 38 ships were damaged and a high-speed transport sunk by these suiciders. But it was not until April 6 that the Japanese were able to launch the first of what eventually would be ten massed attacks (named *kikusui* or floating chrysanthemums) on the ships off Okinawa.

Although April 6 was cloudy and cool, many men on the ships would find themselves sweating profusely when *Kikusui No. 1* howled in that afternoon. This first attack, which continued the next day, consisted of 303 *kamikazes* and 432 other aircraft. The carnage they wreaked in this two-day attack was awesome — six ships sunk and 27 damaged, some badly enough to be knocked out of the war, plus 466 men killed and 568 wounded. Two of the ships sunk were ammunition ships and these losses immediately created an ammunition shortage for the troops on Okinawa. Losses were not one-sided, however. Not one *kamikaze* returned to Japan, as the planners of the *kikusui* attacks expected, and an undetermined number of other attackers were shot down.

The *kikusui* attacks continued with decreasing numbers of aircraft but unswerving ferocity until the last mass attacks on June 21-22. Prime targets for the *kamikazes* were the destroyers and other small vessels acting as radar pickets around Okinawa. Among the ships assigned these "hot spots" were the *Mannert L. Abele*, which went down on April 12, the victim of suicide planes and a nasty new weapon, the rocket-propelled *Ohka;* she was the only ship lost to such a weapon. The *Laffey* — attacked four days later by 22 planes, hit by eight *kamikazes* and four bombs — survived. The *Hugh W. Hadley*, although hit on May 11 by four suiciders and one bomb, shot down 23 of the planes attacking her and also survived.

However, when the *kikusui* campaign finally ground to an end in June, there were many navy ships that had not survived. A sobering total of 34 ships and small craft were sunk, 368 more were damaged. Over 4,900 sailors were killed or missing and another 4,874 wounded (most of these losses the result of the *kamikazes*), making Okinawa the bloodiest battle in the US Navy's history.

If the navy's losses were eye-opening, those of the Japanese were mind-boggling. Japan lost some 7,800 planes, 16 ships sunk, and another four damaged. One of the ships, the giant battleship *Yamato,* went down on her own suicide mission.

In conjunction with the first *kikusui* attacks on April 6-7, the *Yamato,* in company with the cruiser *Yahagi* and seven destroyers, sortied from Japan on the 6th bound for Okinawa. With fuel just for a one-way trip, the battleship was to beach herself on Okinawa and use her huge 18-inch guns on the invasion fleet and the troops on the island.

The *Yamato* and her escorts did not even make it halfway to Okinawa. Spotted first by American submarines, then tracked by search planes, and bereft of any air protection of its own, the Japanese force was overwhelmed by wave after wave of hostile planes. Shortly after noon on April 7, the first of almost 300 attackers from Task Force 58 swept in. It was a slaughter, though it took a lot to put the battleship under — ten torpedo hits, five bomb hits, and an uncountable number of near-misses — but two hours after the opening attack, the *Yamato* sank, taking over three-quarters of her crew with her. She was joined by the *Yahagi* and four

destroyers. Approximately 3,400 officers and men went down with their ships. The Americans lost ten planes and 12 fliers.

While the American sailors underwent their trial by *kamikaze,* the soldiers and marines were also undergoing their own ordeal. By April 7, it was evident that the assault force had come up against the fortified zone centered around the town of Shuri. Progress of the 7th and 96th Infantry Divisions came to be measured in feet as they threw themselves against the enemy positions. Casualty figures began to spiral upward.

To the north of Shuri and not particularly prepossessing in appearance, the Kakazu hill mass nevertheless was one of the strongest defensive positions on Okinawa. Mortars were zeroed in on specified areas; pillboxes, caves, and tunnels contained machine guns that covered all avenues of approach; on call to the defenders were the many artillery pieces in the Shuri area.

Given the task of reducing this seemingly innocuous hill mass was the 96th Infantry Division. The attack began on April 9 with a regimental assault against Kakazu Ridge and Kakazu West (a point a few hundred yards west of the ridge). One company did reach the top of Kakazu West but, almost out of ammunition, was forced back down. No other units got near the top of the ridge. Over the next three days the division tried repeatedly to take Kakazu Ridge and just as repeatedly was repulsed by the Japanese. On the 12th, the attack was called off.

The 7th Infantry Division attack on the eastern flank was also brought to a halt. By April 12, the attack of the Tenth Army had lost its momentum. Although it was estimated that by the 12th almost 6,000 Japanese had perished, compared

Right: Obverse and reverse of a safe conduct pass. This leaflet, written in English and Japanese, promises safe treatment, food, clothes and medical help to those soldiers and civilians who surrender to Americans. *Eugene C. Gibson.*

Above: After its capture, Okinawa became a vast base from which the eventual invasion of the Japanese Home Islands was to be launched. Here the attack transport *Bruleson* uses one of her LCVP landing craft to unload her troops on August 4, 1945.

to a total casualty list of 2,900 (including 451 dead) for the XXIV Corps, the defenders still held out and the weary attackers could not push on.

At this juncture, however, the Japanese did the Americans a favor: a small favor but a favor nonetheless. From the beginning of the invasion, a handful of officers led by Ushijima's fiery chief of staff, Lt. Gen. Isamo Cho, were pressuring Ushijima into ordering a counterattack. Ushijima at last agreed. This counterattack was originally intended to be a six-battalion onslaught, but more cautious planners on Ushijima's staff were able to reduce the force to four battalions. Still, the commanders of the units scheduled for the attack planned to operate as if all six battalions were present.

Following an intense artillery barrage, the Japanese attacked the US positions on the evening of April 12. Only in a few areas were the Japanese successful in penetrating the lines and these successes were soon wiped out. At one point in this action, S/Sgt. Beauford T. Anderson, of the 96th Infantry Division, became trapped at night in one of the many "horseshoe" tombs that dotted the landscape. His supply of grenades exhausted, Anderson pulled the safety pin from a mortar shell, banged the shell against a wall to release the set-back pin, then hurled it toward the advancing Japanese. Fourteen more times he did this with a mortar shell and when dawn came, 25 dead Japanese surrounded his position. Anderson was awarded the Medal of Honor.

When dawn came on the 14th, the counterattack petered out and grenade explosions could be heard all along the front line as some of the enemy committed suicide. The attack was an abysmal failure, costing the Japanese over 500 dead while inflicting minimal losses on the Americans.

By now it was apparent to Gen. Buckner that fresh troops were needed if his army was to breach this defense line. From floating reserve came the 27th Infantry Division which took up position on the right flank of the line near Machinato. The 7th and 96th Infantry Divisions also received replacements but these were still not enough to bring the two units back to full strength. With three divisions on line, Gen. Buckner planned to renew his attack on the 19th.

Despite the greatest artillery barrage ever employed in the Pacific and the largest air strike (about 650 planes) of the entire campaign, the XXIV Corps failed to break through the defenses. The 27th Infantry Division came up against a pair of formidable obstacles — the Urasoe-Mura escarpment and the old nemesis of the 96th Infantry Division, Kakazu Ridge — and was roughly handled by the defenders.

In the center, the 96th Infantry Division faced Tombstone Ridge, Nishibaru Ridge, and the eastern end of the Urasoe-Mura escarpment, which was known as the Maeda escarpment. To the east, Skyline Ridge was the 7th Infantry Division's *bête noire*. On the 19th alone, the XXIV Corps lost 720 dead, missing or wounded. Forward movement was a slow and painful ordeal and for a time the Americans wondered if they could break through. Suddenly, on April 24 the line gave way and the corps was through the first Shuri defense line. However, the ease with which the line broke was caused by the withdrawal of the defenders on the night of April 23-24 to the next ring of positions in the Shuri area.

As April waned, the three Army divisions in the line were battered and in need of rest. Gen. Buckner replaced the 27th Infantry Division with the 1st Marine Division and the 27th spent the rest of the campaign in northern Okinawa ferreting out stragglers. The 97th Infantry Division in the center was replaced by the 77th Infantry Division. For the moment the 7th Infantry Division would stay in the line.

Meanwhile, unhappy with the results of the first counterattack, Gen. Cho and his adherents pressed for a full-scale counter-offensive. Again caving in, Ushijima ordered such an attack to take place on May 4. Although carefully planned, the objectives of the operation were beyond the capabilities of the Japanese. Just before dawn of the 4th, the counter-offensive was launched. Over 15,000 men, including the entire Japanese 24th Division, took part. The attack went well at first, with a deep penetration in one spot, but this was soon sealed off. Attempts at amphibious end-runs around the flanks resulted in complete disaster for the Japanese.

By the next day it was obvious to both sides that the attack was a failure. After losing about 5,000 men killed, the attackers retired back to their defensive positions. The one Japanese tank unit on the island was virtually destroyed, never again to be used in a mobile role. The Americans lost 335 men killed or wounded the first day and 379 the next. Ironically, the 1st Marine Division, involved only peripherally in stopping the counterthrust, incurred 352 casualties while assaulting the enemy positions in its sector. As Ushijima had believed, a defense built around strong positions caused more casualties to the Americans than did a counterattack.

The counteroffensive had little effect on altering Tenth Army plans for its own offensive and the Americans leaped off again on May 6-7. On May 8, the 6th Marine Division (relieved in the north by the 27th Infantry Division) moved alongside the 1st Marine Division, and Gen. Buckner now had a two-corps front. The 96th Infantry Division also came back on the line to give the 7th Infantry Division a breather.

Adms. Turner and Spruance, who were very concerned over the losses the Navy was taking from the *kamikazes*, pressured Buckner to speed up the offense. But Tenth Army was boring into the heart of the Shuri defenses and progress remained slow. There really was not much that could be done to accelerate the battle — the enemy defenses were still strong, only so many divisions could be brought into the front lines, and there was no room to fight a battle of maneuver. The infantrymen still had to take their objective, using what Bucker called the "blowtorch and corkscrew" to dig out the defenders. "Blowtorch" was the flamethrower; "corkscrew" was the use of demolitions to seal the many caves.

As the 6th Marine Division's battle for the hill known as Sugar Loaf showed, Okinawa would be tough to the very end. In the ten-day period from May 9, when it came on line, to May 19, when Sugar Loaf fell, the division lost 2,662 men killed or wounded.

On the 1st Marine Division front, the main Japanese positions were located around Dakeshi Ridge, Wana Ridge, and Wana Draw. The marines launched attack after attack, each time suffering heavy casualties before finally reducing the positions.

The quaintly-named Chocolate Drop Hill belied a not-so-sweet filling — a maze of prepared positions which made it

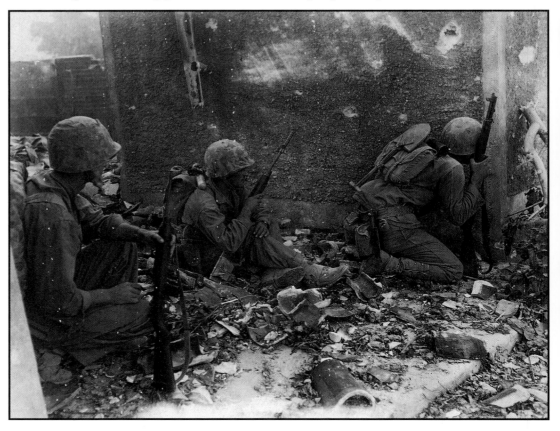

Right: Combat in an urban environment was a comparatively rare event in the Pacific campaign, but here men of the 6th Marine Division take cover in a ruined house during the fighting for Naha, the capital of Okinawa, at the end of May 1945.

almost impregnable. It took almost ten days, until May 20, for the 77th Infantry Division to seal off the hill.

On the far left flank, the 96th Infantry Division ran into Conical Hill. The fighting here was as savage as any on Okinawa and was made worse by the rains that now deluged the island. Under the constant pressure of the American attack, Conical Hill finally fell, but again at great cost to the soldiers. Conical Hill's fall, however, opened up the right flank of the Japanese line and the 7th Infantry Division, brought back on the line, pushed forward to exploit the promising situation.

Heavy rains and the still tenacious defenders kept the division from making a complete breakthrough. Nevertheless, Gen. Ushijima realized he was being flanked by both the 7th Infantry and 6th Marine Divisions and directed an orderly withdrawal to a final line about four miles (6km) south of Shuri centered on the Yaeju Dake-Yuza Dake escarpments. Slow to understand the movement of the Japanese and hampered by the weather, the Americans could not prevent the escape of many of the defenders.

The city of Naha, on the west coast, fell easily to the 6th Marine Division on May 25. The centerpiece of the enemy defenses, Shuri and its ancient castle, were taken by the 1st Marine Division and the 77th Infantry Division by the end of the month. Virtually obliterated, Shuri was hardly recognizable as a town.

For a few days Gen. Buckner and many of his staff believed that with the fall of

Above: Type 97 (1937) antitank rifle, 20mm, semi or full automatic, with spare parts and tool kit. Both armor-piercing and high-explosive shells could be fired. It was magazine-fed (not shown) and had a crew of four men. *West Point Museum.*

Shuri all that was needed now was to clean out the pockets of stragglers. They were roused from that daydream rather abruptly when Tenth Army ran into Yaeju Dake and Yuza Dake. The rain had stopped and the ground was again firm enough for tanks and other vehicles, but the infantrymen still had to climb over and through the rugged terrain to flush out the defenders.

On June 10, the 6th Marine, 1st Marine, 96th Infantry, and 7th Infantry Divisions launched a shoulder-to-shoulder assault on the final defense line. The Japanese fought with their usual tenacity, and Tenth Army gains were measured in yards. But the end was now in sight. By June 13, Yaeju Dake (known as the Big Apple to the Americans) had been wrested from the enemy by the 96th Infantry Division. After a bitterly contested fight that lasted five days, Kunishi Ridge belonged to the 1st Marine Division on June 17.

Suddenly, enemy resistance collapsed. There were those who fought until killed, but more and more prisoners were gathered in every day. Two who were not taken prisoner were Gen. Ushijima and his chief of staff, Gen. Cho. As American patrols prowled around the entrance to Ushijima's headquarters cave, the two

men and their staffs ate a special meal and drank farewell toasts. Then the two generals committed *seppuku* (ritual suicide). It was shortly after 4:00 A.M. on June 22. The same morning, the American flag was formally raised over conquered Okinawa.

Another general, this one American, also did not survive the campaign. As was common for him, Gen. Buckner was in the front lines on the afternoon of June 18, this time watching the progress of a regiment of the 2d Marine Division (which had come ashore on the 16th to take part in the final assault). There was the flat ''whack'' of a Japanese gun firing, an explosion, and Buckner was mortally wounded.

Command of Tenth Army passed to Maj. Gen. Geiger, the senior commander on Okinawa. Geiger became the only marine in World War II to command a field army. His tenure as commander was short, Gen. Joseph W. Stilwell assuming command on the 23rd. It should be noted that Army-Marine relations on Okinawa, unlike at Saipan, were quite good. To be sure, there were the usual charges that one or the other of the services was not doing its share, but these were generally at lower levels. Buckner and Geiger, both front-line generals, had great respect for each other.

The conquest of Okinawa was not cheap. Some 39,420 battle casualties were incurred by all units on the island, with another 26,211 men counted as non-battle casualties. The Japanese suffered even more dearly. Approximately 110,000 Japanese were killed, of which an undetermined number were Okinawan civilians.

Okinawa seemed worth the price in American lives. It was large enough to handle a great number of troops and supplies; its airfields placed the Home Islands within range of even medium bombers and fighters; Nakagusuka Bay (renamed Buckner Bay) provided the Navy with an excellent anchorage. It would have been an outstanding springboard for the invasion of Japan. Then came Hiroshima and Nagasaki, and Okinawa, paid for with the blood of thousands, became just another base whose usefulness had come to an end.

Below: Okinawa was the first truly Japanese island to be invaded by the Americans, who were faced with the problem of dealing not only with the defenders but also with a large civil population, whose apprehensions are evident in the face of these women.

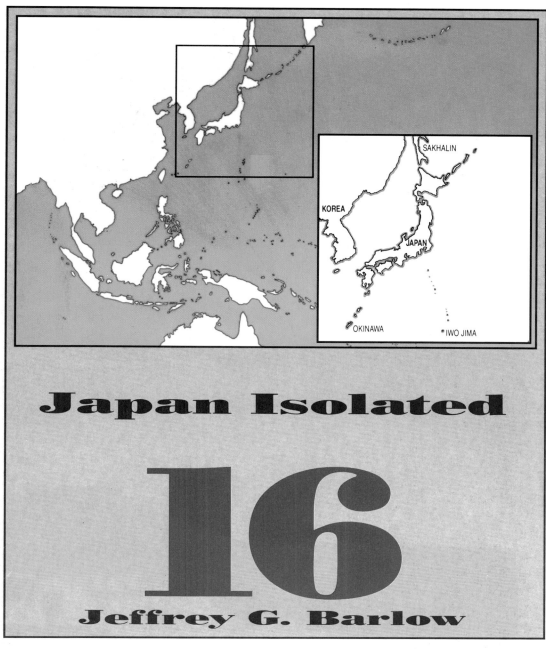

Japan Isolated

16

Jeffrey G. Barlow

In the years after World War I, United States Navy planners refined Plan Orange, the war plan designed to be employed in the event of a conflict between the United States and the Japanese Empire. An Orange war was expected to be "[an] offensive war, primarily naval, directed toward the isolation and harassment of Japan, through control of her vital sea communications and through offensive sea and air operations against her naval forces and economic life." As the planners learned more about Japan's own plans for fighting and defeating a superior US Navy, through the service's radio monitoring of Japanese fleet exercises and its deciphering of Japanese naval codes, Orange Plan was revised to reflect these changing realities. The results of these changes were then tested during the war games which were being regularly played at the Naval War College in Newport, Rhode Island.

The Navy viewed the mission of its submarine force as being to support the operations of the fleet. The main tasks for the submarine force, therefore, were intelligence-gathering — observing the harbors of the Mandated Islands —

operations against the hostile main body, and assisting in the defense of America's principal Pacific bases in Hawaii and the Philippines, as well as protecting the approaches to the Pacific side of the Panama Canal. Surprisingly, since its war plan envisaged the eventual isolation of the Japanese Home Islands, until late 1941 the US Navy did not contemplate the early use of its submarines for major attacks against Japanese commerce. One of the reasons for this omission, however, was the effect of international law. At the London Naval Conference in 1930, Britain, the United States, and Japan had signed a final agreement which contained an article outlawing the use of unrestricted submarine warfare. Under Article 22 of the 1930 London Naval Treaty, submarines were obliged to conform to the same rules of international law as surface ships when it came to actions against merchant vessels. Submarines were forbidden to sink a merchant ship without having first placed its passengers, ship's crew, and papers in a "place of safety." This restriction promised to limit severely the value of a sustained submarine

Japanese Experimental and Prototype Small Arms

1   Clip-fed, gas operated semi-automatic rifle, caliber 6.5mm
2   Type 100 submachine gun of 1940. The weapon has a caliber of 8mm. In this example the curved 30 round magazine is missing
3   Type 5 semi-automatic rifle of 7.7mm caliber. This weapon was adopted in April 1945, and is similar in some respects to the US M1 Garand rifle of the same period
4   Type 38 (1905) rifle, of 6.5mm caliber. This weapon has had the barrel shortened and its floor plate altered so as to accept a 30 round light machine gun magazine, seen here in position on the rifle
5   Type 11 submachine gun, of bull-pup configuration. The weapon has a caliber of 8mm. The magazine in this particular example is missing
6   Incomplete shop model of semi-automatic pistol/sword combination. This unusual experimental weapon has a caliber of 7mm. The sword scabbard appears to be an altered 1886 type

US Army Ordnance Museum

campaign against enemy commerce, since, among other things, it obliged the submarine to expose itself to possible attack by remaining on the surface for a considerable period of time, awaiting the transfer of the intended victim's personnel to the lifeboats or, indeed, taking them on board for delivery to a place of safety.

Top-level Navy thinking began to change on the issue of unrestricted submarine warfare in early 1941, following the submission of a study by the Naval War College which advocated the establishment of "war zones" within which enemy merchant vessels could be

sunk on sight. Although this proposal was not accepted at that time, in May 1941 the Navy approved War Plan Rainbow 5, which authorized the theater commanders to declare "strategical areas" from which merchant ships would have to be excluded, thus incorporating the essential feature of the earlier proposal. In late November 1941, the Chief of Naval Operations, Adm. Harold R. Stark, drafted a cable giving the Commander in Chief of the Asiatic Fleet authorization in the event of a formal war between the United States and Japan to conduct unrestricted submarine and aerial warfare in a

specifically designated Far Eastern strategical area.

In December 1941, the United States Navy had 51 submarines based in the Pacific. These boats were of two basic types — fleet submarines and *S* Class submarines. The fleet submarines, most dating from the mid-1930s and after, were of a number of different classes, ranging in size of from 271 to 381 feet (83 to 116m) in length and up to 2,730 tons in surface displacement. With most of them having a wartime fuel capacity in excess of 90,000 gallons (341,000l), the fleet boats were capable of patrolling 10,000 nautical miles (18,500km) at

The impact of Allied bombing and blockade on the Japanese arms industry led to various innovations and experiments in the attempt to keep production of weapons going with the rapidly diminishing resources available. Some were technically proficient attempts to copy Allied arms — such as the Garand lookalike semi-automatic rifle (*3*), while others such as the strange sword and pistol combination (*6*) had more of the air of desperation about them.

normal cruising speed, without refueling. The older *S* Class submarines, designed primarily for a defensive role and first introduced into the fleet in the early 1920s, were 231 feet (70m) in length and up to 950 tons in surface displacement. They lacked air conditioning, which made submerged patrolling in tropical waters arduous for their crews, because temperatures inside the boats could climb to 110 degrees Fahrenheit (45°C). In addition, because the fuel capacity of the *S* Class submarines was far smaller — less than a third of that of the newer fleet boats — their cruising range was shorter.

At the time of the Japanese attack on Pearl Harbor, 29 of the available US submarines in the Pacific Ocean — 23 fleet boats and six *S* Class boats — were based in the Philippines. The other 22 — 16 fleet subs and six of the *S* Class — were based at Pearl Harbor. On the morning of the attack, however, there were only four submarines in Pearl Harbor, together with the submarine tender *Pelias*. To the attacking Japanese aircraft, the submarines were not high-priority targets, and, as a result, none of them suffered significant damage in the Japanese air raids. Five more Pearl Harbor-based subs were operating in nearby waters that morning and were unaffected by the main attacks. The submarines berthed at Cavite Naval Station in the Philippines were less lucky than their Hawaiian counterparts. When the base was attacked by high-altitude Japanese bombers on December 10, the fleet boat *Sealion* was wrecked beyond repair and had to be scuttled, and her sister *Seadragon* was seriously damaged.

In the aftermath of the aerial destruction at Pearl Harbor, which left all the battleships of the Pacific Fleet sunk or seriously damaged, the submarines at Pearl Harbor and Cavite constituted one of the few offensive forces left in the Pacific to slow down the Japanese onslaught. They were rapidly put to use. Within six hours of the Japanese attack at Pearl Harbor, well before the extent of the damage had even begun to be known, dispatch orders from the Chief

THE US NAVY *GATO* CLASS SUBMARINE

This ocean-going diesel electric submarine (seen on patrol above) was just over 311 feet (94m) long, and was a little over 27 feet (8.2m) in the beam. It could dive to a depth of 300 feet (91m) and traveled at speeds of up to 20 knots surfaced and 8 knots submerged.

Seen here in her 1942 configuration, the *Gato* class had been developed before the war and bore the brunt of the early submarine campaign against Japanese shipping. Each was built of an all-weather construction, at four yards in the United States. She was armed in 1942 with the unreliable Mk XIV steam-driven torpedo, which had a range of between

4,500 yards (4,050m) and 9,000 yards (8,100m) depending on the speed it traveled. This varied from 46-31 knots. The surface weapons on the submarine went through continual upgrading as the war progressed, but in 1942 the class carried a 3-inch/50 gun (far left) and a .50 caliber water-cooled antiaircraft gun (left) abaft the position of the fin.

of Naval Operations to the affected commanders directed *"Execute unrestricted air and submarine warfare against Japan."* The first of the Hawaiian-based subs left on a war patrol on December 11, 1941. Others followed over the next two weeks. In all, four headed for operations around the Marshall Islands, and three more left for patrols in the waters off the Japanese Home Islands. Four other submarines from Pearl Harbor were already operating off Midway Island and Wake Island. The Cavite-based subs were also at sea, preparing unsuccessfully to defend the island of Luzon against invasion. By December 11, 22 of the surviving 28 in the Philippines were operating in waters to the east, west, and south of Luzon.

At the outbreak of the war, the Japanese merchant marine was a choice target for attack. Because of a lack of adequate natural resources, Japan had to import more than two-thirds of her basic requirements of iron ore, petroleum, lead, tin, and manganese and all of her required nickel, wool, and raw cotton. Each of the commodities arrived by ship. To meet her immense transportation needs, Japan had some 6,400,000 tons of merchant shipping in December 1941. Although prewar estimates had set a minimum requirement of three million tons of shipping needed to keep Japan's civilian economy going, initial wartime requirements for the Japanese Imperial Army and Navy forced the drafting of nearly four million tons of shipping for military purposes. This left barely two-and-a-half million tons available to fulfil Japan's domestic economic needs.

From March 1942, the US submarines operated under one of two commands: Commander Submarine Force, Pacific Fleet, headed (after January 1943) by Vice Adm. Charles A. Lockwood at Pearl Harbor, and Commander Submarines, Southwest Pacific (later Commander Submarines, Seventh Fleet), headed for much of the war by Rear Adm. Ralph W. Christie, at Perth-Fremantle, Australia. The Pearl Harbor-based submarines operated in the East China Sea and Empire waters close to the Japanese Home Islands and off the Marshall, Marianas, Palau, and Caroline Islands, with the Japanese fleet base at Truk a target of particular interest. Hunting grounds for the Perth-based submarines included the South China Sea, the Celebes Sea, and the Java Sea. Among the individual target areas were Cam Ranh Bay and the waters off Manila, Davao (in the Philippines), and Surabaya (in Java). Until the arrival of many additional submarines, however, there were simply too many areas for the available boats to cover. As a result, the deployed submarines were spread thin during all of 1942 and much of 1943.

US submarines were slow to take advantage of the promise offered by Japan's merchant shipping in the first months of the Pacific War. For example, during the first three months of fighting, the subs sank only 13 Japanese merchant vessels. There were several important reasons for this slowness. One was the conservative tactics used during the early patrolling. Based on their pre-war training, submarine commanders were overly cautious in their attacks on shipping targets — diving too quickly on the basis of contacts and relying on submerged attacks at night rather than attacks on the surface. Moreover, since the submarines operated singly, there was no chance to practice team tactics to overcome resistance from Japanese escort vessels. With the experience gained from their first few wartime patrols, though, most submarine skippers learned to become more aggressive in attacking convoys, and the sinking failures attributable to over-cautious tactics declined sharply.

The more important reason for this lack of success in sinking Japanese merchant shipping, however, was the Mark XIV torpedo — the principal weapon then used by the fleet boats. The Mark XIV was a steam torpedo armed with a 500-pound warhead and the Mark VI magnetic exploder, which was designed to set off the torpedo's warhead when the "fish" was directly under the target's keel, thus breaking its back. For a variety of economy and security reasons, the interwar-designed Mark XIV torpedo was inadequately tested before it was introduced into the Fleet. Incredibly, its complex magnetic exploder never underwent a live firing test. As the result

Above: In February 1942, an American submarine was used to move gold from Corregidor to an escaping cruiser. The bullion and other valuables belonged to the Philippine Commonwealth, banks, mines, and private individuals.

of these serious lapses, for the first 18 months of the war US fleet submarines were patrolling with defective torpedoes, which ran at depth settings some 11 feet deeper than set and whose magnetic exploders often failed to explode even on those occasions when the torpedoes ran at the proper depth. The number of sinkings by US fleet boats during this period could have been three or four times higher if their torpedoes had not been defective.

A big advantage which the United States submarine fleet had, which partially offset these early problems, was the Navy's ability from the first days of the war to read significant portions of Japanese naval codes and ciphers.

Below: The importance of American submarines in the war against Japan has been much undervalued. Boats such as the *Nautilus*, seen here taking on supplies, decimated Japanese shipping and thus severed Japan from her supplies and forces.

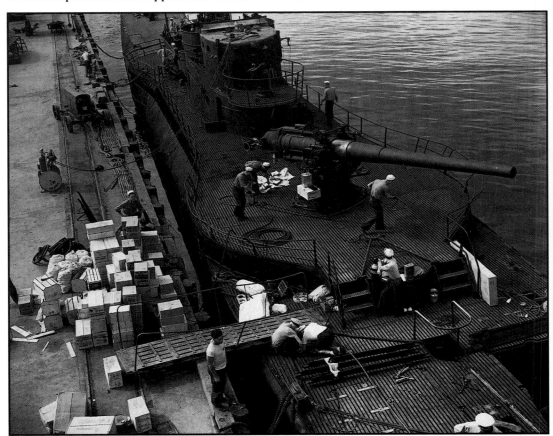

Indeed, the first Japanese warship loss was the submarine *I-173*, sunk by the fleet boat *Gudgeon* which was alerted to the passage of Japanese submarines through waters near Midway by the code breakers of Fleet Radio Unit Pacific (FRUPac). At first, intelligence information (derived from cryptanalysis) on the location of Japanese warships was passed informally and on an *ad hoc* basis from FRUPac to the staff of Commander Submarine Force, Pacific Fleet (ComSubPac). In early 1943, however, FRUPac solved the "maru" code — the special code in which the Japanese transmitted convoy routing messages. By this time, the Japanese had been forced to organize all of their tankers, freighters, and transports (designated "marus" because that was the second word in their names, as in *Hikawa Maru*) into centrally-directed convoys with specified routes and schedules, to protect them against submarine attack. Thus, the solving of the maru code enabled the US Navy cryptanalysts to derive accurate locations and meeting times for Japanese merchant convoys. From this point on, a FRUPac staffer met with a counterpart from ComSubPac on a daily basis to plot the location of such convoys with the known positions of US submarines on patrol. This new information made it possible to direct submarines to mid-ocean contacts with Japanese merchant shipping targets, thereby avoiding long and fruitless searches. As the numbers of available submarines and torpedoes increased and the problems with the Mark XIV torpedo were solved, this intelligence greatly increased the deadliness of the submarine offensive.

The shortage of available submarines gradually eased during 1942 and disappeared by the fall of 1943. Thirty-six new fleet submarines joined the force in the Pacific during 1942. Fifty-two more fleet boats arrived during 1943, and 76 in 1944. At war's end there were 169 fleet submarines in the Pacific, together with 13 *S* Class boats being used for anti-submarine warfare training. As the new fleet subs reported, the inadequate *S* Class boats were transferred to the Aleutians or retired from service. The new arrivals comfortably outpaced submarine losses, although these too mounted proportionally as the war progressed. While only seven subs were lost to enemy action in 1941-42, 13 were lost in 1943 and 19 in 1944.

The original plan for employment of the US submarines had been to place them at the so-called focal points of enemy shipping — the entrances to the Inland Sea and off the principal harbors of the Japanese Mandates, Formosa, the Philippines, and the Dutch East Indies. As increasing numbers of new fleet boats deployed, more and more of these focal points were patrolled simultaneously.

Finally, in late 1943, there were more than enough operational submarines to cover all of these vital target areas. It was at this point that the submarines began operating in coordinated attack groups or "wolf packs". Unlike the German U-boat wolf packs, however, which contained 15 or 20 subs and were centrally controlled by radio communication from shore bases, these US groups consisted of three or four boats coordinated by a leader, often the senior submarine commander in the pack, who maintained local radio contact with his force. When a convoy was encountered by one of the subs in the wolf pack, she would vector her packmates into position for an attack. The attack itself though would not be coordinated though. Each of the subs would attack the convoy independently. Because the Japanese never operated large convoys — four to eight marus escorted by from one to four destroyers or escort vessels was average — there were a number of occasions when a submarine sank a convoy single-handed.

By the fall of 1943, the submarine force also had added a new weapon to its arsenal, the long-delayed Mark XVIII electric torpedo. The Mark XVIII was a mixed blessing to the submariners. Because it was electrically propelled it left no tell-tale track to give away the submarine's position. However, it was a much slower torpedo than the old Mark XIV and thus had a far lower margin of error for target tracking. Yet, with both types of torpedoes in sufficient supply, fleet boats at last were able to go out on patrol armed with full complements of weapons.

The combination of increased numbers of fleet boats, the use of wolf pack tactics, and working torpedoes accomplished wonders in merchant ship

Above: A transportable field telephone exchange, complete with code books and ear and mouth pieces. This was one of the most vital pieces of equipment in the establishment of secure landline communications.
Dale E. Biever.

sinkings in 1944. In 1942, for example, the subs had sunk only 608,536 tons of Japanese shipping. This figure was slightly more than doubled by US submarines in 1943.

However, in 1944 the Japanese merchant fleet lost 2,383,431 tons of shipping to the submarines. As the result of these staggering losses, by the start of 1945 Japan retained only 40 per cent of the shipping tonnage with which she had begun the war; even after the additions to the fleet made by wartime construction, ship salvage, and captures. The US submarine war truly was strangling Japan's economic and military lifelines to the remnants of her overseas empire. In 1940, the last year before the eruption

Right: A vital stage in the preparations for any patrol was the loading of torpedoes. Seen here in November 1942, the *Nautilus* receives one of the 24 weapons for her six 21-inch torpedo tubes (four located in the bows and the other two in the stern).

Japanese Telecommunications Equipment

1 Model 94-3A, No. 36 transmitter-receiver. This equipment is complete with wooden field case and carrying handles. Inside are stored the operator's earphones and sending key, together with spare valves in their original packing
2 Self-contained key-transmitter unit, partially opened to show the interior
3 Portable voltage tester for checking power sources and electrical output
4 Wooden storage box for Type 92 instrument
5 Portable Ohm meter with leather carrying case
6 Model 92 (1932) telephone in metal reinforced wooden box
7 Model 92 (1932) telephone, with lid open and operating handle in position on the side. The mouth and ear pieces are shown together with their electrical connections. Operating instructions can be seen on the inside of the lid
8 Model 92 (1932) telephone with lid open and mouth and ear pieces in the stowed position. The bottom panel on this example has been opened to reveal the electrical components and battery pack

United States Marine Corps Air-Ground Museum

of the Pacific war, Japan had imported some 67 million tons of raw materials for use in her industrial economy. During the last full year of the war, though, her imports were down to barely 27 million tons. The import tonnage decreased even more severely in the war's final months, as the shipping available for carrying raw materials was swept from the seas.

In the spring of 1945, with the Pacific virtually cleared of Japanese shipping by the effects of US and Allied submarine and air attacks, only one important area still remained where Japanese merchant ships traveled largely unmolested — the Sea of Japan. A few US submarines had penetrated the Sea of Japan in the summer of 1943, but the patrols were quickly discontinued because of the dangers posed to the submarines by Japanese minefields laid in all the entrances to the sea. With other shipping targets almost nonexistent, ComSubPac decided to train subs to underrun anchored minefields. After a series of exercises, in June 1945 nine fleet boats equipped with FM sonar for mine detecting, organized into three wolf packs, simultaneously passed through the minefields laid in the Tsushima Strait and entered the Sea of Japan. In 17 days of patrolling there, the subs accounted for 28 ships and 16 smaller craft. They then assembled south of La Perouse Strait (minus *Bonefish* which had been sunk) and made a successful night surface escape in column through La Perouse (which lies between Sakhalin and Hokkaido). This marked the last major submarine offensive of the war. The isolation of the Japanese Home Islands from the empire's supporting territories was almost complete.

By the war's end in August 1945, the US submarine force in the Pacific had compiled an enviable record of success

In their operations, Japanese military forces placed primary emphasis on wire communications. Radio equipment was used initially when communications between units had to be established rapidly. Technically, most of the equipment was obsolete by Western standards, but well-made nevertheless.

US Technical Manuals and Training Equipment

1 US Navy recognition chart of Aichi Type 99 ''Val'' dive bomber
2 War Department booklet on Japanese military forces
3 War Department Japanese language phrase book
4 Aircraft recognition models
5 Allied ship recognition manual
6 War Department loose leaf manual on Japanese military forces
7 Box for Japanese Navy recognition manual
8 War Department guide to the Japanese Army
9 War Department/US Navy recognition manual
10 Manual of international navy recognition. Open at page featuring Japanese Navy uniforms and equipment
11 Carrying box of War Department training aid set on Japanese mines and hand grenade
12 Type 93 antitank mine
13 Fuzes for mine 19
14 Fuze for landmine 16
15 Type 97 hand grenade, with fuze shown in position
16 Type 3 landmine
17 Loose leaf technical manual for training set
18 Type 99 magnetic mine with fuze below
19 Yardstick mine

Eugene C. Gibson Col: 6, 8, 11-19; Andrew W. Xaras Col: 1-5, 7, 9, 10

against Japan's merchant fleet. At the time of her surrender, Japan's merchant tonnage stood at only 1,500,000 tons — less than a quarter of the total with which she had started the war — and half of this remainder was unusable due to damage. In some 42 months of fighting, US submarines had destroyed 54.6 per cent of all Japanese merchant vessels lost during the war — 1,113 ships, totalling 4,779,902 tons — at a total cost of 49 submarines lost. In large measure, the United States submarine offensives had brought the Japanese war machine virtually to a halt.

During 1942 the United States Navy began extensive preparations for a coordinated strategic mining attack on Japan's outer defense zone. The objectives of this mining campaign were "to disorganize the enemy maritime supply system, deny him safe ports and shipping routes for the transport of essential war and economic materials, to sink and damage as many of his ships as he would expose to mine risk, and to impose upon him the military and economic burden incident to the establishment and maintenance of a mine defense."

To accomplish these objectives, there were three distinct types of mining available: attrition mining, closure mining, and interception mining. Attrition minefields were ones specifically designed to sink enemy shipping. Accordingly, they were designed to be laid secretly so that they would remain undetected by the enemy until ships struck the mines. Closure mining was designed to deny enemy ships access to particular areas until the mines could be cleared. Under such circumstances, in which the threat was as important as the tally of victims, a relatively small number of mines could be used to stop shipping by inflicting losses in the chosen areas. Finally, interception minefields were strong fields laid across

As the war progressed, intelligence on Japanese military organization and equipment grew. Where applicable, this information was then passed to the fighting troops by means of a whole host of training aids which used a number of different teaching methods — from posters to models. In the case of training aid set 3 actual replicas of mines were used.

enemy lines of communication to intercept ships attempting to supply advanced enemy positions. The mines themselves were of two basic types: ground mines and moored mines. Ground mines were laid on the bottom in waters not over 25 fathoms in depth. They were designed to be set off by the magnetic or acoustic fields of ships passing overhead. Moored mines were used in deeper water to bring the mine's explosive charge closer to the passing targets. They could be set off either by direct contact with a ship or by a magnetic influence device.

Because of lack of aircraft and bases for aerial minelaying in late 1942, in mid-October submarines from the Seventh Fleet based in Australia began the first strategic minelaying astride Japanese shipping routes in the Gulf of Thailand and the Gulf of Tonkin. At about the same time, Pearl Harbor-based subs laid mines off of the coasts of Japan and China. Because of the limited carrying capacity of the submarines, these minefields were relatively small, ranging in size from 12 to 32 mines each.

The first surface mining by destroyer minesweepers (DMs) took place in the Solomons in early 1943 in an effort to interfere wth the resupply operations to Guadalcanal by the "Tokyo Express". This proved relatively successful because the Japanese were unable to provide minesweeping forces for reopening the mined areas. Aerial mining began in late February 1943, when B-24 Liberators from the Army's Tenth Air Force, operating out of India, laid British mines in the port of Rangoon, Burma, in order to close off Japanese shipping there. This mining attack proved so successful that few large ships ever again attempted to use Rangoon.

By the summer of 1943, the initial steps of an offensive mining campaign had been undertaken in all of the major combat areas of the Pacific. As of October of that year, US and Allied forces had deployed 5 surface-laid minefields in the Solomons, 17 submarine-laid fields in areas such as Borneo, the Gulf of Siam, Indochina, Southern China, and Eastern Japan, and 19 aircraft-laid fields ranging from Java to the Solomons. That same month, the US Fourteenth Air Force inaugurated its minelaying efforts with attacks on the Indochinese port of Haiphong. Thereafter, it operated a small but useful mining effort against targets stretching from the Tonkin Gulf in the south to the Yangtze River in the north.

A strategic planning document issued in November 1943 called for offensive mining to be directed against all four approaches to the Japanese homeland: the Central Pacific via the Mandates, the Southwest Pacific along the New Guinea-Netherlands East Indies-Philippine axis, the North Pacific, and Southeast Asia and China. The same study set forth the localities most favorable for attrition mining, with tentative priorities based upon probable results, as: (1) the coasts and harbors of the Japanese mainland; (2) the coastal waters of French Indochina; (3) the Netherlands Indies; (4) the Kuriles area (especially the island of Paramushiro); and (5) the Marshalls, Carolines, and Marianas.

During much of 1944, the mining campaign against the Japanese Outer Zone saw a rapid increase in attrition mining, particularly minefields laid by aircraft. Planes from the Royal Air Force, the Royal Australian Air Force, the US Tenth and Fourteenth Air Forces and the XX Bomber Command were involved in increased mining efforts in the Southwest Pacific area. The first American acoustic mine was dropped at Balikpapan, Borneo, the site of a high-grade gasoline refinery vital to the Japanese, in April 1944. In August, the first aerial mining by B-29 bombers took place against Palembang, Sumatra.

The culmination of the Outer Zone mining campaign occurred in early 1945, when India-based B-29s from the XX Bomber Command made their first large-scale mining effort. The aircraft planted several hundred magnetic mines in the approaches to Singapore, Saigon, and Cam Ranh Bay.

This set the stage for the offensive mining campaign against Japan's Inner Zone. In November 1944, Adm. Chester Nimitz had suggested to Army Air Forces chief, Gen. Henry H. Arnold, that the Army Air Forces undertake a mining blockade of Japan. This idea was accepted, and, in December, Arnold directed Maj. Gen. Curtis E. LeMay, Commanding General, XXI Bomber Command, to begin planning for mining operations scheduled to begin on or about April 1, 1945. The mission of the XXI Bomber Command was to complete the destruction of Japanese seaborne lines of communication already badly damaged by the US submarine offensive. The three principal objectives of the campaign were: (1) to prevent the importation of raw materials and food to Japan; (2) to prevent the supply and deployment of her military forces; and (3) to disrupt her internal marine transport within the Inland Sea. The mission was assigned to the 313th Bomb Wing.

By this time, Japan's merchant fleet totalled only 2,000,000 gross tons of ships over 1,000 tons in size — most of which had been withdrawn into the relatively-protected waters of the East China Sea, the Yellow Sea, and the Sea of Japan. The shipping annually required to support the tottering Japanese war industry consisted of some 12,000 voyages from ports on the Chinese and Korean coasts via the Shimonoseki Strait, 12,000 local passages between Inland Sea ports, and 15,000 voyages to the Kobe-Osaka region. This shipping offered a valuable target for the mining of the Inner Zone.

Mission planning for the Inner Zone mining offensive eventually produced certain decisions about how the mining would be undertaken. These included the following: to employ single B-29 aircraft, unescorted, coming in at low altitude at night and laying the mines by radar; to use all available mines as early as possible; and to initiate and maintain the mining blockade by successive steps starting with the main enemy shipping artery, the Shimonoseki Strait and ending with the Korean ports, if possible. The 313th Bomb Wing did all the tactical planning for the mining offensive.

The B-29 mining offensive, as accomplished, consisted of five phases. The first phase lasted from March 27 to May 3, 1945. Two planning factors affected this phase of the campaign. The

Left: The sight of a Japanese warship sinking gladdened the heart of many submarine commanders, but in reality the destruction of an increasing proportion of Japan's merchant ships played a more strategically decisive role in defeating Japan.

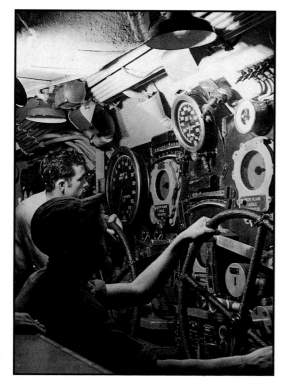

Left: The diving officer and two enlisted men prepare to dive the *Batfish*. Launched in May 1943, this boat was a member of the tactically important *Balao* subclass of the large *Gato* class that was the US Navy's standard submarine type in World War II.

with a loss of only five aircraft. The mining effort provided effective closure of the Shimonoseki Strait for a period of from ten days to two weeks. This resulted in reducing the shipping traffic to 25 per cent of normal. During this phase, some 35 Japanese vessels, totalling 100,000 tons, were sunk or damaged by the mines. The mining also served to bar the Japanese fleet from Shimonoseki. When the super battleship *Yamato* did come out, it sortied by way of the Bungo Strait. After passing along the east and south coasts of Kyushu toward Okinawa, it was sighted by American carrier planes and sunk.

The second phase of the mining campaign, labeled the Industrial Center Blockade, lasted from May 3 to May 12, 1945. In this phase the blockade was extended to the Inland Sea, to Kobe and Osaka, and along the entire Inland Sea routes. Also during Phase II, the blockade of the Shimonoseki Strait was maintained by re-mining, while attrition mining was begun at Tokyo and Nagoya. In all, 195 aircraft laid 1,422 mines without the loss of a single aircraft and eliminated almost completely the large-type shipping between the Asian continent and Japan's Inland Sea ports.

The third phase of the campaign, designated the Northwest Honshu-Kyushu Blockade, ran from May 3 to July 8, 1945. During this period the bulk of the effort was devoted to mining ports in northwest Honshu and Kyushu to which much of the Shimonoseki Strait traffic had been diverted. A total of 209 participating aircraft laid 1,313 mines in the target areas, with a loss of only three planes. Ship casualties increased sharply in Phases II and III over Phase I. An

estimated 75 to 100 vessels of some 300,000 tons were sunk or damaged by mines during the latter two phases.

The fourth phase, labeled the Intensified Northwest Honshu-Kyushu Blockade, lasted from June 7 to July 8, 1945. The mining in this phase was designed to reinforce the targeting of the ports in northwest Honshu and Kyushu. During Phase IV, 404 B-29s laid 3,542 mines in the target areas, with the loss of just one plane. Reconnaissance revealed that Japan was likely to withdraw its shipping from the Yellow Sea to the Sea of Japan and to make increasing use of northwest Honshu ports. Indeed, by early July it was apparent that the Japanese had abandoned the Yellow Sea ports and that almost all exports from the Asian continent would have to be funneled through a limited number of ports on the southern and eastern coasts of Korea.

The fifth and last phase of the Inner Zone mining offensive ran from July 9 to August 5, 1945. During this period, Japanese shipping was becoming less and less visible as few ships passed into the Inland Sea. The mining plan for July was limited by logistic considerations — there were only a limited number of magnetic mines available for use. Accordingly, a much higher proportion of acoustic mines were laid. During Phase V, 474 sorties laid 3,746 mines, with a loss of six planes to enemy flak. The results of the mining in this phase were mixed.

The overall results of the Inner Zone mining campaign, nonetheless, had proven highly satisfactory. Altogether, a total of 1,528 sorties laid 12,053 mines in the target areas during the four-and-a-half months of the campaign, with a loss of only 15 bombers. As the postwar report by the Army Air Forces on the campaign noted, "Mining established an effective blockade at the end of four and a half months, and enemy shipping which remained operable was reduced to the status of blockade running." As the result of the mining blockade of Japan, the early cessation of Japan's industrial production and the starvation of a significant portion of her population became certainties. These sobering facts undoubtedly influenced her final decision to surrender.

The gradual but increasing attrition of Japan's merchant marine by the United States' campaign of unrestricted submarine warfare and the mining blockade of the Home Islands' Inner Zone by US B-29 bombers served to isolate Japan from the raw materials which were vital for her industrial survival. The two campaigns proved highly complementary. The one had managed by late 1944 to drive her ocean-going commerce off the high seas. The other, a few months later, had severed her last links to the Asian continent. With these formidable weapons arrayed against her, it is no wonder that by early 1945 Japan stood as a nation alone.

first was target priority. Since the Inland Sea was the most important target area, the targets of highest priority for the first phase were the Shimonoseki Strait (the narrow sea-lane between Kyushu and Honshu), followed by the Kobe-Osaka area, and then the general shipping routes and smaller ports in the Inland Sea. The second factor was the requirement imposed by Nimitz to plant mines in the Shimonoseki Strait in conjunction with the invasion of Okinawa to prevent main enemy fleet units from sortieing out through the Strait.

During the 37 days of Phase I, 246 aircraft laid 2,030 mines in the target area,

Below: Able to carry a large bomb load over great ranges, the Boeing B-29 Superfortress was the strategic bomber that allowed the USAAF to burn the heart out of Japan's cities, destroy her war industries, and mine her sea lanes and ports.

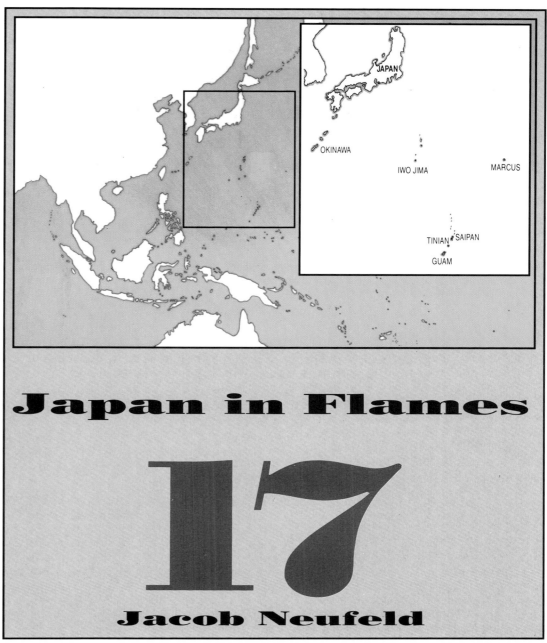

Japan in Flames

17

Jacob Neufeld

In the Boeing B-29 Superfortress, a long-range, very heavy bomber, the United States at last possessed the weapon capable of striking Japan from secure bases. Although B-29 missions were first launched from bases in China on June 15, 1944, the initial attacks were too few and the pace too slow: two strikes in June, two in July, three in August, two in September, four in October, and nine in November. One problem involved the arduous task of transporting the necessary high-octane aviation fuel to China. This required shipment to India by sea and then a 1,200-mile (1,900km) flight across towering mountains using special aerial tankers, cargo airplanes, or the B-29s themselves. The handicaps of supply and distance soon demonstrated that China could not support a B-29 campaign against Japan.

In the meantime, the leadership of the US Navy and the Army Air Forces turned their attention to the Japanese-held islands in the Central Pacific. The Marianas — Saipan, Tinian, and Guam — could provide the bases which would put Japan within range of the Superfortresses. On June 15, 1944 the Americans

began their assault on Saipan, spearheaded by the 2d and 4th Marine Divisions, with the Army's 27th Infantry Division in reserve. Saipan fell to the Americans on July 9, and shortly afterward Japan's premier and former war minister, Hideki Tojo, resigned in disgrace. During the third week of July 1944 forces began to storm Tinian and Guam, and by August 9 had gained control of those islands as well.

Navy Seabees began airfield construction despite continued enemy resistance and bad weather, while Japanese planes from nearby islands mounted "heckling" raids, eluding night fighters to damage or destroy aircraft parked at the new bases and kill or wound American troops. Eventually, five great airfields began operating at full capacity in the Marianas, each occupied by a B-29 bombardment wing: the 73d at Isley Field, Saipan; the 58th at West Field and the 313th at North Field, Tinian; and the 314th at North Field and 315th at Northwest Field, Guam. At each field, some 12,000 men operated and maintained as many as 180 B-29s. The 509th Composite Group (which would drop the

Japanese Military Swords

1 Army officer's *Shin-gunto* (new military sword) c. 1941. Blue tassels indicate company grade officer. Scabbard has leather combat cover on it
2 Naval officer's *Kai-gunto* (sea military sword)
3 Naval officer's *Kyu-gunto* (first military sword) with steel scabbard, a pattern adopted c. 1896
4 Army officer's *Kyu-gunto* with steel scabbard
5 Army officer's sword
6 Army officer's sword: blade c. 1730
7 Army officer's sword with early blade c. 1390
8 Late 1944 pattern army officer's sword. Blade was made in August 1934
9 Standard army officer's sword
10 Standard army officer's sword
11 Army NCO aluminum-hilted *Shin-gunto*
12 Army officer's sword, *Wakizashi* (blade length 16-20 inches — 40-50cm). The blade is c. 1800
13 Army officer's *Wakizashi*. The blade is c. 1690
14 Army officer's sword, *Katana* (blade length 24-30 inches — 60-75cm). The blade is c. 1925
15 Army officer's sword

MacArthur Memorial Collection

All these swords, with the exception of *1* and *14* were collected by General MacArthur and placed at the MacArthur Memorial, Norfolk, Virginia in 1963. All are fine examples of the Japanese weapon, popularly known as the samurai sword. A number boast blades of great age and antiquity which reveal the true art of the Japanese swordsmith. Sword *2*, the naval officer's *Kai-gunto*, is distinguised from its army counterpart by the double ring mounts on the scabbard. The steel scabbard of the *Kyu-gunto 4*, was introduced around 1900, while the mountings on *7*, though of a standard pattern, exhibit a far higher quality than is common. This is fitting, perhaps, given the great age of the blade. Sword *11*, sports a presentation plaque on its scabbard, which reads: "United States forces in the Philippines/Headquarters, Cebu Area Command/Office of the Commanding Officer/To: General Douglas MacArthur, Commander in Chief/USAF Pacific."

atomic bomb) was nominally assigned to the 313th Bomb Group.

Directed from Washington by Gen. Henry H. "Hap" Arnold, the Commanding General of the Army Air Forces, the Twentieth Air Force controlled the B-29s' operations as a global air force responsible to the Joint Chiefs of Staff. The XXI Bomber Command of the Twentieth Air Force, under Brig. Gen. Haywood S. "Possum" Hansell, Jr., controlled the B-29 wings in the Marianas. Hansell arrived in the Marianas on October 12, 1944 when he landed his B-29 the "Joltin' Josie" on Saipan. He wasted little time, for he launched the first mission on October 28 against the island of Truk. However, only 14 of the 18 planes managed to bomb the target, and the results proved disappointing. On November 24, after additional training missions, Gen. Hansell inaugurated the campaign against the Japanese Home Islands. Brig. Gen. Emmet "Rosie" O'Donnell, commander of the 73d Bombardment Wing, led a force of 111 B-29s against Tokyo — the first attack on Tokyo since the Doolittle raid of April 1942 — but only 88 of the planes succeeded in dropping their bombs because of the bad weather, which also reduced accuracy among the aircraft that did attack.

Hansell intended to conduct a classic strategic bombing campaign, sending his B-29s on high-altitude, daylight, precision raids against industrial targets, chiefly aircraft factories and steel plants. However, a combination of factors — the slow buildup of B-29 strength, lack of escort fighters, bad weather which contributed to "deplorable" bombing accuracy, a high abort rate because of engine failure, and the perils of a long flight over the unforgiving sea — reduced the damage he could inflict. Impatient for results, Gen. Arnold in January 1945 brought Maj. Gen. Curtis E. LeMay from China to replace Hansell as commander of the XXI Bomber Command.

One of Hansell's major problems was that many of the damaged Superforts returning from Japan often had to ditch in the sea because they had nowhere to land between the air bases and the target. Although the air-sea rescue service of the Army Air Forces and submarines assigned as lifeguards performed valiantly, losses mounted. One answer to the problem was to seize Iwo Jima, a rocky, eight-square-mile (20km²) island in the Volcano chain midway between the Marianas and Japan, as an advanced base where B-29s could land in an emergency and from which American fighters could be launched against Japanese planes attacking the Marianas. The marines landed on Iwo Jima on February 19, 1945, and bloody fighting continued throughout most of March before the island was declared secure. On March 4, while the battle still raged, the first B-29 made an emergency landing on Iwo Jima.

Meanwhile, in January and February the aerial onslaught against Japan had intensified when, in addition to the B-29 raids, hundreds of carrier-based planes of the American fast carrier task forces joined in. On February 16, Vice Adm. Marc A. Mitscher's Task Force 58 conducted the first carrier strike against Japan since the raid by Halsey and Doolittle in April 1942. Five fighter sweeps drove the defenders from the skies over Tokyo in preparation for attacks on airframe and aircraft engine factories in the vicinity of the Japanese capital. The fighters and bombers returned on February 17; and in two days the Navy pilots claimed the destruction of 341 enemy aircraft in aerial combat and another 190 on the ground at the cost of 88 airplanes shot down or lost in accidents, for a ratio of six Japanese losses for one American. The February attacks not only screened the invasion of Iwo Jima, but further reduced the number of aircraft and pilot available to the Japanese.

In March, in order to protect the invasion of Okinawa, Task Force 58 again attacked Japan; on the 18th bombing airfields on Kyushu and on the following day hitting ships and installations on the Inland Sea. The Navy pilots damaged the aircraft carrier *Amagi*, reduced to a burned-out hulk by subsequent attacks, and the battleship *Yamato*, sunk on April 7 when it sought to intervene in the Okinawa operation. *Kamikazes* or bombers damaged three American carriers — the new *Wasp*, the new *Yorktown*, and *Franklin*, which was shaken by explosions so violent that they could be felt by crewmen on the carrier *Bunker Hill*, 20 miles (32km) away.

While the fast carriers were launching

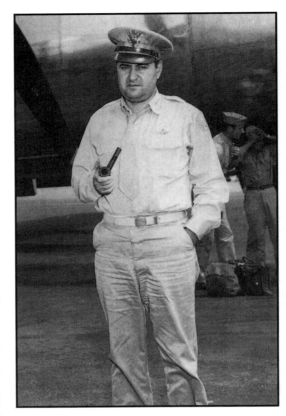

Above: Maj. Gen Curtis LeMay began the war as a group commander in the 8th Air Force in England. Transferred to China in 1944, he developed there the low-level fire-bombing tactics which were to have such a destructive impact on Japan's cities.

Above: Tokyo after a fire raid. During the night of March 9-10, over 300 B-29s from Tinian and Saipan dropped 2,000 tons of incendiaries onto one of the most densely-populated areas in the world. It was only the first of five such raids that were to follow in succession.

their attacks on Japan, LeMay experimented with new tactics. At first he tried to bomb from high altitude — to do what his predecessor had done, only more effectively — but he soon adopted a different approach. By early 1945 planners and analysts at Army Air Forces headquarters expressed great enthusiasm for incendiary bombing attacks against Japan's largest cities, which contained lightly constructed, highly inflammable wooden houses and lacked well-equipped, highly-trained fire fighters. Indeed, Gen. LeMay had

conducted a devastating fire raid on Hankow (Hangzhou) when he operated in China, while Hansell had also experimented with fire raids. Once he decided that he could burn down the cities, LeMay made one of the most important decisions of the war when he launched his B-29s on low-level, night

Right: Fire fighters try to control a blaze at Sukiyabashi in central Tokyo. The civil defenses of the Japanese capital were totally inadequate to cope with the B-29 onslaught — Tokyo only had 8,000 firemen and just over 1,100 vehicles.

Left: The explosion of the world's first atomic device at 5:30 A.M., July 16, 1945. The Trinity Test, as it was known, was completed at Alamogordo in New Mexico and reckoned a success. Targets in Japan were being selected a week later.

At the end of July 1945 Gen. Carl A. "Tooey" Spaatz, fresh from the victory in Europe, took over control of air operations in the Pacific. In addition to the Twentieth Air Force in the Marianas, he controlled the Eighth Air Force which was deploying from Europe to operate against Japan from the Ryukus, joining forces with the Marianas-based B-29s. Earlier the four B-29 groups from India had joined the Twentieth and more units arrived from the United States. Spaatz would direct the final aerial assault on Japan, including the atomic bombing. By now B-29 strength in the Marianas had grown to nearly 1,000 bombers, permitting an armada of as many as 625 B-29s to attack on a single day. In the organizational shuffle that followed the appointment of Spaatz, the XXI Bomber Command was inactivated and LeMay became Chief of Staff of Twentieth Air Force.

The United States had drafted plans for the invasion of Japan beginning with an assault on Kyushu in the fall of 1945; a second invasion, of Honshu, was planned for the Spring of 1946. Japan was thought to have an army of about two million men and 8,000 airplanes for use in the defense of the Home Islands. If the Japanese fought with anything like the tenacity they had displayed at Iwo Jima, American losses would be staggering. No American leader contemplated an early or an easy victory.

Fortunately, a weapon existed that might make an invasion unnecessary. On June 11, 1945, Col. Paul W. Tibbets, Commander of the 509th Composite Group, arrived at North Field on Tinian. His secret mission — to drop the atomic bomb on Japan — was known only to a select few.

On August 13, 1942 the United States initiated the Manhattan Project, an all-out effort to develop the atomic bomb based on the principle of atomic fission. Administered by Brig. Gen. Leslie R. Groves, the head of the Manhattan Engineering District, the project took only three years to complete. Operating under elaborate security measures, the true nature of the project was known to a small number of individuals — neither Secretary of State Cordell Hull nor Vice President Harry S. Truman knew of the undertaking. The secrecy was astoundingly effective, considering that the Manhattan Project employed more than 120,000 people at numerous locations, and was estimated to have cost two billion dollars. Dr. J. Robert Oppenheimer, the physicist entrusted with the task of designing the atomic bomb, gathered a top-level research team at Los Alamos, New Mexico. Basic research was conducted at three centers: Dr. Arthur H. Compton headed the University

attacks with incendiaries. By coming in at low altitude, only 7,000 feet (2,000m), the planes could carry larger bomb loads, and they avoided a long climb at maximum power that strained their temperamental engines. The first attack on March 9-10 by a force of 334 B-29s burned out 16 square miles (40km²) of the heart of Tokyo, destroyed about one-fourth of all the buildings, and took more than 80,000 lives.

The astounding success of this mission established a pattern for the fire-bombing campaign against Japan's cities. Four more incendiary attacks followed in rapid succession and by March 20 the Superforts had flown 1,600 sorties and in the process burned out 32 square miles (80km²) of the industrial areas in Tokyo, Osaka, Nagoya, and Kobe. Because the Japanese air defenses against night attack were poor, the B-29s suffered only minor losses in these attacks. In fact, the Americans were so confident of success that they stripped their B-29s of guns and ammunition and filled the planes with additional bombs. Japan's fighter defenses collapsed so quickly that the P-51 escort fighters became superfluous almost as soon as they began flying from Iwo Jima.

Toward the end of the war, the B-29s began dropping leaflets naming Japanese cities that were targeted and warning the civilian population to flee. By the end of the war the B-29 bombers had dropped 145,000 tons of bombs on Japan and destroyed 105 square miles (260km²) in Japan's six most important industrial centers. Dozens of smaller

cities were laid to waste. Even after June 1945, when the first phase of the destruction of urban areas had ended, LeMay did not ease up. Whenever poor weather was predicted over his primary targets, like airfields or aircraft factories, LeMay continued fire bombing missions against secondary industrial targets and launched precision daylight strikes under visual conditions.

The American Pacific Fleet, assisted since mid-March by the British Pacific Fleet operating as an integral task force, returned to Japanese waters in July and remained there until Japan surrendered. Task Force 38 (made up of the ships of Task Force 58 but commanded by Vice Adm. John S. McCain, instead of Mitscher (just as Adm. Spruance's Fifth Fleet became the Third Fleet when Fleet Adm. Halsey and his slate of officers assumed command), attacked military and industrial targets in Tokyo and elsewhere on the island of Honshu and on Hokkaido to the north. For the British the high point of this foray may have come on July 17 and 18 when their carrier aircraft joined in attacking Tokyo. On July 29, the battleship HMS *King George V* shelled the industrial city of Hamamatsu in central Honshu. Despite reservations on the part of Fleet Adm. Ernest J. King, the American Chief of Naval Operations, that the British could not adapt to American logistical techniques like refueling at sea, they had organized a train of oilers and supply ships and caused a minimum of disruption to the replenishment system as they helped carry the war to Japan.

US Naval Aviator's Uniforms and Equipment

1 Naval officer's service jacket with aviator's wings
2 Naval officer's service trousers
3 AN-H-15 lightweight tropical flying helmet
4 Aviator's goggles
5 Box for goggles 4
6 Lightweight cotton flying suit
7 Inflatable buoyancy vest, with dye markers
8 Smith and Wesson Victory Model .38 caliber revolver
9 Oil bottle for 8
10 Cleaning rod for 8
11 Navy sheath knife and sheath
12 Leather flight helmet with earphones
13 A2 flight jacket
14 Navy leather flight gloves
15 Navy officer's visored cap
16 Navy manual for officers
17 Napkin ring from mess
18 Ashtray
19 Leather sunglass case
20 Aviator's sunglasses with metal case
21 Aviator's log book
22 Silk escape map
23 Lightweight aviator's windbreaker
24 Fleece-lined flying boots
25 Signal flare
26 Fragments of main float from a US Navy Kingfisher float plane

William M. Galbraith: 1-13, 15-24; Andrew W. Xaras: 14

All these items, except the naval flying gloves (*14*) were worn or used by Lt. (j.g.) William M. Galbraith, United States Navy, a contemporary photograph of whom can be seen at left. Lt. Galbraith flew a Vought Kingfisher OS2U-3 floatplane off the battleship *Iowa*, and cruiser *Boston*. In this role he served throughout the campaigns for Hollandia, Truk, Guam, Saipan, the Philippines and Iwo Jima. The metal fragment (*26*) is an actual section from his aircraft's float, which was retrieved after a 'mishap.'

The Vought Kingfisher was a single float seaplane, designed as an observation scout aircraft. It was first delivered into US Navy service in August 1941. With a crew of two, the Kingfisher flew from both ships and land bases, on a wide variety of missions, including bombing missions over the Aleutians.

of Chicago group; Dr. Ernest O. Lawrence supervised the University of California team; and Dr. Harold C. Urey led a team at Columbia University. Each group employed a different method to produce the fissionable materials needed to release the enormous energy that would characterize the atomic bomb. In December 1942 at Chicago, Dr. Enrico Fermi demonstrated the world's first self-sustaining nuclear chain reaction. Following that demonstration, Gen. Groves built a plant to produce plutonium at Hanford, Washington, and another for fissionable materials at Oak Ridge, Tennessee. Then, on July 16,

1945, the United States successfully detonated the world's first atomic bomb, a plutonium device (code named Trinity), at Alamogordo, New Mexico.

Earlier, in May, Secretary of War Henry L. Stimson had established a civilian advisory panel to make recommendations concerning employment of the atomic bomb. This seven-member "interim committee" advised using the bomb as soon as possible; aiming it at a dual — military and civilian — target; and to employ the weapon without prior warning. Arrayed on the other side was a group of 64 scientists involved in the Manhattan Project. The Committee on

Personal Arms of General Hideki Tojo, Prime Minister and War Minister of Japan, 1941-44

1 Army officer's sword and scabbard, *Shin-gunto* pattern (new military sword). Note the general officer's tassel tied to the pommel of the hilt
2 Sword blade with plain wooden storage or 'resting' scabbard and hilt
3 Short dirk or *tanto* in wooden storage scabbard
4 Colt Model 1903 semi-automatic pistol, 7.65mm (.32) caliber; SN 535330. This weapon was used by Tojo in an attempted suicide bid in September 1945 after his arrest by the American occupying forces for war crimes. It may have been given to him by his son. The attempt failed and Tojo lived to face trial
5 Photograph of Tojo's suicide attempt with the actual bullet removed from his body after successful surgery. The bullet later became part of the FBI Collection and was placed in the MacArthur Memorial Collection by J. Edgar Hoover, head of the Federal Bureau of Investigation

MacArthur Memorial Collection

Tojo first came to prominence as the chief of staff of the Kwantung Army in Manchuria in the late 1930s. In 1938 he became Japan's vice minister of war, and was promoted minister of war in 1940. On October 17, 1941 he assumed the position of prime minister as well. In these combined roles, his hold over Japanese war policy was almost total, until the reverses in Burma and the Marianas in mid-1944 forced him to resign. He was replaced as prime minister by Gen. Kaniaki Koiso. After the Japanese defeat and occupation, Tojo was arrested and despite his botched suicide attempt in September 1945, was sent to trial by the International Military Tribunal of the Far East. He was convicted of war crimes, and along with seven others was hanged on December 23, 1948.

Social and Political Implications, as it was called, urged Stimson and the president first to demonstrate the power of the bomb before an international audience on some barren spot. However, the advice of the concerned scientists was rejected on grounds that "the possibility of a dud made an advance notice a bad psychological risk."

Regarded as a kind of ultimate weapon, the atomic bomb might serve as the answer to avoiding the enormous American casualties contemplated in an invasion of Japan. Truman, who had become president after Roosevelt's death in April, learned of the successful atomic bomb test while he attended the conference of Allied leaders which met at Potsdam, near conquered Berlin, between July 17 and August 2. On July 26, President Truman, with Prime Minister Churchill and Generalissimo Chiang Kai-shek, issued an ultimatum (the Potsdam Declaration) for Japan to surrender unconditionally. Truman had decided that if the Japanese failed to accept, "They may expect a rain of ruin from the air, the like of which has never been seen on this earth." The Allies demanded that Japan: limit its sovereignty to Honshu, Hokkaido, Kyushu, and Shikoku; accept Allied occupation; disarm its military forces; destroy its war industry; submit to the trial and punishment of war criminals; institute the freedoms of speech, religion, and thought; and revive democracy. Three days later Prime Minister Kantaro Suzuki rejected the Allied terms, whereupon Truman made the fateful, though all but inevitable, decision to use atomic bombs.

Despite the devastating B-29 attacks, Japan had refused to surrender. The *coup de grace* against Japan was delivered with the dropping of the atomic bombs against Hiroshima on August 6 and Nagasaki on August 9.

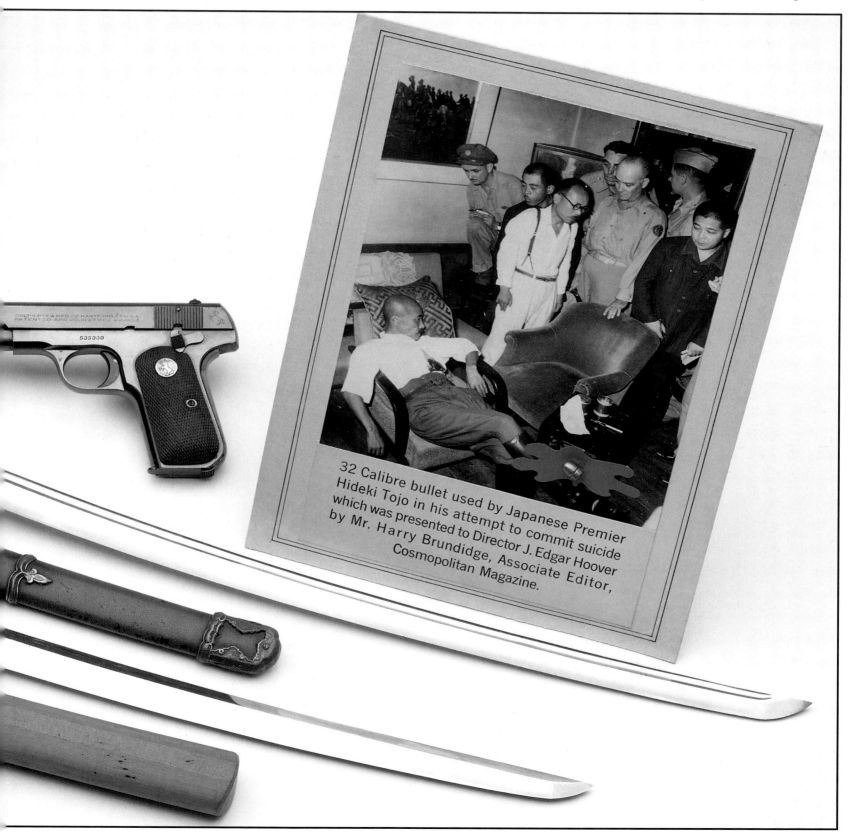

32 Calibre bullet used by Japanese Premier Hideki Tojo in his attempt to commit suicide which was presented to Director J. Edgar Hoover by Mr. Harry Brundidge, Associate Editor, Cosmopolitan Magazine.

OPERATION DOWNFALL — THE INVASION OF JAPAN

Map A

The decision to begin planning the invasion of Japan was taken on May 25, 1945. At this point the B-29 bombing campaign against the Home Islands had been going on from the Marianas since the previous November, the battle for Okinawa was in its final stages, and Luzon was largely secure. The question of how to conquer the Home Islands, however, remained. The mining and submarine blockade, though successful, could only go so far in making Japan submit, and the atomic bomb remained for the time being at least, just an untested theory. Awful though the idea was, there seemed little option for finishing the war other than a full-scale amphibious assault by troops.

And it was an awful prospect. For despite the advantages of total air and *materiel* superiority, and the possibility of a Russian attack on the Japanese forces in Manchuria at the same time, an American casualty figure of over one million was envisaged. The fanatical resistance that American forces had come up against before, would be as nothing to what they would face there.

Map B

The invasion itself would comprise two separate operations on two of the Home Islands. Gen. MacArthur would be in overall command of the land forces, while Adm. Nimitz would command the Pacific Fleet; the Air Forces would be under the command of Gen. Carl Spaatz. The first invasion, Operation Olympic, would be undertaken by the four corps of Sixth Army under the command of Gen. Walter Krueger. The corps would be: V Amphibious Corps comprising three Marine divisions; XI Corps of one armored and one infantry division, together with the Americal Division; I Corps of three infantry divisions; and the reserve IX Corps of three infantry divisions which would make a feint attack before the actual landings. On X-Day, November 1, 1945, these forces would attack the southernmost island of Kyushu.

The second invasion, Operation Coronet, would take place in the following spring of 1946. Y-Day was provisionally set for March 1.

Two armies with a combined strength of five corps would attack the main island of Honshu. In a pincer movement, the Eighth Army with three corps would land to the south of Tokyo Bay, and make an armored thrust north towards Koga. The object would be to isolate Tokyo. At the same time, the two corps of the First Army, which would include III Amphibious Corps of three Marine divisions would land east of the Japanese capital and begin a direct attack towards it.

As in previous amphibious operations, initial attacks would take place on small surrounding islands before the main assaults went in.

Facing these American attacks would be no fewer than six Japanese armies. These troops would be augmented by millions of home defense personnel.

As the war in Europe finished, units were already on their way east to take part in this last great battle of the Pacific. As history records, however, the atomic bomb was a success and their sacrifice was never needed.

Since the loss of Saipan, it had become increasingly obvious to those Japanese leaders willing to face reality that Japan could be destroyed by starvation and bombing, even without an invasion. But influential groups of Japanese militants, determined to fight to the bitter and, refused to give in, and others preferred national suicide to the probable

Below: The vast majority of casualties in Hiroshima were civilians, and apart from those killed in the atom bomb's explosion they were many others who were injured and later died from an assortment of traumatic and radiological problems.

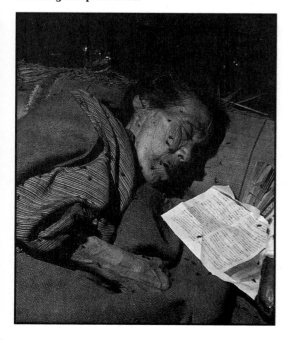

imprisonment and possible execution of the emperor they revered. The final blow that convinced Japan to come to terms was the atomic bomb. On August 6, 1945 the B-29 *Enola Gay*, piloted by Col. Paul W. Tibbets, Jr., took off from Tinian. Its payload was an experimental U-235 atomic bomb named "Little Boy". At 8:15 A.M. Tibbets dropped the bomb. At 2,000 feet (600m) above Hiroshima, the bomb exploded in a blinding flash of light, with a force equal to 20,000 tons of TNT. A huge mushroom-shaped cloud that rose 40,000 feet (12km) marked the bomb's devastation. An hour and a half later Tibbets and his crew were 360 miles away, but they could still see the cloud. The destruction was unprecedented: nearly five square miles of Hiroshima had vanished, 40,000 people were killed instantly, 20,000 others died eventually of gruesome wounds or radiation, and yet another 60,000 were injured. The Japanese literally did not know what hit them, nor did they have any idea how to treat the burned and bleeding hapless victims.

When the Japanese government, paralyzed by indecision, still refused to surrender, Truman directed a second atomic strike. Kokura was the intended target, but Maj. Charles W. Sweeney, piloting the B-29 *Bockscar*, found the city cloud-covered and flew some 80 miles (128km) to the southwest for his secondary target. At 11:00 A.M. on the morning of August 9, Nagasaki was turned into another atomic furnace as the

Above: Lying in a natural bowl that helped to trap some of the bomb's destructive effect, Nagasaki was totally devastated by the atomic bombing on August 9. The Japanese authorities were quite unable at first to grasp the enormity of the occurrence.

plutonium bomb named "Fat Man" did its grisly work. Although the second bombing was less effective, it too produced enormous destruction as 36,000 were killed and 60,000 injured at a single stroke. The bombing of Nagasaki convinced the Japanese leaders of the futility of further resistance.

In a radio broadcast shortly after the bombing, President Truman explained:

"I realize the tragic significance of the atomic bomb . . . . Having found the bomb we have used it. We have used it against those who attacked us without warning at Pearl Harbor, against those who have starved and beaten and executed American prisoners of war, against those who have abandoned all pretense of obeying international laws of warfare. We have used it in order to shorten the agony of young Americans. We shall continue to use it until we completely destroy Japan's power to make war. Only a Japanese surrender will stop us."

On August 8, 1945, in accordance with the Yalta agreement made in February, the Soviet Union declared war on Japan. However, Foreign Minister Vyacheslav

Molotov's announcement to the Japanese ambassador, Naotake Sato, was phrased in a way to make it appear that the Soviets were acting at the behest of the Allies. Immediately, the Red Army invaded Manchuria and in a three-pronged attack demonstrated its superiority over the weakened Kwantung Army as the Russians drove south into Korea, stopping at the 38th parallel. This was in accord with a prior agreement which permitted the United States to liberate South Korea. The Russian-American action effectively overturned the November 23, 1943 Cairo Conference decision to grant Korea its independence. Approximately 25 percent of the Japanese soldiers and settlers in Manchuria, some 80,000 people, were confirmed killed by the advancing Russians, or by the long-suffering Chinese, bent on exacting revenge.

The final, relentless assault on Japan came with aircraft armadas bombing at will in broad daylight. They smashed what was left of Japan's industry — iron, steel, and chemical works. Warships and

BOEING B-29 SUPERFORTRESS

For an aircraft forever associated with the ending of the Pacific War, it is surprising to note that the spearhead of the USAAF's long-range bomber force, the mighty Boeing B-29 Superfortress, did not reach squadron service until July 1943; and that its first combat mission came as late as June 5, 1944 — some two years after the Japanese attack on Pearl Harbor! Yet in the short space of time between its combat debut and VJ-Day, vast aerial armadas of B-29s, many up to 500-strong, pounded Japanese targets relentlessly. Over 3,000 Superfortresses were built, but it took just two to bring the war to and end and to earn the B-29 its place in the annals of aviation history.

carrier aircraft of the US Third and Fifth Fleets and the British Pacific Fleet blasted northern Honshu mercilessly; they dropped millions of leaflets informing the Japanese people that their cause was futile. Allied radio broadcasts beamed the endless message: "quit or die". But the Japanese government could not act. At the imperial conferences on August 10 and 14, Premier Suzuki, Navy Minister Mitsumasa Yonai, and Foreign Minister Shigenori Togo advocated surrender, but other military leaders — the army minister and the two chiefs of staff — refused to accept the humiliation of defeat. In this hour of crisis, Emperior Hirohito broke the tradition that he acted only on the unanimous recommendations of his advisers. Accepting the possibility that he could be tried as a war criminal, late on the night of August 14 Hirohito recorded a cease-fire announcement to be broadcast at noon on the following day. But even this last desperate measure almost failed, for a group of army officers plotted to overthrow the government, kill the

USAAF BOMBER CREWMAN, 1945

Despite operating from tropical locations, bomber crews in the Pacific theater, like those fighting in Europe, wore fleece-lined flying suits when operating in the freezing conditions of high altitude. This figure carries the B-3 flying jacket and wears standard pattern A-6 fur-lined flying boots. Over his khaki drill service dress he wears an inflatable life preserver. He wears the insignia of the 7th Air Force.

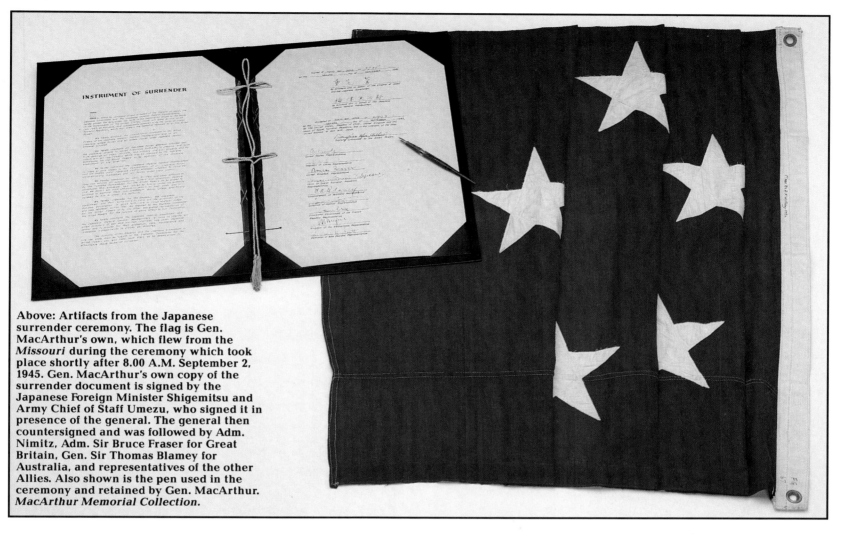

Above: Artifacts from the Japanese surrender ceremony. The flag is Gen. MacArthur's own, which flew from the *Missouri* during the ceremony which took place shortly after 8.00 A.M. September 2, 1945. Gen. MacArthur's own copy of the surrender document is signed by the Japanese Foreign Minister Shigemitsu and Army Chief of Staff Umezu, who signed it in presence of the general. The general then countersigned and was followed by Adm. Nimitz, Adm. Sir Bruce Fraser for Great Britain, Gen. Sir Thomas Blamey for Australia, and representatives of the other Allies. Also shown is the pen used in the ceremony and retained by Gen. MacArthur. *MacArthur Memorial Collection.*

advocates of surrender, and continue the war, using the emperor as their figurehead. Fortunately, the fanatical plot failed, and Hirohito's message was aired on schedule. The Japanese population listened incredulously to the emperor's words, but they accepted his decision.

Below: On board the *Missouri*, the Japanese delegation led by Mamoru Shigemitsu (with cane) and Gen. Yoshijiro Umezu waits to sign the document of surrender. Their signatures are followed by that of Douglas MacArthur (below right), his staff and representatives of each of the allies.

The formal surrender ceremony was staged in Tokyo Bay on the morning of September 2, when General of the Army Douglas MacArthur received the Japanese envoys for the surrender aboard the battleship *Missouri*. After accepting the document, MacArthur said, "Let us pray that peace be now restored to the world and that God will preserve it always." President Truman had named MacArthur Supreme Commander of the Allied Powers for the surrender and occupation of Japan. For the next five years MacArthur directed the dismantling of the Japanese military and converted

Japan to a peacetime economy. Despite wartime promises to establish a Far Eastern Commission and an Allied Council for Japan, in reality the United States exercised sole control as the occupying power in Japan. And although the arrangement irritated some Allies, the Japanese appeared generally pleased with MacArthur's administration, which was firm but fair and statesmanlike.

As the Japanese surrendered on board the *Missouri*, 400 B-29s circled overhead. The B-29 force was celebrated by Gen. Spaatz as "the best organized and most technically and tactically proficient organization that the world has seen to date." Indeed, the B-29 force in the Marianas symbolized the defeat of Japan. It had launched an amazing total of 34,000 effective sorties, dropped 170,000 tons of bombs (most of them during the final six months of the war), leveled some 65 Japanese cities, and killed 300,000 people. While the B-29s crews claimed 2,000 enemy aircraft destroyed or damaged, their own losses amounted to 414 Superfortresses and 3,015 crewmen killed, wounded or missing. American casualties in the Pacific theater totalled 170,596, including 41,322 killed.

These cold statistics can only measure the grim punishment the B-29s meted out against Japan; they cannot describe the brutal human carnage that the campaign caused. Above all other episodes, the atomic bombs served as a signpost for mankind to avoid war.

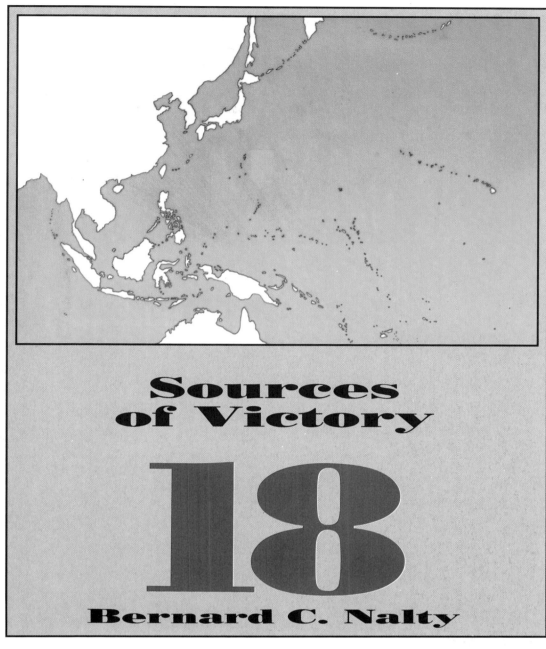

Sources of Victory

18

Bernard C. Nalty

Japan's militarists — who dominated the government by persuasion, tradition, and when necessary, assassination — went to war in accordance with a series of assumptions — really articles of faith — rather than a clearly defined strategy. These leaders proposed to neutralize the Pacific Fleet at Pearl Harbor, an achievable goal, which would give the imperial forces time to seize Burma, Malaya, the Netherlands East Indies, and the Philippines, incorporate the territory into the Greater East Asia Co-Prosperity Sphere, and establish a defensive line embracing the Japanese Mandates, New Guinea, and the Malay barrier. Behind this shield, Japan would subjugate China, exploit the resources of the recent conquests, and enjoy dominance based on a self-contained empire that included: mines, oil wells, and rice fields; smelters, refineries, and mills; and mass markets. As Japan grew stronger, the United States would rebuild its shattered fleet, hammer in vain at the impregnable outer shell of empire, give up in despair, and accept Japanese hegemony in Asia and the far Pacific. This scenario reflected a belief that the Japanese enjoyed a

natural superiority; that they comprised a warrior race, whereas Americans lacked the discipline and character to recover from the initial setbacks and win a long war.

Like the Japanese leaders who gambled their nation's future on a belief in racial superiority, many Americans clung to a conviction that they belonged to a superior race. The notion that Japanese immigrants were unworthy of American citizenship had, in fact, contributed to the souring of relations between the two nations. Those Americans who shared the attitude of superiority tended to dismiss the Japanese as imitators, not innovators; according to legend, they imported American scrap metal to make cheap toys and copies of foreign products for sale in variety stores like F. W. Woolworth or W. T. Grant. The British were not immune to cultural and racial bias either. Adm. Sir Tom Phillips, on the bridge of HMS *Prince of Wales* in December 1941, thought in terms of elderly biplanes like the British Swordfish when he heard that Japanese torpedo planes were operating off the coast of Malaya; since the Japanese

Above: A Marine recruiting poster (left) painted by Sgt. Tom Lovell. Army poster (right) urging greater war production. A 1943 publication of the Government Printing Office, artist unknown. *War Memorial Museum of Virginia.*

could not possibly have anything better, he was unprepared for the fast, modern, twin-engine aircraft that scored fatal hits on his battleship and the accompanying battle cruiser *Repulse*. Similarly, the nimble, long-range Zero fighter shocked Allied airmen, even though Claire Chennault, the American officer serving as air adviser to Chiang Kai-shek had warned of it.

The mutual feeling of racial superiority contributed to acts of cruelty by both sides. After the American surrender on Bataan, a Japanese officer told Brig. Gen. William E. Brougher that the code of the warrior required the humane treatment of captives, but, as the death march immediately revealed, this was rarely the case. Gen. Tomoyuki Yamashita, the conqueror of Malaya, paid scrupulous attention to the rules of warfare, but he nevertheless went to the gallows as a war criminal, largely because of his success on the battlefield. Yamashita was an exception, however; other Japanese officers worked British and Australians to death on the River Kwai and in Borneo, beheaded captured members of B-29 crews as the war drew to an end, and used prisoners as guinea pigs in germ warfare tests or in medical experiments that were exercises in brutality.

For the Americans, the surprise attack on Pearl Harbor justified measures from waging unrestricted submarine warfare,

to razing whole cities with fire bombs, to arresting American citizens of Japanese ancestry living on the West Coast, confiscating their property, and herding them into concentration camps. Conditioned by propaganda to hate the Japanese, aware of instances of enemy brutality, and perhaps a little frightened by his tenacity — even fanaticism — the American soldier, sailor, and marine often harbored a murderous hatred of the Japanese. Indeed, Cdr. Dudley W. Morton, the brilliant and courageous skipper of the ill-fated submarine *Wahoo*, dedicated himself to killing the enemy. On one occasion, shortly before *Wahoo* itself went down, Morton sank a troop transport, fired upon survivors swimming for their lives and rammed lifeboats. Such was the depth of his hatred. At times, misunderstanding intensified the hate felt by so many Americans, as on Guadalcanal, when Marine Col. Frank Goettge mistook what could only have been a battle flag — white with a red orb at the center — for a white flag of surrender and led a rescue party to assist the supposedly helpless Japanese, who opened fire, killing the colonel and all but one of his men. The destruction of the Goettge patrol, which seemed a deliberate trap, provided yet another reason for revenge. Feelings reached such intensity that at times those few Japanese who did surrender, and may

not have been Japanese at all but Korean laborers, were shot out of hand.

Although the attack on Pearl Harbor did neutralize the Pacific Fleet, the sudden onslaught inflamed and unified the American people as nothing else might have done. In December 1941, strong isolationist sentiment existed in the United States, a reluctance to become involved in foreign wars that stemmed in part from the belief that America in 1917 had burned its fingers pulling British chestnuts from the fire. Had Japan ignored Pearl Harbor and the Philippines and attacked the Netherlands East Indies and British Malaya, President Franklin D. Roosevelt might well have found it difficult to persuade Congress and the American people to go to war. Instead, Japan attacked on a day associated with church-going and relaxation, killing and wounding unsuspecting soldiers and sailors. The surprise attack helped Roosevelt weave a fabric of national resolve that survived his death in April 1945, and had only begun to fray when the war ended.

Nor was the attack on Pearl Harbor a complete victory in a tactical sense.

Every battleship anchored there sustained severe damage or was sunk, but the battleship no longer dominated naval warfare. The aircraft carrier had taken its place, as the attack on Hawaii demonstrated, and not one ship of that class was in port when the enemy struck. Moreover, the Japanese failed to attack the oil reserves, the very life's blood of naval operations, or the important repair facilities.

Adm. Isoroku Yamamoto of the Imperial Japanese Navy had just one weapon, the carrier-based airplane, that could knock the Pacific Fleet out of the war and open the way for conquest. He had no bases within bomber range of the Hawaiian anchorage, and the Americans could not fail to discover a surface fleet before it had steamed close enough to use its big guns, with a range of perhaps 20 miles (32km). Only the carriers could avoid the principal shipping lanes, approach Pearl Harbor from an unexpected quarter, and launch the attack from a comparatively safe distance. Only a carrier task force — with fighters, bombers, and torpedo planes flown by resourceful and highly trained airmen —

Below: US Navy poster (left), designed by artist Howard Scott and produced by the Industrial Incentive Division. War Bonds poster (right) painted by Georges Schreiber, a Belgian, then living in New York. *War Memorial Museum of Virginia.*

made the attack at all feasible. The expedition, however, did not have a suitable commander, for Adm. Chuichi Nagumo, a veteran of surface ships but a newcomer to naval aviation, proved incapable of providing Yamamoto with a truly decisive victory. In short, Nagumo failed to follow up his initial success; he settled for setting battleships ablaze when this was not enough.

At most, the crippling of the Pacific Fleet bought time for the Japanese to seize and exploit an empire. Until Japan could tap the resources of the conquered territory, it risked disaster, even though it went to war with an excellent navy, a well trained army, and skilled air forces. The nation's weakness lay in its natural resources, especially oil. The petroleum reserves to sustain the fighting were slender indeed — a mere 50 million barrels, when the Imperial Japanese Navy alone burned 2,900 barrels to keep the fleet steaming for just one hour. The oil of the Netherlands East Indies provided the key to national survival. Imports from the former Dutch colony surpassed 50,000 barrels per day at the end of 1943, but American submarines, along with minefields and aircraft reduced the flow of crude oil and refined petroleum to a mere trickle. By the end of the war, tankers totalling 1.1 million gross tons had gone to the bottom, two-thirds of them sunk by submarines. The refining

of crude oil already on hand, the manufacture of a synthetic fuel made of pine knots, and the manufacture of alcohol to blend with gasoline accounted for only 10,000 barrels per day.

Air power played a critical role in Japan's conquest of the oil and other resources it needed, crippling the battleships of the Pacific Fleet at Pearl Harbor, sinking the *Prince of Wales* and *Repulse*, and providing cover for the invasions of Malaya, the Netherlands East Indies, and the Philippines. Yet, reliance on aircraft represented yet another gamble, not merely because of the shortage of aviation fuel but also because of the nation's weak industrial base. In 1939, Japan, already at war in China, and the United States, manufactured a comparable number of aircraft to those of the United States. Within two years, however, as the United States prepared for a possible war. its production had grown more than four-fold to 26,000 airplanes, whereas Japan had increased its output by fewer than 700 aircraft to slightly more than 5,000. During the war, Japanese production peaked at 28,000 during 1944, compared to 96,000 in the United States. The dismal Japanese production record reflected a persisting shortage of raw materials, a network of small plants that assembled components turned out at scattered sites, and a lack of experience in

Cloth unit shoulder insignia 'patches' were first used in World War I. Before that cap badges on headgear had been used to identify various commands, and before that distinctive unit flags were utilized.

The shoulder patch is not only a means of identification, but also a source of unit pride. The design of the patch usually has some basis in unit history, and national colors of red, white and blue are evident in many examples.

operating a continuous assembly line under a single roof. Meddling by the army and navy further disrupted the aircraft industry, for the Japanese services put their individual requirements first and refused to agree on such basic matters as a common voltage for electrical systems or a standard machine gun. Not until it was too late did the admirals and generals turn to the civilian industrialists who, if given the chance, might have marshaled the available resources and to some extent accelerated production.

The comparative strength of the rival navies afforded another demonstration of the difference in industrial capacity between the United States and Japan. When the Japanese attacked Pearl Harbor, the US Navy had 17 battleships and the Imperial Navy 12. Adm. Nagumo's airmen sank USS *Arizona* on December 7 and damaged *Oklahoma* so badly that the ship had to be written off. When the war ended, however, the American Navy had 23 ships of this class, including eight newly constructed battleships and six that had sustained varying degrees of damage at Pearl Harbor. In contrast, Japan had proved unable to replace any of the nine battleships sunk during the war, and at the time of surrender, only three remained afloat, all of them badly battered. Besides increasing the number of battleships, the American shipbuilding industry turned out three submarines for each of the 52 lost to accidents or enemy action, and produced an armada of landing craft ranging from amphibian tractors used to assault the invasion beaches to huge LSDs (Landing Ships Dock) that carried the tractors in their cavernous interiors and launched them at the objective.

During the war, the aircraft carrier supplanted the battleship as the decisive weapon of naval warfare. When the fighting ended, Japan had not one undamaged carrier still afloat; fifteen such

These insignia are representative of most of the major American commands active in the Pacific theater during World War II. There are countless small unit insignia, official and unauthorized, of units which contributed greatly to the war effort. There are also unit designating insignia of Commonwealth countries, Japanese forces and other participants, which are a whole field of military heraldry. The patches shown are but a small example.

Japanese Naval Aviator's Flight Equipment and Personal Effects

1 Japanese naval aviator's intermediate weight flight suit. Well-made of quality materials, this suit is typical of the first-rate equipment of the naval aviator
2 Naval aviator's leather flying helmet
3 Naval aviator's flying goggles
4 Storage box and cleaning cloth for goggles, 3
5 Handkerchief used to wrap photographs of father, mother and brother. Photographs were carried by the aviator in his flying suit
6 Photograph of Japanese naval aviator in the flight suit shown here
7 Personal flight log/ledger
8 Patriotic headband, often worn or carried as a good luck token
9 Personal wallet of aviator, including bank notes and change
10 Pocket knife carried with other personal items
11 Pencils for note-taking in flight log
12 Packet of dried herbal infusion
13 Small personal Japanese national flag, carried in pocket of flying suit

Andrew W. Xaras Collection

ships had joined the fleet after the attack on Pearl Harbor, but only six survived. The American Navy lost four of the seven large aircraft carriers in service when the war began, and the Japanese also sank the diminutive USS *Langley*, converted from a collier in 1920. Shipyards in the United States produced 17 large carriers, built as such from the keel up, nine light carriers that utilized cruiser hulls, and 114 escort carriers converted from merchantmen. Of the escort carriers, 38 were handed over to the British. The Japanese sank one of the newly constructed light carriers and five escort carriers, and inflicted crippling damage on several others, including large carriers, but American ship-building capacity more than met the challenge.

Japan's industrial infrastructure proved too fragile to sustain modern warfare. Stockpiles, especially of oil, could be replenished only through conquest, and the very act of conquering drew upon these reserves. Handicapped by industries that produced just 3.5 percent of the world's manufactures, compared to 32.2 percent for the United States, plagued by shortages of essential materials, the Japanese had no strategy, a shortcoming masked by tactical successes like the devastation of Battleship Row at Pearl Harbor and the conquest of Malaya. Instead of clearly defining a strategic objective and marshaling the resources need to achieve it, Japan devoutly believed that the warrior spirit would prevail, that Americans lacked courage and resolve and would accept a negotiated settlement leaving the Japanese in control of Asia and the western Pacific.

Despite its superiority in manufacturing and war materials, the United States had to conserve its resources by rationing food and fuel, collecting old tires and scrap metal, and increasing taxes and

Naval aviators, within the Japanese military organization, were considered an elite force. Careful initial selection, especially rigorous training, and first rate equipment were standard requirements for this excellent fighting group. They were probably among the best combat pilots in the world at the beginning of the war, but suffered appalling losses in the big carrier battles of the conflict, as American pilots grew in experience and their aircraft outstripped those of the Japanese in performance and hitting power. Even during the final stages of the war, however, naval pilots still received the best quality training and equipment.

**Above: A series of Japanese English-language color propaganda leaflets aimed at Australian and New Zealand troops fighting in New Guinea. Particular attention is focused on American military activities at home with the wives of girlfriends of the men in the jungle. They also seek to play on the appalling conditions in which the soldiers are fighting, and try to persuade the troops that to sacrifice their lives in such a wilderness is both futile and meaningless to the final outcome of the war. They are fairly crude attempts to split the allies and to create morale problems among the troops.
*Dale E. Biever Collection.***

selling treasury bonds to finance the conflict. These measures conserved oil, rubber, and aluminium, helped curb consumption, and prevented the bidding up of prices for scarce goods. More important, they enabled the populace to enjoy, at minimal inconvenience, a sense of truly participating in the war effort. Although often symbolic, as when air raid wardens scanned the friendly skies, this kinship with the fighting men was important for civilian morale. Although the air raid warden served as a symbol in the United States, he played a vital role in Japan, where fire rained down from the sky, where food grew scarcer as the war progressed, and where, in the summer of 1945, schoolboys were being trained to fight the American invaders.

Besides having overwhelming material and industrial resources, as demonstrated by the vast numbers of ships and aircraft made in America, the United States succeeded in marshaling science in support of the war to a degree barely dreamed of in Japan. The Manhattan Project, which produced the atomic bomb, served as the most devastating example of science in the service of Mars, but American scientists and engineers also advanced the piston-engine aircraft to its practical limits and developed the radar proximity fuze, which greatly increased the deadliness of antiaircraft fire. Indeed, every form of radar improved radically during the war, whether shipboard models to locate targets for naval gunfire or airborne types for bombing through cloud cover.

The United States also had a strategy, Germany first, and a clearly defined war aim — unconditional surrender. Because

Below: Japan's whole social structure emphasized the value of an unswerving national loyalty. Seen in November 1942, these primary school children are receiving basic military training that helped to cement their devotion to the services.

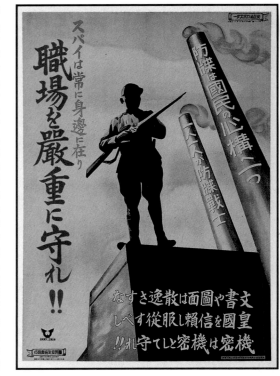

**Above: Japanese poster in translation reads: ''Each of us is a soldier against counterintelligence. We must always be watchful for spies. Firmly protect your workplace. Obey and trust the Empire.''
*War Memorial Museum of Virginia.***

of the basic strategy, the European and Mediterranean theaters had first call on troops, Army aircraft, and landing craft, although the war in the Pacific laid claim to the fast carrier task forces, the fleet submarines, and the long-range B-29 bombers. A shortage of landing craft sometimes disrupted plans, like those for an assault on the Andaman Islands in 1944, but the American forces in the Pacific managed to schedule their operations to make the most efficient use of the available resources. The decision to defeat Germany first had a decreasing impact on the war against Japan as

USSR

OUTER MONGOLIA

**SOVIET
OFFENSIVE**
August 1 1945

MANCHURIA
(MANCHUKUO)

Japanese surrender
August 18

INNER MONGOLIA

Peking

KOREA

JAPAN

TIBET

CHINA

Chengchow

Nanking

Shanghai

Yangtze

Chungking

**OPERATION
*ICHI-GO***
April 1944-April 1945

Ledo

LEDO
ROAD

BURMA ROAD

Kunming

Hengyang

Sui-chuan

OKINAWA

Ling-ling

Kweilin

Liuchow

FORMOSA

Mandalay

Lashio

Canton

Hong Kong

**BURMA
LIBERATED**

BURMA

FRENCH
INDOCHINA

Hanoi

HAINAN

LUZON

THAILAND

Rangoon

0	Miles	600
0	Km	400

THE POSITION ON THE ASIAN MAINLAND, AUGUST 1945

The last years of the war against Japan saw several major events in the region. The Japanese launched a big offensive in southern China in April 1944; British and Allied forces in Burma took Mandalay on March 29, 1945, and began a race to reoccupy Rangoon; while the Soviet Union, for so long occupied with its own survival in the west, after the defeat of Nazi Germany, began turning its forces east in June 1945 and declared war on Japan in August.

The last Japanese offensive in China, *Ichi-Go*, was designed to create a land-route into Southeast Asia and to destroy the airbases threatening the Home Islands. The offensive was a success, as far as it went in an increasingly peripheral theater of war, though one of its targets — the B-29s, were moved to the Mariana Islands before they could be reached.

By the beginning of April 1945, the British Fourteenth Army under Slim had the Japanese in full retreat in Burma. Supplied and supported by air and using tactics of encirclement and infiltration, British and Allied forces were pushing the Japanese south. An armored column of the 17th Indian Divison, XXXIII Corps was racing down the line of the Rangoon-Mandalay railway in attempt to take the city before the onset of the monsoon. At the same time, an amphibious landing (Operation Dracula) by the 26th Indian Division, XV Corps on May 2, was aimed at taking the city from the south. This division entered Rangoon on May 3, unopposed, the Japanese having fled. With Rangoon again in Allied hands, and the remaining Japanese forces bottled up in the Arakan and Shan Hills, the fight for Burma was over.

On August 9, 1945, the Soviets launched their attack against the Japanese in Manchuria (Manchukuo) across three fronts. The first advanced from Vladivostok towards Korea; the second attacked from the north; while the third and main force attacked from Outer Mongolia towards the south to cut off the Japanese Kwantung Army. The Japanese fell back to defend Korea, and finally surrendered on August 20, after a direct order from the emperor.

American factories began turning out the implements of war in quantities that satisfied worldwide demand. The fate of Japan was sealed well before Germany surrendered, although an invasion of the Home Islands might yet have proved necessary except for the atomic bomb and the emperor's decision to surrender. By stopping short of requiring unconditional surrender and allowing Emperor Hirohito to remain, the United States capitalized upon his reluctance to demand futile sacrifice from his people — and on the reverence and obedience they displayed toward him — to avoid a final town-by-town, house-by-house battle for Japan.

Just as the American war effort required a balancing of the campaign against Germany and the war against Japan, with the former enjoying a higher priority, the fighting in the Pacific involved the coordination of two offensives, one directed by Gen. of the Army Douglas MacArthur and the other by Fleet Adm. Chester W. Nimitz. Advancing westward through the Japanese Mandates, Nimitz and his principal subordinates, Adm. Raymond A. Spruance and William F. Halsey, made deadly use of the fast carrier task force, the fire support ships (especially the old battleships), and the tactics and equipment of amphibious warfare. The drive across the central Pacific resembled the offensive envisioned in the old Orange

Plans, save that it aimed for Iwo Jima, Okinawa, and ultimately Japan, rather than Manila Bay in the Philippines.

The other offensive led to the Philippines by way of New Guinea and the Solomon Islands, achieving the objective of the Orange Plans but from a different direction. In 1942, Australia had to be saved from the Japanese, and the build-up for that purpose provided the resources to begin the northward advance that MacArthur launched to fulfill his vow to return to the Philippines. The general had left the islands as an American hero, whatever his failings in conducting the defense of Luzon. Because of his popularity, and the debt owed those Filipinos who had rallied to the American cause and now lay in subjugation, MacArthur could not be ignored, but what he could do depended upon his access to the fast carriers, as least until the escort carriers became available in vast numbers. At the outset, therefore, he made short moves under cover of land-based aircraft, using a minimum of carriers and landing craft as he seized a succession of airfield sites progressively closer to his goal.

Although the two offensives required a juggling of American resources, especially in terms of fast carriers and landing craft, they imposed impossible demands on Japan's ever-shrinking fleet and dwindling supply of airplanes. Moreover, the Americans bypassed

strongpoints like Rabaul on New Britain, Kavieng on New Ireland, and the powerful base at Truk in the Carolines. As Japanese seapower declined, garrisons like these could no longer be withdrawn, as isolated outposts in the Solomons had been earlier in the war, or supplied.

Even as the United States used the mobility of amphibious warfare to deprive the Japanese of manpower, it voluntarily deprived itself of the services of roughly ten percent of its populace by failing to take full advantage of the African American minority. President Franklin D. Roosevelt promised American blacks better treatment and greater opportunity, within the confines of racial segregation, both in the military and in war industries under contract to the federal government, but the continued existence of segregation ensured discrimination against blacks. In the armed forces, racism tended to divert African Americans into menial jobs like truck driver, although there were exceptions, especially in Europe.

In the war against Japan, only the Navy abandoned racial segregation,

Below: American artillery and armored vehicles. (Top left) 75mm pack howitzer, range 9,475 yards (8,527m). (Bottom left) M4 Sherman Medium Tank, entered service in 1942. (Top right) M3 Half-Track Armored personnel Carrier, mounting in a Browning .30 caliber machine gun. The carrier entered service in 1941. (Bottom right) M3 37mm antitank gun. *US Marine Corps Air-Ground Museum.*

Above: Japanese weapons. (Top left) **70mm howitzer, used in infantry support.** (Top right) **Ohka Model 11 piloted suicide bomb, designed to be carried and launched from beneath a bomber. Around 750 of them were built.** *US Marine Corps Air-Ground Museum.* (Bottom left) **Type 1 Medium Tank.** (Bottom right) **Type 95 *HA-GO* Light Tank.** *US Army Ordnance Museum.*

though to a limited degree, when in 1944 it sought to apportion the burden of sea duty between whites and blacks by integrating the crews of certain fleet auxiliaries, like oilers and ammunition ships. The Navy's racial policy changed slowly. Dorie Miller, a mess attendant, earned the Navy Cross at Pearl Harbor when he manned a machine gun and opened fire on the Japanese. Despite his willingness to fight, he was still a messman in November 1943, when he died in the sinking of the escort carrier *Liscome Bay*. During the war in the Pacific, race, rather than ability or the needs of the services, all too often determined how Americans were trained and assigned.

The American skill in coordinating every aspect of the war against Japan — the air and submarine campaigns and the major advances westward from Hawaii and northward from Australia — resulted in part from the interception, decoding, and translation of Japanese radio traffic. The information obtained from military and naval messages contributed to the strategic victory at

Midway and helped win tactical successes in New Guinea and the Bismarck Sea. As a result of these early successes, American planners trusted the information on ship movements obtained from this source in directing submarine and mine warfare against Japanese merchantmen. Moreover, the code-breakers enabled the destroyer escort USS *England* to intercept and sink six Japanese submarines in 12 days, inspiring Fleet Adm. Ernest J. King, of the Chief of Naval Operations, to declare: "There'll always be an *England* — in the United States Navy."

Cryptanalysis, however, remained a conjurer's trick unless the information it provided reached the right people in time to be of use, and the recipients drew the proper conclusions. In the final weeks of the war, the system broke down, and the lapse cost American lives. The codebreakers learned that the Japanese submarine *I-58* had sailed to a patrol area in the southern Philippine Sea, but this information never reached the heavy cruiser *Indianapolis*, steaming through the danger zone after delivering components of the Hiroshima bomb to Tinian. When that submarine reported sinking "a battleship of the *Idaho* class," the decoded message seemed to be another exaggeration, like an earlier report that suicide craft launched from this same submarine had attacked and

sunk a tanker. If a tanker actually were attacked, the incident went unnoticed by the intended victim, and the unverified claim undermined the credibility of the second message, which was true except for the identity of the American ship. Actually *I-58* had torpedoed *Indianapolis*, which sank in 15 minutes without getting off a distress call and carried some 300 men to their deaths. Not until 84 hours had passed did a Navy plane on routine patrol happen across the survivors. By the time rescuers arrived, another 500 of the 1,100 crewmen had died from exposure or shark attack.

The Japanese diligently monitored American radio traffic, but their signal analysts had not cracked the codes. Instead of extracting the contents of messages, like their American counterparts, they had to interpret the volume of traffic, the frequently used call signs, and the bearing of the source of the transmission. Although they supplemented this information with translations of uncoded messages, especially from aircraft, the Japanese could produce only a general indication of what the Americans intended to do. The Japanese Navy received no revelations like those presented to Adm. Nimitz before the Battle of Midway; consequently, the enemy had little confidence in communications intelligence.

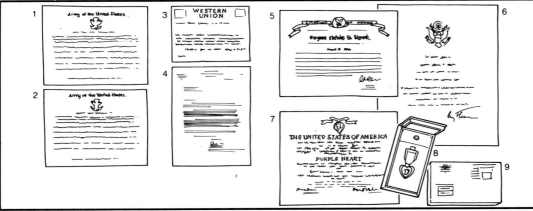

The Vozniak Citations

These documents chart the military career and death in combat of Sergeant Nicholas S. Vozniak, US Army Air Corps. They include his posthumous Purple Heart, together with the notification, condolence, and award documents. The medal group is significant because of its completeness. While many Purple Hearts still exist with their cases, to find a medal with both case, carton and documentation is unusual

1 Promotion certificate from private to corporal, dated July 1, 1942
2 Promotion certificate to sergeant, dated September 15, 1942
3 Notification telegram of armed forces personnel missing in action
4 Letter of the Secretary of War advising of the action
5 Army Air Corps Certificate signed by General Arnold
6 Presidential certificate signed by President Truman
7 Award certificate to accompany the Purple Heart decoration
8 Order of the Purple Heart, awarded for wounds or death from enemy action
9 Shipping carton for 8

Andrew L. Chernak Collection

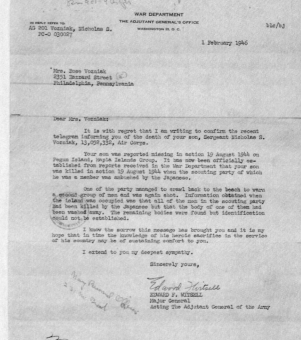

Authorized in 1932, the Purple Heart was awarded for combat action only. It was designed by Elizabeth Will and is probably the most readily recognized US decoration.

Sergeant Vozniak was killed in action on August 19, 1944, on Pegun Island, one of the Mapia group which lies to the north of the Vogelkop Peninsula in New Guinea. It is interesting to note the amount of time between his death and its official notification — in this case 18 months.

The war against Japan was largely an American fight, in part by necessity, in part by choice. When Japan struck, Australia and New Zealand had committed large numbers of troops to fight the Germans in the North African desert, leaving a vacuum that American forces filled. The performance of the first Australian soldiers to do battle against the Japanese disappointed MacArthur, who did not appreciate the difficulty of waging war in the jungles of New Guinea. Even though American troops experienced an equally disheartening introduction to combat, he continued to cast the Australians in a subordinate role. Meanwhile, the strategy of Germany first tied down British forces, although the defense of India and, insofar as resources permitted, the reconquest of Burma became the responsibility of Lord Louis Mountbatten, the Allied Supreme Commander in South East Asia. Once the Allies had gained control of the Mediterranean, units of the Royal Navy might have become available for operations in the Pacific, but Adm. King discouraged such a move. He believed that British warships lacked the endurance of their American counterparts, remained tied to fixed bases, and could not make full use of the US Navy's techniques of refueling and replenishment at sea. Despite King's misgivings, however, the British Pacific Fleet did successfully participate in the battle off Okinawa.

If the United States failed to make full use of its British and Australian allies in the war against Japan, it expected far too much from Nationalist China for far too long. Sustaining operations in China required that fuel and other cargo travel halfway around the world. Moreover, between the closing of the Burma Road in 1942 and the opening of the Ledo Road and pipeline in 1945, every bullet and drum of gasoline destined for China had to cross the Himalayas by air. Actually, the completion of the Ledo Road had little impact as Japan was already careering headlong toward defeat. Further to complicate the logistics problem, the priorities of Chiang Kai-shek's Nationalist government did not coincide with those of the United States. For Chiang, the more dangerous enemy was Mao Tse-tung and his communists, and the decisive battle would be fought after Japan had gone down to defeat. Instead of hurling their armies against the Japanese, the Nationalists intended to save them to fight the Chinese communists. Although operations in China proved inconclusive, at times frustrating, from an American point of view, the United States could put up with the drain on its resources.

A comparison of natural, industrial, military, and naval power reveals that the advantage lay with the United States in almost every category from shipbuilding, to nuclear physics, to code breaking. Another factor that favored the Americans might be called the fortunes of war or just plain luck. Almost inevitably, it seems, the Japanese made the wrong decision when the time came to choose and suffered disastrous consequences. In contrast, the Americans, despite their mistakes, never really jeopardized ultimate victory.

Twice in the course of the war, Adm. Chuichi Nagumo had to decide whether or not to renew an attack, and both times he made the wrong choice. At Pearl Harbor, he left the fuel storage tanks and repair facilities intact; six months later, at Midway, he elected to hit the island a second time, and as sailors were changing bomb loads on his carriers, the Americans struck. His principal opponent at Midway, Adm. Spruance, has been criticized for a lack of aggressiveness, but he would have risked his all-important carriers by trying to pursue the Japanese. Similarly, Spruance annihilated Japan's corps of naval aviators, painfully reconstituted after the fight at Midway, in the Battle of the Philippine Sea; again he did not pursue, but he could have accomplished nothing more by hunting down the carriers, for Japanese naval aviation had been destroyed. The conclusive demonstration that fortune favored the United States came off Leyte in the Philippines, where Adm. Halsey left the landing force exposed to attack as he steamed off to destroy Japanese aircraft carriers that were devoid of pilots. Halsey's mistake made no difference, however; confronted by gallant resistance from the escort carriers and their screen, the enemy commander,

Above: US decorations and campaign medals. Top row from the left: Distinguished Flying Cross; Distinguished Service Cross; Silver Star; Bronze Star — 'V' device on ribbon indicates valor. Center: Purple Heart. Second row from the left: Air Medal; American Campaign Medal — awarded to all members of the armed forces who, between December 7, 1941 and March 2, 1946, served within the continental limits of the United States; Army Medal of Honor — highest award for gallantry, awarded to those who distinguish themselves conspicuously by gallantry, at the risk of their lives above and beyond the call of duty, while engaged in combat against an armed enemy; Army Occupation Service Medal — awarded for thirty day consecutive service in occupied territories after World War II; Philippine Liberation Medal — awarded for action in the liberation of those islands, October 17, 1944 to September 3, 1945. Bottom row from the left: Navy Distinguished Service Medal, American Defense Service Medal; Army Distinguished Service Medal; Asiatic-Pacific Campaign Medal — awarded for thirty days active service in the prescribed area or aboard certain ships between December 7, 1941 and November 8, 1945; World War II Victory Medal. *Andrew L. Chernak.*

Right: The victory over Nazi Germany complete, the Allies under Clement Attlee, Harry S. Truman, and Stalin meet at Potsdam July 17-August 2 1945, to discuss the war against Japan. It was here that Truman revealed the success of the Trinity Test.

Above: The end of a long struggle is signalled as the New York City crowd gathers in Times Square to celebrate VJ Day on August 15, 1945. The last stage of World War II had ended in Allied victory.

Adm. Takeo Kurita, decided to break off the action.

During the war in the Pacific, both sides displayed stirring gallantry and sickening brutality. The victory of the Allies did not result from moral ascendancy or greater courage. The ultimate source of victory was a tremendous material and technological superiority that the Americans employed to devastating effect. The nation's industrial and scientific base supported the war effort with such varied weapons as the amphibian tractor and the atomic bomb. Japanese science and manufacturing, handicapped by shortages of war materials, simply could not keep pace. If any single factor symbolized the American victory, it was the assembly line, undisturbed by bombing or crippling shortages of resources, which overwhelmed Japan with an endless succession of ships and airplanes, bombs and cartridges, and even immersion heaters to provide hot water in the field.

Bibliography

1: SOURCES OF CONFLICT

Agawa, Hiroyuki. *The Reluctant Admiral: Yamamoto and the Imperial Navy*, translated by John Bester. Tokyo, 1979.
Allen, Louis. *Japan: The Years of Triumph, From Feudal Isolation to Pacific Empire*. London, 1971.
Barker, A. J. *Ballentine's Illustrated History of the Violent Century; War Leaders: Yamashita*. New York, 1973
Coox, Alvin D. *Ballentine's Illuctrated History of the Violent Century; War Leader: Tojo*. New York, 1975.
Hayashi, Saburo, and Alvin D. Coox. *Kogun: The Japanese Army in the Pacific War.* Quantico, Virginia, 1959.
Ienaga, Saburo. *The Pacific War: World War II and the Japanese, 1931-1945*. New York, 1978.
Toland, John. *The Rising Sun: The Decline and Fall of the Japanese Empire, 1936-1945*. New York, 1970.

2: TORA! TORA! TORA!

Heinrichs, Waldo. *Threshold of War.* New York, 1988.
Lord, Walter. *Day of Infamy.* New York, 1957.
Morison, Samuel Eliot. *History of United States Naval Operations in World War II*, vol III, *The Rising Sun in the Pacific, 1931-April 1942*. Boston, 1950.
Prange, Gordon W., in collaboration with Donald M. Goldstein and Katherine V. Dillon. *At Dawn We Slept: The Untold Story of Pearl Harbor.* New York, 1981.
Spector, Ronald H. *Eagle Against the Sun: The American War with Japan.* New York, 1985.

3: DELAYING ACTION OR FOUL DECEPTION

Baldwin, Hanson W. *"The Rock: The Fall of Corregidor,"* in *Battles Lost and Won: Great Campaigns of World War II.* New York, 1966.
Beck, John Jacob. *MacArthur and Wainwright: The Sacrifice of the Philippines.* Alburquerque, 1974.
Brereton, Lewis H. *The Brereton Diaries.* New York, 1946.
Cline, Ray S. *US Army in World War II: Washington Command Post: The Operations Division.* Washington, 1951.
Ind, Allison. *Bataan: The Judgement Seat.* New York, 1944.
Craven, Wesley Frank and James Lea Cate. *The Army Air Forces in World War II:* vol I, *Plans and Early Operations.* Chicago, 1948.
Falk, Stanley L. *Bataan: The March of Death.* New York, 1962.
James, D. Clayton. *The Years of MacArthur*, vol II, *1941-45.* Boston, 1975.
Kennedy, Paul. *Pacific Onslaught, 7th Dec. 1941/7th Feb 1941.* New York, 1972.
Leary, William M., ed. *We Shall Return! MacArthur's Commanders and the Defeat of Japan.* Lexington, Kentucky, 1988.
Love, Robert W. ed. *The Chiefs of Naval Operations.* Annapolis, 1980.
Lundstrom, John B. *The First South Pacific Campaign: Pacific Fleet Strategy, December, 1941-June 1942.* Annapolis, 1976.
Morton, Louis, *US Army in World War II: The Fall of the Philippines.* Washington, 1953.
Morton, Louis. *US Army in World War II: Strategy and Command: The First Two Years.* Washington, DC, 1962.
Petillo, Carol Morris *Douglas MacArthur: The Philippine Years.* Bloomington, Indiana 1981.
Toland, John. *Infamy: Pearl Harbor and Its Aftermath.* Garden City, New Jersey, 1982.
Wainwright, Jonathan M. *General Wainwright's Story.* Garden City, New Jersey, 1946.
Watson, Richard L., Jr. *Army Air Action in the Philippines and Netherlands East Indies, 1941-42.* Washington, 1956.

4: THE JAPANESE OCTOPUS

Caidin, Martin, et al. *"The Sinking of the Prince of Wales and the Repulse,"* in *Gene Gurney, ed. Great Air Battles.* New York, 1963.
Churchill, Winston. *The Second World War: The Grand Alliance.* Boston, 1950.
Morison, Samuel Eliot. *History of United States Naval Operations in World War II*, vol III, *The Rising Sun in the Pacific, 1931-April 1942.* Boston, 1950.
Office of Chief of Military History, *Japanese Monograph no. 107, Malay Naval Invasion Operations.* HQ Far East Command, October 1952.
Roskill, S. W. *The War at Sea, 1939-1945*, vol I, *The Defensive.* London, 1954.

5: MIDWAY: THE TURNING POINT

Buell, Thomas B. *The Quiet Warrior.* Boston, 1974.
Craven, Wesley Frank, and James Lea Cate. *The Army Air Forces in World War II:* vol IV, *The Pacific: Guadalcanal To Saipan August 1942 to July 1944.* Washington, reprinted, 1983.
Dull, Paul S. *A Battle History of the Imperial Japanese Navy 1941-1945.* Annapolis, Maryland, 1978.
Forrestel, E. P. *Admiral Raymond A. Spruance, USN: A Study in Command.* Washington, 1966.
Fuchida, Mitsuo and Masatake Okumiya. *Midway: The Battle that Doomed Japan.* New York, 1955.
Heinl, Robert D., Jr. *Marines at Midway.* Washington: 1948.
Hough, Frank O., Verle E. Ludwig, and Henry I. Shaw, Jr. *History of the US Marine Corps Operations in World War II*, vol I, *Pearl Harbor to Guadalcanal.* Washington.
Holmes, W. J. *Double-Edged Secrets: US Naval Intelligence Operations in the Pacific during World War II.* Annapolis, Maryland, 1979.
Lewin, Ronald. *The American Magic: Codes, Ciphers and the Defeat of Japan.* New York, 1982.
Morison, Samuel Eliot. *A History of United States Naval Operations in World War II*, vols IV, VIII. Boston, 1959.
Prange, Gordon W. with Donald M. Goldstein and Katherine V. Dillon. *Miracle At Midway.* New York, 1982.

6: INTO THE JUNGLE: NEW GUINEA

Boeicho, Boei kenshujo senshishitsu, ed. Senshi sosho, vol XIV, *Official Military History: Army Operations in the South Pacific: Port Moresby — First Stage Operations at Guadalcanal.* Tokyo, 1968.
Ibid., vol XXI, *Army Operations north of Australia.* Tokyo, 1968.
Ibid., vol XXVIII, *Army Operations in the South Pacific: Guadalcanal and Buna operations.* Tokyo, 1968.

Ibid., vol LIV, *Southwest area fleet operations.* Tokyo, 1972.
Barbey, Daniel E. *MacArthur's Amphibious Navy: Seventh Amphibious Force Operations, 1943-1945.* Annapolis, Maryland, 1969.
Craven, Wesley Frank, and James Lea Cate, eds. *The Army Air Forces in World War II*, vol IV, *The Pacific: Guadalcanal to Saipan, August 1942 to July 1944.* Chicago, 1950 (re-printed Washington, 1983).
Dexter, David. *Australia in the War of 1939-1945; Army: The New Guinea Offensives.* Canberra, 1961.
Drea, Edward J. *"Defending Driniumor: Covering Force Operations in New Guinea, 1944" Leavenworth Paper No. 9.* Washington, 1983.
Krueger, Walter. *From Down Under to Japan: The Story of Sixth Army in World War II.* Washington, 1953.
Luvaas, Jay, ed. *Dear Miss Em: General Eichelberger's War in the Pacific, 1942-1945.* Westport, Connecticut, 1972.
McCarthy, Dudley. *Australia in the War of 1939-1945; Army: Southwest Pacific Area — First Year: Kokoda to Wau.* Canberra, 1959.
Miller, John, Jr. *The United States Army in World War II; The War in the Pacific; Cartwheel: The Reduction of Rabaul.* Washington, 1959.
Milner, Samuel. *The United States Army in World War II; The War in the Pacific: Victory in Papua.* Washington, 1957.
Morison, Samuel Eliot. *A History of US Naval Operations in World War II*, vols VI, VIII. Boston, 1957, 1964.
Smith, Robert Ross. *The United States Army in World War II; The War in the Pacific: The Approach to the Philippines.* Washington, 1953.
Supreme Commander for the Allied Powers. *Reports of General MacArthur: The Campaigns of MacArthur in the Pacific*, vols I, II. Washington, 1966.

7: THE ADVANCE THROUGH THE SOLOMONS

Dyer, George C. *The Amphibians Came to Conquer: The Story of Admiral Richmond Kelly Turner*, two vols. Washington, 1969.
Griffith, Samuel B., II. *The Battle for Guadalcanal.* Philadephia, 1963.
Halsey, William F., and J. Bryan, III. *Admiral Halsey's Story.* New York, 1947.
Isely, Jeter A., and Philip Crowl, *US Marines and Amphibious Warfare: Its Theory, and Its Practice in the Pacific.* Princeton, New Jersey, 1951.
Miller, John, Jr., *The United States Army in World War II; The War in the Pacific: Guadalcanal: The First Offensive.* Washington, 1949.
History of the United States Naval Operations in World War II, vol V, *The Struggle for Guadalcanal, August 1942, February 1943*, Boston, 1950.
Shaw, Henry I., and Douglas T. Kane. *History of US Marine Corps Operations in World War II: The Isolation of Rabaul.* Washington, 1963.

8: THE GILBERTS AND THE MARSHALLS

Crowl, Philip A., and Edmund G. Love. *The United States Army in World War II; The War in the Pacific: Seizure of the Gilberts and Marshalls.* Washington, 1955.
Heinl, Robert D. Jr., and John A. Crown. *The Marshalls: Increasing the Tempo.* Washington, 1954.
Morison, Samuel Eliot. *A History of US Naval Operations in World War II*, vol VII, *Aleutians, Gilberts, and Marshalls.* Boston, 1951.
Reynolds, Clark G. *Fast Carriers: Forging the Air Navy.* New York, 1968.
Shaw, Henry I. Jr., Bernard C. Nalty, and Edwin T. Turnbladh. *History of US Marine Corps Operations in World War II*, vol III, *Central Pacific Drive.* Washington, 1966.
Sherrod, Robert. *Tarawa: The Story of a Battle.* New York, 1944.
Smith, Holland M., and Percy Finch. *Coral and Brass.* New York, 1949.
Stockman, James R. *The Battle for Tarawa.* Washington, 1947.

9: WAR ON THE ASIAN MAINLAND

Allen, Louis. *Burma: The Longest War, 1941-45.* New York, 1984.
Byrd, Martha. *Chennault: Giving Wings to the Tiger.* Tuscaloosa, 1987.
Callahan, Raymond. *Burma, 1942-1945.* Newark, Delaware, 1978.
Chennault, Claire Lee. Robert Hotz, ed. *Way of a Fighter.* New York, 1949.
Craven, Wesley Frank and James Lea Cate, eds. *The Army Air Forces in World War II*, vols IV, V, VII. Chicago, 1950-8.
Feis, Herbert. *The China Tangle: The American Effort in China from Pearl Harbor to the Marshall Mission.* Princeton, 1953.
Kirby, S. Woodburn. *History of the Second World War: The War Against Japan.* vols II-IV. London, 1958-65.
LeMay, Curtis E. with MacKinlay Kantor. *Mission With LeMay.* Garden City, New York, 1965.
Romanus, Charles F. and Riley Sunderland. *United States Army in World War II: China-Burma-India Theater.* vols I-III. Washington, 1953-9.
Slim, William J. *Defeat into Victory.* New York, 1961.
Thorne, Christopher. *Allies of a Kind: The United States, Britain, and the War Against Japan, 1941-1945.* Oxford, 1978.
Tuchman, Barbara W. *Stilwell and the American Experience in China, 1911-45.* New York, 1970.
Turner, William H. *Over the Hump.* New York, 1964.
White, Theodore H., ed. *The Stilwell Papers.* New York, 1948.
Ziegler, Philip. *Mountbatten.* New York, 1985.

10: WITHIN STRIKING DISTANCE OF JAPAN

Crowl, Philip A. *Campaign in the Marianas, United States Army in World War II, The War in the Pacific.* Washington, 1960.
Morison, Samuel Eliot. *History of United States Naval Operations in World War II*, vol VIII, *New Guinea and the Marianas.* Boston, 1964.
Y'Blood, William T. *Red Sun Setting: The Battle of the Philippine Sea.* Annapolis, 1981.

11: SECURING MACARTHUR'S FLANK

Gailey, Harry A. *Peleliu 1944.* Annapolis, 1983.
Garand, George W., and Truman R. Strobridge. *Western Pacific Operations, History of US Marine Corps Operations in World War II.* Washington, 1971.
Morison, Samuel Eliot. *History of United States Naval Operations*

in *World War II*, vol. XII. *Leyte: June 1944-January 1945.* Boston, 1958.
Smith, Robert Ross. *The Approach to the Philippines, United States Army in World War II, The War in the Pacific.* Washington, 1953.

12: THE RETURN TO THE PHILIPPINES

Cannon, M. Hamlin. *Leyte: The Return to the Philippines, United States Army in World War II, The War in the Pacific.* Washington, 1954.
Falk, Stanley L. *Decision at Leyte.* New York, 1966.
Hayes, Grace Person. *The History of the Joint Chiefs of Staff in World War II, The War Against Japan.* Annapolis, 1982.
Morison, Samuel Eliot. *History of United States Naval Operations in World War II*, vol. XII, *Leyte: June 1944-January 1945.* Boston, 1958.
Warner, Denis and Peggy Warner. *The Sacred Warriors.* New York, 1982.
Y'Blood, William T. *The Little Giants.* Annapolis, 1987.

13: THE PHILIPPINES RECONQUERED

Barker, A. J. *Ballentine's Illustrated History of the Violent Century; War Leaders: Yamashita.* New York, 1973.
Boggs, Charles W., Jr. *Marine Aviation in the Philippines.* Washington, 1951.
Craven, Wesley Frank, and James Lea Cate, eds. *The Army Air Forces in World War II*, vol V, *The Pacific: Matterhorn to Nagasaki.* Chicago, 1953 (reprinted Washington, 1983).
Eichelberger, Robert L. *Our Jungle Road to Tokyo.* New York, 1950.
James, D. Clayton. *The Years of MacArthur*, vol II, *1941-1945.* Boston, 1975.
Krueger, Walter. *From Down Under to Japan: The Story of Sixth Army.* Washington, 1953.
Lael, Richard L. *The Yamashita Precedent: War Crimes and Command Responsibility.* Wilmington, Delaware, 1982.
Manchester, William. *American Caesar: Douglas MacArthur, 1880-1964.* Boston, 1978.
Morison, Samuel Eliot. *The History of US Naval Operations in World War II*, vol XIII, *The Liberation of the Philippines.* Boston, 1969.
Smith, Robert Ross. *The US Army in World War II; The War in the Pacific: Triumph in the Philippines.* Washington, 1963.

14: UNCOMMON VALOR

Bartley, Whitman S. *Iwo Jima: Amphibious Epic.* Washington, 1954.
Craven, Wesley Frank, and James Lea Cate, eds. *The Army Air Forces in World War II*, vol V, *The Pacific: Matterhorn to Nagasaki.* Chicago, 1953 (reprinted Washington, 1983).
Garand, George, and Truman R. Strobridge. *History of US Marine Corps Operations in World War II*, vol IV, *Western Pacific Operations.* Washington, 1971.
Morison, Samuel Eliot. *A History of US Naval Operations in World War II*, vol XV, *Victory in the Pacific*, Boston, 1975.
Newcombe, Richard F. *Iwo Jima.* New York, 1965.
Ross, Bill D. *Iwo Jima: Legacy of Valor.* New York, 1985.
Wheeler, Richard. *Iwo.* New York, 1980.

15: THE LAST INVASION

Appelman, Roy, et al. *The United States Army in World War II; The War in the Pacific: Okinawa: The Last Battle.* Washington, 1948.
Frank, Benis M., and Henry I. Shaw, Jr. *History of US Marine Corps Operations in World War II*, vol V, *Victory and Occupation.* Washington, 1968.
Gow, Ian. *Okinawa 1945: Gateway to Japan.* Garden City, 1985.
Morison, Samuel Eliot. *History of United States Naval Operations in World War II*, vol. XIV, *Victory in the Pacific, 1945.* Boston, 1960.

16: JAPAN ISOLATED

Blair, Clay, Jr. *Silent Victory: The US Submarine War Against Japan.* Philadelphia, 1975.
Holmes, W. J. *Double-Edged Secrets: US Naval Intelligence Operations in the Pacific during World War II.* Annapolis, Maryland, 1979.
Johnson Ellis A. and David A. Katcher. *Mines against Japan.* Silver Spring, Maryland, 1973.
Lockwood, Charles A. *Sink 'Em All: Submarine Warfare In The Pacific.* New York, 1951.
Parillo, Mark P. *"The Japanese Merchant Marine In World War II."* Ph.D. Diss., The Ohio State University, 1987.
Twentieth Air Force. *Starvation: Phase Analysis of Strategic Mining Blockade of the Japanese Empire.* Washington, 1947.
The Joint Army-Navy Assessment Committee. *Japanese Naval And Merchant Shipping Losses During World War II By All Causes.* Washington, 1947.

17: JAPAN IN FLAMES

Berger, Carl. *Ballentine's Illustrated History of the Violent Century; Weapons: B-29: The Superfortress*, New York, 1970.
Coox, Alvin. *Japan: The Final Agony.* New York, 1970.
Department of State Bulletin, August 12, 1945.
Feis, Herbert. *The Atomic Bomb and the End of World War II.* Princeton, New Jersey, 1961.
Goldberg, Alfred. *A History of the United States Air Force, 1907-1978.* Princeton, New Jersey, 1957.
Ienaga, Saburo. *The Pacific War: World War II and the Japanese, 1931-1945.* New York, 1978.
Roskill, S. W. *The War at Sea, 1939-1945*, vol III, *The Offensive. pt II, 1st June 1944-14th August 1945.* London, 1961.
The United States Strategic Bombing Surveys. Air University Press, Maxwell Air Force Base, Alabama, reprinted October 1987.

18: SOURCES OF VICTORY

Dower, John W. *War Without Mercy: Race and Power in the Pacific War.* New York, 1986.
Holmes, W. J. *Double-Edged Secrets: US Naval Intelligence in the Pacific during World War II.* Annapolis, Maryland, 1979.
Lewin, Ronald. *The American Magic: Codes, Ciphers, and the Defeat of Japan.* New York, 1982.
Morison, Samuel Eliot. *Strategy and Compromise.* Boston, 1958.
Overy, R. J. *The Air War, 1939-1945.* New York, 1981.

AUTHOR BIOGRAPHIES

Bernard C. Nalty: Consultant Editor and author of Chapters 1,8,13,14, and 18. Currently a member of the Office of Air Force History, and a former member of the Marine Corps Historical Branch. Mr. Nalty has also contributed as consultant editor to another Salamander Book: *The Vietnam War.*

Dr. Thomas C. Hone: author, Chapter 2. Dr. Hone is currently an instructor in the Defense Systems Management College, Department of Defense. He formerly taught at the Naval War College.

Dr. Daniel R. Mortensen: author, Chapter 3. Dr. Mortensen is currently a historian at the Office of Air Force History.

Jacob Neufield: author, Chapters 4 and 17. Mr. Neufield is the Chief of the Headquarters USAF Branch, Office of Air Force History.

Dr. George H. Watson, Jr.: author, Chapter 5. Dr. Watson is currently the Chief of the Office of History for the Surgeon General of the US Air Force. He is also a veteran of the 101st Airborne Division and served during the Vietnam War.

Dr. Edward J. Drea: author, Chapter 6. Dr. Drea is the Chief, Staff Support Branch, US Army Center of Military History. He has taught at the Combat Studies Institute, US Army Command and General Staff School, and at the US Army War College. Fluent in Japanese, he studied in Tokyo and served as an intelligence officer in the US Air Force.

Dr. Edward J. Marolda: author, Chapter 7. Dr. Marolda is currently in charge of the Contemporary History Branch, Naval Historical Center, Department of the Navy. He also served in Vietnam as an Army officer.

Dr. Wayne Thompson: author, Chapter 9. Dr. Thompson is a member of the Office of Air Force History.

William T. Y' Blood: author, Chapters 10, 11, 12, and 15. After flying B-47s for the Strategic Air Command, Mr. Y' Blood was a commercial pilot for 18 years. He is currently a member for the Office of Air Force History.

Dr. Jeffrey G. Barlow: author, Chapter 16. Dr. Barlow is a historian in the Contemporary History Branch, Naval Historical Center, Department of the Navy.

Russ A. Pritchard: Technical Consultant. Mr. Pritchard serves on the Board of Governors for the Civil War Library and Museum, Philadelphia and is a consultant to The Museum of the Confederacy, Richmond. He is a member of the American Society of Arms Collectors, Fellow of the Company of Military Historians, Life Member of the National Rifle Association and member of the board of the National Firearms Museum of the National Rifle Association. Mr. Pritchard has also been the technical and arms advisor on Salamander's Civil War Series: *Rebels & Yankees.*

Acknowledgments

INSTITUTIONAL COLLECTIONS
GENERAL DOUGLAS MacARTHUR MEMORIAL
Norfolk, Virginia
Edward M. Condra, III, Colonel, USMC (Ret.), Director
Edward J. Boone, Jr., Archivist
Jeffrey Acosta, Curator

MILWAUKEE PUBLIC MUSEUM
Milwaukee, Wisconsin
H. Michael Madaus, Assistant Curator of History

US ARMY ORDNANCE MUSEUM
Aberdeen Proving Ground, Maryland
William F. Atwater, Ph.D, Director
Roger A. Godin, Curator
Armando E. Framarini, Museum Specialist
Lesley M. LeRoy, Administrative Assistant

US ARMY QUARTERMASTER MUSEUM
Fort Lee, Virginia
Phillip M. Cavanaugh, Director
Luther Hanson, Museum Technician

**UNITED STATES MARINE CORPS
AIR-GROUND MUSEUM**
Quantico, Virginia
Colonel Brooke Nihart,
  Deputy Director for Marine Corps Museums
Lieutenant Colonel William A. Beebe, II,
  Officer-in-Charge
Kenneth L. Smith-Christmas,
  Curator of Material History
Nancy F. King, Museum Specialist (General)
Michael Starn, Museum Specialist (Aviation)
John G. Griffiths, Museum Specialist (Ordnance)

US MARINE RAIDER MUSEUM
The American Historical Foundation,
Richmond, Virginia
Robert A. Buerlein, President
J. E. B. Stuart, Executive Vice President
R. G. Rosenquist, Curator
Catherine Meador, Executive Assistant

WAR MEMORIAL MUSEUM OF VIRGINIA
Newport News, Virginia
John V. Quarstein, Chief Executive Officer
Arthur LaBonte, Curator
William C. Barker, Registrar

WEST POINT MUSEUM
United States Military Academy,
West Point, New York
Michael E. Moss, Director
Robert W. Fisch, Curator of Arms
Michael J. McAfee, Curator of Uniforms and History
Walter J. Nock, Museum Specialist Conservator

PRIVATE COLLECTIONS
Dale E. Biever, Boyertown, Pennsylvania
Laurence J. Beyer, Havertown, Pennsylvania
Andrew L. Chernak, Springfield, Pennsylvania
Allan D. Cors, McLean, Virginia
Scott A. Duff, Export, Pennsylvania
George J. Fistrovich, Winterthur, Delaware
John T. Frawner, Hanover, Virginia
John Frost, Historical Newspaper Service,
  New Barnet, Hertfordshire, England
William M. Galbraith, Devon, Pennsylvania
Eugene C. Gibson, Jr., Ambler, Pennsylvania
Howard O. Hendricks, Richmond, Virginia
Richard Kos, Quantico, Virginia
Elliott R. Laine, Quantico, Virginia
William A. LePard, Ardmore, Pennsylvania
Gary S. Pagel, Milwaukee, Wisconsin
Russ A. Pritchard, Jr., Bryn Mawr, Pennsylvania
Russ A. Pritchard, III, Bryn Mawr, Pennsylvania
Michael F. Pritchard, Bryn Mawr, Pennsylvania
William Ricca
Robert Seijas
Richard Slack
Thomas Staats, Milwaukee, Wisconsin
William Thomas
Andrew W. Xaras, Philadelphia, Pennsylvania
Theodore A. Xaras, Philadelphia, Pennsylvania

PICTURE CREDITS
a, Above; b, Below; l, Left; r, Right; al, Above left; ar, Above right; ac, Above center; bl, Below left; br, Below right; t, Top; tl, Top left; c, Center; cl, Center left.
All photographs are by courtesy of the National Archives, Washington, DC, except: **8**, (b) Keystone Press Agency; **9**, (ac) Novosti Press Agency, (ar) Library of Congress, (b) Salamander Books; **10**, (ar) Hulton Picture Library, (b) Bettman Archive; **11**, (a) Bettman, (b) Hulton; **12**, (a) US Navy, (USN), (b) The Mainichi Newspaper, Tokyo; **15**, (b) Mainichi; **16**, (a) USN; **17**, (tl) Fujiphotos, Tokyo, (cl) Library of Congress; **18**, (a) Hulton; **18-19**, (b) Novosti; **20**, (a) Imperial War Museum, London, (IWM), (b) Mainichi; **21**, IWM; **24**, Mainichi; **25**, (a) USN, (r) Mainichi, (br) USN; **28**, (a, b) Salamander; **29**, (al, b) Mainichi, (ar) IWM; **30**, (bl) USN; **31**, (t) IWM, (c, l) Mainichi, (bl) USN; **32**, (al) Mainichi, (bl) USN; **36**, (b) Mainichi; **37**, (al) USN; **39**, USN; **40**, (c) USN; **41**, (b) USN; **45**, (b) US Army, (USA); **54**, (al) Salamander, (b) USN; **55**, (a) USN; **58**, (a) Mainichi; **59**, (b) Dr. Diosdado M. Yap, Editor-Publisher, Bataan Magazine, Washington DC; **61**, (tr, cl) USN; **66**, IWM; **67**, IWM; **72**, (a) Mainichi, (b) Australian War Memorial, Canberra, (AWM); **75**, (t) Fujiphoto, (c, b) IWM; **76**, (b) Mainichi (al) Netherlands State Institute for War Documentation, Amsterdam, (ar) IWM, (b) Mainichi; **82**, USN; **83** (b) National Air & Space Museum, Washington DC, (b) USN; **86**, USN; **98**, (a) AWM, (b) USN; **100-1**, (a) US Air Force, (USAF), (b) AWM; **103**, (a) AWM, (b) Mainichi; **108**, USA; **111**, USAF; **117**, (a) USN; **121**, USN; **126**, US Marine Corps (USMC); **134**, USN; **143**, USA; **145**, (b) USN; **150**, (b) IWM; **155**, IWM; **160**, (ar) USA; **161**, (al) USAF; **166**, USN; **170**, USN; **176**, USA; **183**, USN; **189**, (a) USN, (b) USMC; **191**, (a) USMC; **196**, (b) IWM; **200**, (a) Bettman, (b) USA; **204**, USN; **207**, (a) USN; **214**, USN; **217**, (a) USAF, (b) USN; **223**, AWM; **224-5**, USMC; **228**, (a) USN, (b) Salamander; **229**, (b) USN; **233**, USMC; **238**, (a) USMC; **239**, (b) USAF; **240-1**, USMC; **244**, (b) USN; **250**, (a) USMC, (b) USN; **252**, USMC; **254-5**, USN; **259**, Salamander; **260**, USN; **267**, (l) USN, (b) Smithsonian Institute; **272**, (b) Mainichi; **273**, USA; **274**, (inset) William Galbraith; **279**, (a) USAF; **283**, (bl, br) USN; **292**, (b) Mainichi; **299**, USA.

Index